SITTING IN THE EARTH AND LAUGHING

Books by A. Roy Eckardt

Christianity and the Children of Israel

The Surge of Piety in America

Elder and Younger Brothers

The Theologian at Work (editor)

Christianity in Israel (editor)

Your People, My People

Jews and Christians

For Righteousness' Sake

Black-Woman-Jew

Reclaiming the Jesus of History

Sitting in the Earth and Laughing

By Alice L. Eckardt and A. Roy Eckardt

Encounter With Israel

Long Night's Journey Into Day

SITTING IN THE EARTH AND LAUGHING

A Handbook of Humor

A. Roy Eckardt

Transaction Publishers
New Brunswick (U.S.A.) and London (U.K.)

Library of Congress Catalog Number: 91–14626
ISBN: 1–56000–001–5
Printed in the United States of America

Library of Congress Cataloging-in-Publication Data

Eckardt, A. Roy (Arthur Roy), 1918 –
    Sitting in the Earth and laughing: a handbook of humor / A. Roy Eckardt.
      p.   cm.
    Includes bibliographical references and index.
    ISBN 1–56000–001–5
    1. Wit and humor — History and criticism. 2. Laughter. 3. Comic,
The. I. Title.
PN6147.E34   1991
809.7 — dc20   91–14626
                                            CIP

For my grandchildren

Elizabeth Nicole Eckardt

Jesse Aaron Strock

And, in their name, for the

children who perished in the Shoah

*The funniest joke of all is the absolute truth
stated simply and gracefully.*

— Carl Reiner

*Real comedy can't be learned; it comes from
a need for justice.*

— Elayne Boosler

*The invention of a fable is to me the most
enviable exertion of human genius: it is the
discovering of a truth to which there is no
clue, and which, when once found out, can
never be forgotten.*

— William Hazlitt

Contents

Preface

I express appreciation to President and Mrs. David Patterson and the staff of the Centre for Postgraduate Hebrew Studies at the University of Oxford, where I prepared this book. For my wife, Alice L. Eckardt, and myself, I offer thanks to Elisabeth and Robert Maxwell for enabling the two of us to be the first Maxwell Fellows in the Study and Teaching of the Holocaust (1989–1990) at the Centre. My wife is as helpful and influential here as she has been in all my previous writings. I also thank my friend Marlyn Robinson of Baltimore, Maryland, for encouraging me; Glenda Abramson of the University of Oxford for her substantial aid and critical counsel; and Carol Troen at the Oxford Centre for her probing questions and suggestions.

Materials of both a serious and a comic nature that are not attributed to other sources are my concoctions, and I bear the only responsibility for them. Though somewhat more audibly and persistently, the present exercise sounds a note found in my book *For Righteousness' Sake* (1987) and may accordingly be treated as a sequel to that work.

A. Roy Eckardt

xi

Introduction

Somewhere I saw the aphorism: "When we meet, humanity reveals itself to humanity; when we pray, humanity reveals itself to God; when we study, God reveals Godself to humanity."

What happens when we laugh?

The practical way to come to terms with this little handbook upon the sense and nonsense of humor is to read it straight through, ringing all the shifts and changes, in the interests of a variety that will be conspicuous but also of a gestalt that will become evident. To direct one's work to specialist and general reader alike, as I do here, is to walk a tightrope. But I think there is much in this exposition for both parties. The fact remains that humor is an amorphous business; to write about it is to risk a certain lack of focus. I have sought to temper the problem by being as systematic as I can. This introduction and chapters 1 through 8 concentrate upon the theory and practice of humor; chapters 9 and 10 bring together fools, clowns, and children; and the remaining chapters venture more upon moral and theological dimensions of the subject.

Among its other motivations, this book may be construed as a fragment of response to a question: How is it possible to live today in the shadow of the *Shoah* (Holocaust), as of other recent horrible events? (Dictators and inquisitors share a nontoleration of the jest that has them as its object. Ironically, the same is true of revolutionists.)

Any job description for the "field" of humor will inevitably suffer from vagueness and/or controversy. I have no special competence in this area. (I was, however, born and raised in Brooklyn, which could help a little.) Fortunately, there are many knowledgeable thinkers and writers around who are able to lend a hand as we grapple with the many facets of the question of humor. Throughout I rely on a number of these people. Though the book is not an anthology, I include copious quotations from them. My own background in philosophy may be

of some aid. The consideration of humor is a "natural" for philosophy
(particularly for psychological and moral themes within philosophy,
touching, at a minimum, upon epistemology, ethics, aesthetics, and
general personality and social theory). Again, I have had a little experience as a sit-down comic before family and friends. Such encounters
can be frightening yet also cathartic; they teach instantly and power-
fully the differences between "funny" and "unfunny." Finally, through
the years I have collected a fair-sized file on the subject of comic
laughter; I put it to use here.

The title of the book, *Sitting in the Earth and Laughing,* is not meant
to suggest that stand-up comedians would be better advised to sit
down and be quiet. My title merely converts to earthly use Psalm 2:4,
"He that sits in the heavens laughs." The verse is what makes the title
possible — which could imply, but does not perforce imply, that it is
divine comedy that legitimates human comedy. (*Comedy* is traceable to
the Greek kōm[os], "a revel.") As a matter of fact, the laughter of
Psalm 2:4 is sardonic in character. This is made clear by the accompanying parallelism, "the Lord has them in derision." (The Greek root of
sardonic is *sardónios,* a plant of Sardinia the consumption of which
was reputed to induce compulsive laughter culminating in death.)

The life of humor cannot be reduced to mere laughter, most especially to hearty laughter.[1] This state of affairs prompts a question: Ought
a book *on* humor be *of* humor? That is to say, is it to be unfunny or
funny? I am not sure. In the interests of both these possibilities I have
decided to alternate my chapters between "unfunny" exposition and
more or less "funny," or at least laughter-related, content. (Perhaps,
therefore, chapters 2, 4, 6, etc. could be placed under some such general title as "Life Among the Wollenjoobies," or another the reader
may wish to create.) One conceivable problem with my alternating
method is that it could act to obscure or interfere with any overall
effort at continuity and coherence. Yet the approach can well have the
paradoxical effect of aiding and abetting the "cause" of laughter itself,
which is always cutting unceremoniously into the rest of life. Some
interpreters go so far as to claim that the very substance of humor is
surprise. I contrive an example:

> Having eaten a buttery crumpet,
> Bumpet the musical strumpet
> Stood up to play — the xylophone.

For Kierkegaard, the comical is present wherever there is contradiction.[2] Peter Berger writes that "the essence of the comic is always some sort of discrepancy." Berger makes the same point in a stronger way: "The comic world is one of magic."[3]

An added problem is that the reader may decide that some of the "unfunny" parts of this book are actually to be laughed at, while many of the "funny" parts do not make it as humor. I should merely respond that the main thing is to get on with our subject and then be better able to determine whether such judgments are in order.

> *Reader:* This book is a joke.
> *Author*: How very kind of you!

That the book as a whole may be taken as a joke (a "joke book") rests upon the incongruity between the "unfunny" parts and the "funny" parts.

I further go hiding behind Shel Silverstein's goat. He — Silverstein, not the goat — wrote "a beautiful book for you," but the goat ate it. He — Silverstein, not the goat — proceeded to write another book as fast as possible, yet it never could equal the beauty of the original. However, it was not his fault: "Blame the goat!"[4]

I remain a little unsure of whether the present effort can attain unto or reflect a concrete purpose — beyond the fact that I enjoy writing books, which is, I take it, a means of finding out something about oneself and one's lived world. Perhaps the reason for my uncertainty is the unsettled and indeed unsettling question of whether humor can or ought to boast discrete or objective aims or virtues beyond itself. Beneath this question lies the entire unresolved issue of the "essence" or "nature" of laughter and humor. "What laughter is and why it is, what a sense of humor is and how it comes to be, what a joke is and why it is a joke — these questions are most problematic" (Jackson Lee Ice).[5]

Marie Collins Swabey argues that issues "of the natural origin and practical purposes of laughter . . . are irrelevant to its essential comicality."[6] Less negatively put, the "purpose" of my book is tied to the "purpose" of laughter and humor, granted that these phenomena offer *some* discernible end(s) or function(s).

There is a sense in which a great deal of today's "comedy" has an all-too-blatant motive: to get a laugh — sometimes at almost any cost or anyone's expense. But this does not explain very much. Why should some people want other people to laugh? Again, I am aware of Konrad Lorenz's contention in *On Aggression* that the survival of civilization depends to a large degree upon our capacity for humor. Yet neither does this throw very much light upon the inner quality or meaning of laughter.[7]

Another way to state our problem is to ask whether humor and laughter are to be treated from the standpoint of the left side of the human brain (L-mode), the right side (R-mode), or both. These two realms are usually identified as involving, respectively, temporal, logical, linear-specific, rational-analytic, and even aggressive powers; and extraverbal, wholistic, intuitive, global, and nonaggressive powers. The faculty of laughter tends, I should think, to be particularly affinal to the R-mode — something like the artistic faculty as such, though not for the most part an extraverbal one — yet the faculty of laughter, and especially the study of it, can hardly avoid the L-mode.

My own predisposition is that — to speak a little metaphysically — humor and laughter fall in the category of peculiarly human mysteries, yet not wholly incomprehensible mysteries. Why is it, for example, that if two vehicles collide on the street it is not funny, but if a block away they collide a second time, it may seem funny? Why is it that accidentally to knock over a glass of milk is not funny, but if a moment later the replenished glass is accidentally knocked over a second time, it may seem funny? And how about a *third* time respecting both these kinds of accident? Yet the humor fades very quickly. Nothing funny is left in ten, or even five, glasses of spilled milk. *What is the secret of the relation between repetition and humor?* Already we are plunged into the province of mystery. More broadly, why is it that contradiction or incongruity or some other condition should incite laughter or be identified as humorous? Who has the answer to this question? These are mysteries. (Humor and laughter are not the only human reactions to incongruity. There are, for example, the reactions of anger, fear, and puzzlement.)

Professor Ice continues: "Man is the only animal that weeps and laughs and knows that he weeps and laughs, and wonders why. He is the only creature that weeps over the fact that he weeps, and laughs over the fact that he laughs. He is the most humor-seeking, humor-making, and humor-giving species that has walked the earth, ever ready to provoke or be provoked with laughter; even in the midst of fear and pain he is capable of incongruously ameliorating his misery by a smile, pun, or joke. He is the jester in the courts of creation."[8] For all the sexism of Ice's language, we are helpfully reminded that humor is a faculty constituent to human being as such. (This need not rule out its possible presence in other creatures. In strict honesty we simply do not know what it is to be a nonhuman creature.) To be human is evidently to live in a funny (i.e., incongruous and hence, in principle, comic—though also tragic) situation.[9]

One day not long ago a neighbor of mine needed help with a chore. I heard myself blurting out, "Sorry, I'm fighting a deadline." At the time the exaggeration impressed me as somewhat brazen (or brazenly spontaneous) until all at once the fact hit me that I was right in any case: A man in his seventies is indeed fighting a deadline.

> We are but older children, dear,
> Who fret to find our bedtime near.[10]

At the moment I am working on two dreams: to ride the train from "London to Paris and return" when the Channel Tunnel opens in (reportedly) 1993; and, less attainably, to write a letter or check (preferably the former; what could be sweeter than to leave this world *owing money*?) bearing the astonishing date 1 January 2000. The only warrant for mentioning these personal trivia is the painful bond that humor has with death. At this particular level, humor is linked to *Galgenhumor*, the laughter of the gallows. The psychiatrist Martin Grotjahn observes that some people "can always fight the anxiety of death by finding something to joke about."[11] As late as age eighty-five, Rex Stout, creator of Nero Wolfe, declared: "One trouble with living beyond your deserved number of years is that there's always some reason to live another year. And I'd like to live another year so that Nixon won't be President. If he's re-elected, I'll have to live another four years."[12] In its very guise of "trouble" the *élan vital* here succeeds in mustering a small laugh at death itself—though hardly a last laugh. (As one physician noted, "We're all terminal.")

In the meantime, have you heard the one about the two old men? One confides to the other, "I'd *love* to live in the past. The trouble is I can't remember it!"

NOTES

1. Where full bibliographical information is lacking in the notes to this book, the data are found in the listing "For Further Reading." In a brief "general" or "popular" study of this kind it would be tedious and disrupting to keep distinguishing analytically among humor, laughter, and comedy. As we shall see, different interpreters treat these concepts in varied ways. Several of the contributions to John Morreáll, ed., *The Philosophy of Laughter and Humor* have relevance to the problem of definitions; see the sections, "Contemporary Theories of Laughter and Humor" and "Amusement and Other Mental States." Morreall points out that to treat all cases of laughter as cases of humor is a very common mistake. "Kant and Schopenhauer, for example, present their Incongruity Theories as if they were theories of laughter generally, when at most they could hope to serve as theories of humor. Bergson titles his book *Laughter*, when a more accurate title would have been *Humor*, or better, *Comedy*" (ibid., p. 5).
2. Søren Kierkegaard, *Concluding Unscientific Postscript*, trans. David F. Swenson (Princeton: Princeton University Press, 1941), pp. 459–68.
3. Peter L. Berger, *The Precarious Vision*, pp. 74, 77. "While there are many human activities in which magic plays an important part, in the legal enterprise it is the essence of the matter" (ibid., p. 79).
4. Shel Silverstein, "Blame," *A Light in the Attic*, p. 34.
5. Jackson Lee Ice, "Notes Toward a Theology of Humor," *Religion in Life* 42 (1973): 392.
6. Marie Collins Swabey, *Comic Laughter*, p. v. Cf. ibid., chap. 6, "The Genesis of Laughter."
7. Lorenz construes laughter as a controlled kind of aggression.
8. Ice, "Notes," p. 392.
9. When I use the word "funny" in this book, I mean primarily "funny ha-ha." But that meaning of "funny" cannot be wholly divorced from "funny peculiar or strange." For a powerful critique of the traditional assumption that rationality and other "human" faculties are unique to humankind, including criticism of the effort to separate humanity from the rest of nature, consult Alan Freeman and Betty Mensch, "Scratching the Belly of the Beast," *Tikkun* 4 (Sept./Oct. 1989): 34–38, 92–96.
10. Lewis Carroll, *Through the Looking-Glass*, p. 6.
11. Martin Grotjahn, as cited in Glenn Collins, "The Joke as Healthy Aggression," *The New York Times* (7 September 1981).
12. Israel Shenker, "Rex Stout, 85, Gives Clues on Good Writing," *The New York Times* (1 December 1971).

1

From Proto-Joke to Defiance to Carnival: Tentative Stages in a Life Story of Laughter

> *Existence is comic inherently . . . , the oddest of possibilities masquerading momentarily as fact.*
> —George Santayana

> *If they [children with cancer] pass a mirror reflecting their bald head, they will stick out their tongue in defiance.*
> — Erma Bombeck

> *God shows the angels how to eat spaghetti.*
> — A child named Alan

Beyond my preliminary comments in the introduction, the listing to follow may be of orienting help. It appears that there are at least Ten Primordial Jokes, or Proto-Jokes, consanguine to one another.

1. The most original, or First Joke (= Incongruity), is Being Amidst Nothingness. How could there ever be such an incongruity as this? Why is there something rather than nothing? Here, perhaps, lies the *Urgrund*, the ultimate ground of human laughter (as also of human tears).

2. The Second Joke involves The Dialectic of Order and Chaos — or perhaps of rules versus anarchy. This is described by Conrad Hyers:

> In the comic tradition, [the] elements of randomness and happenstance that swirl through much of our lives are made the special focus of attention . . . , elements that our theologies often ignore — or attribute to sinister forces — in favor of a singular emphasis upon cosmic orders, divine plans, historical patterns, and ultimate destinies. . . . Hence all those quirks of fate, meandering plots, petty interruptions, and odd circumstances that proliferate themselves in comedies. Comedy comes directly to terms with the arbitrariness of life. . . . Apart from this side of things, there would be no adventure, no risk, no challenge, no drama. . . . If in the beginning God created order out of chaos (Gen. 1:2), God also created chaos. Chaos is the other side of order.[1]

Any who question the abiding influence of chaos are asked to have a look at the classic Marx Brothers' movies.

3. The Third Joke is The Absence of Any Say in One's Birth. No one asks to be born. (It would be a bit odd if one *could* so ask — a joke against the Joke.) Accordingly, the human person is, with every creature, left with the task of "making the best" of things. Arguably, one way (among many) to do this is laughter. There is also weeping, making the worst of things. Sooner or later the "sense" that we call humor, an authentic sixth sense, may be empowered either to reject or accept the universe, or to do both these things successively or alternately.

4. For humans, as for other creatures, the Fourth Joke is Death Amidst Life. The ongoing, seemingly imperishable *élan vital* is interrupted, indeed annihilated, by its end (*finis*), Death. Stephen Leacock holds that humor stems finally from "the incongruous contrast between the eager fret of our life and its final nothingness."[2]

5. The Fifth Joke is The "Is" Versus the "Ought" — the eternal incongruity between the world and people as they are, and the world and people as they could or may become. Here is a place where human suffering and humor so often meet. William Hazlitt finds the secret of human laughter/weeping in humanity's being struck with the difference between things as they are and things as they ought to be.[3]

6. The Sixth Joke, particularly affinal to the fifth, is Self-abnega-

tion Versus Self-centeredness — the will (instinct?) to sacrifice ourselves for the sake of others, counteracted and fought by the urge
(instinct?) to sacrifice others for the sake of ourselves.

7. The Seventh Joke is the Human Thrust/Wish to Partake of, or
Relate to, Infinity. This is why so much in religion is funny — or, put
somewhat more forcibly, why religion is a joke.

8. The Eighth Joke is Body in Juxtaposition to Spirit. For instance,
the same human voice that in one moment self-exaltingly enunciates
"eternal verities" may in the next moment cough itself to pieces. Professor Hyers points out that while tragedy inclines toward abstracting
spirit from body, comedy does the opposite. "The archaic staples of
comedy are . . . the earthen trinity of sex, food, and body wastes.
Added to this are the requirements of clothing, shelter, and sleep — the
first two as reminders of our nakedness, the third a reminder of our
nightly helplessness and unconsciousness. Mixed in are all those
troublesome inevitabilities of burping, itching, scratching, sniffling,
twitching, yawning, dozing, stretching, hiccuping, nose-wiping, ear-
picking, sneezing, snorting, coughing, choking, spitting, belching,
farting — ad infinitum and ad nauseam."[4]
Under the promptings of this catalogue from Hyers we are helped to
catch the point that embedded in the relation between the scatological
and the eschatological lies the comical. If "scatology represents a form
of aggression against propriety" (Sarah Blacher Cohen), eschatology
embodies, I should say, a kind of ultimate propriety and check against
human aggression.
A possible corollary to, or subheading under, the Eighth Joke is the
juxtaposition between human beings treated as subjects or persons and
human beings treated as objects (Carol Troen) — in Martin Buber's
phraseology, the difference between "I/Thou" and "I/it" relations. Much
humor may arise — so it can be adjudged — out of this dialectic. One is
further reminded of Henri Bergson's axiom that laughter is induced
when a person gives, or is made to give, the impression of being a
thing.

9. The Ninth Joke, more or less peculiar to humans, is Clothing.
Here we have, *au fond*, a naked body that is forced and/or enabled to

appear, behave, and masquerade in and through a congeries of wholly extrinsic, assorted colors, shapes, sizes, and materials.

10. The Tenth Joke is The Human/Domestic Animal Symbiosis. How can there be such accord between these disparities? How could it ever be that *this* kitten should lie purring upon *this* child's lap? Is it not a miracle? At the least, it stands amongst life's unpierced secrets.

If the philosophic enterprise begins in wonder, the above little decalogue may help to sharpen the wonder of everything there is. Particular jokes are ultimately traceable to, or made possible by, one or another of these fundamentals. (The reader may wish to suggest others.) One implication of my decalogue is to apprehend the kingdom of humor as much wider and deeper than is often assumed. An analogy or parallel here is that once religious faith is equated with being human — true, a debatable claim — religion as a mere segment of life or culture tends to lose its separate meaning or its "mereness."

The life of one who gives herself or himself to the cause of laughter is helped in getting started by certain objective conditions or raw materials "out there." This usually implies the presence of other human beings but it does not have to do so. That nonhuman creatures can be "funny," objectively speaking,[5] is a highly viable eventuality. If children, kittens, and puppies *are* funny, it can hardly be because we humans made them that way. Swabey writes, if we say "ducks are funny" we mean "to call attention to an imbalance in them, an incongruity. This incongruity [we find] between the duck's airborne structure as a bird of flight and its aquatic structure as a swimmer, in the contrast between its flat bill, web feet, dumpiness, ungainly waddle on the one hand, and its wingedness, glossy feathers, far-sighted restless eyes on the other, a contrast culminating in its voice, that crowning absurdity, the quack."[6] (The funniness of humans may be approached through corresponding antinomies.) The many birds who, while indescribably majestic in flight,[7] waddle hopelessly when on the ground furnish a juxtaposition, an incongruity, that may make for humor. I say "*may* make" because some human antinomies do not perforce issue in something humorous; for example, truth/falsehood.[8] Again, we may take pity upon the waddling bird rather than laugh at it.

A not unrelated way to conceptualize the present point is to apprehend comic potentiality as a function of distance/proximity. The greater the distance an object stands from us, the more difficult it becomes for us to complete the circle of incongruity. (There is a link here to the phenomenon of pornography, which simply cannot do its reprehensible mischief when great distances are present. Pornography lives as a parasite upon closeness.)

If humor is a function of space it may also be a function of time, as when it is manifest in the form of satire. In the words of Lenny Bruce, "Satire is tragedy plus time. You give it enough time, the public, the reviewers will allow you to satirize it."[9] Time and space comprise the ultimate playing fields of humor; humor is hostage to, but also creative pupil of, these supreme categories. (But, then, who or what isn't?) The bond between human laughter and the final dual category of space/time points up the ontological standing of human laughter.

The import of the reality of incongruity in the realm of nature is that it helps establish an objective rationale, perhaps even a scientific one, for humor and laughter. Nevertheless, it appears extreme to identify "life" as a whole as inherently "funny" on the univocal ground that it operates in the presence of its opposite, death. The difficulty here is that humor would then tend to lose its discreteness as a meaningful human category. A much more fitting opposite for funniness is sadness, for now the very sensible and nagging question poses itself of whether there can be comedy without tragedy, or tragedy without comedy.

What, then, is the task, the calling of representatives of comic laughter—the Dave Allens, the Woody Allens, the Carol Burnetts, the John Reeses, the Carl Reiners, the Rita Rudners, the Lily Tomlins, the Victoria Woods?

In accounting for the Hasidic storyteller, Elie Wiesel identifies that individual's calling as having but "one motivation: to tell of himself while telling of others."[10] In continuity with this identification, yet in partial contrast to it, I think we may say that the vocation of the servant of comic laughter is, or ought to be, to tell of others while telling of herself or himself. For Leo Rosten, humor is "the affectionate communication of insight."[11] To serve laughter is to serve life in a special way. Thus is this servant a humanist, yet more than that. For, as we have already intimated, the universe of this person extends to creatures other than human ones (for example, to tiny, delightful bugs).

Charlie Chaplin said that the best definition of humor he ever heard was "getting people in and out of trouble."[12] One psychiatrist has declared that "humor helps survival—even in Auschwitz." However, I have the impression that the creative and therapeutic values of humor sometimes get overstated. It seems to me that the only responsible answer to the question, "Is there anything funny about dying?," is a categorical No.[13] We sometimes tend to idealize humor and laughter, perhaps due to their pleasantness and seemingly remedial powers. They ask to be sentimentalized, utopianized. Humor can do nothing whatever to counteract the categorical sentence of death that Auschwitz pronounced. On the other hand, we are afforded documented claims of the power of humor to overcome sickness—as in the noted case of Norman Cousins, who contended that humor therapy helped him overcome a terminal illness.[14]

The loosest and most truistic definition of comedy is drama with a happy ending, in contrast to tragedy as drama with a sad or terrible ending.[15] The questionability in such a differentiation is that comic laughter is never safe from the end we call despair, while the tears of tragedy just may be dried by the sunshine. However, in tragedy fate (*moira*) is regnant, though not without catharsis. Comedy boasts freedom, spontaneity, a measure of mastery. A threat to comedy is its trivialization into "happy endings," just as a menace to tragedy is sublimity and destruction apart from fate.

There is the enigma of whether laughter could ever become omnipresent and thereby dominate us.

> Somewhere in this world, Rabbi Nachman of Bratzlav used to say, there is a certain city which encompasses all other cities in the world. And in that city there is a street which encompasses all other streets in the city. And on that street there stands a house which dominates all other houses on the street. And that house has a room which comprises all other rooms in the house. And in that room there lives a man in whom all other men recognize themselves. And that man is laughing. That's all he ever does, ever did. He roars with laughter when seen by others, but also when alone.[16]

Were laughter to be everywhere, to encompass and govern everything, how could there be any such thing as laughter? Yet weeping runs up against no less formidable an obstacle.

Julian Green wrote that after Auschwitz "only tears have meaning."

Who would quarrel with him? Yet what are we to think and do should someone dare the alternative, "After Auschwitz, only laughter has meaning"? When tears act, imperialistically, to determine all things, they appear to overreach themselves. Nevertheless, when humor is bereft of pain it comes to share the plight that descends upon "the good" once its antagonist "evil" is somehow removed. Imperializing laughter is not real laughter, just as imperializing tears are not real tears. Soft laughter seems to be somewhat healthier, and soft tears as well. As Howard Moss puts it, humor, like innocence, is by nature fragile.[17] Shel Silverstein tells of "The Land of Happy," where day after day after day after day everyone is "jolly and gay" — and he concludes: "What a bore!"[18]

True laughter, like true weeping, is often marked by fragility and scarcity (though not so much so in the instance of children). At the beginning of Elie Wiesel's *The Testament,* Viktor Zupanev reports, pitifully, that he has never laughed in his entire life. It is not until the final page of the tale that he is enabled to fill this emptiness: "My heart is broken but I know that I shall laugh. And suddenly it happens: I am laughing, I am laughing at last."[19]

The patriarch Abraham is allegedly told by God to sacrifice his son in the fire (Gen. 22) — one of the most terrifying of the biblical stories (Robert McAfee Brown).[20] Yet the son bears the name Isaac (Itzhak, "he laughs"). How can these two eventualities exist together?

The story is familiar. Just in time, an angel stays the hand of the executioner, and a ram is substituted for Isaac. I lift out only three *midrashim* (interpretive comments) upon the one who will laugh. (I have to pass over Woody Allen's suggestion that Abraham knew he must sacrifice his son because God's order came in a resonant, well-modulated voice.)

a. The occasion was hardly one for the *ram* to laugh — or its mother and father, or its never-to-be-born offspring. The anthropocentrism of the entire affair is patent.

b. Wiesel points to the subsequent (necessary?) estrangement of father and son: Isaac remained alive, but he no longer journeyed with his father.[21] The life of laughter often carries a steep price.

c. "Why was the most tragic of our ancestors named Isaac. . . ? Here is why. As the first survivor, he had to teach us, the future survivors of Jewish history, that it is possible to suffer and despair an entire lifetime, and still not give up the art of laughter. Of course, Isaac never freed himself from the traumatizing scenes that violated his youth; the holocaust had marked him and continued to haunt him forever. Yet he remained capable of laughter. And in spite of everything, he did laugh."[22] Yes, Isaac is indeed the one who will laugh. Yet the life of laughter often inflicts deep scars.

To homogenize these three *midrashim*: Laughter can be *an in spite of everything* — in other terminology, the polar opposite of every TV "laugh track."

Elie Wiesel comments upon the *akedah*, the binding of Isaac: "Laughter becomes a defiance. A defiance and a victory. The only way to be victorious over God is to laugh, not at Him, but with Him. Laughter is also a sort of anguish."[23] Robert McAfee Brown proffers a *midrash* upon the *midrash*:

> There is frequent laughter in Wiesel's novels. Much of it is the laughter of madmen. Often it is the laughter of despair acknowledging that all doors are closed. But sometimes it is the laughter of anticipation that new doors are opening. . . . Laughter *at* God will get us nowhere. But laughter *with* God. . . . Where might that take us? . . . It could at least help us explore suffering in a new fashion. Suffering can never be "justified" — a thousand theodicies to the contrary notwithstanding. Nor, apparently, can suffering be ended, as a thousand experiences confirm. However, by remaining defiant in the face of suffering, seeking to limit it, refusing to accept it as a justifiable end or a necessary means, we can still deal with it. . . . There is massive evidence to justify giving way to despair. . . . And yet, and yet . . . the messenger urges us to sing a song of joy! There is no absolute victory, he has already told us, but there can be a "small means of victory." In spite of everything.[24]

I have much difficulty with efforts to equate (1) the laughter of defiance or anguish and (2) laughing *with* God. Humor readily and radically excels defiance. It often exudes a carefreeness, a lightheartedness, that is spontaneous, a form of pure joy that bears its own meaning and its own justification. There is nothing of anguish in the pristine laughter of children. Is adult laughter to be the critic and criterion of child laughter, or is child laughter to be the critic and criterion of adult laughter? (And where does this leave the awkward yet integral laughter of the adolescent?) We can scarcely restrict the domain of humor to the adult world of trials and tribulations. Nevertheless, a caution against sentimentality, trivialization, and frivolousness remains in force. The laughter of the child lives in the very same house as the child's sadness.

In *Souls on Fire,* Wiesel is himself more expansive than we have noted above: "To submit blindly to God, without questioning the meaning of this submission, would be to diminish Him. To want to understand Him would be to reduce His intentions, His vision to the level of ours. How then can man [*sic*] take himself seriously? Revolt is not a solution, neither is submission. [There] remains laughter, metaphysical laughter."[25] From the latter perspective, the defiance of God does not really go against God but is itself affirming of God.

Morton Gurewitch understands comedy's "ultimate variousness" as resting upon "the tendency to exploit both celebration and scorn."[26] In referring to the "complete equality" that is a mark of carnival, W. H. Auden makes a similar point. He identifies two dimensions of laughter in its completeness:

> Essentially, what is carnival about? . . . It is a common celebration of our common fate as members of our species. Here we are, mortal, born into the world, we must die, and this applies to everybody, so that there is a mixture. This is what laughter also implies, because laughter is both an act of protest and an act of acceptance.

> There is joy in the fact that we are all in the same boat, that there are no exceptions made. On the other hand, we cannot help wishing that we had no problems — let us say, that either we were in a way unthinking like the animals or that we were disembodied angels. But this is impossible; so we laugh because we simultaneously protest and accept.[27]

Laughter may perhaps be compared to song, though also contrasted with it. Singing incarnates the two elements, but on the whole it is more accepting than protesting. There are elements of hostility in comedy, yet comedy can be loving as well.[28] Authentic humor has a twin sibling that haunts us. The twin goes by the name of Sorrow. (We can laugh so hard that we cry. But can we cry so hard that we laugh?) Interpreting Elie Wiesel, John K. Roth declares: "Without God, humanity is and can be nothing. The catch — and the challenge — is that even with God humanity may also become nothing. Therefore, life must be lived so that it can be celebrated; it must be celebrated so that it can be lived. Otherwise humanity defeats itself and the goodness of God as well."[29]

All in all, a life story of laughter such as is being told here—the journey from Proto-Joke to defiance to carnival—is grounded in the peculiar dimension of human freedom, in freedom's catholicity, a freedom that in turn flies upon the twin engines of responsibility and fate, creativity and givenness, protest and acceptance.[30]

NOTES

1. Conrad Hyers, *The Comic Vision and the Christian Faith*, pp. 169–70.
2. Stephen Leacock, *Humor and Humanity* (New York: Holt, 1938), pp. 219–20.
3. William Hazlitt, *Lectures on the English Comic Writers* (1885), in *Philosophy of Laughter and Humor*, John Morreall, ed., p. 65.
4. Hyers, *Comic Vision*, pp. 88–89, 90.
5. If there is "funniness" "out there," the element of *to us* is yet ineluctably present.
6. Swabey, *Comic Laughter*, p. 10.
7. A flock of flying birds does something that no creatures have ever done before or can ever do again: it cleaves just *this* single configuration of space/time. The spoken word has an analogous effect upon silence (cf. Frederick Buechner, *Telling the Truth*). A philosophic hypothesis using data such as these is that there are no exactly repeatable events. This state of affairs appears not unrelated to the uniqueness of the life of humor.
8. The antinomy of true/false is, however, subject to comic application, as are all human antinomies.
9. John Cohen, ed., *The Essential Lenny Bruce*, p. 116.
10. Elie Wiesel, *Souls on Fire*, p. 259.
11. Leo Rosten, *Leo Rosten's Giant Book of Laughter*, p. 1.
12. *The New Yorker* (25 February 1950), p. 25.
13. The theme, "Is There Anything Funny About Dying?," made up part of a conference on humor and pastoral care at Anaheim, California, Nov. 14–15, 1989, sponsored by the Institute for the Advancement of Human Behavior and the American Association for Therapeutic Humor. Jackson Lee Ice takes a markedly optimistic position respecting the creative value of the comic faculty: "Humor and religion, each in its own way, are profoundly regenerative; they are the two most effectively therapeutic means at man's disposal for responding to his finitude" (Ice, "Notes," pp. 395–96). Consult Thomas Kuhlman, *Humor and Psychotherapy* (Homewood, Ill.: Dow Jones-Irwin, 1984).
14. Norman Cousins, *Anatomy of an Illness as Perceived by the Patient* (New York: Norton, 1979).
15. However, an old tradition has it that tragedy produces the *right* ending (Swabey, *Comic Laughter*, p. 187; see chaps. 7 and 9). The comedy/tragedy

dialectic raises the question of sport and play. Since in baseball leagues, for example, all teams save one must lose the final championship, baseball may be viewed as prevailingly tragic — but only when the enterprise is taken with undue seriousness. When it is not taken too seriously, there is no tragedy. However, at a more general level it is often observed that athletes are, in a manner of speaking, forced to die young. Cf. Johan Huizinga: Play is the activity that stands outside the normal intensity of life, since it is not serious, but nevertheless absorbs the players intensely and utterly (*Homo Ludens*, p. 13). Consult Michael Novak, *The Joy of Sports* (Lanham, Md.: University Press of America, 1988).

16. Elie Wiesel, *A Beggar in Jerusalem*, p. 30.
17. Howard Moss, foreword to *The Nonsense Books of Edward Lear*, p. vii.
18. Shel Silverstein, "The Land of Happy," *Where the Sidewalk Ends*, p. 143.
19. Elie Wiesel, *The Testament*, pp. 28, 346. "It is laughter signaling a cunning victory, laughter revealing something more powerful than the NKVD and the Politburo, more powerful even than Stalin. And that something is the insignificant court stenographer, who, by his very insignificance, survives the purging of the purgers and tells the story nobody was supposed to hear" (Robert McAfee Brown, *Elie Wiesel: Messenger to All Humanity* [Notre Dame: University of Notre Dame Press, 1983], p. 132).
20. See Brown's commentary upon Elie Wiesel's reading of the *akedah*, the binding of Isaac (*Elie Wiesel*, pp. 124–29).
21. Elie Wiesel, *Messengers of God*, p. 83.
22. Ibid., p. 97.
23. Elie Wiesel, in Harry James Cargas, ed., *Responses to Elie Wiesel* (New York: Persea Books, 1978), p. 156.
24. Brown, *Elie Wiesel*, pp. 223, 224–25.
25. Wiesel, *Souls on Fire*, pp. 198–99.
26. Morton Gurewitch, *Comedy: The Irrational Vision*, p. 35.
27. W. H. Auden, "Forgotten Laughter, Forgotten Prayer," *The New York Times* (2 February 1971).
28. But not for S. J. Perelman: "I don't believe in kindly humor. I don't think it exists" (as cited in William Zinsser, "That Perelman of Great Price is 65," *The New York Times Magazine* [26 January 1969], p. 76).
29. John K. Roth, *A Consuming Fire: Encounters with Elie Wiesel and the Holocaust* (Atlanta: John Knox Press, 1979), p. 143.
30. As Gurewitch expresses it, humor "either copes with disaster or thrives on whimsy and joy" (*Comedy*, p. 9).

2

Five Reflections upon the Wet Queen

Others write clever things for foolish people. I write foolish things for clever people.

—Moishe Nadir

1. THE WET QUEEN, A RIGHT COLLARBONE, AND THE SACRED CANOPY

Why should anybody be commended for exposing his right collarbone as a target for the Wet Queen?

I call her the Wet Queen because "Queen" does not quite seem to do it. This woman is invariably soaking wet; hence, it would be out of the question to call her, say, the Arid Queen. For only four things in the Universe are permitted to be wet and dry at one and the same time: wine, beer, the martini, and a bather from Bensonhurst up to his middle at Coney Island.

Yet it is not at all the Monarch's wetness that authorizes the name Wet Queen; it is instead my own abiding desire to plunge into that wetness, an urge that has beset me for more years than I care to mention — but shall mention anyway: thirty-seven gedillion.

It so happens that I am Chief of a small Group of souls who forever and ever have been guiding and guarding the Wet Queen in her every queenly move — and in some moves not so queenly. (Put a little less circumspectly, I am in charge of the Universe as a whole — the dream

13

come true of every male being, though probably not of every female being.) For the present, our Group goes by the name, the Sacred Canopy.

You could say that it must have been something suicidal that drove me to jog past the Wet Queen's palace window during that fateful night of the 23rd of Dissembler. (All right, go ahead and say it: "It must have been something suicidal that drove you, Excellency, to jog past the Wet Queen's window during that fateful night of the—what was that date again?—23rd of Dissembler.") I ought to have remembered that the Wet Queen and her deadly Magnum-Bow would be waiting for me. . . .

Was I talking about anything? O yes, the Wet Queen winged me in the right collarbone. Now I am aware as well as you that an invaded right collarbone is not the most grievous of injuries. At least, I seriously doubt that either of us has ever heard it said, "The invasion of the right collarbone is the worst hurt a human or divine person can experience." Tell me: How could anyone be so foolhardy as to *believe* that an invasion of the right collarbone is the most terrible injury possible?

However, an invaded *left* collarbone is quite a different kettle of marrow. In my case, it would have inevitably brought about a worldshaking reversal of roles as between the Wet Queen and me as Chief—as I shall shortly explain. More fateful than anything else was a certain by-product of my "accident." For ever since that wholly gratuitous episode, I find that I am programmed to refer to my Group as the Sacred Can . . . Can . . . Canopwhy—now you have heard with your own ears the exact nature of my affliction—assuming that you can hear something that is being written to you. And it is most embarrassing. For example, in presiding at daily sessions of the Group, I find myself having to say, "Will the Sacred Canopwhy please come to order?" And upon each and every such occasion I am given no choice but to be forcibly, even tiresomely, reminded of one Ed Wynn, the Perfect Fool, and his repeated visits to Eggwhypt.

Yet I suppose I could be a lot worse off. It could well have been the left collarbone. I am aware as well as you that an invaded left collarbone is indeed the most grievous of injuries. At the very least, you and I have heard it said a thousand times, "The invasion of the left collarbone is the worst hurt a person could ever experience." Tell me: How could anyone ever be so silly as to come to *believe* that an invasion of the left collarbone is *not* the most terrible injury possible?

In this very connection we have to bear in mind that, in my case, an invaded left collarbone would mean that the party calling *My* Organization to order would be none other than the Wet Queen herself. Before me is a well-documented intelligence report showing that she intends to stoop to the sacrilege of changing the name of our beloved Sacred Canopy to the Wet Blanket. You can understand the agonizing dilemma in which this will have placed me — on the one hand, Lover of Wetness yet, on the other hand, Defender of Traditional Language.

In retrospect or even willy nilly, I thank myself for having bared my *right* collarbone to the Wet Queen. And I imagine it is only a question of time — give or take a few million years — when I will once again be pronouncing Canopwhy as Canopy. There now, the time passed rather quickly after all.

2. A LOST CONVERSATION?

The other day the Wet Queen telephoned. She said, "This is Ploonhoven." I responded, "I am Ramphont."

Ploonhoven and Ramphont proceeded to have a long talk. I do not know what they said. After all, I am not Ramphont. For that matter, neither is the Wet Queen Ploonhoven. And yet, once you put it that way — "Wet Queen Ploonhoven" — the two do seem to merge. And is this not also the case with "I am Ramphont."

Conclusion: I am simply not telling the truth when I plead above that I did not know what Ploonhoven and Ramphont said to one another.

3. IS THE WET QUEEN YET IN CUSTODY?

The reason we of the Sacred Canopy have adjudged that the Wet Queen will have to abdicate is that she keeps going over to the Herzegovinians.

You know intimately the continuing conflict between Bosnia and Herzegovinia. The Sacred Canopy is, of course, allied with the Bosnians. Just within the past fortnight — in the U.W.Q. we would never say "weeks" — the Wet Queen has gone over to the Herzegovinians no less than 684 times. Fortunately for our side, Bosnian technology recently fabricated the Wet Queen Catapult, installing it under the cover of darkness barely within Herzegovinian lines, just beyond No-People's-Land. Now each time this woman goes over to the other side, she is thrown back by the Catapult, being deposited uninjured, and increasingly less surprised, well within Bosnian territory.

So in keeping with the terms of the U.W.Q.-Bosnia extradition agreement of 1269, the Wet Queen languishes in our custody — at least for the moment.

Until she is exiled permanently to the Isle of Woman, the Wet Queen is to expend a preparatory time of penance in the Rewot fo Nodnol. However, Bosnian intelligence now advises us that the Wet Queen and her Rather Damp Cohorts are planning an escape attempt for her precisely at the line between the Rewot and the Inclined Plane. The Inclined Plane is the *Anknüpfungspunkt* between Nodnol as such and its Rewot. To locate the Inclined Plane, sneer with the left side of your face. The resultant line of your lips will roughly indicate the effective working angle of that Plane.

The reason the Wet Queen and her debased followers have selected for the escape attempt the demarcation line between the Inclined Plane and the Rewot is that precisely at that juncture a change of jurisdiction is in force between the authority of the Sacred Canopy and the authority of the Rewot. In fact, it is widely rumored that the Rewot Repeek (or Repeek fo eht Rewot; or, for that matter, Rewot eht fo Repeek; but never Repeek Rewot — unless, of course, you read it Repeek Rewot), Sir Reginald Damp-Saddle, is secretly allied with the Wet Queen, and through her with the Herzegovinians.

But we of the Sacred Canopy are not left without resources. I am personally ordering elite companies of the 23rd Scottish Lowlanders, the 17th Upland Brigadoons, the 13th Irish Dragoons, the 26th Vessex Regular Goons, and the 39th Cornish Hens to stand guard at the entrance to the Rewot — alert for any and every eventuality. Or was it the 24th Orkney Islanders, the 18th Grampian Grenadiers, the 14th Welsh Lancers, the 27th Norwich Irregulars, and the 40th Nodnol Artillery? No, it was not. Just this morning I came to realize that it was in fact the 22nd Hebridean Outlanders, the 16th Cracked Rifles, the 12th Fifth of Forth Sharpshooters, the 25th Unseemly Limericks, and the 38th Royal Rhode Island Reds.

If only in order that we may all be reassured and carry on, please add together all these possibilities. You just may find yourself coming out with the 316th Royal Foreflushers, a tidy, aggressive bunch readily capable of subduing each and every Wet Queen. (You are entirely correct in your objection. Ought not the total be 354? However, word is now in that the 38th Royal Rhode Island Reds have gone over to the Herzegovinians.)

4. SEVEN INCHES FOR THE UNIVERSE

In opposition to everything for which the Wet Queen stands, I plan to expand the Universe by seven inches.

I am probably more aware than anyone that I am already expanding the Universe, and quite rapidly at that. What I intend to do is simply to add on seven inches all the way round — perpetually *out in front* of any and every ongoing expansion. Seven inches may not sound like very much to you, but when you keep in mind the size of the entire business, I think you will agree that this will be quite a notable addition.

In a word — more accurately, in twenty-four words: Contra the Wet Queen, the expanse of the expanse of the expanding Universe will be significantly expanded beyond the expanse of its present expanse. And the expansion will be dry, basically dry, that is, vulnerable to the charge of selfhatred.

5. THE WET QUEEN'S FAILURE TO DIE

> The day that slate and chalk do meet,
> The sound of Death shall oft repeat.
> But death to Death is generate,
> When slate and chalk do separate.
> — Bjorn of Bjutland (d. 563)

Though an expert upon, as well as longtime student and friend of, Bjorn of Bjutland, I had never succeeded in puzzling out the inner meaning of his most renowned quatrain — not until a certain incident took place at my summer home in Slob one fair afternoon last Leo.

Seated in my study chair, I was remarking dryly to a visitor, "The

Wet Queen is not dead." Then, suddenly sneezing, I repeated, but now wetly, "No, the Wet Queen is not dead."

The Intruder (Death) snorted. He then proceeded to scrape the soul of his left boot upon my highly unpolished slate floor. The sound became maddening, like the screech sometimes made by chalk on a blackboard. I was at once carried back to the halcyon days when I used to drive students to distraction with this very weapon. I saw the word "Screech" being spelled out boldly on the floor between the Intruder and me. And I heard my ears ringing with that same piercing, hollow sound. I would be inclined to say, my ears heard my ears ringing, yet, while this is perfectly correct, it sounds a bit strained. I think I shall say it anyway: My ears heard my ears ringing. In any event, this was how I became aware that my visitor was wearing chalk souls upon his boots.

The Intruder continued with his scoffing. "Of course the Wet Queen is dead! Did not we ourselves (Death prefers the editorial "we") hear the shots ring out? Ding, Gong! Ding, Gong! We saw the blood spurt from the tightly-corseted torso, all the more so as she was falling to the pavement. We were less than ten feet from her all the time. True, the press of the crowd made it most difficult, even impossible, to reach her side. Indeed, it became necessary for us to go round the other way."

I looked up from my private game of Dizzical Brown, with which I had been idly toying; my face, or more accurately my forehead, showed a quizzical frown:

"The other *way*?"

"Yes, at the very moment of her assassination we were directly east of the Wet Queen. In order to get to her we were forced to head eastward, eventually circumnavigating the entire globe. It was fascinating, of course: Biarritz — Baluchistan — Calcutta — Vladivostok — Honolulu — San Francisco — San Antonio — New Orleans — Macungie, Pennsylvania. Unfortunately, when some eighty days later we managed to get back to Roundstone Square in Nodnol the place was entirely deserted — except, it goes without saying, for the pigeons. One of these — he must have been the homing kind — directed us to the morgue. But of course the Revolutionary Tribunal had long since disposed of the Wet Queen's remains and removed every trace of the attack."

Suddenly and menacingly, the Intruder rose and began to dance indecently upon my floor, with *both* boots: "Screech! Screech!" But somehow a strange calm had come over me. Tempted as I had been to break the Intruder's head, I merely broke my silence. "Baluchistan all well and good, but never Macungie. You are not a reliable witness!"

Tale between his legs, the Intruder quickly and quietly left, without so much as another screech upon my floor of slate. He *flew* out — all of which served to confirm the uncanny prophecy of Bjorn of Bjutland.

3

The Anatomy of Laughter

To classify and explain the many and various kinds of laughter and humor can become boring, a menace to what is funny, even a goad to depression. The analytic dissection of humor may simply kill it. "Humor can be dissected, as a frog can, but the thing dies in the process and the innards are discouraging to any but the pure scientific mind" (E. B. White).[1] Yet I don't quite know how to escape this anatomical chore. Perhaps we may say that any such analysis is the tribute an ever-imaginative right side of the brain must pay to the left side for the latter's necessarily *being there* to the end of human completeness and good order. Maurice Samuel has suggested that while talking around a joke tends to blunt its point, perhaps enough of it will remain to justify the effort.[2] Jackson Lee Ice writes that "apparently humor is only to be enjoyed, not understood — the proto-exemplification of the epigram 'ignorance is bliss.' "[3] I should add, though, that in and through the very enjoyment of laughter different efforts at human understanding can be encouraged.

We may bear in mind a caution of Morton Gurewitch: "The energies of comedy are too diverse to permit procrustean interpretations."[4] The same is the case with respect to theory. Divergent viewpoints upon the nature and function of humor are legion. The "serious" chapters of the present handbook underscore this fact.

Humor and laughter are subject to treatment from a variety of methodological perspectives: anthropology, biology, drama, history, literature, philosophy, physiology, psychology, sociology, theology. I put these in alphabetical order in order to underline my assumption that on the face of things, no one approach is more insightful than any other. For example, the philosopher or theologian does well to be aware of psychological, biological, and physiological data. Thus, correlations have been found between galvanic skin response and the experience of humor, and the same is the case with heart rate. Again, in one experiment a group injected with epinephrine found a particular film funnier than those who had been injected with saline. Nitrous oxide is known to be readily productive of laughter.[5] Psychiatric understandings of laughter are well-known and influential, particularly the Freudian contention that the basic element in humor is the reduction of anxiety, and hence that at least amongst healthy people, humor can offset human destructiveness.[6]

Conrad Hyers offers a tenfold representation of special practitioners of laughter: humorist, fool (jester), clown, child, comedian, simpleton, comic hero, divine hero, underdog, and trickster. The general standpoint of Hyers is one of comparative mythology and the history of religions, with stress upon myth, ritual, and symbol, and with a focus upon the religious significance of different comic forms. "The larger questions have to do with the *meaning* of this side of existence. What are the implications of the comic perspective for those peculiarly human issues of sacred and profane, 'truth, beauty, and goodness,' 'nature, man, and God'? What does this angle of vision reveal about human existence, or existence as such?"[7]

We concentrate here upon Hyers's treatment of the *humorist*, wherein some helpful distinctions are provided.

The first of these distinctions is between "low" laughter and "high" laughter. There is the "low" laughter that can be "arrogant, taunting, scornful, contemptuous, sneering, vulgar, cruel, nervous, giddy, hysterical, malicious, bitter, and insane." "Low" laughter is a ready tool of aggression, a reinforcement of prejudice and of a sense of superiority. Instead of unmasking pride and pretension, "low" laughter only masks them more effectively. This genre of laughter "can become an easy path of escape from intellectual labor, moral accountability, and profound commitment. It can degenerate into a frivolous diversion from the tortuous and seemingly intractable issues that confront us." Finally, such laughter may merely be trivial — "witticisms of the moment that are quickly forgotten because they do not touch us at the core of our being. They provide only a convenient diversion, a false sense of security."

Hyers emphasizes that the authentic and responsible humorist will simply refuse to trade in any and every sort of laughter. However, to ridicule, say, an oppressor is not really "low" laughter but is "aimed at a restoration of balance and a renewed sense of dignity and fair play. Comic *justice* is served."[8]

In "high" laughter "the humorist laughs *with* and not just *at* other people." Thus is humor "opened up to sympathy and goodwill. . . . A humor that heretofore has moved within the context of comic release and comic justice now moves within a context of empathy and kindred feeling." It has become the "humor of humility and compassion." To practice comic twists for the admiring masses is not the same as the true art of humor, wherein the humorist succeeds "in personally existentializing the comic spirit and perspective" and provides a perspective on the whole of life. "High" laughter has a redemptive quality. Accordingly, Thomas Hobbes's definition of laughter as a sudden glory arising at the sight of an inferior is, for Hyers (and I agree), "a garbage collector's view of the comic sensibility. Everything is thrown away but the trash." I may interpose here Morton Gurewitch's comment upon "sick humor." It is a "pathological variety of gallows humor: it does not so much exorcise dread and the fear of death as pander to a dehumanizing appetite for the macabre."[9]

In his accounting of Garrison Keillor's humor of compassion, William Lee Miller writes:

> There is indeed an aspect of humor that *divides* — that makes someone the butt of a joke while the rest of us laugh at him or her. But is there not, at a more profound level, an aspect of high humor that unites, that brings a shock of recognition of our common humanity? Often there is a sudden rush not only of recognition — *Yes, that's the way it is, exaggerated now so we can see it clearly* — but also of fellow-feeling, even of surprise identification: *Yes, it must be that way with them, and it would be so with us, in that condition; yes, we share those human responses.*[10]

Conrad Hyers further distinguishes among three storeys of humor. In the *laughter of paradise* humor is "a playful return to a past innocence and unity," "a form of playing for the sake of playing." Here human beings are free to "play the fool, indulge in silliness, act with childlike abandon, and deliver themselves to the caprice of the instant." At this level of comic banter, "distinctions between significant and trivial, serious and frivolous, holy and unholy, are not available. They have been set aside in the recollected laughter of children." (Cf. *Monty Python's Flying Circus.*)

In the present handbook, which extends to the nonsense of humor as well as to the sense of humor, a comment upon the quality of nonsense appears apropos at this point. Howard Moss suggests that nonsense requires two qualities: "the ability to think and feel like a child and a highly developed sense of language."[11] We might note here that Lewis Carroll specifically identified his *Through the Looking-Glass* as a "book of nonsense."[12]

At the second storey, the *laughter of paradise lost*, there is "reflection and release of present tensions and contradictions." Humor now becomes a means of expressing frustration, fear, and even antagonism. But at a higher plane this humor is seen as a means of dispensing a sort of poetic justice. It fastens upon hypocrisy and injustice. It begins to come to direct terms with the ambiguity and ambivalence that pervade human life. It becomes a reminder of the basic awkwardness of human nature and its place in the cosmos, "especially for those inclined to forget it (its *iconoclastic* or *prophetic* function, which it shares with satire and irony). And it offers a means of accepting this awkwardness and coping with it (its *cathartic* or *purgative* function)." Humor further tries to come to terms with absurdity, evil, suffering, and death. A certain defiance of the evil and torments of life manifests itself, as we witness in certain forms of Jewish and Black humor. "Where there is humor there is still hope" (cf. chapter 1 above).

A third storey of humor, the *laughter of paradise regained*, may be achieved only rarely. For it attains unto "a recovery on a higher level of lost innocence and unity." It is a laughter of maturity, corresponding mythically to paradise regained. We are brought, in a sense, to "the final goal and fulfillment of humor. Humor moves from playful innocence through truth and justice to humility and compassion." Such humor is generated by an inner harmony, a profound sense of security. "It presupposes faith in some sacred order or depth-dimension of being, some common basis of worth and dignity, at the same time that it represents a persistent unwillingness to dogmatize its understanding of that faith and worth." The element of judgment in humor passes over into mercy and love. At this level there is a kind of recovery of

childlikeness. "Because children are not given to absolutizing themselves and their situations, reconciliation comes easily and the festival
can begin once more."

> The world ruled by seriousness alone grows old, faded, wooden, rigid, lifeless.
> The grave world is indeed the world of the grave. But the world in the reign of
> the comic spirit grows young again — lively, vital, creative, dancing, joyful. It
> is a world that is guarded not, like Eden, by some angel of judgment with a
> flaming sword, but by the high priests of comedy who invite all to come in
> who will lay down their rifles and rattles, their poses and posturings, their
> masks and trumpetings. It is a world which, as Johan Huizinga said of poetry,
> "lies beyond seriousness, on that more primitive and original level where the
> child, the animal, the savage and the seer belong, in the region of dream,
> enchantment, ecstasy, laughter." (cf. Edward Hicks, *The Peaceable King-
> dom.* — A.R.E.)[13]

NOTES

1. E. B. White, *The Second Tree from the Corner*, p. 173. "Any exegesis of hu-
    mor is both fatal and dull" (S. J. Perelman).
2. Maurice Samuel, *The World of Sholom Aleichem*, p. 184.
3. Ice, "Notes," p. 389.
4. Gurewitch, *Comedy*, p. 9.
5. Consult N. N. Holland, *Laughing: A Psychology of Humor.*
6. Ice, "Notes," p. 395.
7. Hyers, *Comic Vision*, p. 19. Gurewitch puts forward a simpler typology:
    comedy is generated by the four impulses of farce, humor, satire, and irony
    (*Comedy*, p. 13).
8. Cf. Ronald de Sousa, "When Is It Wrong to Laugh?," in *Philosophy of
    Laughter and Humor*, John Morreall, ed., pp. 226–49.
9. Gurewitch, *Comedy*, p. 100.
10. William Lee Miller, "*Sola Gratia* in Lake Wobegon," *The Christian Century*
    104 (1987): 528.
11. Moss, foreword to *The Nonsense Books of Edward Lear*, p. vii. Edward Lear
    "never forgot his childhood — the mark of all good writers. What a child feels
    is not often the same as what he can say. What an adult can say is not always
    the same as what he feels. Lear came to the rescue" (ibid., p. xix).
12. At the end, in his "Easter greeting to every child who loves 'Alice.' "
13. Hyers, *Comic Vision*, chap. 1.

4

Collected Works, Uncollected Works

COLLECTED WORKS

A Beginning Word List

Abracadábra. A foundation garment worn by an abracada.

Cóndominíum. A very small contraceptive that is neither male nor female.

Detáched rétina. A condition of the eye that couldn't care less.

Eárwig. Special aid for those whose hearing is getting bald.

Fíghting Báptist. A person who joins the Navy's submarine service in order to be under water as often as possible.

Foúrflúsher. A person who has the compulsion to pull the chain, pull the chain, pull the chain, pull the chain.

Gum árabic. An alternative to pidgin English, wherein the use of the tongue is forbidden.

Indéntured sérvant. An individual who bites the hand that feeds him.

27

Nápkin. A group of relatives taking a siesta together.

Nítwit. A very intelligent lover of louse eggs.

Oxymóron. An individual who becomes stupefied, and hence momentarily stupid, from breathing too deeply.

Píltdown man. A prehistoric featherweight.

Rotúnda. Fatter, in Brooklyn.

Wómbat. (1) A highly indecisive person who vacillates between being a womb and a bat. (2) a female pinchhitter/designated hitter.

Short Stories

THE REVENGE OF MONSIEUR ANCIEN

Monsieur Ancien and Monsieur Jeune met one day.

Monsieur Jeune said: "You do not look at all well. But then, you are not getting any younger!"

Monsieur Ancien replied: "You look marvelous. But then, you are not getting any older!"

The bullet from Monsieur Ancien's pistol went straight to its mark, and Monsieur Jeune fell down dead.

(You are watching an animated short; quickly, Monsieur Jeune got up, the two friends shook hands, and went off to drink a bottle of wine.)

IRONY IN THE WILD WEST

Ottomar the Outlaw came rushing in with guns blazing, caught fire, and burned to death.

(You are not watching an animated short. Ottomar was cooked, once and for all.)

CRISIS IN THE GALILEE

Rabbi Israel ben Judah said: "Man is greater than the phallus."

Rabbi Judah ben Israel answered: "The phallus seems to be greater than man."

Rabbi Joseph Ben Zaddik intervened: "You are both right. Man is greater than the phallus *precisely because* the phallus appears to be greater than man."

Rabbi ben Zaddik's colleagues were perplexed at this, and questioned him. He replied: "Rabbi Yeshua ben Joseph taught, 'Which of you by taking thought can add one cubit unto his stature?' (Matt. 6:27). True, the phallus periodically increases its stature — twofold, sometimes even three fold. [Cf. Hyam Maccoby: "In Bava Metsia, 84a: 'Rabbi Johanan said: "The penis of Rabbi Ishmael was like a wine-skin of nine Kavs' (pints') capacity." ' "[1]] However, it is still man who, by taking thought, enables the phallus to add to its stature. Therefore, man is greater than the phallus."

SPOTTED DICK: AN ENGLISH SWEET

Richard's phallus has been spotted in Birmingham, Norwich, Blackpool, and Southampton. But it has been observed unspotted in Spokane, Pisa, Nicosia, and Vladivostok.

A TALE OF SAHARAN HOSPITALITY

Guest to host and hostess: Well, kind friends, I think I will say goodnight.

Host and hostess: Goodnight.

Guest: Look here, I didn't say "Goodnight." I merely said I was *thinking* of saying "Goodnight."

Host and hostess: Nostra culpa Emiliae Postae!

Guest: Goodnight.

Host and hostess: Goodnight.

Host: And may the Sandman bury you, your children, and your children's children in the deepest dune of the desert!

Verse

LINES COMPOSED AFTER TEN WINTERS
OF HAULING WOOD FOR A PAIR OF WOOD STOVES

Once
All wood
Was good.

Now
No good
Is wood.

IN CELEBRATION OF NEIGHBORHOOD ROPE JUMPING

The temperature out is in.
The temperature in is out.
So whether you're in,
Or whether you're out,
The old man has the gout.

SEDENTARY INSIGHT

For many years I aspired
To know why I was forever tired.
The answer came at last:
I've been sitting in my gyms,
Crossing and uncrossing
Two very heavy limbs.

MEMOIR OF A BLOATED DIETETIC

My flabbergas is ted.
My flabberg is asted.
My flabber is gasted.
My flab is bergasted.

I am fat.

Instructions to a Blind Devil About to Take a Bath

Grab hold ze tub,
Beelzebub.
Then zit and rub.

Toward Cleanliness in the Royal Pies

Prince Vince hince,
But more than hince,
"Rince the mince!
Forget the quince!
Or you will wince,
forever since!"

Ultimatum to a Chattering Spouse

Unless you culminate,
I shall fulminate.

Metaphysical Musings

'Midst the wonderful world of monads,
Leibniz noticed his duplex gonads.
    But the first was green,
    The second was blue.
He'd been feasting on colored doughnads.

The Art of Compromise

You demand
One pound of flesh,
Do you?

How about
Two pounds of
Doo-doo?

———————

Essays

On Anatomical Relativity

"Off with his head!"—that's all right from the perspective of the body. But from the perspective of the head, "Off with his body!" is much more fitting.

Operation State Department

In the realm of sex, Romain Forbush became a supreme practitioner of the art of negotiation—so much so that already by age 23, he and most of his friends agreed that he did not have a scrotum. His was a Diplomatic Pouch.

Mares in the Night

One recalls with distaste those bands of detached penises that (in large contrast to detached retinas) thunder through the darkness bent (in a manner of speaking) upon fearsome exploits, which the Berengailias call sanssadonn jinbladdies.

Canines and Felines

What is the difference between dogs and cats?

God has a preferential option for cats when they are kittens and dogs when they are puppies, but ever so slightly favors dogs when they are grown up.

Nevertheless: Any cat is as much a miracle as any dog.

Toward an Epidermal Revolution

Contrary to an opinion popular among the Lettuces, an itch does not have to precede a scratch.

By scratching, you can readily get an itch going, and that gives you something to scratch.

Note: Did you know—I am sure you did—that ever since 1740, "Old Scratch" has been colloquial for the "devil"? (I am not joking here.) But the devil is also known as "the dickens." This could warrant the following:

What the Dickens!

Contrary to a widespread opinion amongst the Trobriondes, an old itch does not have to precede Old Scratch. For Old Scratch is Father of all itches, particularly those underneath bandages and casts.

Alone Abroad
(March 14, 1976)

In the English language the words "Am I homesick!" simply mean "I am homesick." But another interpretation is to say that the words call into existence another person. For they could also read, "Boy, am I homesick!"

Where is this boy and what is his name? He is right here, and he bears the name "Gosh." How do we know that? We know it because the words could read, equally well, "Gosh, am I homesick!"

Toward the Rectification of Rectal Talk

In the *Random House Dictionary* "s---" is given a place whereas "doo-doo" is barred. I find this disconcerting, not to mention unclean, not to mention immoral.

I have always been antagonized by "s---"—the word, that is. My mother Marina and my father Josephus never allowed me to utter this dreadful word, and still, centuries later, I refuse to say it. At the same time, if the dictionary is going to do away with doo-doo, how are we supposed to communicate upon such a matter as this? "Feces" is much too highbrow, and in any case is better left for the Hegelians and all their Feces-Antifeces-Synfeces.

I submit, however, that doo-doo involves us in a serious communication problem all its own. The problem is already manifest above where the phrase appears, "do away with doo-doo." After all, in spoken English there is no way to distinguish between "do" and "doo." And the problem is compounded whenever someone admits, as he must sooner or later, "I do doo-doo." Which is the "do" and which is the "doo"? And is the person in fact saying, with an ear to the Muse, "I doo-doo do"? Alternatively, is he perhaps influenced by the words of the old song, "How come you do me like you do doo-doo?"—one of the few instances in the history of music where doo-doo was granted a voice of its own.

In 1567 Harold of Gondgge proposed a solution to this problem. Always say "my" after the first "do": "I do *my* doo-doo." This procedure has had enormous influence, and Harold's wording is long since authoritative throughout the English-speaking world. But while this is all well and good when we are dealing with the present, and perhaps even the future, it simply does not work once the doos-doos have been done (or dood, as some purists insist). For by that time any doo-doo in question is no longer "mine." It belongs, instead, to the environment, not to mention the whole world, not to mention God.

There is, I suggest, a way of getting around this difficulty: After any given doo-doo is done, let us be bold, even windbreaking, and identify it as did-did. "I did my did-did" — no problem at all now, since everyone will know that "my" refers only to the past, and hence no longer constitutes a claim to personal ownership.

As for the future, I am working on that. For the present, as perhaps also for the past, I offer the following proposal for the future, yet only tentatively and heuristically: "I will do my will-doo — will-doo."

Until this last, eschatological aspect of the scatological question will have been resolved, I might add the judgment that almost as revolting as "s---" is the wording "poo-poo." For, not unlike "pee-pee," "poo-poo" is harsh, crude, antagonistic, subversive. By contrast, in its present tense "doo-doo" is friendly, comforting, supportive, constitutional — rather like "wee-wee." Children who do poo-poo and pee-pee already carry ugly blemishes in their little hearts. They are marked for trouble. But children who regularly do their [*sic*] doo-doo and wee-wee are blessed They can only be destined for a peaceable tomorrow. In this connection it is fully acknowledged that recipients of the Presidential Freedom Medal are restricted to doers of doo-doo and wee-ers of wee-wee.[2]

Miscellaneous

What did the Israeli ski racer say when she hung up her skis for the last time?

"Shalom, slalom."

What did Winnie the Pooh say when he saw the herd of elephants approach?

"Here come the Heffalumps."

INNOCENT ABROAD

If you can get an American martini[3] in England, why not do that? Why stay home? (If you have the money—which most people don't.)

Cf. E. B. White: "There is no such thing as one martini." (A theological precedent/justification here is: "And God saw everything that he had made, and behold it was very good" [Gen. 1:31].)

How could there be martinis upon earth and not in heaven? Since when is earth superior?

Prudence Crowther tells the oldie: If you get lonely, start fixing a martini, and somebody is sure to come up behind you and say, "That's not how you make a martini."[4]

MONTHS OF THE YEAR

1. Yallhere
2. Unanfang
3. Moosh
4. Aliza
5. Perhaps
6. Moon
7. Eeeyeeeeyeohh
8. Leo
9. Still-leavesio
10. Off-leavesio
11. No-leavesio
12. Dissembler

WORKING EPITAPH

Procrastination finally paid off.

EPITAPH OF A PROCRASTINATOR

Procrasti

UNCOLLECTED WORKS

The difference between Collected Works and Uncollected Works is that the materials to follow have not been classified. Somehow, I doubt that they will be.

THE PRAGMATIC QUESTION

Is   Is it
Footle   OR   Futile to
Futile?   Footle?
(Thereby
   celebrating
      noun and
         verb
            together)

GARDEN NEIGHBORS

Simple Wimple went calling on six herbal friends.
   Lamentably, Lavender was temporarily off color.
   Mint only tickled his nose, and besides had
      already been tithed.
   Sage merely outthought him.
   Tarragon proved to be long absent.
   Thyme just stood and looked at him clockwise.
Rosemary alone welcomed him in.

THE ENIGMA OF AFRO-ASIA

Here is a question that has puzzled phallicist investigators for some twenty-four centuries:
Were the human penis able to talk, would it necessarily speak Coptic?

HUMAN RELATIVITY

A, more
Fuddled than B,
Is yet more
Befuddled
Than C, D, or E.

Animal Economics

Question: If you are charged by a lion, what is your best move?
Answer: Whip out your American Express or Barclay card.
Question: If you are charged by a cheetah, what is your best move?
Answer: Demand a re-accounting.
Question: If you are charged by a tiger, what is your best move?
Answer: Jump ahead three spaces to Africa.

Civility Under the Dreaming Spires of Oxford
(January 9, 1990; nonfiction)

"Excuse me, Sir, would you have some loose change?"
"No, I'm very sorry, I don't."
"Don't be sorry. It's perfectly all right."

A Theory of History

Today is not so much the day before tomorrow as it is the day before Everyday. Everyday except those days that have been — which include raggedy undershorts with inelastic elastic.

Persecution

He was a druid
Until, all at once,
They drained his fluid.

No Place

The best food is corn,
It comes straight from utopia.
In this way was born
The blessed cornucopia.

The Construction of the Alimentary Canal:
A Great Feat of Engineering

The peasant Daddios Diskonect-Rekonect Schlol had ten mouths to feed. But the food would keep falling through the orifices onto the floor, and the family of Daddios Diskonect-Rekonect Schlol was threatened with malnutrition. Moreover, the kitchen had long since become a mess. Daddios Diskonect-Rekonect Schlol hit upon a daring but practical solution. He would permit no mouth to come to the table that had not firmly attached itself to a body. In this way, Daddios Diskonect-Rekonect Schlol was able to nourish his family well, and they lived happily ever after.

A Do-It-Yourselfer's Tribute to the Prophets

I did the floor in asphalt tile.
I crafted next formicah.
I did it in aluminile,
And also forelijah.

Not to mention Isaiah.

Why the Revolution Failed

The reason the Revolution did not make it is that no leader could ever know what he was himself saying, not to mention what others would hear him saying.

The proof of this is that, whenever they were asked to repeat words they had just uttered, the would-be revolutionists could not manage it.

Here is a sample conversation from one of their press conferences:

Comrade Stillatto: Sklandoon aboozádut witha Minooney sed withouta Minooney.

Foreign reporter: Coodzevoos repetoot u mism tinkle?

Comrade Stillatto: Vett?

Foreign reporter: Iddy poon, pliz, coodzevoos repetoot u mism tinkle?

Comrade Stillatto: Whatever. Ast aleestozcdaan Kleepidee sed abbozáwt klopadoowant alzo.

Foreign reporter: Tanckdoo muchie-muchie sed no tanckdoo.

Small wonder the Revolution never got off the ground. No one could ever learn or understand the Kalcifragian language. To this day, no one understands it. I am told that it may not even be a language.

FATE OF A REVOLUTIONIST

From insurrection
He yearned to pass
To resurrection.

But that direction
Was blocked, alas,
By vivisection.

THE RAW MATERIAL OF ESPIONAGE

This politician leaked,
That politician leaked.
    (All politicians leak.)
This politician leaked a leak,
That politician merely leaked.
This politician leaked a secret,
That politician simply took a leak.
    (Though we do not know where he took it.)
This politician did not take a leak,
He gave a leak.
    (Nothing meek about his leak.)

WAITING FOR DISSOLUTION

He cannot repose
In his repository.

We may suppose it's
That new suppository.

REGULARITY

I
Metamucil
En route to the fair.

Mucils are regular people.

COMPARATIVE POLITICAL THEORY

Body English is a weak form of the body politic.
Body French is a moderately strong form of the body politic.
Body Italian is the strongest form of the body politic.
Where does that leave body American?

DISILLUSIONMENT

You had a man so truly thine.
   I mean,
   You rhad that man.
But things got bad, and things got worse.
Richard was not thy valentine,
He proved to be rhadamanthine.

THE AGE OF THE COMPUTER

It comes down to the same old conflict between work and home.
Cedric and Molly have both proved to be IBM compatible, but they
are still conjugally incompatible.

INTERPLANETARY CONVERSATION

Small Creature: Extent of the pressure [pre-shúr], extent of the
power, extent of the glory. Extent of the ability to be taken, to be
gotten, to be grabbed—these are the basics, these are the fundamentals. Without them no Etchem can be counted upon to survive more
than twenty-three months.
Large Creature: No *Etchem*?
Small Creature: Yes, that's like an Ation, or even a Nation."
Large Creature: Why only twenty-three?
Small Creature: Skiddoo!

RELIGIOUS WARFARE

Was always / is always / will always be the Buddha?
It all depends:
   Was he born?
   Was he not born?
If born, he is a pesht,

His birthplace known:
'Tis Budapest.
If unborn, he was / is /
Will be the besht.
Yet how can that be?
I though the Baal Shem Tov
Was Besht.

Cross-Examination

Having tested his testicles,
And tickled his tickletests,
He testtickled his testtesticles,
And tickletested his tickletickletests.

The Unvarnished Truth
(or Painters on Strike)

The difference between Me as equal and in some respects superior
to God and you pitiful millions (minions) who try so stubbornly to
play God is that you commit blasphemy and I embody the Truth.

Contra Platonic Dualism

S.O.S.! Save our souls!
Forget our bodies!
But then:
Why send an S.O.S.?

Feet, Foot, Foe, Fum

Interviewer: Do you have athlete's foot?
Thinclad: No.
Interviewer: Do you have athlete's feet?
Thinclad: What do you mean? If one of my feet is not an athlete's
foot, how can my two feet together be athlete's feet?
Interviewer: Let me proceed a little differently. Do you have the
feet of an athlete?

Thinclad: Yes.

Interviewer: You are saying that each of your two feet is an athlete's foot?

Thinclad: Yes.

Interviewer: Then why can't we use the term "athlete's foot" with respect to you?

Thinclad: For a very simple reason. I don't have athlete's foot.

THE LIMITS OF EDUCATION

While in school
He was taught
Nothing a-
Bout his tool.

Small wonder
He is such
A tool fool.

Wrong.

No school pool
Can put out
A tumescent,
Pubescent,
Burning tool.

THE CONFLICT BETWEEN FISHING AND HOUSING

A piece
Of cod
Is not a
Codpiece.

A MOTHER AND HER SON

"Come here, Bedaft."

"I will come, but I will not be daft. As a matter of fact, I am undaft."

"Undaft, come here."

"If you want me, you had better call me by my right name."

DAYS OF THE WEEK

1. Christianposeday
2. Noday
3. Up and about day
4. Girlboyday
5. Thirstday
6. Muslimandfrenchfryday
7. Jewishandseventhdayadventistday
8. Frogday (used only in Leapweek)[5]

TWELVE NAMES

1. Continent Puddle
2. Incontinent Piddle
3. Handdown Colinqualot
4. Osh Besucht
5. Countercock Squeemish
6. Consoodla Temperory
7. Aristova B'Singledouble
8. Caspar Unmcveety Sea
9. Sanddune Mayshee Wave
10. Expandine l'Difference
11. Isayza Ceremonyel
12. Aintayza Plainsong

I could mention Gonza Prettl but that would spoil things by giving us more than twelve names. The same goes for Thucid Awdlebawd. And for Brigid Frigidclone.

ACHIEVING AN UNSPLIT PERSONALITY

Slim was flimsy,
Slam was flamsy,
'Til they got his act together:
Slim-Slam Dan, the flim-flam man.

Cushioned by Whoopie

I am uncomfortable in saying this, but I have learned that the origin of *petard* (as in the phrase, "hoist by its own petard") is *pet(er)*, (to) break wind.

Query: Why am I uncomfortable in reporting same? Yet would not Miss America be equally uncomfortable, not to mention Miss Universe? (It is sobering but revealing that I should remand this item to my uncollected works.)

Supply and Demand

There once was a man with a goat
   Ee. Send gifts to him, the address
   Ee. Return again to your teep
   Ee. Then go and do your wee-w
   Ee.

On Resolving the National Debt

I would merely remind the ministers that the reduction we propose signally reduces the already reduced reduction, in contrast to the reduced reduction previously reduced from all earlier reductions. Accordingly, we will do better to reduce the reduction that had been proposed on Tuesday, in order that we may emerge with a greatly reduced reduction among all feasible, alternative reductions.

The instituting of the above concrete plan will mean that we can count upon a minimum balance in the Royal Treasury of no less than £3.61.

Double Jeopardy

Even
My
Sag
Sags.

HUMAN ADAPTABILITY

What with the bulldozer in short supply these days, the human penis is filling in admirably, if bruisingly.

But not in the case of Lord Uxxxley. He has mislaid his. According to one report, he left it out in Mooldavia.

The high irony here is that Uxxxley himself is the inventor of the Detachable Penis.

HUMAN HOPE

To be bald
Is rather nice:
No dandruff,
No head lice.

NOTES

1. Hyam Maccoby, ed. and trans. *The Day God Laughed*, p. 89.
2. Cf. Yehoshua Bar-Yosef: "In Brussels there is the famous Manneken-Pis statute of a mere child doing a wee pee [NB] on nobody at all" ("The Drunkards," in *Waiter, There is [a] Fly in My Orange Juice*, Maurice Carr, ed., p. 219).
3. Consult Lowell Edmunds, *The Silver Bullet: The Martini in American Civilization* (Westport, Conn.: Greenwood Press, 1981).
4. Prudence Crowther, preface to *Don't Tread on Me: The Selected Letters of S. J. Perelman* (London: Penguin Books, 1988), p. ix.
5. This listing may be contrasted with that provided by the devil during the infancy of the universe. The days of the week were Courgette, Dishwasher, Drain, Particle, Lawnmower, Gastritis, and Wubblypoop (*Satan: The Hiss and Tell Memoirs*, p. 39n).

5

Comic Laughter as Moral Brainwork

For an epigraph to this chapter, I introduce Woody Allen's plenary aphorism: "Great humor is intellectual without trying to be."[1] For there is a close bond between comic laughter and the life of reason, including the moral reason. (Caution: To say this is not to reduce humor to "reason" or to something narrowly "reasonable.")

A helpful guide here is Marie Collins Swabey, who in her *Comic Laughter: A Philosophical Essay* distinguishes comic laughter from such other forms as infantile, drunken, hysterical, and nonsense laughter. To her, "comic insight turns on the falsity of contradictions in the world." "What is genuinely funny in words, character, or situation must have a logical point, drift, nub, or pertinence and yield some insight into values." The important thing is that "in the laughter of comic insight we achieve a logical moment of truth; while metaphysically, through some darting thought, we detect an incongruence as cancelled by an underlying congruence. We gain an inkling, as it were, of the hang of things, sometimes even a hint of cosmic benefi- cence. In short, perception of the ludicrous helps us to comprehend both ourselves and the world, making us, at least in the highest reaches of humor, feel more at home in the universe by aiding in the discern- ment of values."[2]

Humor parades before us its own brands of seeming illogic, yet unless it nurtures *some* kind of deeper logic it fails to realize itself.

Experience of the comic "centers in the perception of a contradic- tion or absurdity." And until there is "penetration of a confused state of affairs and its transcendence, there is no relish of the ludicrous." By and large, "the ludicrous" and "the comic" may be used interchangeably; both categories signify what is "worthy of exciting laughter because of a certain inconsistency or absurdity in its referent." Because the ludicrous involves the perception of absurdities, "it excludes utter foolishness, pure silliness, senselessness. The ludicrous encounter must yield not blindness but an insight."

The best generic definition of "the comic" is "the presence of an incongruity, contradiction or absurdity that is humanly relevant without being oppressively grave or momentous." It is in this strict sense that "the comic" and "the ludicrous" are one and the same. The ludicrous takes many forms: the comic (in a narrow sense), wit, satire, irony, and so on.[3] In addition to the comprehensive meaning of the comic or ludicrous, the comic in a narrower sense need not always require verbal or symbolic expression. Thus, while wit lives through its witticisms, satire through its satirical works, and irony through its figures of speech, "the comic may inhere in characters, situations, or events, and be appreciated even though beyond linguistic reach." What Swabey says here is reminiscent of right-brain activity, and is exemplified in cartoons that are able to do their job while remaining wordless. Moreover, as against satire or irony, comic insight "yields a spontaneous satisfaction largely unmixed with pain and free of derogatory intent."[4]

Swabey differentiates among nonsense, sadism, and incongruity as competing forms of the comic. At issue is "what is worth laughing at, what states of affairs are essentially ludicrous or deserving of mirth." This question is one, not of fact, but of value. Again, for any apprehension of contradictions, "logical thinking and not mere animal sufferance" is demanded.

By exposing fallacies in thought, language, and ways of living, minds alert to the ludicrous may contribute not a little to human progress. . . . By uncovering neglected hypocrisies, illusions, vanities, and deceptions in the behavior of persons and societies, avoidance of error is promoted as well as knowledge of the truth. Neat presentations by the humorist of instances of men's vain conceit of their appearance, wealth, or wisdom, their pretensions to be what they are not, their illusions of grandeur, good looks, sagacity . . . remove in part our blindness with regard to certain factual and moral weaknesses in mankind. Similarly the sudden grasp of cases of contradiction between word and deed, of men not practicing what they preach, of talking one way and acting another, in tickling our sense of the ludicrous may enlighten us as to sources of wrongdoing in ourselves and others.

To apply Swabey's reasoning by resorting for a moment to theo-logical-anthropological terminology: Comic laughter is a dam against human sin. That the dam very often leaks and humankind's evil most usually spills over it—a condition itself eligible for comic treatment and comic relief—is not able to abolish comic laughter's philosophi-cal/police function.

The deepest source of the knowledge that perceives and publicizes the ludicrous has to do with the "structure of truth and reality." At its higher reaches, the comic adopts a universal outlook and surveys events impartially. Comic perception entails "a transcendental element of cosmic perspective." The comic "grasps incongruities in a more com-prehensive congruity, and finds contradictory sub-systems resolved in a non-contradictory entirety. In brief, he takes the world both from an over-all view and from a slant, both locally, empirically, and as a logician and metaphysician." Ideally, the comic "grasps what is wor-thy of laughter, what . . . is laugh*able* and not merely what makes us as organic creatures laugh." Incongruity presupposes, and lives upon, congruity.

Thus is Swabey insistent that if human experience "is not to dis-solve into a welter without distinctive meaning, reference, or definition of terms," the realm of the comic must observe both logical laws and moral standards. Amongst the relevant principles of rationality are those of consistency and inference. These are "canons of validity, constituting the comprehensive framework of both thought and things," principles that are only confirmed by their very denial. "That these principles are not mere optional conveniences for ordering discourse and behavior but constitutive necessities is shown by their universal acceptance as criteria" *in the very effort to refute them*. In this connec-tion, "the inventions of physical science can never assess the logical laws upon which the ludicrous turns, for the reason that science in attempting to test such laws already grants their validity."[5]

More discretely, throughout the realm of the comic two sets of assumptions operate, and the awareness of comic incongruity is aroused by any attempt to violate either or both of these: *truth* in the senses of integrity, consistency, and systematic harmony; and *morality* "in the obligation of promise-keeping, of uniformity in conforming to the code laid down, doing what you agreed to do, or otherwise being guilty of a breach of contract."

To wit:

1. On the one hand, the incongruity that is comic arises from a transgression against local commitments, as when people deviate from accepted codes, or when two or more such codes collide. For instance, the humorist may deliberately depart "from his accepted rules of language, syntax, rhyme, meaning of terms, or realm of discourse." Swabey alludes to Ogden Nash's noted utilization of deviant rhymes and nonsense words within material ostensibly committed to conventional language and rhyming, with a resulting comic effect. In his "Lines Written to Console Ladies Distressed by the Lines 'Men seldom make passes at girls who wear glasses,' " Nash declares:

> A girl who is bespectacled
> She may not get her nectacled
> But safety pins and basinets
> Await the girl who fascinets.

2. On the other hand, we can "become aware of an infringement in the content of our thought of the basic inclusive logic — whereby we are guilty of the formal incongruity of *reductio ad absurdum*" or a re-affirmation-in-denial that is self-refuting. As examples, we have the man on the gallows saying "This will certainly be a lesson to me"; Carl Sandburg's "man so tall he had to climb a ladder to shave himself"; and Mark Twain's account, "We were twins, defunct and I. One of us drowned in the bathtub. That was I."

To any critic who asks why comics "cannot be totally freed from moral and rational canons," Swabey replies that "a completely hodge-podge world would have no discriminable qualities or meanings sufficient to denote the comic." This response is not unreminiscent of my own intimation in chapter 1 that laughter (together with weeping) cannot be all-encompassing. To laugh at everything is no longer to laugh; to weep at everything is no longer to weep: these negations/affirmations are reflective of structures within (psychologically speaking) the human, interior universe, or within (ontologically speaking) the realm of objective being as such. Put in other terms, there is no way to play the game that is, *in essentia*, comic laughter without there being rules. As Swabey sums up: "Because reason is universal and thinking operates through the universal, the comic cannot be freed from moral categories. . . . In the long run the logic of a realm in which vice is treated like virtue, inhumanity like humanity, the fiendish like the friendly, the decent like the depraved must finally, by evading all responsibility to law and order, drown itself in a chaos of nonsense."

The life of comic laughter, contra nonsense and contra sadism, is the world of incongruity, but also of the true and the moral within and despite that world. Yet incongruence is firmed up and in a sense redeemed "by an underlying congruency." Truth and morality ever stand on trial, yet, blessedly, they are sometimes able to emerge with finite victories. In this emergence, wrong moves to the scaffold, truth moves to the throne.

Swabey concludes her study:

> Though a mixed value, the negative side of the ludicrous can never overrule its positive aspect. Let satire and irony do their worst, there still remains the jollity of the comic spirit, the serenity of humor. Undeniably, a chief function of laughter is to help sweep the world free of shams, superstitions, outworn customs, and false beliefs, a process which leaves us with a chill sense of fewer supports to lean on. Nevertheless along with this goes — even in the exchange of common, street-corner jesting — a fresh conviction of the camaraderie of truth, a renewal of hope, of springtime in life, which despite all reverses finds the world good, reason in its heaven, and man eager to fare forth on new adventures.[6]

I include two critical comments upon Swabey's analysis. First, I think she is not right in disallowing nonsense an integral place within comic laughter. Nonsense is not to be confused with senselessness. It does not have to be ridiculous. Nonsense makes much moral and intellectual sense. Since good nonsense is highly clever, there is no way to cut it off from the life of the mind. We may note that Sigmund Freud finds nonsense not merely enjoyable but also reasonable; it permits us "to withdraw from the pressure of critical reason."[7] Morton Gurewitch supports Freud in the contention that it is necessary periodically to abandon and dismantle reason and reality.[8] I would simply add that such negation in and through nonsense is not possible without serious intellectual exertion.

My second comment simply repeats the allusion in chapter 1 to the mystery of why incongruity should incite laughter or be identified as humorous. Yet this lack of explanation applies not alone to Swabey but to us all. Even Herbert Spencer, for all his attempt to physiologize the phenomenon of laughter, acknowledged the mystery that is present: "How come a sense of the incongruous" is followed "by these peculiar bodily actions?"[9]

Steve Allen writes that comedy "is about tragedy. Most of the things we laugh at are actual or make-believe disasters of one degree or another. What else are jokes about? They're about fat people, stingy people, dumbbells, small hotel rooms, drunks, sexual problems, high prices, war, marital tensions, laziness, or, as Christian tradition lists them, pride, covetousness, lust, anger, gluttony, envy, and sloth. In other words, there's nothing amusing about perfection. Things are funny in some sort of loose relationship to how far they fall short of perfection. There may not be laughter in hell, but there couldn't possibly be any in heaven."[10] One difficulty here is that Allen's observation cuts in more than one way. It is obviously descriptive of much that we find humorous. But it also reminds us of the critical role of comic laughter in exposing human imperfections and willful distortions.

The lament is often heard that our generation (more particularly, its younger members) is seriously defunct in knowledge, historical and other. There is much truth in the finding. One counter to this condition is that people, in Renata Adler's phrasing, "see the world still in words, as writers, arguers, archivists—even, perhaps even especially, those who do not write."[11] And no group sustains and even protects the human *logos* (word) more than the practitioners of comic laughter. They are a powerful counterforce to the *illiterati*. Andrew Greeley has contended that the passion for respectability among middle class and well-to-do Irish tended to deprive them of their flair and wit.[12] It is a pity that the wish for respectability was ever given a chance to play such a deprivative role.

In anticipation of chapter 7, I include a passage from John Morreall, whose argument that humor involves, not the suspension of reason, but a nonserious utilization of reason may be placed beside Swabey's exposition:

> Clearly, reason is necessary for humor; without it we could not even recognize incongruity, much less enjoy it or create it for enjoyment. Infants and the higher animals, which have much in common with human adults, including a capacity for emotions, lack a capacity for humor, because they lack our ratio-

nality. They can learn, they have expectations, and they can be surprised. But because they don't have our conceptual system with its class concepts, causal patterns, and so on, they don't appreciate incongruity; at most they react to the violation of their expectations with puzzlement, frustration, or distress. We, by contrast, can enjoy having our expectations violated, sometimes even when the incongruity involves our own failure, because we can look beyond the mere practical aspects of individual situations to understand the world in a *general* way, abstracted from its particular relations to ourselves.[13]

We may conclude our visit with Marie Collins Swabey by repeating one of the epigraphs of this book. Carl Reiner sums up well the cause of comic laughter: "The funniest joke of all is the absolute truth stated simply and gracefully." Humor is a truth, a blessing, brought to birth by the human imagination.

A Freudian, Predictably Elongated Endnote. Marie Collins Swabey tends toward optimism. She pays tribute to the reasonableness of the human species and identifies comic laughter as socially redeeming. Humor is a creative, useful sociomoral instrument.

In the interests of objectivity or balance, of allowing for alternative views, we may ponder the argument of Morton Gurewitch in *Comedy: The Irrational Vision.* Gurewitch finds comedy at once conservative and radical, rational and illogical. He does not deny to comedy elements of constructiveness and criticism, but he seeks to balance these with an irrational factor: "Although comedy is often generated by the forces of civilized sanity and searching criticism, it is also activated, perhaps just as often, by a drive to celebrate irrationalism." Gurewitch's primary theme is the bond between comedy and irrationality; accordingly, he makes "a more than casual use" of the thinking of Sigmund Freud, to whom the major concern of humor is the repudiation of suffering, rather than the clarification of truth. For example, to Gurewitch, satire, "whether blistering or benign, is anger that has been alchemized into comedy." And farcical comedy or nonsense is especially devastating: "It promotes a subversion of mind itself by seeking out the powerful pleasures of irrationality."[14] However, even for Gurewitch "the complete sequence, from stereotyped normality to uninhibited revelry and then back to refreshed responsibility, is highly parabolic: misrule is futile unless it generates a sane and, ideally, a more wholesome acceptance of rule, of civilized order and grace. Festivity must finally yield to civility." Again, we "must not enthrone irrationality at the heart of comedy." Comedy may serve in "the testing and clarification of ideas and forms of conduct." Nevertheless, "comedy may also function as a sanctuary where the rigors of reality yield to, or where the joys of life fulfill, the illogical requirements of the heart."[15]

Gurewitch faults Swabey for limiting the supreme attributes of wit to rational cogency and logical truth. In truth, such innocent conceptual wit is fully accepted by Freud as, potentially, intellectually valuable. It is claimed that Swabey fails to distinguish between innocent wit and tendentious wit (the latter of which is, for Freud, created through various "inhibited instincts"). And in attacking Freud's theory of wit as "essentially a weapon *against logic*," she is held somewhat to misinterpret Freud. "For though it is true," Gurewitch continues, "that logic in tendentious wit is usually the tool of instinct, logic is also perfectly at home (and untouched by motivated malignity) in innocent conceptual wit. If Freud does not elaborate on the wit maker's capacity for heightened lucidity and logical congruence, that is because his major interest is in tendentious wit; and tendentious wit, which is far more potent than innocent wit, is above all a psychological, not a logical, phenomenon."[16]

So there is a conflict. I suggest, however, that Swabey and Gurewitch may be at least in part reconciled in and through a shared assumption that the highest — or lowest — reaches of human irrationality are yet treatable, if never finally conquered, by human moral brainwork — to the extent that each effort is able to keep the instinctual unconscious from taking over the entire game. Any drive to celebrate irrationalism requires the rational mind as well as the id and the stern cultural superego.

Gurewitch's praise of Freud would be impossible, I should have thought, apart from Freud's appurtenance to the Jewish *Anschauung*: "Freud upholds humor's metamorphosis of pain into pleasure as the noblest of man's defensive processes. He considers humor to be superior to wit, for example, because while the latter is invaluable as a force for the recoupment of instinct and the cancellation of guilt, it is also vindictive. [Swabey too has misgivings respecting the morality of wit — A.R.E.] Humor, on the other hand, is a liberation from the wounds of life, not a release for lawless desires; and it does not outjest agony at the expense of others. This is why humor's ability to transmute misfortune into gaiety . . . makes it incomparable among the uses of adversity." Freud sternly resists "the kind of humor that suggests a camouflaged surrender to evil and oppression, or a willingness to accept the hardships of existence because disasters are forever to be swallowed and never regurgitated."[17] In Freud's own words, humor brings with it something that is "fine and elevating." "By its repudiation of the possibility of suffering, it [humor] takes its place in the great series of methods devised by the mind of man for evading the compulsion to suffer."[18]

As a conclusion to this chapter as a whole, I suggest that comedy is a celebration of Life, which is in turn at once rational, irrational, and transrational.

NOTES

1. Woody Allen, as cited in Penelope Gilliott, "Profiles," *The New Yorker* (4 February 1974), p. 42.
2. Swabey, *Comic Laughter,* pp. v, 238.
3. See ibid., chap. 4, "Irony and Satire," and chap. 5, "Wit and Humor." For Swabey's consideration of the types of comic incongruity, see her chap. 6.
4. Ibid., pp. 3–5, 16, 28. See ibid., chap. 3, "The Comic in the Wider and the Narrower Sense."
5. "Whereas coherence presupposes the laws of logic, these laws are themselves established by the test of coherence: by the operation of the *reductio* and reaffirmation in denial. (That is to say, by *reductio* in that since denial of the laws of thought leads to contradiction, their denial is false, while in complementary fashion, the attempt to think through their denial reaffirms them)" (ibid., p. 235).
6. Ibid., chap. 2 and pp. 40, 247; see also pp. 115, 164, and passim.
7. Sigmund Freud, *Jokes and Their Relation to the Unconscious,* p. 126.
8. Gurewitch, *Comedy,* p. 112.
9. Herbert Spencer, *Essays: Scientific, Political, and Speculative* (New York: Appleton, 1892), II, p. 455; cf. Swabey, *Comic Laughter,* on Spencer, pp. 199–203, 206–9, 213–14, 224. Swabey writes that the difficulty with Charles Darwin and Herbert Spencer is that, by translating incongruity "into psychological and somatic terms, they rob it of logical efficacy. In their hands, logical distinctions are existentialized: incongruities are viewed as feelings of contrast, as phenomenal events in the experience of human perceivers, but without implications of intellectual insight or objective axiological significance" (ibid., pp. 207–8).
10. Steve Allen, *Mark It and Strike It,* p. 338.
11. Renata Adler, *Toward a Radical Middle,* as cited in Richard Schickel, "The Basic Woody Allen Joke," *The New York Times Magazine* (7 January 1973), p. 37.

12. On the humorous genius of the Irish, see Christie Davies, *Ethnic Humor Around the World,* pp. 88–89.

13. John Morreall, *Taking Laughter Seriously*, p . 99.

14. "Defined somewhat simply, farce is tendentious wit writ large — at least as far as psychological factors are concerned" (Gurewitch, *Comedy*, p. 127). "Social farce says to heil with society — and therefore also to a good deal of history. Society is imaged as organized bunk or as a chimera draining the life out of natural man; and history is figured as a series of abominable grotesqueries. Unlike conventional social satire, which seeks to purify the idols and idioms of the tribe, social farce aims to pulverize the very idea of idols and idioms" (ibid., p. 159).

15. Ibid., pp. 42, 9, 10, 99, 45, 85, 108, 46, 232.

16. Ibid., p. 66; Swabey, *Comic Laughter*, p. 71. For Swabey's critique of Freud, see ibid., pp. 70–73, 220–21. Swabey can hardly be faulted for protesting Freud's bent "to psychoanalyze and biologize the realm of meaning and values." For her, Freud's unconscious consciousness "is quite incomprehensible" (p. 220).

17. Gurewitch, *Comedy*, pp. 99, 107.

18. Sigmund Freud, "Humor," in *Philosophy of Laughter and Humor*, John Morreall, ed., p. 113. The following piece may be regarded as an extension of Freud's essay on humor: Robert Alter, "Jewish Humor and the Domestication of Myth," in Sarah Blacher Cohen, ed., *Jewish Wry*.

6

Adventures of Youth

The following fabrications are not arranged in any particular order. The nonderogatory meaning of *fabricate* is to manufacture, as when we fabricate steel. Most of the items are garnered from student examination papers. No contributor is represented more than once.

The Virgin Birth means that Jesus is the Son of God on his mother's side.

God is the highest being capable of conceiving.

Evil does more harm than good.

The Ten Commandments in the Torah are very similar to the Ten Commandments in the Old Testament.

The nave of the church is the little rascal who runs around during the service pinching all the old ladies.

The San Headren.

The punishment of criminals is needed all right, but is it necessary?

Catholics and Episcopalians alike believe in Apostate Succession.

Man must recreate the world by repeating the cosmogony. This presupposes a difference between where he has never been.

Sex can be considered as a method of release from everyday tensions. It is a way of forgetting, temporarily at least, the problems of our ordinary, everyday life. The church recognizes this and realizes its importance. In our fast-moving modern world tensions mount quickly and there must be a satisfactory way to ease them. Sex is one of the better ways of doing this. It is better than trying to forget our troubles by drinking or other such unsatisfactory means.

Confusionism has been more like what is considered a religion than what we believe Confusionism was like.

Japan formerly held the Cuspidores Islands.

Heresy is anything contrary to the basic tenements of the church.

The Puritans enjoyed working hard because it cleanses the body.

The main reason the Romans persecuted the Christian church was its failure to worship the czar.

Judaism is a religion because it believes in a God who has sent down a set of moral platitudes for Jews to follow.

Immanuel Kant sought to explain God as the absence of something else.

Wilkins believed that faith is only for the ignorant or intellectual people.

The Protestant view is that man is shaved by faith alone.

Isaiah characterizes God as omnipotent, very brilliant, and therapeutical. Relations with this God can only be salubrious.

Judaism and Protestantism say that sex is sinful but not bad.

To Jews, God is more a Deity than anything else.

William Jennings Bryan was prosecuting attorney at the Spook Trial.

Protestants view marriage as a reality.

We have been studying the evils of sex, virginity, etc.

If owning your own land is good, you should own it.

God is transient.

One requirement for being a monk is starvation.

Marriage is a sacred bondage.

The dogma of the Virgin Birth means that Mary conceived without labor pains.

Religion involves the ability to copulate death.

The Pharisees are the judiciary branch of the Methodist general organization.

The Seventh Day Adventists are named for the saying that when Christ died, "on the seventh day he shall rise."

Hell is fairly easy to get to.

For Catholics, Extreme Unction is the same as Holy Matrimony.

These people believe in eternal life with the one true polytheistic God.

Until two years ago the Presbyterians believed in predestination.

Query: How is it that so many of these creations — gathered at random — should echo the voices and styles of two gentlemen from the world of baseball, Yogi Berra and Casey Stengal?

FINAL EXAMINATION[1]

Instructions: Read each question carefully. Answer any ten. Time limit, two hours. Begin immediately.

1. *History*
   Describe the history of the papacy from its origin to the present day, concentrating especially but not exclusively on its social, political, economic, religious, and philosophical impact on Europe, Asia, America, and Africa. Be brief, concise, and specific.

2. *Medicine*
   You have been provided with a razor blade, a piece of gauze, and a bottle of Scotch. Remove your appendix. Do not suture until your work has been inspected. You have fifteen minutes.

3. *Public Speaking*
   2,500 riot-crazed aborigines are storming the classroom. Calm them. You may use any ancient language except Latin or Greek.

4. *Biology*
   Create life. Estimate the differences in subsequent human culture if this form of life had developed 500 million years earlier, with special attention to its probable effect on the English parliamentary system. Prove your thesis.

5. *Music*
   Write a piano concerto. Orchestrate and perform it with flute and drum. You will find a piano under your seat.

6. *Psychology*
   Based on your knowledge of their works, evaluate the emotional stability, degree of adjustment, and repressed frustrations of each of the following: Alexander of Aphrodisias, Ramses II, Gregory of Nicea, Hammurabi. Support your evaluation with quotations from each man's work, making appropriate references. It is not necessary to translate.

7. *Sociology*
   Estimate the sociological problems that might accompany the end of the world. Construct an experiment to test your theory.

8. *Management Science*
   Define management. Define science. How do they relate? Why? Create a generalized algorithm to optimize all managerial decisions. Assuming an 1130 CPU supporting fifty terminals, each terminal to activate your algorithm; design the communications interface and all necessary control programs.

9. *Engineering*
   The disassembled parts of a high-powered rifle have been placed in a box on your desk. You will also find an instruction manual, printed in Swahili. In ten minutes a hungry Bengal tiger will be admitted to the room. Take whatever action you feel appropriate. Be prepared to justify your decision.

10. *Economics*
    Develop a realistic plan for refinancing the national debt. Trace the possible effects of your plan in the following areas: Cubism, Donatist controversy, the wave theory of light. Outline a method for preventing these effects. Criticize the method from all possible points of view.

11. *Political Science*
    There is a red telephone on the desk beside you. Start World War III. Report at length on its sociopolitical effects, if any.

12. *Epistemology*
    Take a position for or against truth. Prove the validity of your position.

13. *Physics*
    Explain the nature of matter. Include in your answer an evaluation of the impact of the development of mathematics on science.

14. *Philosophy*
    Sketch the development of human thought; estimate its significance.
    Compare with the development of any other kind of thought.

15. *General Knowledge*
    Describe in detail. Be objective and specific.

Extra Credit: Define the universe; give three examples.

NOTE

1. From *Lehigh Horizons* (Lehigh University), December 1982, p. 5.

7

Toward a Comprehensive Theory of Laughter

Humor is purely a point of view, and only the pedants try to classify it.
— S. J. Perelman

It is essential that we be comprehensive in our theoretical and substantive characterization of humor and laughter; otherwise we distort or lose the picture as a whole. S. J. Perelman's above disclaimer maintains humor's subjectivity but fails to allow for its objective qualities.

In *Taking Laughter Seriously* John Morreall endeavors to provide a philosophic, or philosophic-psychological, theory of humor specific enough to provide explanatory power yet comprehensive enough to avoid reducing all cases of laughter to a single kind. Morreall finds the latter fault present in the three major traditional theories of laughter.[1]

1. There is the notion, traceable to Plato and Aristotle and developed classically in Hobbes, that laughter expresses an individual's feeling of superiority or "sudden glory" over others. The fallacy here is that many cases of laughter, humorous and nonhumorous alike, do not carry with them any consciousness of superiority.

2. In contrast to the emotional or "feeling" side of laughter, the incongruity theory identifies amusement as "an intellectual reaction to something that is unexpected, illogical, or inappropriate in some way." The most well-known proponents of this theory in the eighteenth and

nineteenth centuries were Kant and Schopenhauer. Kant interprets laughter "as an affection arising from the sudden transformation of a strained expectation into nothing."[2] In other pages of the present handbook some indication is found of support for this view. But as already stated, I think that an abiding difficulty faced by such an interpretation is just why illogicality or incongruity should entail or at least issue in laughter. To Morreall, the central weakness of the incongruity interpretation is that, while incongruity may indeed be involved in all humor, the viewpoint is not sufficiently comprehensive to account for all kinds of laughter. As long as we limit ourselves to humorous laughter, there is much to be said for the theory; a stumbling block is the many instances of nonhumorous laughter that do not involve incongruity. Furthermore, a number of cases of incongruity — those that fall within such categories as fear, pity, moral disapprobation, and disgust — are not laugh-provoking.

3. The relief theory addresses a question largely ignored in other theories: "Why does laughter take the physical form it does, and what is its biological function?" Representative of the position are Herbert Spencer and Sigmund Freud. For Freud, jokes are (acceptable) expressions of hidden aggression. Morreall allows a clear connection between some laughter and the relief of tension or the expenditure of energy, but he denies that all laughter must entail the release of emotional nervous energy. Thus, much nonhumorous laughter is simply unconnected to pent-up emotions. Like the two foregoing views, the relief theory fails to stand up as a comprehensive theory of laughter.[3]

Morreall now offers his own general theory of laughter. He discerns three features in laughter situations that can help structure a comprehensive theory.

a. The laugher undergoes a change in her or his psychological state. The change may be primarily cognitive, as shown in the incongruity theory. The change may be primarily affective, as contended by both the superiority and the relief theories. Or the change can be at once cognitive and affective (as typified in hostile humor).

b. The alteration must be sudden. "To laugh, we must be caught off guard by the change so that we cannot smoothly adjust to what we are experiencing."

c. The psychological shift must be pleasant.

Morreall epitomizes his general theory via the proposition: *Laughter results from a pleasant psychological shift.* We have to distinguish carefully between laughter as physical behavior and the feeling— Morreall calls it "amusement"—that laughter expresses.

Due to the cast of Morreall's subsequent analysis and apologia, it is well to reproduce at this point the listing he has provided back at the start of his book.

NONHUMOROUS LAUGHTER SITUATIONS	HUMOROUS LAUGHTER SITUATIONS
Tickling	Hearing a joke
Peekaboo (in babies)	Listening to someone ruin a joke
Being tossed and caught (babies)	Watching someone who doesn't get a joke
Seeing a magic trick	Watching a practical joke played on someone
Regaining safety after being in danger	Seeing someone in odd-looking clothes
Solving a puzzle or problem	Seeing adult twins dressed alike
Winning an athletic contest or a game	Seeing someone mimic someone else
Running into an old friend on the street	Seeing other people experience misfortune
Discovering that one has won a lottery	Hearing outlandish boasting or "tall tales"
Anticipating some enjoyable activity	Hearing clever insults
Feeling embarrassed	Hearing triple rhymes or excessive alliteration
Hysteria	Hearing spoonerisms and puns
Breathing nitrous oxide	Hearing a child use some adult phrase correctly
	Simply feeling in a silly mood and laughing at just about anything[4]

Morreall reviews various cases of nonhumorous laughter in babies. For there to be humor, a conceptual shift is required. By the age of three or four the child is able to know that objects exist independently of his perceiving them. More importantly, he has developed a primordial set of concepts for apprehending things, properties, and events in his experience. And the child does more than acquire labels for naming these things; he comes to discern certain patterns among them. Once he has developed a conceptual system, or picture of the world (*Anschauung*), he can begin to enjoy humor.

Most adult humor in our culture, Morreall continues,

is based on experiencing or imagining incongruity . . . but children often find something humorous because they have not experienced anything like it before. The conceptual shift in adult humor is usually from what the person would expect a given thing or situation to be like, to an awareness that the thing or situation is not like that, that it has incongruous features. . . . The surprise here is based on having part of one's conceptual system violated. But in [simple children's humor] the shift is . . . from an ordinary state of awareness . . . to a surprised state of confronting some new *kind* of thing or event. . . . And so when he sees something like an ostrich for the first time. . . . it will be a brand-new kind of thing, and . . . it will shift him from an ordinary state of awareness to one of astonishment. If this shift is pleasant to him, and not, say, threatening, he will laugh. . . .

The child cannot enjoy humor, or even experience it as humor, until he catches on to the fact that the incongruities he is being presented with are only a playful arranging of reality and not, say, a confusing bunch of preposterous lies. Before the child can play around with his conceptual system, in short, he has to have a pretty solid grasp of that system, and has to feel comfortable in having it violated.

I suggest, accordingly, that ofttimes adult humor may be fostered by a drive to return, so to speak, to the totally fresh and new experiences of little children — for instance, by engaging oneself with "life among the Wollenjoobies," as this is presented in chapters 2, 4, 10, 12, and 14 of this book. The favorite phrase of Lewis Carroll's Alice is "Let's pretend." Again, Steven S. Schwarzschild writes that the modernist revolution in art "broke decisively with the pervasive Greek principle of mimesis-imitation in favor of creativity, the production of something new not given by nature."[5] Such newness in artistic creation may make a positive contribution to the "cause" of humor (cf. Morreall's chapter, "Humor as Aesthetic Experience").

John Morreall next concentrates on emotional shifts, upon the ground that without concerted attention to such shifts we cannot understand most of the instances of nonhumorous laughter in the list above, or cases (cf. hostile humor) in which conceptual shifts are accompanied by emotional shifts.[6] Thus, in the instance of regaining safety after being in danger, one experiences a quick emotional change from fearful tension to relaxed security. "Emotions are based on perceptions; but here it is the emotional shift that is experienced as pleasurable and leads to the laughter." Similar kinds of emotional shifts take place upon solving a frustrating puzzle or difficult problem, or upon winning a contest or game that has involved great struggle. But the shift that causes laughter may be from a nonemotional state to a positive emotional state, as when one runs into an old friend on the street, or in the sudden news that one has won a lottery. Furthermore, in many instances of humorous laughter the enjoying of a conceptual shift is accompanied and reinforced by the enjoying of an emotional shift. However, while the latter kind of enjoyment is neither necessary nor sufficient for humor, our enjoying of a conceptual shift *is* necessary and sufficient. Morreall here makes a notable acknowledgment: "The essence of humor lies in the enjoyment of incongruity."

In the interests of understanding not just laughter in general but the final three items on his list of nonhumorous laughter situations, Morreall examines in greater detail the two elements of suddenness and pleasure.

Sudden psychological changes are such that it is hard to assimilate them into our experience; they happen too quickly for us to make an adjustment. The need for suddenness — what William Zinsser and others dub "surprise" — helps explain why most pieces of humor affect us fully only once and also why the perpetrator of the humor usually does not laugh.

While laughter in older children and adults perpetuates the natural expression of pleasure at a psychological shift, it is no longer merely an involuntary response to a stimulus. It is also a piece of learned behavior, at least partly under the individual's control. Furthermore, in order to block laughter a psychological shift does not have to induce such negative emotions as anger and pity; attitudes of puzzlement, wonder, curiosity, or problem-solving may keep laughter from coming. An essentially cognitive challenge is present. Morreall stresses that the factor of personal security is a prerequisite of normal laughter — in crying, by contrast, we feel helpless — but nevertheless humor is a world apart from immediate practicality. "In order to enjoy a psychological shift . . . we need to be without urgent practical needs." Studies of both children and adults reveal the link between laughter and the individual's sense of security and control.

Children and adults too can recapture a feeling of security by being made to laugh. That laughter can be the *product* of feelings of security as of pleasure ought not tempt us to posit a one-way causal relation. Along with crying, "laughter is not a mere epiphenomenon of some completely nonbehavioral internal feeling." William James went too far in claiming that a person does not cry because he is sad, but is sad because he cries. Yet his comment correctly moves us away from assuming that our behavior has no effect on our feelings. In truth, there is two-way causality between our feelings and the behavior that expresses feelings. By changing someone's behavior from crying to laughing, we at least partly change his feelings and thereby make him less upset. "There is a causal loop here. Laughing is a behavior that expresses pleasant feelings. But this behavior is itself pleasant, and so tends to increase pleasant feelings. It is possible, then, to break into the loop by starting with just the laughter (performed voluntarily or caused physiologically), which will induce pleasant feelings, which feelings may in turn cause more laughter."

Morreall is now ready to consider the final three items upon the one side of his listing: embarrassment, hysteria, and the inhaling of nitrous oxide. For all the presence of distress and the absence of pleasure in embarrassment and hysteria, both phenomena embody coping techniques. The laughter of embarrassment serves the function of helping the individual to rise above distress, and of appearing to others that one is not upset but amused by the situation.

In hysteria, laughter is not at all a chosen act, for all rational control is in fact lost. The hysterical person is rejecting the reality of a shocking event; nevertheless, the afflicted person is granted "some distance, at least temporarily, from the horror" — in analogous fashion to the way hysterical paralysis may "work" for the individual who cannot face having to use his limbs. Even though it is not voluntary, hysterical laughter remains a fully human, psychological response. Morreall seems to be saying that the laughter of embarrassment and more especially hysterical laughter are boundary cases that test his comprehensive theory but do not annul it. At this place he offers the general judgment that "laughter, as we have set out to account for it, is a human behavior that is a reaction of a person to his perceptions of the world around him — a motor response, to put it crudely, to sensory input." This means that where acts of laughter are directly caused by certain drugs or by abnormal impulses in the brain, we do not have laughter "as a piece of human behavior."

This brings up the case of laughter through breathing nitrous oxide, which Morreall treats under the same rubric as marijuana and alcohol. The sudden onset of a carefree feeling can become pleasant enough to trigger laughter. Under mood-altering drugs laughter can be nonhumorous yet it is often humorous, though not necessarily to the observer. "We might describe both nonhumorous and humorous laughter in altered moods by saying that, by objective standards of the stimulation required to trigger laughter, the person has a much lower threshold of amusement."

Morreall concludes his chapter on "a new theory" of laughter in a way that relates humor to human freedom as such, a subject treated more fully by him later on (as it will be when we are further along in this book):

> Because laughing is not only a natural expression of pleasure, but is also under our voluntary control, and even under the control of unconscious coping mechanisms, it can occur in the absence of pleasure. I can force a laugh to please my boss or to make myself feel less tense. But such cases . . . are parasitic on laughter as the natural expression of pleasure, for they all work by using laughter to feign pleasure, or by breaking into the causal loop between pleasure and laughter to induce pleasure by performing laughter. Because laughter is partially voluntary, too, it can not only be forced when the person is not amused, but can also be suppressed when he is amused. . . . There is no one-to-one correspondence, in short, between instances of amusement and instances of laughter. Nevertheless, our formula that laughter is the natural expression of amusement provides the key to understanding all cases of laughter.[7]

In his following chapter, Morreall deals with the variety of humor, an exposition that is of direct relevance to humorous laughter (cf. right side of the listing above). He indicates at the outset that the only kind of humor he will talk about from now on is the humor of incongruity. In this way he downplays somewhat his earlier critique of the incongruity theory; also, he sets aside child humor. (Why is not child humor as humanly significant as adult humor? Is a child not fully a human person?)

Of great import within the domain of incongruity is that things and events are "not incongruous *simpliciter*, but only relative to someone's conceptual scheme." This is why people from different cultures often fail to appreciate one another's humor. What people find incongruous is dependent upon what they find congruous.

Morreall distinguishes between "incongruity in things" and "incongruity in presentation." (In chapter 1, I allude to incongruity "out there.") He contrasts comedians, who "say funny things," with comics, who "say things funny." Perhaps the kind of "incongruity in things" that is most often conducive to laughter points to some deficiency in a person or object. Probably the oldest kinds of human shortcoming to be found humorous are physical deformity, underdevelopment, and weakness. Closely allied is laughter at ignorance and stupidity (cf. such "ethnic humor" as "Polish jokes" and "Irish jokes"). Again, there is laughter over alleged moral shortcomings. And there is laughter over actions that fail or are incongruous (as in the case of a luckless person trying to use a defective tool).

Another kind of "incongruity in things" is one thing appearing to be another. Four cases in point are the humor (1) of mimicry; (2) of the impostor (cf. W. C. Fields as flim-flam man par excellence); (3) of coincidence or unanticipated repetition (cf. my example of successively spilled glasses of milk, Morreall's illustration of a person successively meeting at random three people all of whom tell him they have just had their appendix out, and Henri Bergson's contention that identical twins look manufactured, contra what we expect of human beings); and (4) of strange juxtapositions (cf. the sight of these two dogs together: a Saint Bernard and a Mexican chihuahua).

Then there is "incongruity in presentation." Central here are various endeavors to manipulate language (cf. some of the "funny stuff" in the present book). Morreall separates "puns and lower forms of humor" that basically play with words from "higher forms of humor" (traditionally called "wit") that basically play with ideas. Most effective is the kind of wit that violates logic but is just logical enough to sound plausible. (Woman to an interviewer: "I never watch TV. I turn it off more than I turn it on.") Of further comic effectiveness are disparities between serious words delivered in a funny way, or funny words delivered in a serious way; also wording containing built-in incongruities. (Sign on a post office door: "No dogs allowed, except seeing-eye dogs.") In general, "incongruity in presentation" operates quite well when a principle is to be violated or a regularity upset. Indeed, humor can often be gleaned from the failure of a piece of humor to work — a device commonly fallen back upon by comedians.[8]

In his final four chapters, John Morreall considers the role of humor in human life: humor as aesthetic experience,[9] humor and freedom, the social value of humor, and humor as offering human beings a constructive approach to life as a whole. A review of this fourfold exposition is not immediately necessary to a knowledge of Morreall's comprehensive theory of humor, with one salient exception: his relating of humor to human freedom. I say this on the basis of a possible problem with his theory — a problem that lies beyond, but is nevertheless related to, the tendency toward psychologism in his "new theory" of laughter.[10] Morreall is very helpful in providing us with a general phenomenological accounting of the psychological, moral, and social mechanisms of laughter. But will his comprehensive-hedonist theory do anything to penetrate or reveal the inner precincts of (the mystery of) laughter? Can the latter ever be done? (I wish that in stating his comprehensive theory, "Laughter results from a pleasant psychological shift," Morreall had used some such term as "delightful" rather than "pleasant," since this alternative has a somewhat more objective connotation. "Delight" means not only "intense pleasure" but "that which is a source of pleasure." "Delight" and "delightful" further point to the uniqueness of humor and laughter, as against "pleasure" and "pleasant" as such.)

Professor Morreall finds enlightening the affinity between the humorous attitude and the philosophic attitude. "The person who looks at his life philosophically does not let his emotions color his view; he is distanced ... from the practical aspects of his situation. And this calmness makes his assessment of his situation more objective, more like that of an unbiased observer. In both respects the humorous attitude is like the philosophical: the person who can appreciate the humor in his own situation is liberated from the dominance of his emotions, and so he has a more objective view of himself." Morreall is here touching upon the relation of humor and laughter to the human capacity for self-transcendence, the ability to stand "outside" ourselves and judge and evaluate ourselves. I suggest that a fuller development of this form of argumentation by Morreall would have had positive relevance for the issue of the essential uniqueness of the reality of humor.

Humor is indeed the child of freedom, which also makes it a child of mystery. Bearing upon this matter is Morreall's emphasis upon the need to be without urgent practical concerns if the incongruity of a situation is to be enjoyed. But he is himself cautious concerning the applicability of his point: "There are times when humor can disengage us from what should be our moral concerns, and then it is not appropriate. To be able to stand back and laugh at things is one of the most valuable traits of our species; still, this is not a proper reaction in every situation."[11]

All in all, John Morreall is contending that humor and laughter are valuable to human life in a way nothing else is. Indeed, it is not an exaggeration to say that "humor is essential to maintaining a healthy outlook on things."

NOTES

1. In an essay "Humour and Incongruity," Michael Clark also evaluates these three traditional theories. His own view is a version of the incongruity theory (*Philosophy* 45 [1970]:20–32). In "Humour and the Aesthetic Enjoyment of Incongruities," Mike W. Martin challenges the views that amusement is to be construed as the enjoyment of incongruity, and that amusement is a kind of aesthetic experience. Both these essays are reproduced in *Philosophy of Laughter and Humor,* John Morreall, ed. Part One of the last-mentioned volume contains a convenient collection of excerpts from philosophers in different periods.
2. Immanuel Kant, as quoted by Israel Knox, "The Traditional Roots of Jewish Humor," in *Holy Laughter*, Conrad Hyers, ed., p. 163.
3. Morreall, *Taking Laughter Seriously,* chaps. 2–4. Morreall offers a lengthy critique of Freud, pp. 27–37. Central is Morreall's judgment that Freud "cannot *define* humor in terms of a release of emotional energy in order to defend his theory that humor involves a release of emotional energy; if he did so, he would be left not with a theory of humor, but merely with the tautology that situations involving the release of emotional energy involve the release of emotional energy" (p. 36).
4. Ibid., pp. 1–2.
5. Steven S. Schwarzschild, "Aesthetics," in *Contemporary Jewish Religious Thought,* Arthur A. Cohen and Paul Mendes-Flohr, eds. (New York: Free Press, 1987), p. 4.
6. Morreall here states that since chapter 6 of his book will consider conceptual shifts in different kinds of humor, there is no need to detail at this juncture how the proposition that laughter stems from a pleasant psychological shift applies to each of the instances of humorous laughter on the foregoing list.
7. Morreall, *Taking Laughter Seriously*, chap. 5. We have to remember here that amusement need not issue in laughter.

8. Ibid., chap. 6.

9. Morreall proposes that when the necessary conditions for humor are met, that is, when incongruity is enjoyed for its own sake, the enjoyment of humor is seen to be a kind of aesthetic experience. The faculty of imagination is central to both the aesthetic life and humor (ibid., pp. 93, 90; in general, chap. 7).

10. Cf. Swabey: "The judgment arousing comic laughter contains an objective insight into the rational order of things" (*Comic Laughter*, p . 104) .

11. Morreall, *Taking Laughter Seriously*, chap. 8. Further to Morreall's views, consult his two essays, "Funny Ha-Ha, Funny Strange, and Other Reactions to Incongruity" and "Humor and Emotion," in *Philosophy of Laughter and Humor*, John Morreall, ed., pp. 188–207, 212–24.

8

Pilferage

The limerick that follows will introduce the contents of this chapter.

> A wonderful bird is the *ibid*.
> In appearance it's pale and insibid.
> It stands as a sage
> At the foot of the page
> To tell where the passage was cribbed.[1]

Aristides writes concerning *The Big Book of Jewish Humor* that he became bored with it rather quickly. "Reading joke after joke, comic piece after comic piece, is like eating a cookie that is all chocolate chips — it doesn't take long for one's teeth to begin aching and one's lips to parse like those of a bank loan officer greeting a couple who has missed their last eleven mortgage payments."[2]

Why do I reproduce this passage? Perhaps by way of reminding my readers of the calculated parsimony of the present book's jokes. Aristideedeezzes's comment may help justify why the little encyclopedia about to come is highly selective and even runs on too short. But on the other side of the argument I cite the film critic Vincent Canby: "As comedy is impossible to analyze without killing the humor, laughter cannot easily be explained except to people who share the laughter with you. That's why it's sometimes necessary . . . to include some samples of the things that have made one laugh. In quoting specific lines of dialogue, the critic runs the risk of forever spoiling the reader's pleasure in discovering those lines for himself. Yet because comedy is far more difficult than straight drama or melodrama to describe accurately, the risk must be taken from time to time."[3]

I further repeat a disclaimer from Leo Rosten relevant to the difficulty in *written* jokes: "Just consider the arsenal of props available to you when you tell a story [orally]: the calculated pause, the ironic inflection, the ingenuous smile, the warning frown, the accented adjective, the changes in pace — in accelerated rhythm or decelerated momentum. All of these devices serve to cue and control your listeners: gestures, nods, smiles, cunning chuckles, grunts or murmers, the gasp of affected astonishment, the moan of pretended dismay." The poor writer lacks every one of these tools.[4]

Finally, a rule of middle finger is that the recounting of a new joke is not necessarily superior to the retelling of an old one.

Cecil Adams

Reader: How come people always say "Jesus H. Christ"? Why not Jesus Q. Christ or Jesus R. Christ or something else?

Adams: The *H* stands for Harold, as in, "Our Father, Harold be thy name."

Dave Allen

When it comes to birth control, I say to the pope: "If you don't play the game, don't make the rules."[5]

(On the same reasoning, can married people have any proper say about celibacy? Well, at least once upon a time they were celibate — A.R.E.)

Fred Allen

He was so small that he was a waste of skin.

This scarecrow scared some crows so badly they brought back the corn they'd stolen two years ago.

Steve Allen

A quadrilingual woman is one who speaks a single language but has four tongues.

We just had a very successful membership drive. We drove out forty-nine members.

Woody Allen

My wife is very childish. I was taking a bath and she came in and sank all my boats.

Sex between a man and a woman can be wonderful, provided you get between the right man and the right woman.

Interviewer: What is the most depressing thing that ever happened to you?
Allen: The day I realized I was starting to breathe like my father.

I knew my parents loved me because after I was kidnapped they waited a whole week to rent out my room. When the gang that kidnapped me was finally jailed, they escaped from the chain gang, getting past the guards by posing as an immense charm bracelet.

A fine example of a demonstration was The Boston Tea Party where outraged Americans disguised as Indians dumped British tea into the harbor. Later, Indians disguised as outraged Americans dumped actual British into the harbor. Following that, the British disguised as tea dumped each other into the harbor. Finally, German mercenaries clad only in costumes from "The Trojan Women" leapt into the harbor for no apparent reason.

"All I want is a chair," he told his father. "It's not so much that I mind stooping to work, but when I relax and put my feet up on the desk I fall over backward."

Kurt Andersen

Astrologers with goatees are scary.

Anonymous [6]

When the Communists were in control of Poland a man went to church but did not kneel. He was asked about this. He replied, "I don't believe in religion."
"Why, then," came the further question, "do you go to church?"
He answered, "I don't believe in the government either."

I never forget a face, but in your case I'm ready to make an exception.

Man to woman: May I join you?
Woman to man: I wasn't aware I'd come apart.

First grandson: Gran'pa needs water.
Second grandson: Why, is he thirsty?
First grandson: No, he's on fire.
Second grandson: Oh. Lemme know when he's thirsty.

Life is a losing cause. That's why they have cemeteries and Wrigley Field.

If Jesus was a Jew, how come he has a Puerto Rican name?

A certain frightened citizen sought to escape being lynched due to his controversial remarks. He protested, "I didn't say I was against the Monroe Doctrine. I love the Monroe Doctrine. I would die for the Monroe Doctrine. I merely said I didn't know what it was."

The East German pole-vaulting champion today became the West German pole-vaulting champion. (I needed a dated joke—A.R.E.)

An aide to Bismarck: Sir, do you want war?
Bismarck: Certainly not. I want victory.

Trees are made by gods like me, but only a fool like you can make a poem.

This life is a test. It is only a test. Were it an actual life, you would have received instructions on where to go and what to do.

Aristides

The story is told of a dinner party by Prime Minister and Mrs. Harold Macmillan for General and Mme de Gaulle, at which Mrs. Macmillan is supposed to have said to Mme de Gaulle: "Your husband has accomplished so much. You have both lived such rich and full lives. Is there anything left for you? Is there anything you still desire?" To which Mme de Gaulle is said to have replied, "Yes, one thing: a penis." After a brief stunned silence, General de Gaulle interjected: "*Non, non, ma chérie*, the word is pronounced *Happiness.*"

A story is told about [W. C.] Fields's last words on his deathbed in New York. His doctor, his mistress, a few close friends are in the room. Outside it is cold and snowing, the newsboys, hawking their papers, are crying out "Wuxtry! Wuxtry!" Fields, who has been dozing, on the edge of death, opens his eyes and signals the people in the room to gather round his bed. In a barely audible whisper, he says: "Poor little urchins out there. No doubt improperly clad and ill-nourished. Something's got to be done about them! Something's got to be done!" Fields closes his eyes. His friends return to their chairs. Twenty seconds later, he opens his eyes, signaling his company back to his bedside. They lean in to hear what he now has to say. "On second thought," Fields whispers, "screw 'em!"

"You know, Dottie," Robert Benchley said to Dorothy Parker after her third or fourth attempt at suicide, "you keep this up, you're going to make yourself very sick."

C. M. Bowra is supposed to have said of another Oxford don: "He is the kind of man who will stab you in the front."

The best sex jokes demonstrate a tasteful perversity, such as the joke about the nonagenerian who reports to his physician that he notices himself beginning to slow down sexually. "When did you first begin to notice this?" asks the physician. "Last night," the man says, "and then again this morning."[7]

Alan Berger

One day a white South African bus driver pulled over to the side of the road and announced to his passengers: "I am sick and tired of all this black against white business. From now on, everyone is green. Light green people will sit in the front of the bus, dark green people in the rear."

Peter L. Berger

What did the Indians say when Columbus landed in America? "Thank God, we're discovered!"

Bethlehem (Pa.) Globe Times (1 October 1987)

VATICAN CITY — Pope John Paul II today convened a synod of bishops on the role of women and laity in the Roman Catholic Church, declaring his "profound esteem for our lay brothers and sisters." John Paul and 232 bishops from around the world celebrated ass together in St. Peter's Basilica to formally open the month-long meeting.

Ambrose Bierce

Hippogriff, *n.* An animal (now extinct) which was half horse and half griffen. The griffen was itself a compound creature, half lion and half eagle. The hippogriff was actually, therefore, only one-quarter eagle, which is two dollars and fifty cents in gold. The study of zoology is full of surprises.

Historian, *n.* A broad-gauge gossip.

Non-Combatant, *n.* A dead Quaker.[8]

Victor Borge

I'm a little short of breath because it's been a long day, and I've been breathing all that time.

I wonder why there are three pedals on the piano, when I have only two feet.

Craig Brown

This year, the editor of *The Times Literary Supplement* is particularly anxious lest the unpleasantness of last year's notorious seasonal correspondence should repeat itself.

The furious to and fro began quietly enough on the Letters page of November 15, when veteran academic Professor Hobart Place wrote:

> Sir, May I take this opportunity to wish all your readers and contributors a Merry Christmas and a Happy New Year?

Few could have predicted the outcry that was to result from this greeting. In the November 22 issue, a rejoinder was published from leading critic Kingley Court:

> Sir, My attention has been drawn to Professor Place's ill-considered little piece of November 15. I do not intend to list all the inaccuracies contained therein — neither time nor space would allow — but his use of the word "Merry" cannot be allowed to pass without reproof. The true meaning of the word — of which he cannot but be aware — is, in its original Gaelic (*meorargh*) — "lonely and/or dejected." It ill becomes one of his, albeit highly compromised, stature to belittle the seasonal hopes of others less pampered than himself by recourse to such abuse.

The following week, the literary skirmish provoked by the professor's letter had failed to die down:

> Sir [wrote veteran etymologist Walnut Grove], In your columns of Novem-

ber 22, Mr. Kingley Court suggests a wholly misleading interpretation of the word "Merry" as in "Merry Christmas," Far from meaning, as he erroneously claims, "lonely and/or dejected," the word meant, until as late as the 12th century, "pertaining to the use of a donkey or mule for the transportation of sundry items," and those of us who value the language still employ it in this meaning to this day.

Alas, the benevolent tone of Mr. Walnut Grove's letter was not duplicated in the letter printed alongside it from Professor Sir Bexley Heath:

Sir, It saddened me to read that Professor Hobart Place, whom I have not met, should seek to damage his by no means sturdy reputation by impugning the character of your readers and contributors. He loftily wishes us "a Merry Christmas and a Happy New Year," as if it would not be within our ability to enjoy these occasions without his sanction. Needless to say, his letter contains many errors of logic. In wishing us a "Happy" New Year but only a "Merry" (sic) Christmas is he contending that the two states — happiness and merriness — are mutually exclusive?

By November 29, Professor Place's reputation had entered a spiral of decline, and veteran sociologist Sheridan Road's letter offered little succour:

Sir, My attention has been drawn to Professor Place's letter of the fifteenth in which he wishes one and all — and I quote — "a Merry Christmas and a Happy New Year" without any proper acknowledgment of the source — indeed, as if it were his own sentiment entirely.

Over a long disgruntled career, I have always found it painful to point to plagiarism in a fellow scholar but, far from being an original work, "A Merry Christmas and a Happy New Year" is a standard greeting, origin obscure, to be found on a variety of "cards" (pieces of stiffened paper or fabric on sale in retail outlets, often supplemented by a verse or "motto" and seasonal illustration). A number of these "cards" are posted by members of the nonacademic community to one another at this time of year.

By the middle of December, a Paraguayan novelist of international standing had revealed that the professor's phrase was an anagram, in Urdu, of "I am a fraud"; a tutor in psychology had ascribed the tendency to wish strangers well as an early step on the road to chronic kleptomania, and a letter signed by more than a dozen top playwrights had bitterly condemned the professor's intrusion into the private lives and dreams of those unable to defend themselves. Professor Place's letter of resignation in which he expressed his regrets for his recent foolhardiness, was printed on December 23.

In the New Year issue of the *TLS*, the first of many letters was printed in which the professor's use of the phrase "deeply regret" was condemned as "provocative, isolationist and open to question." Happily, so far this winter, seasonal greetings in the *TLS* Letters page have been few and far between.[9]

Bill Bryson

Conversation with a waitress in Sonora, California:
"I'd like the chicken fried steak," I said.
"You'd like the chicken fried steak?"
"Yes. And I would like French fries with it."
"You want French fries with it?"
"Yes. And I would like a salad with Thousand Island dressing."
"You want a salad with Thousand Island dressing?"
"Yes, and a Coke to drink."
"You want a Coke to drink?"
"Excuse me, miss, but I've had a bad day and if you don't stop repeating everything I say, I'm going to take this ketchup bottle and squirt it all down the front of your blouse."
"You're going to take that ketchup bottle and squirt it all down the front of my blouse?"[10]

George Burns

I went to all that trouble to bring a piano player to Philadelphia, only to find out that he doesn't like music.

I can't die yet . . . I'm booked!

George: Gracie, this family of yours . . .
Gracie (Allen): When Willie was a baby my father took him riding in his carriage, and two hours later my father came back with a different baby and a different carriage.
George: Well, what did your mother say?
Gracie: My mother didn't say anything because it was a better carriage.

George: A better carriage?

Gracie: Yes . . . and the little baby my father brought home was a little French baby so my mother took up French.

George: Why?

Gracie : So she would be able to understand the baby . . .

George: . . . when the baby started to talk.

Gracie : Yeah.[11]

Godfrey Cambridge

I have biblical thoughts once in a while, like wondering what Lot might have said to Blue Cross after his wife turned to salt.

Johny Check

Did you ever wonder why golf courses don't have 10 or 13 holes instead of 18? It seems that back in 1858, the board of one of the oldest and most venerable courses in Scotland sat all day trying to settle this very question. There were then 7-hole courses, 13-hole courses and 15-hole courses. At one time the famous St. Andrews itself was made up of 22 holes and Montrose had 25.

Finally, after a fruitless all-day discussion, it is said that one of the Scottish board members, and elder of very good standing, arose and spoke as follows: "You good gentlemen have been considering this situation for many hours. I have been hoping you would decide along lines agreeable to me without any insistence on my part. I see, however, that I must now speak for myself. As you know, it has long been my custom to start out for a game of golf with a full bottle of whisky in my bag, treating myself to a wee nip on each tee. Naturally, I find it pleasant to play golf so long as there is a drink left in the bottle. And it makes no sense to continue the game when the bottle is exhausted. Now, gentlemen, I have here a small glass, which contains about an ounce and a half when not filled so full that a drop may escape. I have found that one bottle will fill this little glass just 18 times, so it has been my custom to play 18 holes each afternoon, no more, no less. I see no possible way of deviating from this custom, unless the bottles are made larger, which I fear would be too marked a change in our manufacturing life. That, my friends, is how golf courses came to have 18 holes. Don't believe it? Well, just take an ounce and a half jigger, fill it full, but not too full, and see if you don't get 18 drinks out of a 'fifth' of whisky."[12]

John Cooper Charles

Tadpoles are the thinking man's caviar.

Will Cuppy

The main ambition of every Egyptian was to be a mummy, but only the rich could afford it.

Huns looked more imposing on horseback. Who doesn't?

There is something about Lapland that seems to destroy one's perspective.

During part of her childhood, [Queen] Elizabeth was illegitimate. In 1534, Parliament ruled that it was treason to believe her illegitimate. In 1536, it was treason to believe her legitimate. Signals were changed again in 1543, and again in 1553. After that you could believe anything.

Montezuma had the courage of his convictions, but he had no convictions.[13]

P. D. East

Kierkegaard must have been very disappointed if he found any other people in heaven.

W. Burnet Easton, Jr.

A man had a tire puncture on a road outside the fence of a mental institution. While changing the tire he accidentally kicked the four wheel lugs and they went rolling down into a muddy stream that flowed nearby. He was at a loss what to do. Several hospital inmates behind the fence advised him to take one lug off each of the other three wheels and put them on the afflicted wheel. When the man thanked his helpers, they responded in unison, "Just because we're crazy doesn't mean that we're stupid."

W. C. Fields

Charlie (McCarthy, Edgar Bergen's dummy): What makes your nose so red?

Fields: That's a very good question, Charles. My scarlet proboscis is a result of an unfortunate accident in my youth.

Charlie: What did you do? Fall off the wagon?

Fields: Very funny, very funny — tell me, Charles, is it true that your father was a gate leg table?

Charlie: If it is — your father was under it.

Fields: Why you stunted spruce — I'll throw a Japanese beetle on you.

Charlie: Why you bar fly — I'll stick a wick in your mouth and use you for an alcohol lamp

Bergen: Charlie — apologize to Mr. Fields this minute.

Fields: Don't waste your breath, Edgar. Everything you tell that kid goes in one knot hole — and out the other.[14]

Sigmund Freud

A man at the dinner table who was being handed fish slipped his hands twice in the mayonnaise and then ran them through his hair. When his neighbor looked at him in astonishment, he seemed to notice his mistake and apologized: "I'm so sorry. I thought it was spinach."

(To Freud, this is "idiocy masquerading as a joke."[15] I disagree — A.R.E.)

God

The most asked question in history is this: Does God exist? And my answer? Do I exist? Is the Pope Catholic? Well, as it turns out, he is. Which is a shock because he was supposed to be Jewish. A massive cock-up while I wasn't watching. But I can't be everywhere, can I? All right, I *can* but it's very tiring when you get to My age. Which you won't.

As we say up here, "the Impossible we can do immediately, miracles take a little longer."

So I blew mightily upon the Red Sea and the waters parted and the Israelites rushed across. When they were on the opposite bank, I stopped blowing and the waters gushed back again, drowning all the Egyptians and their horses. Which was a bit unfortunate but I was completely out of breath, not being as young as I once was and having a sedentary job in which I don't get enough exercise.

And Moses turned over the tablet and read: "The Eleventh Commandment: Thou Shalt Not Turn Thy Sony Walkman Up So Loud That it Annoyeth Others."

(God is evidently not the best speller in — or beyond — the world. She spells the New Testament book "Revelation" with an s: "Revelations." This could be, I suppose, a publication error, but would not God have proofread her own materials? — A.R.E.)[16]

Rich Hall

ananánany — the inability to stop spelling the word "banana" once you start.

fígforce — mysterious magnetic force that holds two or more Fig Newtons together.

pótentater — the largest french fry in the bag.[17]

Melvyn Helitzer

Alexander Graham Bell to his mistress: "What do you mean my three minutes are up?"

Letitia Hernandez

Dear New York Times Diary:

Getting off the Lexington Avenue subway at rush hour, I spotted a young blind man with a cane having difficulty finding the stairs.

"Need some help?" I offered.

"Thanks."

Once he was on his way, he was fast, leaving me behind, gasping for breath, as he raced up 9,000 steps with sheer abandon.

"Which way?" I said when we were in the street.

He asked me to point him toward Third Avenue. I was heading in that direction and offered to walk with him. He proved to be as sprightly a walker as he was a climber.

"Your perfume," he said after a while. "I don't recognize it. It's very nice. What's the name of it?"

"Jean-Marc Sinan," I told him.

"I know Opium, Giorgio, Obsession, Chlöe," he said. "You're my first Jean-Marc Sinan."

"You seem to know a lot about women's perfumes," I said.

"It's always women who offer to help me. Ninety-nine percent of the time. Hardly ever a man. I don't know why. Why do you think it is?"

I looked at him. How strange it must feel to know you're being looked at and not be able to see the reaction.

"Probably because you're so handsome." I knew at once that I had said the right thing. He blushed and then he grinned from ear to ear.

"Thanks," he said, and we parted. He had made my day.[18]

Brian Inglis

(The following account helps to introduce the link between humor and "coincidence" or "chance" — A.R.E.)

Strolling one day along a Paris boulevard, the romantic poet and librettist Emile Deschamps saw a plum pudding in a restaurant window. Remembering how he had liked the taste when, as a schoolboy 10 years earlier, he had been given a slice by an emigré back from England, M. de Fontgibu, he turned in to the restaurant to ask if he could have another. The *dame du comptoir* called across to one of her customers: "M. de Fontgibu! Would you have the goodness to share your plum pudding with this gentleman?"

Many years later — Deschamps related to his friend the astronomer Camille Flammarion — his hostess at dinner in a Paris apartment told him, he would be having plum pudding. In that case, he jested, M. de Fontgibu would surely be one of the party! When the plum pudding was on the table, and the other guests were enjoying the tale, a servant appeared and announced: "M. de Fontgibu!"

Deschamps' first thought was that his hostess was playing a trick on him; but when he saw it really was Fontgibu, by this time a feeble old man, tottering bemused round the table, his hair stood on end. It turned out that Fontgibu happened to have been invited to dinner in the same house, but had come to the wrong apartment.

There is no way of telling whether Deschamps embroidered the story, consciously or unconsciously. Yet as John Beloff, though doubtful of its authenticity, has remarked, it is "likely to remain for all time the *ne plus ultra* of coincidences with its unique combination of the comic and the preposterous." And, he might have added, of the uncanny. Many a person hearing it must have wondered whether it really was pure chance that was to provide Fontgibu with his small niche in history.[19]

William Johnson

One Sunday just before Henry Ward Beecher entered his pulpit at Plymouth Church in Brooklyn, he opened a letter to him that contained the single word "Fool."

Quietly and with proper seriousness, Beecher announced this event to his people and then said: "I have known many an instance of a man writing a letter and forgetting to sign his name. This is the only instance I have ever known of a man signing his name and forgetting to write the letter."

Erica Jong

An 80-year-old widow goes on a blind date to a drive-in movie with an 80-year-old widower. When she comes home, her daughter asks how it went.

"Terrible," says the mother. "I had to slap his face three times."

"You mean he got fresh?"

"No, I thought he was dead."

Garrison Keillor

WHO DO YOU THINK YOU ARE?

. . . There was this man who trained his dog to go around the corner to Bud's Lounge with a dollar bill under his collar and get a pack of cigarettes and bring them home, until one day the man only had a five, so he put it under the dog's collar and sent him down, waited an hour, and no dog, so he got mad and went to Bud's and there was the pooch sitting upon a stool drinking a vodka gimlet. He said, "You've never done this before!" The dog looked straight ahead and said, "I never had the money before."

O THE PORCH

The porch promotes grace and comfort. It promotes good conversation simply by virtue of the fact that on a porch there is no need for it.

Look at the sorry bunch in the living room standing in little clumps and holding drinks, and see how hard they work to keep up a steady dribble of talk. There, silence indicates boredom and unhappiness, and hosts are quick to detect silence and rush over to subdue it into speech. Now look at our little bunch on this porch. Me and the missus float back and forth on the swing. Mark and Rhonda are collapsed at opposite ends of the couch, Malene peruses her paperback novel in which an astounding event is about to occur, young Jeb sits at the table gluing the struts on his Curtiss biplane. The cats lie on the floor listening to birdies, and I say, "It's a heck of a deal, ain't it, a heck of a deal." A golden creamy silence suffuses this happy scene, and only on a porch is it possible. . . .

After a Fall

. . . When I dropped the window off that falling ladder back in 1971, I didn't know that my son had come round the corner of the house and was standing at the foot of the ladder watching me. The window hit the ground and burst, the ladder hit the ground and bounced, and his father landed face first in the chrysanthemums; all three missed him by a few feet. Quite a spectacle for a little boy to see up close, and he laughed out loud and clapped his hands. I moved my arms to make sure they weren't broken into little pieces, and I clapped, too. Hurray for God! So many fiction writers nowadays would have sent the window down on that boy's head as if it were a pulley and the rope were around his neck, but God let three heavy objects fall at his feet and not so much as scratch him. He laughed to see me and I laughed to see him.[20]

Edward Lear

A vile beastly rottenheaded foolbegotten pernicious priggish screaming, tearing, roaring, perplexing, splitmecrackle, crachimecriggle insane ass of a woman is practising howling below-stairs with a brute of a singing master so horribly, that my head is nearly off.[21]

Groucho Marx

> *Man to Groucho*: Well I'll be a monkey's uncle!
> *Groucho*: Keep your family out of this!

Groucho to Mrs. Vandergraff: "Your eyes, your throat, your lips — everything about you reminds me of you. Except you. How do you account for that?"[22]

Michel de Montaigne

When I consider . . . that our joys and excrements are lodged together pell-mell, and that sensual pleasure at its height is attended, like pain, with faintness and moaning, I believe it is true what Plato says, that man is the plaything of the gods. [23]

The New Yorker (17 November 1980)

LONDON (AP) — The Soviet Union has welded a massive naval force "far beyond the needs of defense of the Soviet sea frontiers," and is beefing up its armada with a powerful new nuclear-powered aircraft carrier and two giant battle cruisers, the authoritative "Jane's Fighting Ships" reported Thursday.

"The Soviet navy at the start of the 1980s is truly a formidable force," said the usually-tryly is a unique formidable is too smoothy as the usually are lenience on truly a formidable Thursday's naives is frames analysis of the world's annual reference work, said the first frames of the world's navies in its 1980–81 edition.

"The Soviet navy at the start usually-repair-led Capt. John Moore, a retired British Royal News Services.

"The Soviet navy as the navy of the struggled started," she reportable Thursday.

"The Soviet navy at the start of the 1980s is truly a formidable force," said beef carry on the adults of defense block identical analysis 1980s is truly formidable force, said the usually-reliable of the 1980s is unusually reliable, lake his off the world's reported Thursday. — *Santa Ana (Calif.) Register.*

"Briton Expounds Thinking Theory," *New York Times* (10 November 1968)

A merchant with a beautiful, loving daughter owes money he cannot repay to an ugly, old moneylender. The moneylender fancies the daughter and makes the merchant an offer:

All three will meet on a pebble path and the girl will select one of two stones from a bag. One is black and one is white. If she picks the black one, she must marry the moneylender and her father's debt is canceled. If she selects the white one, she is free and the debt is canceled. If she refuses to select either, her father will go to jail.

Just before choosing, the girl notices that the moneylender has put two black stones into the bag — a clear case of cheating. But under the circumstances she cannot expose the fraud. What should she do?

A conventional thinker would concentrate on the stone that must be removed from the bag and would get nowhere, according to Dr. Edward de Bono, an eminent British physician and author of an imaginative theory on the thinking process.

But a lateral thinker, using Dr. de Bono's classification, would take a different tack and soon zero in on the stone left in the bag.

The solution: The young lady should choose a stone, fumble with it, drop it and explain, sweetly apologetic, "Oh how clumsy of me. But you can tell which one I picked by the color of the one left in the bag."

"Metropolitan Diary," New York Times (26 April 1989)

The bus was heading uptown on Third Avenue. Somewhere before Bloomingdale's it stopped for a traffic light and it was then that the passengers first became aware of the pedestrian: he dashed from the sidewalk out to the middle of the street and knocked on the bus door. The bus driver ignored him. The man knocked again. "This is not a bus stop," the driver shouted. The light changed and the bus took off.

The passengers with window seats could see the man running after the bus. Each time it reached a designated stop the runner was not far behind; each time he missed it by seconds. Soon almost everyone on the bus was watching the would-be passenger.

"Where is he now?" a voice from the front asked. "He's catching up!" someone in back said excitedly. When the sprinter missed out at the third stop, passengers began to cry out, "Wait for him! Please wait for him!" or "Let him on, let him on!"

At the next stop, the driver gave in to their pleas. He waited for the man to catch up and when, breathing heavily, the man finally came aboard, the passengers burst into applause.

With that, the man angrily whipped a pad and pencil from his pocket. "What's your name?" he shouted at the driver. "I want your number." Even louder, with waving fist: "I'm going to report you!"

Further threats were interrupted by groans from the other passengers. "Throw him off!" they now shouted. Also: "Why did we wait for him?" Mostly: "Who wanted him anyway?"

Sean O'Faolain

The well-known story about Noah Webster and the maidservant alleges that when Mrs. Webster caught him kissing the maid she said, "Noah, I am surprised." To which Noah, deeply pained, replied, "No, my dear! *I* am surprised. *You* are astonished."

Harold C. Palmer

Do you know the one about the learned butler? When the boiled tongue fell off the platter on to the table, he said calmly, "Sorry, sir, merely a *lapsus linguae*."

James Parkes

Life should be a continued siesta interrupted only by periods for food and rest. (There is a Yiddish proverb, "A job is fine but interferes with your time." — A.R.E.)

Sign on front door of Park Hotel, Voss, Norway: "Restrooms are not available for non-resistance!"

Matthew Parris

Mistaken identity in the House of Commons: I glanced suspiciously at the elegant red braces of the magnificent Nicholas Soames sitting behind David Maclean. Soames seemed vast today, even for Soames. I looked again. It wasn't Soames. It was two thin Tories in thin red ties, sitting next to each other. I hope that's clear on TV.[24]

S. J. Perelman

"I'm sorry," he added Quigley.
"Why did you add Quigley?" I begged him.
He apologized and subtracted Quigley, then divided Hogan.
"Are you mad, Russell?" I stopped him haughtily.
He bit his lip in a manner that awakened my maternal sympathy, and I helped him bite it.

Emo Philips

I'm not a fatalist. And even if I was, what could I do about it?

James Reston

The great thing about Calvinism, my 94-year-old mother said, is that you expect so little that you're always ahead of the game. (The limitation upon this outlook is that the worst can and does happen — A.R.E.)

Ralph Robin

TAKE NOTICE

I will legislate in this poem:

Large feet are beautiful. Be it enacted and decreed
That from this day on
Beauty shall begin from size ten
— No, strike that out — size nine
And esthetic judgment, under penalties subsequently provided,
Will found itself in perpetuity upon my ground:
Beyond any appeal or repeal.

To which, I affix my seal.

Leo Rosten (his favorite joke)

Two young women meet on the street.
First woman: Is it true that you are going to have a baby?
Second woman: Yes!
First woman: Are you hoping for a boy or a girl?
Second woman: Certainly.

Norman Rosten

Why do people smile when you say you're from Brooklyn — people who would react normally enough if you claimed to be from any of the other five boroughs that make up the city of New York?

It's not only that we are receptive to the image of the underdog; we even anoint our heroes in that light. Where else would a baseball team like the Brooklyn Dodgers, with its pennant and World Series victories, be proudly referred to as "Bums"? Are they called "bums" in Los Angeles? No. That Johnny-come-lately city would never see it that way. Los Angeles has never truly suffered.

A tree growing in Brooklyn is somehow more appealing than a tree anywhere else. . . . Of course, the idea of a tree in any densely urban area is awe-inspiring: the courage, the daring, blindly asserting itself into poisoned air, attacked by dirt, dogs, mischievous children, careening motorists, lovers with pen knives.

Brooklyn Bridge

It stands above a century of winds,
colossus anchored in tides,
still surprising the landscape.

Light upon the cables,
weight gathered within
The stone towers: a tension
spooled out as steel,
now compacted into giant shoulders.
On some days a lithograph,
on others a choir of strings,
our Gothic incarnation;
finally, a curve of silence
upholding a world, as Roebling dreamed . . .

The dream to reach beyond structure,
arrive at a waiting future:
and it is here
    Aloof to the age,
its beauty and line intact,
we see again the pink-veined stone
flowering to the arch, holding
the strands of cable woven by
forgotten fingers. The city flows
to the horizon, heavy with smoke
and the death of architecture,
yet the Bridge will soar, and sing,
rising with dawns and mists,
poised for another leap of time.

Wheels accelerate on the span,
rasping like wasps in their madness,
drone of the living and the dead.
The century, begun on these cobbles,
turns on that weightless arc,
turns with the sun, with light,
as ghosts of the sailing ships
ride the same harbor.[25]

Rita Rudner

Everything kept going wrong with our marriage. My husband and I couldn't even light the fire. One night our neighbor's house caught fire, so we ran round there and said, "How did you do that?"

I have a method of weighing myself in the morning. I hang off the shower curtain and gradually lower myself to the scale. When it gets to the right weight I try to black out.

Mark Russell

After the rift between Blacks and Jews, Sammy Davis, Jr. refused to eat with himself.

De Gaulle always wanted to die in his own arms.

A real conservative is a person whose idea of gun control is a steady aim.

Mort Sahl, with Alexander Haig

Haig: Did you know that Henry Kissinger was born in the United States?
Sahl: Then how is it he has a German accent?
Haig: That comes from not listening to anyone.

Sahl: How come you are smoking a Castro cigar?
Haig: I prefer to think of it as burning his crops to the ground.

Satan

My philosophy is: don't knock it until you've tried it.[26]

Edward Shapiro

A man left a will requesting that his ashes be scattered over Bloomingdale's so that his wife would visit him once in a while.

James Thurber

Medium at a seance: I can't get in touch with your uncle, but there's a horse here that wants to say hello.

This is the only stuffed bird I ever saw with its eyes closed, but whoever had it stuffed probably wanted it stuffed that way.[27]

Lily Tomlin

I had a terrible dream last night. I dreamed that the man who invented Muzak invented something else.

Mark Twain

If you pick up a starving dog and make him prosperous, he will not bite you. This is the principal difference between a dog and a man.

All kings is mostly rapscallions (Huck Finn).

A German joke is no laughing matter.

Wagner's music is better than it sounds.

Peter Ustinov

A diver was exploring a wreck deep under the ocean, when he got an urgent call on the diving phone from his captain in the ship above.
"Come up! Come up now!" the captain said.
"Why?" asked the diver.
"Why? Because the ship is sinking!"

Jane Walmsley

Doctor: You're in great shape. You'll live to be ninety.
Patient: I *am* ninety.
Doctor: Oh, well. That's it, then.

The American senior citizen's greatest fear in life is being marooned someplace where he can't get dental floss.

For the True Brit, only two things really count: the Royal Family and the Pub. For the True American, only one thing counts: Ice Cream.[28]

E. B. White

A book should be the occasion of rejoicing, but it is seldom that, imparting a feeling of completion but not of satisfaction. I suppose a writer, almost by definition, is a person incapable of satisfaction — which is what keeps him at his post.

My night nurse's name began with "A" and ended in a thornbush.

He [Matty, the Seattle *Times* photographer] loved pregnant women — I mean he really had a sort of fondness for them. "I love 'em!" he would shout. "God, I love 'em!" I think the intimation of new life appealed to his sporting spirit — he was glad with a wild, eerie joy, that a baby was on the way. He could always spot ladies who were *enceinte* and would warp his Franklin [auto] alongside and cry out, "H'ya, Mom, h'ya, sweetheart, that's the ticket, that's the old ticket!"

Conch

Hold a baby to your ear
   As you would a shell:
Sounds of centuries you hear
   New centuries foretell.

Who can break a baby's code?
   And which is the older —
The listener or his small load?
   The held or the holder?

Sadness of Parting

The barber was cutting our hair, and our eyes were closed — as they are likely to be. We had passed into that deep and bountiful world of repose which one finds only at the end of the tonsorial trail. The scissors, stroking, had entered into the deliberate phase well behind the ears; our head was bowed; and peace had settled over the chair, with only the asthmatic inhalations of the barber marking life's beat. Deep in a world of our own, we heard, from far away, a voice saying goodbye. It was a customer of the shop, leaving. "Goodbye," he said to the barbers. "Goodbye," echoed the barbers. And without ever returning to consciousness, or opening our eyes, or thinking, we joined in. "Goodbye," we said, before we could catch ourself. Then, all at once, the sadness of the occasion struck us, the awful dolor of bidding farewell to someone we had never seen. We have since wondered what he looked like, and whether it was really goodbye.[29]

Oscar Wilde

The only way to get rid of a temptation is to yield to it.

Ed Wynn

He was beside himself and both of them looked terrible.

NOTES

1. *Newsletter,* Institute of Early American History and Culture (2 June 1958). Cf. Uriel Tal: "Scholarship is gossip with footnotes."
2. Aristides, "What's So Funny?," *The American Scholar* (Autumn 1984), p. 444.
3. Vincent Canby, *The New York Times* (25 January 1981).
4. *Leo Rosten's Giant Book,* pp. 1–2.
5. Dave Allen, BBC Television, 6 January 1990.
6. In some cases the label "Anonymous" means that I have simply not succeeded in locating the source.
7. Aristides, "What's So Funny?," pp. 439, 440–41, 442, 444.
8. Ambrose Bierce, *The Devil's Dictionary.*
9. Craig Brown, "Festive Season's Bleatings," *The Times* (London) (6 December 1989).
10. Bill Bryson, *The Lost Continent,* pp. 226–27.
11. Cited in Barry Took, *Comedy Greats,* p. 18.
12. *Bethlehem (Pa.) Globe Times* (4 September 1964).
13. Will Cuppy, *The Decline and Fall of Practically Everybody,* pp. 10n, 72n, 154n, 172–73, 202n.
14. Cited in Took, *Comedy Greats,* p. 108.
15. Freud, *Jokes,* pp. 138–39.
16. *God: The Ultimate Autobiography,* pp. 9, 15n, 23, 102, 110.
17. Rich Hall, *Unexplained Singlets of the Universe.*
18. Letitia Hernandez, "Metropolitan Diary," *The New York Times* (28 October 1987).
19. Brian Inglis, "A Matter of Chance or Destiny," *Observer* (London) (24 December 1989).
20. Garrison Keillor, *We Are Still Married,* pp. 119–20, 144, 316.
21. Lear, foreword to *Nonsense Books,* p. ix.
22. The second item is from *Flywheel, Shyster, and Flywheel,* Michael Barson, ed., p. 274.
23. Michel de Montaigne, *Essays* III:5, as cited in Berger, *Precarious Vision,* p. 73.
24. Matthew Parris, "Not to be read over breakfast," *The Times* (London) (12 January 1990)
25. Norman Rosten, *Neighborhood Tales,* pp. 139, 153, 19, 121.
26. *Satan,* p. 11.
27. James Thurber, *Collecting Himself,* pp. xvi, 204.
28. Jane Walmsley, *Brit-Think, Ameri-Think,* pp. 113, 126–27, 129–30.
29. White, *Second Tree from the Corner,* pp. xviii, 8, 13, 195, 223.

9

Fool-Clown-Child

Only a rebirth of festivity can move us beyond the religious crisis we call the death of God.

— Harvey Cox

Clownage is less frivolous than the deification of humanity.

— Enid Welsford

All of us are children, only our bodies get older.

— George Booth

When you do comedy, you are not sitting at the grownups' table.

— Woody Allen

The realities of fool, clown, and child lend themselves in some ways to shared treatment.

In the phrasing of Conrad Hyers, the fool is "jester to the kingdoms of earth." The fool was already known in ancient China, Greece, and Rome, and later in the Christian and Muslim worlds. It is hard for us today to realize how prevalent the "office" of the fool was in ancient, medieval, and renaissance society. Fools were to be found amongst the wealthy, at the side of popes, cardinals, and lesser clergy, and indeed within the following of almost anyone of stature. Themselves without rank or power, jesters could yet serve to maintain a delicate balance of power, on either side of which lay tyranny and anarchy. Thus did they play a kind of prophetic role, representative of a wider spirit and a higher wisdom, until they went out of fashion beginning in the eighteenth century. Today their role is filled by a variety of persons: comic actors, comedians, clowns, mimes, et alii.

Within Christianity the early Franciscans dubbed themselves "fools of the world" (*mundi moriones*), men who, wholly devoid of the riches and power of this dispensation, followed in the path of their humiliated master Jesus. In the medieval church three post-Christmas festivals were observed: Holy Innocents Day, when boy bishops would assume the positions and functions of ecclesiastical office; the Feast of Fools, when lower clergy would burlesque the offices of their superiors; and the Feast of Asses, when, in the presence of an ass ridden by a young girl holding an infant boy, mass was sung in dog-Latin rhyme, and priest and congregation would bray the refrain, "Haw, Sir Ass, he-haw."

Beginning in sixth-century Greek Orthodoxy and culminating in Russian Orthodoxy between the fourteenth and seventeenth centuries, the custom appeared of sainting a number of persons as holy fools. Calling up Paul's idea of the foolishness of the Christian gospel and of disciples as "fools for Christ's sake," "a type of sainthood developed in which the expression of piety was that of publicly making a fool of oneself. The monk or priest manifested his sincerity not by projecting an atmosphere of intense seriousness and sanctity, but by playing the part of the buffoon. . . . He humbled himself, as it were, in a comic identification with the humility and humiliation of Jesus."[1]

Conrad Hyers's presentation of the clown parallels and diverges from that of the fool. The clown

dares to sport in the inner sanctum of our being. . . . [He] identifies our tensions and our ambivalences. . . . Then suddenly we find ourselves put back together again in a hilarious slam-bang fashion. . . .

The key to the paradox of the clown's person and performance is a disturbing yet liberating ambiguity. . . . [He] is lord of that no-man's-land between contending forces, moving back and forth along all those human lines drawn (not without arbitrariness) between law and order, social and antisocial, reason and irrationality, friend and foe, fashionable and unfashionable, important and unimportant. . . .

The clown reduces life to its basics. Hence the common association of clowning with food, sex, and evacuation in exaggerated proportions (gluttony, obscenity, and scatological play). For all our pious creeds and momentous concerns, the basic requirements of our lives are relatively simple: a good meal and restful sleep, freedom from anxiety and freedom from constipation, the enjoyment of sex and the laughter of children, the satisfaction of work and the pleasure of play, the conviviality of friends and a moment's peace. . . . Without life, after all, there is no reason, no morality, no religion. And without fertility and food and the elimination of bodily wastes, there is no life. Life and the sources of life are primary. We cannot live by spirit alone.

In a word, "clowns move between fantasy and reality, the sublime and the commonplace. This is a part of their mediation, their dialectic, their salvation."[2]

We come now to the question of humor and the child. Carol Troen, a colleague at the Oxford Centre, suggested to me a possible correlation between the child's gradual discovery and apprehension of one or more of my Proto-Jokes (cf. chapter 1) and the inception of humor in its life. For example, in the peekaboo, people appear to go in and out of existence.

It appears to me that the child incarnates many features of fool and clown, but not deliberately or vocationally so, and hence much more gracefully and liberatingly so. The grace of the child is in no way utilitarian. Evolutionist interpreters of humor[3] tend, I think incorrectly, to dismiss child humor as being inauthentic because it is "undeveloped." (To such interpreters, aspects of the humor of adults are often dismissed on the ground of being "infantile.") William Hazlitt supplies an example: A child who is hiding during play finds it very hard to keep from giving itself away by laughing, whereas a grown person in hiding from assassins will never betray himself by laughing.[4] I ask: Who is to say that the child's behavior here is any less "human" than the adult's?

However, the *primary* sense of the unbelievable grace of children is a function *neither* of (a) childlike "normality," *nor* of (b) childlike "innocence/goodness," *nor* of (c) childlike "hope." Let us consider these negatives.

A. Children with cancer are not "normal," not, at least, statistically speaking. But Erma Bombeck can write the very opposite of what we should expect:

This is a warning. If you can't handle optimism, don't go around children with cancer. If you feel tears are more appropriate than laughter, don't even think of dropping in on a camp where they are. If you don't want to put yourself at risk for feeling good about yourself, your life and the world . . . wear a mask! . . .

When Daniel came home from kindergarten one day, his mother announced excitedly, "Daniel, your sister is in remission." Daniel screamed "Yea!" and ran outside on the porch to shout to a group of his friends, "My sister is in remission!" Joyously, everyone jumped up and down, clapped their hands and danced on the lawn until Daniel stopped and said soberly, "Momma, what's remission?" . . .

If they have one leg, they will jump into a puddle of water with it. If they pass a mirror reflecting their bald head, they will stick out their tongue in defiance. If you put 'em in a wheelchair, they'll find another one to race.

Here is a twelve-year-old girl's poem:

> On the Twelfth Day of Cancer my doctor gave to me,
> Twelve months of remission,
> Eleven frustrated doctors,
> Ten Ewing's tumors,
> Nine prosthetic limbs,
> Eight bald children,
> Seven pairs of crutches,
> Six amputees,
> Five joking nurses,
> Four fuzzy wigs,
> Three blood tests,
> Two rounds of chemo
> And a big needle for my arm.

Bombeck concludes: "To me, the animal 'Hope' is small. Sometimes it has two legs, sometimes not. Sometimes it has hair and sometimes it is bald. It can laugh and cry in the same breath. It doesn't have to talk. Its very presence is enough to change the course of your life. . . . It has a name. It is called a child fighting cancer."[5]

B. Just as questionable as any recourse to "normality" is any attempt to make the grace of children contingent upon their "innocence/goodness."

The "innocence/goodness" of children is distinguished by its actual absence — save perhaps amongst very little ones.[6] Here is the theme song of "Bullies," a BBC documentary upon the ways children "get it" from other children in playgrounds, on the way to school, or in school itself:

> You get it for being Jewish,
> You get it for being black,
> You get it for being chicken,
> You get it for fighting back.
> You get it for being big and fat,
> You get it for being small.
> You get it, you get it, you get it,
> For any damn thing at all.[7]

John Morreall observes that "children who have been speaking for only a few years are already proficient at making up nicknames with which to taunt other children and adults who have physical deformities, or whose clothing, language, or behavior is different from their own." Some studies have shown "that what young children find most amusing is someone else's suffering."[8]

C. It is equally questionable to make "hope" *the* key to the child. Robert Fulghum writes:

> It's hard to share everything and play fair if you don't have anything to share and life is itself unjust. I think of the children of this earth who see the world through barbed wire, who live in a filthy rubbled mess not of their own making and that they can never clean up. They do not wash their hands before they eat. There is no water. Or soap. And some do not have hands to wash. They do not know about warm cookies and cold milk, only stale scraps and hunger. They have no blankie to wrap themselves in, and do not take naps because it is too dangerous to close their eyes.[9]

To be positive now, we may have to sound tautological: The grace that the child brings is the grace of the child as such, nothing else. Here is a *childness* that drives above and beyond any and all spatio-temporal conditions, that bursts out beyond any and all spatio-temporal eventualities. ("Childness" seems better to convey my intention here, which is ontological, than the alternative, "childhood," which sounds more periodic than is proper in the present context.)[10] In the symbolization of Conrad Hyers, the laughter and humor of children manifest a collective memory of paradise.

Once we are emboldened to bring childness, humor, and cancer within a single (and singular) shared, conceptual and moral world, the barrier falls away to any exclusion of, say, the poems of the children of Terezín (Theresienstadt), a transit camp or holding place for Auschwitz.

THE BUTTERFLY

The last, the very last,
So richly, brightly, dazzingly yellow.
    Perhaps if the sun's tears would sing
    against a white stone . . .

Such, such a yellow
Is carried lightly, 'way up high.
It went away I'm sure because it wished to
    kiss the world goodbye.

For seven weeks I've lived in here,
Penned up inside this ghetto
But I have found my people here.
The dandelions call to me
And the white chestnut candles in the court.
Only I never saw another butterfly.

That butterfly was the last one.
Butterflies don't live in here,
    In the ghetto.

— Pavel Friedmann

TO OLGA

Listen!
The boat whistle has sounded now
And we must sail
Out toward an unknown port.

We'll sail a long, long way
And dreams will turn to truth.
Oh, how sweet the name Morocco!
Listen!
Now it's time.

The wind sings songs of far away,
Just look up to heaven
And think about the violets.

Listen!
Now it's time.

— Alena Synková

THE GARDEN

A little garden,
Fragrant and full of roses.
The path is narrow
And a little boy walks along it.

A little boy, a sweet boy,
Like that growing blossom.
When the blossom comes to bloom,
The little boy will be no more.

— Franta Bass[11]

We may dare to open a place within a "handbook of humor" for the children beset by the German Nazi horror only because *in and of themselves,* that is to say, by virtue strictly of their being, the children are (living/dying) warriors against the devil. The mystery of human life and grandeur here opens itself to our view. The same child who is never to see another butterfly yet "finds his people here." The same child who will never sail again yet testifies to the sweetness of the name Morocco. The same child who "will be no more" yet knows the narrow path to a small garden full of roses. At approximately the same time a five-year-old orphan in the ghetto of Lodz is comforting her rag doll: "Don't cry, my little doll. When the Germans come to grab you, I won't leave you. I'll go with you, like Rosie's mother."[12] One rejoinder to Auschwitz is the powerful pathos of a hymn to joy.

To return to Conrad Hyers: The child acts out in all naturalness the liturgy of the fool, and the child does quite naturally all the wonderful things the clown performs as a vocational responsibility. The clown and the child are intrinsic companions. For in the clown's world we are brought to rediscover the "child's delight in life's little bits and pieces." With the child, the clown's task is to defend the ordinary. The maturity that clown and fool represent — I believe we may number the child here as well — consists in a reversal of the process of restlessness and disenchantment, "a de-escalation. Instead of terminating in a kind of cynicism or despair over life, as if caught in a speeded-up merry-go-round from which one yearns to get off, one is reawakened to a new zest for life. Or instead of the world's being scorned in favor of some spiritual regions judged to be eternally satisfying, the world is reopened in its fullness. It is a recovery, at a higher level, of the child's sense of wonder and worth relative to the whole of life, even the slightest particular." At this place, fool, clown, and child are joined by the sage: "Each in their own way performs that peculiar religious function of treating the marvelous as commonplace, and the commonplace as marvelous, and sensing in everything a great mystery." Children are born philosophers.

The basic affinity is that of child and clown:

> The child exists in those wonderfully in-between years — as the clown is an in-between figure: in between infancy and adolescence, in between asexuality and puberty, in between innocence and the knowledge of good and evil, in between seriousness and frivolity. Because of this in-betweenness the child and the clown stand also, paradoxically, both between the human and animal sphere on the one hand, and the human and divine sphere on the other. They suggest a mediating category that is not quite human in its innocence and amorphousness and yet more than human in its transcendence of rigid structures and narrow identities. As in the mythical motif of the Divine Child, child and clown seem privy to a higher wisdom and freedom and power. . . .

> Why, of all things, bananas? Yet though the oddness and mysteriousness of existence overwhelm us, they do not lead to a sense of bewilderment, nor do they issue in a sense of anxiety or alienation or despair. The context is one of celebration, and the feeling is one of a joyful absurdity in things, a playful surprise, a happy unintelligibility. . . . We laugh in awe and wonder.[13]

We tell a joke and we laugh. But isn't there a sense in which the laughter is beside the point? Why tell the joke in the first place? And what are the lessons in the joke? These questions are extremely serious ones; there is nothing funny about them. They are life-and-death questions. For nothing less than human destiny and fate are caught up in them. In them and through them laughter is seen to transcend itself and emerge with something that is anything but humorous. Yet all this is true only for what might be called *serious humor*, which stands among the great paradoxes of human life. However, there is also *humorous humor*, the laughter peculiar to the little child. Now the question of what are the lessons in one or another joke is told to be quiet. In its place laughter and humor are seen to be — laughter and humor, ends in themselves.

There is humor that endeavors to *say* something (other than itself) and there is humor that is like children romping at play; it is simply being itself. Utilitarian or pragmatic humor is not humor-in-and-of-itself; it has a purpose beyond itself — in contrast to what is dubbed just above humorous humor, or laughable laughter. The prototype of this latter, integral humor remains the child, at least the small child.

Children do much more than bring a fiery judgment upon the evils and pretensions of an "adult world." As though *ex nihilo*, they fashion spontaneously the ecstasy that, freed from all ulterior purpose, yet vanquishes adult dourness and cynicism. In this, the child lives and moves in the one rank with sister fool and brother clown. The word for childness is Joy.

NOTES

1. Hyers, *Comic Vision*, chap. 2. Cf. Harvey Cox, *Feast of Fools*. For a full accounting of folly and holy fools throughout two main strands of the Christian tradition, see John Sayward, *Perfect Fools: Folly for Christ's Sake in Catholic and Orthodox Spirituality*.
2. Hyers, *Comic Vision*, chap. 3 and p. 74.
3. Cf. Swabey, *Comic Laughter*, chap. 10.
4. Hazlitt, *Lectures*, in *Philosophy Of Laughter and Humor*, John Morreall, ed., p. 81.
5. Erma Bombeck, *I Want to Grow Hair, I Want to Grow Up, I Want to Go to Boise: Children Surviving Cancer*, pp. 7–8, 95, 109, 137, 144.
6. Cf. Reinhold Niebuhr: "It is significant that little children are really very sober though they freely indulge in a laughter which expresses a pure animal joy of existence. But they do not develop the capacity of real humour until

the fifth or sixth year, at which time they may be able to laugh at themselves and at others. At about this age their intense preoccupation with self and with an immediate task at hand is partly mitigated. The sense of humour grows, in other words, with the capacity of self-transcendence" ("Humour and Faith," in *Holy Laughter*, Conrad Hyers, ed., p. 141).

7. *The Times* (London) (29 November 1989).
8. Morreall, *Taking Laughter Seriously*, pp. 9–10.
9. Robert Fulghum, *It Was on Fire When I Lay Down on It*, p. 108.
10. We may recall Ambrose Bierce's fierce definition of childhood in *The Devil's Dictionary*: "the period of human life intermediate between the idiocy of infancy and the folly of youth — two removes from the sin of manhood and three from the remorse of age."
11. Hana Volavková, ed., . . . *I never saw another butterfly . . . Children's Drawings and Poems from Terezín Concentration Camp 1942–1944* (New York: McGraw-Hill Book Company, 1976). Some 15,000 children under the age of 15 passed through Theresienstadt; about 100 survived. Of the approximately 6,000,000 Jews killed in the *Shoah*, 1,500,000 were children. Consult Frances Gaeger Grossman, "The Art of the Children of Terezín: A Psychological Study," *Holocaust and Genocide Studies* 4 (1989): 213–29: "One's expectation that the art would reflect the horrors of life at the camp was borne out by the work of the adult artists, but not by that of the children. . . . The major themes . . . are a preoccupation with food, intense feelings of claustrophobia, a desire to be free . . . a sense of the fragility of one's physical existence at the camp, and the lack of human value of the camp inmates." Yet for the most part the children's art is "lacking in deviance or pathology."
12. George Eisen, *Children and Play in the Holocaust: Games Among the Shadows* (Amherst: University of Massachusetts Press, 1988), p. 97.
13. Hyers, *Comic Vision*, chap. 4.

10

From and for the Littler Ones

POETRY

THE BIRTH OF LIGHT

With a blink, a shimmer and a
   CRACK!
A dazzling brightness burst into the
   world
"It is my death," cried Darkness
But he saw a reflection in a far lake
"Ahh, it is a beautiful death," he sighed
And so, it came to pass that light was
   a gift to the world.

Light is like a cherub being born
Or cool as the spangling stars
That give way to the blazing brass sun
It is the red pinpoint of a guttering
   match.

Light is the shine on a rosy apple
It is the multi-coloured stream
Running down the cold walls of a
   cathedral
Or a shaft of green cast through trees

into a clearing
A delicate orchid in a dank wood.

The mystic sheen of ghosts is
    shiver-casting
Eerie as the glow of St Elmo's fire
    that haunts sailors
The ghastly glint of steel is the light of
    destruction
And up rises Darkness again.
                              — Grace Trinnaman (age 8)[1]

I Like Christmas

If I were a Christmas tree
I'd shake my ornaments and run away.
                              —Jeffrey Hatch (Third Grade)

Come with Me

. . . Come with me to a place
I know. It's a very mysterious place.
I get there through the back roads of my mind.

Come with me, I'll take you to a
world, not a world that you know. Not
a world that I know. But a world
that nobody knows, not me or you.
It's a world of our own to live the
way we want. . . .
                              —Vivien Tuft (Sixth Grade)[2]

The Naming of Cats

. . . When you notice a cat in profound meditation,
    The reason, I tell you, is always the same:
His mind is engaged in a rapt contemplation
    Of the thought, of the thought, of the thought of his name:
        His ineffable effable

Effanineffable
Deep and inscrutable singular Name.[3]

LETTER PRAYERS

Dear God:
   I wished on a star two times but nothing happened. Now what?

Anna

Dear God:
   If you made the rule for kids to take out garbage, please change it.

Maurice

Dear God:
   Charles my cat got run over. And if you made it happen you have to tell me why.

Harvey

Dear God:
   Do good people have to die young? I heard my mommy say that. I am not always good.

Yours truly, Barbara

Dear God:
   I am writing to you even though you can't write back, I think, and you are not a person. But I wanted to write anyway.

Love, Karen

Dear God:
   I read your book and I like it. I would like to write a book some day with the same kind of stories. Where do you get your ideas?

Best wishes, Mark[4]

Dear God:
   Some of the time your really horrible but most of the time your quite nice.

Love, Mark

Dear Jesus:

I would like everything I like.

Love, Graham

Dear God:

My cats would like you to make them bigger so they can chase dogs around.

Love, Christo

Dear God:

The world isn't how it was when you drowned it, there's more foolish people now. It's worse now.

Fiona

Dear God:

The devil thinks he is the right way and Jesus is the wrong way.

Alan

Dear God:

Can you tell me what forever is? No-one else can.

Mary

Dear God:

It makes me cross that there are all these droughts and you don't seem to be doing anything about them. Then there's floods in other places, like all this rain we are getting so why can't you send it half way round the world. It seems ridiculous.

David

Dear God:

I wonder why you made animals that eat people.

Christo

(How about people that eat animals? — A.R.E.)

Dear God:

If you walked in now and said "Hello I'm God" I'd say "Stop pulling my leg!"

Judy[5]

OBSERVATIONS

Christopher: "I think heaven is higher than space. It's the highest thing in the world."
Alan: "You can't get further than space!"
Christopher: "You can't get further than heaven! Space doesn't go on forever it stops at heaven."

I ask God things inside my head and he can mindread and it worked once. I asked him for some dominoes and I got some Pooh Bear ones.

Mark

We make God angry.

Esther

If you are very good in hell God will help you to escape he'll give you a secret message.

Alan

He likes comedy — things like batman and superman.

Darren[6]

HOW *THROUGH THE LOOKING-GLASS* CAME TO BE LOOKED THROUGH

Do you know the probable inspiration of this work of Lewis Carroll? I had forgotten, until I found the following in an old file:

This little Alice lived at 95 Onslow Square, South Kensington, in a house that backed on to a large garden shared by all the neighbors. At 101 lived Lewis Carroll's favorite uncle, and one morning while he was staying at this uncle's home Dodgson [Carroll] went out into the garden and encountered the little girl with the magical name. Many years later, she herself recalled what happened:

"As children we . . . used to play in the garden behind the house. Charles Dodgson used to . . . walk up and down, his hands behind him, on the strip of lawn. One day, hearing my name, he called me to him saying, 'So you are another Alice. I'm very fond of Alice. Would you like to come and see something which is rather puzzling?' We followed him into the house which opened, as ours did, upon the garden, into a room full of furniture with a tall mirror standing across one corner.

" 'Now,' he said, giving me an orange, 'first tell me which hand you have got that in.' 'The right,' I said. 'Now,' he said, 'go and stand before that glass, and tell me which hand the little girl you see there has got it in.' After some perplexed contemplation, I said, 'The left hand.' 'Exactly,' he said, 'and how do you explain that?' I couldn't explain it, but seeing that some solution was expected, I ventured, 'If I was on the other side of the glass, wouldn't the orange still be in my right hand?' I remember his laugh. 'Well done, little Alice,' he said. 'The best answer I've had yet.' "[7]

SELECTIONS

> "The time has come," the Walrus said,
>   To talk of many things:
> Of shoes — and ships — and sealing-wax —
>   Of cabbages — and kings —
> And why the sea is boiling hot —
>   And whether pigs have wings."

"I am real!" said Alice, and began to cry.

"You won't make yourself a bit realler by crying," Tweedledee remarked: "there's nothing to cry about."

"If I weren't real," Alice said- —half laughing through her tears, it all seemed so ridiculous —"I shouldn't be able to cry."

"Why, sometimes I've believed as many as six impossible things before breakfast." (The White Queen)

"When *I* use a word," Humpty Dumpty said, in a rather scornful tone, "it means just what I choose it to mean —neither more nor less."

[Queen] Alice glanced nervously along the table as she walked up the large hall, and noticed that there were about fifty guests, of all kinds: some were animals, some birds, and there were even a few flowers among them. "I'm glad they've come without waiting to be asked," she thought: "I should never have known who were the right people to invite!"[8]

THE NONSENSE BOOKS OF EDWARD LEAR

From "The Story of the Four Little Children Who Went Round the World"

By-and-by the Four Children came to a country where there were no houses, but only an incredibly innumerable number of large bottles without corks, and of a dazzling and sweetly susceptible blue colour. Each of these blue bottles contained a Blue-Bottle-Fly, and all these interesting animals live continually together in the most copious and rural harmony, nor perhaps in many parts of the world is such perfect and abject happiness to be found. Violet and Slingsby, and Guy, and Lionel, were greatly struck with this singular and instructive settlement, and having previously asked permission of the Blue-Bottle-Flies (which was most courteously granted), the Boat was drawn up to the shore and they proceeded to make tea in front of the Bottles; but as they had no tea-leaves, they merely placed some pebbles in the hot water, and the Quangle-Wangle played some tunes over it on an Accordion, by which of course tea was made directly, and of the very best quality.

———————

From "The History of the Seven Families of the Lake Pipple-Popple"

The Seven Young Parrots had not gone far, when they saw a tree with a single Cherry on it, which the oldest Parrot picked instantly, but the other six, being extremely hungry, tried to get it also. On which the Seven began to fight, and
they scuffled,
   and huffled,
      and ruffled,
         and shuffled,
            and puffled,
               and muffled,
                  and buffled,
                     and duffled,
                        and fluffled,
                          and guffled,

and bruffled, and screamed, and shrieked, and squealed, and squeaked, and clawed, and snapped, and bit, and bumped and thumped, and dumped, and flumped each other, till they were all torn into little bits, and at last there was nothing left to record this painful incident, except the Cherry and seven small green feathers.

And that was the vicious and voluble end of the Seven Young Parrots.[9]

FROM *WINNIE-THE-POOH*

(Please note: According to the inside front cover, Where the Woozle Wasn't is between Piglet's House and the Floody Place.)

"It is hard to be brave," said Piglet, sniffing slightly, "when you're only a Very Small Animal."

PLAN TO CAPTURE BABY ROO

1. *General Remarks*. Kanga runs faster than any of us even me [Rabbit].

2. *More General Remarks*. Kanga never takes her eye off Baby Roo, except when he's safely buttoned up in her pocket.

3. *Therefore*. If we are to capture Baby Roo, we must get a Long Start, because Kanga runs faster than any of Us, even Me. (*See* 1.)

4. *A Thought*. If Roo had jumped out of Kanga's pocket and Piglet had jumped in, Kanga wouldn't know the difference, because Piglet is a Very Small Animal.

5. Like Roo.

6. But Kanga would have to be looking the other way first, so as not to see Piglet jumping in.

7. See 2.

8. *Another thought.* But if Pooh was talking to her very excitedly, she *might* look the other way for a moment.

9. And then I could run away with Roo.

10. Quickly.

11. *And Kanga wouldn't discover the difference until Afterwards.*

And then this Bear, Pooh Bear, Winnie the Pooh, F.O.P. (Friend of
Piglet's), R.C. (Rabbit's Companion), P.D. (Pole Discoverer), E.C.
and T.F. (Eeyore's Comforter and Tail Finder) — in fact, Pooh himself — said something so clever that Christopher Robin could only look
at him with mouth open and eyes staring, wondering if this was really
the Bear of Very Little Brain whom he had known and loved so
long.[10]

THE POETRY OF SHEL SILVERSTEIN

I place here an example of Silverstein's verse, though, laughing as it
does at any line between children's humor and adult humor, it could
fit elsewhere or everywhere.

PICTURE PUZZLE PIECE

One picture puzzle piece
Lyin' on the sidewalk,
One picture puzzle piece
Soakin' in the rain.
It might be a button of blue
On the coat of the woman
Who lived in a shoe.
It might be a magical bean,
Or a fold in the red
Velvet robe of a queen.
It might be the one little bite

Of the apple her stepmother
Gave to Snow White.
It might be the veil of a bride
Or a bottle with some evil genie inside.
It might be a small tuft of hair
On the big bouncy belly
Of Bobo the Bear.
It might be a bit of the cloak
Of the Witch of the West
As she melted to smoke.
It might be a shadowy trace
Of a tear that runs down an angel's face.
Nothing has more possibilities
Than one old wet picture puzzle piece.[11]

JAMES THURBER

THE MOTH AND THE STAR

A young and impressionable moth once set his heart on a certain star. He told his mother about this and she counseled him to set his heart on a bridge lamp instead. "Stars aren't the thing to hang around," she said. "Lamps are the thing to hang around." "You get somewhere that way," said the moth's father. "You don't get anywhere chasing stars." But the moth would not heed the words of either parent. Every evening at dusk when the star came out he would start flying toward it and every morning at dawn he would crawl back home worn out with his vain endeavor. One day his father said to him, "You haven't burned a wing in months, boy, and it looks to me as if you were never going to. All your brothers have been badly burned flying around street lamps and all your sisters have been terribly singed flying around house lamps. Come on, now, get out of here and get yourself scorched! A big strapping moth like you without a mark on him!"

The moth left his father's house, but he would not fly around street lamps and he would not fly around house lamps. He went right on trying to reach the star, which was four and one-third light years, or twenty-five trillion miles, away. The moth thought it was just caught in the top branches of the elm. He never did reach the star, but he went right on trying, night after night, and when he was a very, very old moth he began to think that he really had reached the star and he went around saying so. This gave him a deep and lasting pleasure, and he lived to a great old age. His parents and his brothers and his sisters had all been burned to death when they were quite young.

MORAL: *Who flies afar from the sphere of our sorrow is here today and here tomorrow.*[12]

DELIA EPHRON

HOW TO HANG UP THE TELEPHONE

"Good-bye."

" 'Bye."

"Are you still there?"

"Are you?"

"Yeah. Why didn't you hang up?"

"Why didn't you?"

"I was waiting for you."

"I was waiting for *you*. You go first."

"No, you first."

"No, you first."

"No, you first."

"OK, I know. I'll count to three and we'll both hang up at the same time. Ready? One, two, three, 'bye."

" 'Bye." . . .

"Are you still there?"

"Yeah."

"Why didn't you?"

"What do you mean, me?"

"OK, do it again. This time for real. One, two, two and a half, two and three quarters, three. 'Bye."

" 'Bye."

"Hello."

"Hello."

"Are you still there?"

"Yeah."[13]

GARRISON KEILLOR

FROM LAKE WOBEGON DAYS

I liked Mrs. Meiers a lot. . . . She was a plump lady with bags of fat on her arms that danced when she wrote on the board. . . . That gave her a good mark for friendliness in my book, whereas Miss Conway of fourth grade struck me as suspiciously thin. What was her problem? Nerves, I suppose. She bit her lip and squinted and snaked her skinny hand into her dress to shore up a strap, and she was easily startled by loud noises. Two or three times a day, Paul or Jim or Lance would let go with a book, dropping it flat for maximum whack, and yell, "Sorry, Miss Conway!" as the poor woman jerked like a fish on the line. It could be done by slamming a door or dropping the window, too, or even scraping a chair, and once a loud slam made *her* drop a stack of books, which gave us a double jerk. It worked better if we were very quiet before the noise. Often, the class would be so quiet, our little heads bent over our work, that she would look up and congratulate us on our excellent behavior, and when she looked back down at her book, *wham!* and she did the best jerk we had ever seen. There were five classes of spasms. The Jerk, The Jump, The High Jump, The Pants Jump, and The Loopdeloop, and we knew when she was prime for a big one. It was after we had put her through a hard morning workout, including several good jumps, and a noisy lunch period, and she had lectured us in her thin weepy voice, then we knew she was all wound up for the Loopdeloop. All it required was an extra effort: *throwing* a dictionary flat at the floor or dropping the globe, which sounded like a car crash.

We thought about possibly driving Miss Conway to a nervous breakdown, an event we were curious about because our mothers spoke of it often. "You're driving me to a nervous breakdown!" they'd yell, but then, to prevent one, they'd grab us and shake us silly. Miss Conway seemed a better candidate. We speculated about what a breakdown might include—some good jumps for sure, maybe a couple hundred, and talking gibberish with spit running down her chin.

Miss Conway's nervous breakdown was prevented by Mrs. Meiers, who . . . sat us boys down after lunch period and said that if she heard any more loud noises from Room 4, she would keep us after school for a half hour. "Why not the girls?" Lance asked. "Because I know that you boys can accept responsibility," Mrs. Meiers said. And that was the end of the jumps.[14]

MARY NORTON

THE BORROWERS

(Have you ever wondered where all those odd little items from around the house have vanished to, and that you never find no matter how hard you search? Mary Norton has the answer in "The Borrowers." — A.R.E.)

Young Kate decided that there *must* be such people as the Borrowers. "Because of all the things that disappear. Safety pins, for instance. Every day people buy safety pins, and yet, somehow, there never is a safety pin just when you want one. . . . Where do they go to? . . . All the needles my mother has ever bought . . . can't just be lying somewhere about this house. . . . And all the other things . . . like pencils and matchboxes and sealing wax and hair slides and drawing pins [thumbtacks] and thimbles — "

"And hatpins . . . and blotting paper," added Mrs. May.

But where do such little beings live? Well, the Clock family lived under the kitchen stove and had their entrance under the great grandfather clock in the hall, through a hole below the wainscot. But the entrance was a long way from the home itself. One went down "yards of dark and dusty passageway, with wooden doors between the joists and metal gates against the mice [made of] a flat leaf of a folding cheese grater, the hinged lid of a small cashbox, squares of pierced zinc from an old meat safe, a wire fly swatter. . . . [In] the sitting room the walls had been papered with scraps of old letters out of wastepaper baskets . . . arranged [with] the handwriting sideways in vertical stripes. . . . On the walls hung several portraits of Queen Victoria. . . . these were postage stamps, borrowed by Pod . . . from the stamp box on the desk in the morning room. There was a lacquer trinket box, padded inside and with the lid open, which they used as a settle; and that useful stand-by — a chest of drawers made of matchboxes. There was a round table with a red velvet cloth which Pod had made from the wooden bottom of a pillbox supported on the carved pedestal of a knight from the chess set. . . . The knight itself . . . stood on a column in the corner. . . .

"They kept the fuel, assorted slack and crumbled candle grease, in a pewter mustard pot and shoveled it out with the spoon. . . . It was a charming fireplace, made by Arrietty's grandfather, with a cogwheel from the stables, part of an old cider press. The spokes of the cogwheel stood out in starry rays, and the fire nestled in the center. Above there was a chimney piece made from a small brass funnel, inverted. . . . An arrangement of pipes, from the spout of the funnel carried the fumes into the kitchen flues above. The fire was laid with matchsticks . . . and as it burned up, the iron would become hot, and Homily would simmer soup on the spokes, in a silver thimble, and Arrietty would broil nuts. . . .

"Water they had in plenty, hot and cold, thanks to Pod's father, who had tapped the pipes from the kitchen boiler. . . ."

It was cosy when the family gathered for tea time, with the light from homemade candles securely fastened to upturned drawing pins adding to the glow from the fire. The teapot was made from a hollow oak gall with a feather quill for the spout, and wire for the handle. Roasted chestnuts were sliced for buttered toast, topped with cinnamon bread crumbs, and served on silver florin and half-crown plates.

In their store rooms were kept other borrowings that might be useful one day: scraps of silk and lace; odd kid gloves that could be made into knickers or bloomers or the soft leather shoes buttoned with beads that Pod made so cleverly; razor blades; hairpins and needles; hazel nuts and raisins; pen nibs, which made handy flour scoops; bottle tops that served as wash basins as well as many other purposes; and lots of spools of thread and balls of wool.

Once other Borrower families had lived in other parts of the house before they had had to leave for one reason or another: the Linen-Presses (who changed their name to Harpischord), the Overmantels (who had lived in the wall of the drawing room and put on grand airs), the Bell-Pulls, the Sinks (in the scullery), the Rain-pipes (from the stables), and the Broom-Cupboard boys.

In the Borrowers' view they were not stealing, since stealing was only taking things from other Borrowers, whereas taking things from human beings was only borrowing. Why? As Arrietty explained, "Human beings are *for* Borrowers — like bread for butter!"[15]

ISAAC BASHEVIS SINGER

There are five hundred reasons why I began to write for children, but to save time, I will mention only ten of them.

Number one: Children read books, not reviews. They don't give a hoot about the critics.

Number two: They don't read to find their identity.

Number three: They don't read to free themselves of guilt, to quench the thirst for rebellion, or to get rid of alienation.

Number four: They have no use for psychology.

Number five: They detest sociology.

Number six: They don't try to understand Kafka or *Finnegan's Wake.*

Number seven: They still believe in God, the family, angels, devils, and witches.

Number eight: They love interesting stories, not commentary, guides, or footnotes.

Number nine: When a book is boring, they yawn openly without any shame or fear of authority.

Number ten: They don't expect their beloved writer to redeem humanity. Young as they are, they know that it is not in his power. Only adults have such childish delusions.[16]

MAURICE SAMUEL

Grown-ups are always queer to children; they are queer, in particular, because of their dependence on things, their inelastic submission to the law of "having" instead of the law of "being."[17]

(Query: What is it that actualizes the plunge from "being" to "having"? — A.R.E.)

ROBERT FULGHUM, ADVICE FOR MOTHERS AND FATHERS

1. Children are not pets.
2. The life they actually live and the life you perceive them to be living is not the same life.
3. Don't take what your children do too personally.
4. Don't keep scorecards on them — a short memory is useful.
5. Dirt and mess are a breeding ground for well-being.
6. Stay out of their rooms after puberty.
7. Stay out of their friendships and love-life unless invited in.
8. Don't worry that they never listen to you; worry that they are always watching you.
9. Learn from them; they have much to teach you.
10. Love them long; let them go early.[18]

PETER L. BERGER

There remains something in all of us of the childish belief that there is a world of grownups *who know*. There *must* be — because we, evidently, *don't know*. It is very shocking then to suspect that the knowers do not exist at all. Everyone is groping around in the dark, just as we are. In the political area that is, perhaps, the most subversive of thoughts — the dawning realization that the great policy-makers may be as uncertain as we are as to what their next move is going to be![19]

NOTES

1. First prize, 10 years and under, Observer National Children's Poetry Competition, *Observer Magazine* (London) (17 December 1989).
2. The poems by Jeffrey Hatch and Vivien Tuft are taken from TIME (24 December 1973).
3. From T. S. Eliot, "The Naming of Cats," in *The Illustrated Old Possum: Old Possum's Book of Practical Cats,* pp. 9–10. The musical *Cats* is based on Eliot's work. What a pity that he was not prepared to honor justice and understanding for the Jewish people in the ways that he allowed for cats.
4. The foregoing six prayers are from Eric Marshall and Stuart Hample, eds., *More Children's Letters to God* (New York: Simon & Schuster, 1967).
5. The foregoing nine prayers are from Maggie Durran, compiler, *dear god Most of the time your quite nice* (London: Collins, 1985).

6. The foregoing five observations are from ibid.
7. Morton N. Cohen, "So You Are Another Alice," *The New York Times Book Review* (7 November 1971).
8. Carroll, *Through the Looking-Glass*, pp. 89, 94–95, 113, 137, 219.
9. Edward Lear, *The Nonsense Books of Edward Lear*, pp. 117–18, 130–31.
10. A. A. Milne, *Winnie-the-Pooh*, pp. 92, 93–94, 142.
11. Shel Silverstein, *A Light in the Attic*, p. 21.
12. James Thurber, "The Moth and the Star," in *The Random House Book of Humor for Children*, Pamela Pollack, compiler, pp. 93–94.
13. Delia Ephron, "How to Hang Up the Telephone," in *The Random House Book of Humor for Children*, Pamela Pollack, compiler, pp. 268–69.
14. Garrison Keillor, *Lake Wobegon Days*, pp. 173–74.
15. These materials comprise part-paraphrase and part-citation of a segment of Mary Norton, "The Borrowers," *Woman's Day,* July 1953; copyright Mary Norton, 1952, pp. 55–93, 42–141.
16. Isaac Bashevis Singer, as cited in Mark Bernheim, "Writing for Children: Singer's '500 reasons,' " *The Christian Century* 98 (1981): 1189.
17. Samuel, *World of Sholom Aleichem,* pp. 190–91.
18. Fulghum, *It Was On Fire*, pp. 103–4.
19. Berger, *Precarious Vision*, pp. 83–84.

11

Today's Heirs of Itzhak: Laughter and Tears

The most typical weapon of Jewish spirituality is humor.
— Lionel Blue

Jewish humor favors paradox because it knows that only paradox can do justice to the injustices of life.
— Leo Rosten

There are different ways of pursuing the intriguing philosophic, historical, and cultural-anthropological question of the uniqueness or singularity of a given people's humor. One way is comparative method, whereby two or more peoples are studied — say, the English, the Irish, the Welsh — in order to ascertain continuities and discontinuities between and among their forms and expressions of humor.[1] Another way is social biography, the examination of a single people's story and cultural-historical edifices. The phenomena involved can speak autonomously and then serve as raw materials of interpretation. The present chapter follows the latter approach, concentrating upon the humor of the Jewish people, with the American scene particularly in mind (especially in part II).

The question of Jewish humor is a special variation upon the persisting question of Jewish singularity. It is often maintained that only a member of a given people can really understand its life, including its humor. This limitation may, severely, apply here; I am not Jewish, although I have for years lived and worked upon the threshold of the

Jewish community—not inside yet not entirely outside. However, I might add that while a hoary definition would make a comic with a Jewish mother a Jewish comic, this does not guarantee that his or her comedy will be itself Jewish.

I

To what does the wording "Jewish humor" point? (Perhaps the phrase "humor amongst Jews" is better than "Jewish humor"; it is less constricting, less stereotyping.) The expression "Jewish humor" is hardly self-authenticating. Steven S. Schwarzschild asks: "If something is beautiful, what does its putative Jewishness have to do with its beauty? ... How then Jewish aesthetics?"[2] One might apply the same reasoning to our present subject: If something is funny, what does its putative Jewishness have 'to do with its humor? How then Jewish humor? Again, Peter L. Berger writes:

> It is hardly a coincidence that some of the best jokes are Jewish jokes. The margins of society have been the Jewish habitat for many centuries. From a marginal position one sees things more clearly—and therefore more comically! It may well be that the same social forces which have produced such a great number of Jewish analysts and interpreters of society also underlie the phenomenon of Jewish humor. The humorous capacity to put oneself in the other's position, to look at oneself doubtfully and self-critically, to take all serious matters with a grain of salt—these classically Jewish characteristics may all be seen as the fruits of marginality. [3]

Jewish humor is here accounted for on the ground, not of something peculiarly Jewish, but of a particular sociohistorical condition called marginality, which is independent of Jewishness in and of itself. Solely within the limits of this finding, Jewish humor would fall under an analytical category that Jews share with, say, American Blacks and American Hispanics. The world contains many marginal peoples. But it may be further pointed out that in the matter of their contribution to American humor, Jews have become anything but marginalized. Indeed, in the United States, Jews as a people are less and less marginalized.

The question of the singularity of Jewish humor is thus not met through the concept of marginality as such or alone (or, for that matter, through any other generalizing category). For the problem remains of how or whether there are elements within Jewish life (even marginalized Jewish life) that are distinguishable from the marginal lives of others. What is there, if there is anything, in the Jewish ethos and history, the story of the Jewish people, that sets them apart from other more or less marginalized peoples (granted that such marginality also entails continuities with the life and fate of all marginalized groupings)? Henry D. Spalding's summarization accords with the foregoing question: "The true Jewish joke mirrors the history of the Jewish people. It is a reflection of *their* joy and anguish, *their* aspirations and discouragements, *their* all too brief periods of social and economic well-being. It expresses *their* age-old yearning for a world in which justice, mercy, understanding and equality will prevail — not only for themselves but for all people. It portrays *their* quest for eternal truths."[4]

Spalding continues, in a rather more objective or self-critical vein: The Jew

> can smile at the *schlemiel* who testifies as a minor witness in court at his friend's trial and winds up as the convicted party; the *shlimazel*, Jewry's original Hard Luck Harry, whose pants fall down during his wedding ceremony; the convert to Christianity who now insists on his right to eat ham — but on matzoh; the rabbi who demands a mink *yarmulkeh*; the cantor who fancies himself as a reincarnated Caruso; the fancy *mohel* on Park Avenue who insists on using pinking shears for circumcisions; the *nouveau riche*, the parvenu, the status-seeker, the chronic imbiber, the atheist, the thief and the inveterate liar. And the merriment they invoke is tolerant rather than overly critical, because in many of them the Jewish listener recognizes a little *eppes* [something] of himself.[5]

We may allude to several further (perhaps equally debatable) representations of the qualities of Jewish humor, before entering upon a (hopefully) constructive addition to such views.

Chaim Bermant utilizes Sholom Aleichem (1859–1916) as a point of departure for his own exposition:

> In reading Sholom Aleichem one can find the wryness, the sharpness, the rancor, the irony, the self-deprecation, the world-weary cynicism, and the pathos which characterize Jewish humor. It has a bitter-sweet quality with rather more bitterness than sweetness. There is no hearty joviality or cheerful stoicism, but rather a sort of resigned stoicism; and while there is faith that the Lord will ultimately provide, there is also impatience and one can hear voices murmuring: "Who will provide till the Lord provides?"
>
> Jewish humor is perhaps a reaction to the soul-searching, breast-beating expiation and lamentation required by Jewish tradition, and a defence against the

humiliations and torments of their own experience so that in laughing at themselves Jews were able to withstand more readily the scorn of others. Laughter, of course, has always been the weapon of the weak against the strong, and the clown, provided he is sufficiently amusing, is forgiven everything, even — where necessary — his Jewishness.[6]

Israel Knox proffers a threefold understanding of the traditional roots of Jewish humor. First, he associates the biblical prophets with that humor in its ironic aspects:

> The prophet's message is replete with irony, but it is not for degrading others so as to inflate one's own self-esteem (as Hobbes would have it), nor is it for the pleasure in beholding the stupidities and discomfiture of others without danger to the spectator (as Plato suggests in the *Philebus*), nor is it a gesture of corrective animosity for persons entangled in machine-like behavior (as Bergson describes it). The prophet's irony is directed against idolatry, against the allurements of pagan civilization. Its aim is to lift man up, not to push him down, to remind him of his commitments: "God hath a controversy with you" [cf. Hos. 12:2].
>
> Irony is no affront when it is a summons to our dignity and a spur to our latent possibilities. The prophet's irony is a way of telling the truth, of closing the gap between the human and divine perspective, of lessening and modulating the controversy between God and the people.

While there was no levity in the prophet's protest against idolatry, yet there was a certain pleasure "in the play of contrast, in showing off the pretentious as being vapid and ludicrous."

Second, Knox identifies Jewish humor as a form of "tragic optimism."[7] The Jewish vision of life and destiny was expressed in the Messianic idea of this-worldly redemption, as in the irony of Jewish humor. The irony "takes the measure of the distance between the actual and the ideal, between the idolatry we serve and the Kingship of God we strive for, between the injustice that prevails and the righteousness that we desire." The world is moving toward a Messianic fulfillment — yet the future comes only one day at a time. The Jewish people live amidst the persistent ambiguity between "the Promise and the Pale, the divine promise that Israel was to be a Chosen people . . . and the actuality of its condition as a dispersed people" in a hostile world. To surrender the promise would be to turn history into a terrible farce, depriving it of meaning. But yet failure to be responsible to and for the world and the demands of living would mean extinction. "And so the optimism of Judaism remained firm and steadfast, but always with a tragic dimension to it." For while "the beginning of redemption . . . is everywhere . . . its consummation is yet nowhere." In Jewish irony "there is a clinging to the Promise, but not without a smile — a bit skeptical and a bit jovial. The irony and the smile are manifest in the wry remark of the *Maggid* of Kosenitz: 'Dear God, if you do not want to redeem your people Israel, then at least redeem the Gentiles.' "

Third, Knox emphasizes that Jewish humor entails an intermingling of "is" and "ought" (cf. chapter 1, the Fifth Proto-Joke):

> If righteousness is the goal of history . . . there will be *estrangement* from the world as it is, and there will also be *involvement* in the world for what it may be if *we* will it. . . . [There] is no absolute chasm between the natural and the supernatural, and the God of Judaism is a God of history. It is no unwarranted stretching of the doctrine of Judaism to link the ideal with the natural. The ideal is not the opposite of the natural but a possibility within things natural, and the redemption of the world is not outside history as a Divine initiative solely but as a drama and process within history.[8]

The argumentation of Israel Knox may be contrasted with the "lachrymous conception of Jewish history" as identified but deplored by the historian Salo W. Baron. Baron characteristically stressed that while "suffering is part of the destiny" of the Jewish people, "so is repeated joy as well as ultimate redemption."[9] (Cf. the venerable saying, *"Leid macht auch lachen."*) This much we may attest: The historical roots of Jewish humor are linked to the incongruity between the Jewish people's exalted theological origins and their misery under the power of other peoples and of the vicissitudes of life.[10] Among the difficulties with a strictly lachrymous reading of Jewish history is its large irrelevance amidst the opportunities in a country like the United States, during the period when Jews were changing from *Yidn* to Yankees. "It also leaves us unenlightened about how one ethnic group's comedy of anguish gained such eager applause from the non-anguished and the non-Jewish."[11] Sarah Blacher Cohen's further judgment is pertinent: Jewish humor "is not only based on the masochistic characteristics of the Jews expressed in their self-critical jokes. It has also been a principal source of salvation. By laughing at their dire circumstances, Jews have been able to liberate themselves from them. Their humor has been a balance to counter external adversity and internal sadness."[12]

In the course of his rendering of the Jewish imagination, Geoffrey H. Hartman complements in succinct fashion other interpretations of Jewish humor:

> [This] humor bypasses silence and assuages the anguish of profanation. Jokes, Freud saw, escape the censor. They are often (when Jewish) self-deprecating; they reconcile disparities, as in matchmaker stories that put the best face (or legs) on everything, yet they skirt blasphemy, since anything can be their target. They are brief, moreover, and so resemble the sayings important to Jewish life and its storytellers. Even when as lengthy as Agnon's "Forevermore" they seem to be brief, twisting and turning ironically. They can mock the exquisite *pilpul* of talmudic commentary while celebrating, or reducing to absurdity, the wary ingenuity of the oppressed, as in Freud's Pinsk/Minsk joke. Above all, they share with midrash its unusual habit of inventing dialogues of the most colloquial sort — dialogues that are intimate even in sacred contexts. . . . [A] further characteristic of the Jewish imagination . . . [is the] reticence within its ascendental or Messianic fervor. This holding back can appear as a lack of faith. . . . It can also be a justifiable wariness of false promises or prophets, or more profoundly a knowledge that God is not above "testing" his servants. It may express itself as lack of interest in personal salvation. What matters is the covenant, the return of the entire community to Israel. He who gives up heaven for *erez Yisrael* shows an *ahavat Zion* (love of Zion) that is surely redemptive.[13]

Finally, the exposition of William Novak and Moshe Waldoks has the advantage of taking us closer to the American scene. For these two interpreters, contemporary American Jewish humor "is overtly Jewish in its concerns, characters, definitions, language, values or symbols." Negatively speaking, it is generally not escapist, slapstick, physical, or cruel, and it does not attack the weak and the infirm. Neither is it the case that American Jewish humor is self-hating. There is *some* truth in the allegation of masochism, and Jewish humor is often self-critical. But one scholar responds to the question, "Isn't Jewish humor masochistic?" as follows: "No, and if I hear that line once more I'm going to kill myself!" Novak and Waldoks insist that "masochism" is simply not the right way "to describe an uninhibited and frequently critical treatment of Jewish life."

Positively speaking, several broad judgments may be offered "in full awareness of the futility of the exercise": Jewish humor is usually substantive; it is *about* something. It is "fascinated by the intricacies of the mind and by logic." As a form of social or religious commentary, it may be sarcastic, complaining, resigned, or descriptive. It tends

to be anti-authoritarian, ridicules grandiosity and self-indulgence, exposes hypocrisy, "kicks pomposity in the pants," and is workably
democratic. It frequently has a critical edge that tends to create dis-
comfort. For much Jewish humor "is intended to give offense." Lastly,
it mocks everyone—including God and religion, while nevertheless
"seeking a new understanding of the difference between the holy and
the mundane."[14]

II

As a means of working up to an interpretation of American Jewish
humor with which I am in sympathy, I include a few remarks about
the American situation.

It is a striking fact that while Jews comprise only 2.7 percent of the
population of the United States, as many as 80 percent of the country's
comedians are Jewish. One listing, in *The Big Book of Jewish Humor*,
contains some 125 names of prominent Jewish comic figures. Some
on the list are deceased but other persons are coming along to fill their
places. And the list could be greatly extended by inclusion of the
many Jewish joke writers and creators of TV, cinematic, theatrical,
and radio comedies, not to mention Jewish authors of humorous fiction.[15] Itzhak has many heirs in North America (as of course in Israel
and to a lesser extent in other countries such as the United Kingdom
and the Soviet Union).[16] Needless to say (then why is there need to
say it?), it would be gratuitous to describe all American humor—*not
excepting the humor of some Jews*—as strictly Jewish.

The lingua franca of the East European Jewry that came to North
America in the nineteenth and twentieth centuries was Yiddish. The
first, and European, age of Jewish humor—itself made possible by a
4,000-year history—has been succeeded by a second golden age, primarily in the Western Hemisphere. Accordingly, Novak and Waldoks
can identify their 1981 book of Jewish humor

as a kind of gregarious family reunion which brings together disparate and
dispersed relatives and guests of all ages and orientations. At the long and
crowded dinner table, the Wise Men of Chelm and Hershele Ostropoler swap
jokes with the Marx Brothers and Mel Brooks. Sholom Aleichem, at the other
end of the table, pokes Philip Roth in the ribs, as the impertinent waiter,
assisted by Sam Levenson, clears away the first course. Off in a corner, Isaac
Babel chats about Cossacks with Woody Allen, while back at the table, Yankele

the *schnorrer*, reaching for a boiled potato for tomorrow's lunch, inadvertently spills his soup in S. J. Perelman's lap.[17]

To turn to the point of view respecting recent and contemporary American Jewish humor that I wish to put forward, aided by Mark Shechner and others, I should like to introduce the hypothesis of what might be called the Three Brows: highbrowlichkeit, lowbrowlichkeit, middlebrowlichkeit. The hypothesis is meant to take into account Jewish history and tradition as well as American Jewish life today.

In a recent essay that reckons with Jewish comedy and the contradictions of culture, Mark Shechner propounds the following ratio: As dreams are to the individual unconscious, so comedy is to the collective unconscious. "For in the comic, where all is essentialized and drawn in bold strokes, the basic terms of a culture are most available for inspection. Comedy discloses culture the way . . . iron filings trace the force fields of a magnet, mapping its auras and trajectories, its nodes of energy and its fingers of attraction." Shechner fabricates this aphorism: The comedian's — any comedian's — golden rule is, "*the more familiar, the more strange.*"[18] Shechner's argumentation develops the meaning of his proposed ratio and his proposed aphorism. There is, he declares,

a structure of perception that . . . [sustains] a particular sort of Jewish imagining, and I stress *particular sort*, since it should be evident that the Jewish mind is not and has never been a simple entity. I call that structure "ghetto cosmopolitanism" and think of it as a conjunction of identities within the same individual: contrasting internal frames of reference whose abutment and interplay give form and inspiration to Jewish imagining. Ghetto cosmopolitanism arose out of the striking conjunctions of oppression and spirituality in the ghettos and *shtetls* of Ashkenazic Jewry in Eastern Europe and Russia, and it persists among contemporary American Jews. . . . The ghetto cosmopolitan is at once an insular and a worldly individual. He combines a parochialism bred of poverty and confinement with a universal consciousness bred of study and intellectual ambition. In him, vulgarity and sensibility go hand in hand; his coarseness of manner is not inconsistent with high orders of intellectual and aesthetic discrimination.

To Shechner's end point, I should add "moral discrimination." He continues: "The Ashkenazim of Eastern Europe dwelled in two worlds simultaneously. One was the world of labor and trade, money, politics, love, marriage, family, trouble, death. Its domain was the six days from Saturday night through Friday, and its language was commonly

Yiddish, though the Jews also spoke Polish, Russian, Czech, Magyar, German, Ukrainian, and to some degree had their imaginations shaped by these languages as well. The other was the world of the Sabbath, the world of prayer and study, Torah and Talmud, faith and prophecy. It was exalted and transcendent, and it had its own language, Hebrew." Shechner concludes that "what one finds in a mind nurtured upon a higher and a lower language is one that is rather accustomed to shuttling between the transcendent and the worldly and defining its relationship to reality in terms of the ironies generated by such travel."[19] (Ofttimes I think we may agree that irony is the very soul of humor. All my Proto-Jokes in chapter 1 are ironic, are they not?)

The description of the dialectic here is rather reminiscent of Arthur A. Cohen's phrasing, "the natural and the supernatural Jew."[20] But the highbrow/lowbrow components reflect no abstract dualism; they are fully manifest within the real world in and through the historical contextuality of middlebrow, or middle class, America. Here are joined what might be called the Hebrewist-transcendent-highbrowlich factor, the Yiddishist-immanent-lowbrowlich factor, and the ineluctable sociocultural-political structures of middlebrowlich North America—most formidably, of the United States. Novak and Waldoks helpfully clarify the third factor:

> Although it began as an extension of the folk humor of Eastern Europe, twentieth-century Jewish humor underwent certain immediate changes and transformations in America. . . . Antisemitism became far less central to the immigrants in America, as jokes about assimilation, name-changing, and even conversion soon took its place. Jokes about fundraisers replaced stories of *schnorrers.* Jokes about mothers became popular, replacing jibes at mothers-in-law. The twitting of pretentious rabbis and the well-to-do was broadened as economic and social opportunities enabled the common people to become targets of satire. . . . [Jewish comedians'] primary loyalties were not always to the Jewish community, and there began a complicated and often adversary relationship between the community and its humorists. . . . America has made available a popular culture that has been not only open to Jews but positively *inviting* to Jewish performers and Jewish themes to a degree that was unimaginable in Eastern Europe. There has been, of course, a price to pay for accepting this invitation, which has resulted in the *parevezation*, or neutering, of much of the material. . . . [But] it is difficult to imagine what would remain of American humor in the twentieth century without its Jewish component.[21]

All Three Brows are vividly present—appropriately raising and lowering themselves—in the remark of an elderly Jewish lady art collector who, when apprised of a chance to secure another Picasso, responded "I'm up to my ass in Picassos already." Here is (quoting Mark Shechner) "a by-product of American upward mobility: the language of Delancey Street brought up into the drawing rooms of Sutton Place."[22]

Elsewhere, Professor Shechner writes that "Jewish comedy's entire repertoire of mannerisms originates in the Yiddish language, whose earthiness and realism made it the perfect vehicle for comic deflation." It was, indeed, the "juxtaposition of higher and lower worlds within the mental economy of the Jewish people that established the terms for a *comedy of deflation*, whose basic trope was a sudden thrusting downward from the exalted to the workaday. From Sholom Aleichem to Woody Allen, this comedy of internal juxtaposition has been fundamental."[23]

From this point of view, Woody Allen may be seen as a culminative archetype of American Jewish humor. A single and singular personality exemplifies a trinity that goes to comprise this humor. A perfect representation of the Three Brows within an overall "comedy of deflation" is Allen's pronunciamento, "Not only is there no God, but try getting a plumber on weekends."[24] (1) The "death of God" echoes straight post-Holocaust "theology" à la Richard L. Rubenstein and others.[25] (2) Typologically speaking, plumbers are not exactly rabbis or scholars. (3) Nevertheless, the American phenomenon/ideal of upward mobility is open to plumbers as it is, in principle, to everybody else. Plumbers have at least as much right as corporation executives to a five-day week. The "weekend" constitutes a sacred structure of American middle-class urban and suburban life, for the "weekend" is specially dedicated to serving the various hedonist deities of the indigenous culture: Enjoy! Enjoy!

The act of "comic deflation" from spiritual/intellectual heights down to "the more familiar, the more strange" is a fitting description for much of the methodology in Woody Allen's art. Here are added examples:

In the one-act play *God*, a rendition of Greek tragedy gets away from both cast and playwright. Zeus, who comes down to rectify matters, is accidentally strangled in the stage machinery. Tragically, an actor must announce, "God is dead." Whereupon a physician from the audience runs up and asks, "Is he covered by anything?"[26]

On the question of the creation of the universe: "Did matter begin with an explosion or by the word of God? And if by the latter, could He not have begun it just two weeks earlier to take advantage of some of the warmer weather?"[27]

From within the combined realms of prayer and the mundane, the American world of advertising-cum-snobbery is given triumphant voice:

And it came to pass that a man who sold shirts was smitten by hard times. Neither did any of his merchandise move nor did he prosper. And he prayed and said, "Lord, why hast thou left me to suffer thus? All mine enemies sell their goods except me. And it's the height of the season. My shirts are good shirts. Take a look at this rayon. I got button-downs, flare collars, nothing sells. Yet I have kept thy commandments. Why can I not earn a living when mine younger brother cleans up in children's ready-to-wear?"

And the Lord heard the man and said, "About thy shirts. . . ."

"Yes, Lord," the man said, falling to his knees.

"Put an alligator over the pocket."

"Pardon me, Lord?"

"Just do what I'm telling you. You won't be sorry."

And the man sewed on to all his shirts a small alligator symbol and, lo and behold, suddenly his merchandise moved liked gangbusters, and there was much rejoicing, while amongst his enemies there was wailing and gnashing of teeth, and one said, "The Lord is merciful. He maketh me to lie down in green pastures. The problem is, I can't get up."[28]

Here is a conversation between Woody Allen and a woman in the film *Play It Again, Sam,* as they admire together a Jackson Pollock painting:

Allen: What does it say to you?

Woman: It restates the negativeness of the universe. The hideous lonely emptiness of existence. Nothingness. The predicament of Man forced to live in a barren, Godless, eternity like a tiny flame flickering in an immense void with nothing but waste, horror and degradation, forming a useless bleak straitjacket in a bleak absurd cosmos.

Allen: What're you doing Saturday night?

Woman: Committing suicide.

Allen: What about Friday night?[29]

(If the last part of this conversation exudes humor, why would that be any less the case with the first part?)

Rabbi Baumel of Vitebsk undertakes a fast to protest the Russian regulation forbidding Jews to wear loafers outside the ghetto. And the great and renowned mystic Rabbi Yitzchok Ben Levi applies cabalistic numerology to the horse racing at Aquaduct, winning the daily double fifty-two days in a row.[30]

Mark Shechner brings our analysis together: The larger point to be drawn is that *culture is comedy; the more familiar, the more strange.* What the great comedian tells us "is that the familiar really *is* strange, and if only for an instant the scales would fall from our eyes, we would see with the clarity of naked vision how outrageous is the world around us." For in a *comedy of culture,* "the joke does not create the humor; it formulates a humor that is already there, defamiliarizing the familiar to make it seem suddenly alien. Cultural comedy is the disclosure of ironic conjunctions, not their invention. Where such a comedy is at its richest, the technique is the content; a heightening and distillation of common anomalies. Technique, to reapply an old formula for fiction, is discovery."

All this helps make apparent the relation of Jewish comedy to the religion of Judaism. "It is its inversion, its negative, its shadow. The reversal of figure and ground. Where both comedy and religion acknowledge the interdependence of two worlds, a higher and a lower, each gives primacy to a different world. Religion subordinates this world to another; it translates upwards, while comedy undercuts the transcendent, criticizes it, subordinates it to the common. The one, in effect, Hebraizes, the other Yiddishizes." [31]

It would be wrongheaded to conclude that the Jewishness of one or another joke is merely a function of its Jewish furnishings or content (e.g., references to rabbis). The fact is that most of the Woody Allen jokes reproduced above lack specifically Jewish content. (Allen's own personal obsession with death is hardly more Jewish than goyish.) And yet we are justified in referring to these jokes as instances of applying the Jewish humorous dialectic of heavenly and earthly. I have simply been alluding to the internal logic of given comic material. I have not maintained that particular jokes are inherently Jewish, in contrast to other allegedly non-Jewish jokes. All I have suggested is that certain jokes can exemplify or point to the cultural-historical background, ethos, and *Anschauung* of the Jewish people. Were another people under examination, it would not be impossible (even if unlikely) for there to be the same jokes, illustrating the quite different cultural-historical background and ethos of other (non-Jewish) people. Indeed, it is not out of the question to hypothesize that the formal identity and perhaps even the discrete content of jokes are universal rather than the property or invention of one or another people. We may think once again of the ten (or more?) Proto-Jokes. If human laughter is itself a universal, why cannot its incarnations be universally present? However, I have not been arguing here in behalf of the hypothesis of universality.

An additional caveat is called for. Today (the 1990s) Woody Allen has moved far beyond "comedy" in any narrow or doctrinaire sense. Particularly in his films, he now addresses the entire dialectic of human comedy/human tragedy (an impulse present in embryonic form, to be sure, in his earlier work). Consult, in this connection, Graham McCann, *Woody Allen* (1990).

A moral contribution of the Jewish comedy of America is its aid in subduing antisemitism, though of course not destroying it.[32] This has been done by the simple if incredible expedient of, so to speak, making everybody Jewish. Most people would rather be caught dead than be accused of lacking a sense of humor. To wear the cloak of Jewish (as of other) humor helps to counteract that condition. The expressed sense of humor of Americans has become, content-wise as well as attitude-wise, heavily Jewish. A new human species has stridden upon the stage: *Americanus schlemielus-shlimazelus-sphritzus.*[33] One need not go to the length of identifying Woody Allen as Messiah in order to celebrate him and his colleagues for serving the Messianic cause of human justice, together with the human cause of love. As Graham McCann points out, in refusing to suspend the ethical and indeed in making civilization depend upon it, Allen is being most Jewish. "What he is struggling to achieve is the dignity of the ordinary."[34]

In general, American Jewish humor has reached a plateau; its zenith was the sixties. Yet it seems to be holding its own. As I write, the element of Jewish dramatization and identity within American television is becoming more and more noticeable. Albert Goldman goes as far as to regard Jewishness as a metaphor for modern life as a whole. I think that his exposition of more than two decades back still marshalls much truth:

The individual Jew — the alien in search of identity — has become a symbolic protagonist. As he dares more and more to expose his inner turmoil to self-satire, the Jew is discovering in turn that Americans are more and more receptive to his comic consciousness: to ironic mockery[35] of personal plights, to bitter-sweet retreats from painful realities, and to angry thrusts at broken dreams. The Jew having become a symbolic representative for our time, his humor — his great cultural weapon and consolation — can now be appreciated in its raw form by millions of people who have no connection with the Jewish community.[36]

Or as Lionel Blue portrays us, every so often the whole world "tries with the Jews to sing the Lord's song in a strange land."[37]

III

Thus far we have stressed some of the senses in which Jewish humor *is* humorous, living as it does upon the incongruity between two integral worlds. There is also a decisive sense in which Jewish "humor" is anything but humorous. The latter condition will take us back, in contrast, to the humor of children (chapter 9).

We sometimes hear it said that Jewish humor is a humor of aggression — against others but even against Jews. It is not easy to dissociate this charge from antisemitism but it is sometimes seen as reflecting Jewish self-hatred or at least self-mockery. Irving Howe opens the way to a necessary modification of the idea of "aggression": Having indicated that their humor "is often a thrust at the Jews themselves," Howe argues that "the Jewish joke is not merely self-criticism; it is at the same time self-justification. Or more accurately, it is in a state of constant tension between criticism and self-justification."[38]

Jewish self-criticism is tied to varied historical influences, among them long years of oppression (externally speaking) and the religio-moral aversion to idolatry (internally speaking). The Freudian *Tendenz* to connect humor to human aggression, to see joking as tendentious, appears, when applied to the history of the Jewish people, as markedly less than a half-truth. The Jewish "humor" of "aggression" is not that; it is in truth a form of counteraggression — the historically enduring act of fighting off the enemies of Jews. Counteraggression is a moral response to the aggression of others. The laughter involved is in essence sardonic, a mark of triumph over persecution. In this, Jewish "humor" joins forces with the humor of other persecuted peoples, such as American blacks. On the Jewish side, Lenny Bruce can "observe" to an audience, "You and I know what a Jew is — *One Who Killed Our Lord*":

> All right, I'll clear the air once and for all, and confess. Yes, we did it. I did it, my family. I found a note in my basement. It said:
> "We killed him.
> Signed,
> Morty."[39]

And over on the Black side, Redd Foxx can "observe" to an audience, "Ugly, Ugly. You are the ugliest Negroes I have ever seen. I thought Negroes in Los Angeles were ugly. But you Long Beach Negroes are even uglier."[40]

Until his premature death, Lenny Bruce actually served both of the above (and other) causes as prophet for human justice: "If President Kennedy got on television and said, 'Tonight I'd like to introduce the niggers in my cabinet,' and he yelled 'niggerniggerniggerniggernigger' at every nigger he saw and 'boogeyboogeyboogey, niggerniggernigger' 'till nigger lost its meaning — you'd never make any four-year-old nigger cry when he came home from school."[41] Bruce appeared as hostility incarnate, but his hostility was not Jewish as such, though it was yoked to the biblical prophets. It was a hatred of hypocrisy and evil. It was counteraggression in pristine form.[42]

In each of the above instances the foe, the bearer of actual aggression, is vanquished by means of a *reductio ad absurdum*. To make a joke of the oppressor's charge is to reveal the ridiculousness of the charge. The watchword is, Destroy the enemy's cause by stealing his thunder. The victim defeats the victimizer by getting in the first blows; the persecuted take the offensive away from the persecutor. Moral *counteraggression* is at the opposite pole from *aggression.*

Now the ground for adjudging counteraggressive Jewish "humor" to be in essence nonhumorous is simply that its rationale and purpose are the antimony of anything and everything comic or funny. The rationale and the purpose are alike dead serious; they are life-and-death instrumentalities, existential weapons. Thus we have no choice but to draw an all-critical distinction: between teleological-ideological "humor" and integral or ontological or nonutilitarian humor. Teleological-ideological "humor" is, in conception, totally humor*less*, totally serious, for it is aimed at a moral goal wholly beyond itself. It is strictly an incarnation of politics, of the unending power-political struggle against injustice. It is what Joseph Boskin calls the "humor of militancy." Teleological-ideological "humor" stands in contrast to integral humor, the latter of which, like foals gamboling in the fields, is directed to no special end beyond itself but only *to* itself in spontaneity and joy. Here we have as prototype the laughter of small children, the laughter of unalloyed grace, the embodiment of *homo ludens,* humankind as play-er, as sport, even as practitioner of delightful nonsense. In this alternative context neither aggression nor counteraggression is immediately at question. We have cited the metaphor of Conrad Hyers: The laughter of children manifests a collective memory of paradise. Yet even here the worldly (sacred) work of a Woody Allen may reenter the picture, as in his testimony, "When you do comedy, you are not sitting at the grownups' table." This testimony is indicative of the paradox that integral humor and teleological "humor" are not finally estranged or ultimately divisible.

Robert Alter writes: "If disaster, whatever the scale, seems to be our general fate, the persistence of the comic reflex is itself evidence of the perdurability of the stuff of humanity: a shrug is a small and subtle gesture, but, in the face of the harshest history, it may take a world of strength to make."[43] A shrug of the shoulders combined with raised eyebrows and upturned palms — perhaps these constitute the ultimate image and representation of Jewish humor, its dignity and its power, encompassing yet perhaps also transcending the Three Brows.

IV

I close this chapter with brief reflection upon Jewish humor in the shadow of the *Shoah.*

In the first chapter I cited the anguished judgment of Julian Green (as of others) that after Auschwitz, only tears have meaning. But I also posed the daring (or perhaps outrageous) alternative that after the *Shoah* only laughter has meaning.

The one principle of the Holocaust was the annihilation of every last Jew. Here was an ultimate End, an End that not only took precedence over every Nazi goal but comprised the final *raison d'être* of Nazism. It is well known that even German military needs were sacrificed to the "needs" of the *Endlösung der Judenfrage*. The *Vernichtung* of the Jews constituted an Absolute. Within such a frame of reference, all humor comes, of course, to an end. If the *Shoah* is an ultimate joke, this is because it is the devil's own joke: The people who have been elected to life (*haim*) are also elected to death. True, the Jewish victims would make secret fun and even, astoundingly, open fun of the victimizers. There developed a kind of *Galgenhumor*, a humor of the gallows. But all this was no more than a pitiful act. Before the Nazi Absolute of death to the Jew as Jew, this *Aktion* pales into insignificance. Revealingly, even Viktor E. Frankl, who, from within Nazi concentration and death camps, saw humor as "another of the soul's weapons in the fight for self-preservation," had to concede that the humor would last "only for a few seconds"[44] — no more than a quick flashback to a world that once had been.

From the standpoint of the Nazi Absolute, we see the terrible force of the judgment that in and after Auschwitz "only tears have meaning." However, we must see as well that strictly within the context of the Nazi Absolute, even tears turn meaningless. For with the programmatic annihilation of every Jew, Jewish tears become, like Jewish laughter, no more than a memory. Elie Wiesel has spoken of the *Shoah* as the place where all the tears have been exhausted. Within the bounds of the Holocaust universe there remains only the Absolute.

On the other side, Emil L. Fackenheim represents the moral demand to forbid any posthumous victory to Adolf Hitler and his ilk. Were the judgment "only tears have meaning" to be extended into the present and the future, the cause of the Nazis would triumph. There would be surrender to suffering as a universal horror and to Nazism as a concrete horror. Human tears have meaning only where laughter is possible; human laughter has meaning only where tears are possible — this suggests, in both cases alike, a state of affairs that wars against every destructive Absolute. The living dialectic between Jewish tears and Jewish laughter is restored only with the victory over Nazism. (That victory is hardly complete; the world continues to be afflicted with a neo-Nazi presence.)

The question is not whether to engage in humor but in what manner one is to engage in humor. In the shadow of the *Shoah* all laughter is washed in tears, and must remain in that condition.

This brings me to say a word concerning Jewishness and the category of tragedy — tragedy in a much more profound sense than something "sad" or "unfortunate."

The *Shoah* had nothing to do with tragedy in the classic sense but was a nihilistic, purposive, calculated, and demonic End to any and all distinctions between comedy and tragedy, between humor and no humor. Jewish life and thought are fully aware of tragic elements within the human enterprise. For example, it is said that the very ground of Sholom Aleichem's humor was the idea that "the prevailing social conditions oppressed and crippled . . . [the Jew] until he became not only miserable but ridiculous."[45] But Jewry never grants ultimacy to the dimension of tragedy.[46] For within the *Weltanschauung* of tragedy, human reality (also divine reality) falls under the hegemony of an impersonal, remorseless Fate (*moira*), which contains as well the power of Nemesis, retribution. Against this whole eventuality, Jewishness is life-affirming. Neither Judaism nor the Jewish ethos exalts the "tragic hero." Judaism has always insisted that even mourning is to be limited, that is, to be kept within bearable bounds. Judaism and Jewishness attest to human freedom and human responsibility, even amidst tragedy and suffering. To turn Jewish life into tears alone would be to subject it to Fate. Even the power of fatefulness within the Nazi Absolute was overpowered. And since that time, the act of remembrance (*zachor*) perpetuates the struggle: The tears of today are dried with laughter. Life in its wholeness is restored. Jewish humor embodies "a prevailing optimism that this too, no matter how horrible, shall pass, and that Jews as a people will endure."[47]

The possibility of Jewishness remains the possibility of comedy, not of tragedy. This is not to say that human beings are not evil or that suffering is not real. Humankind is afflicted with an evil urge. But humankind is also blessed with an urge to goodness. The question is always one of choice. Humanness is freedom, freedom is humanness. Freedom entails: responsibility (obligation *and* culpability), hope, creativity, openness to the future, life as meaningful, life as, in the end, subject to redemption, to final wholeness. Comedy boasts freedom, spontaneity, a measure of mastery or at least potential mastery.

Elie Wiesel declares: "A Jew is he — or she — whose song cannot be muted, nor can his or her joy be killed by the enemy . . . ever."[48]

Analytically speaking, Jewish humor engages us further in chapter 13.

NOTES

1. Social experience and tradition come much to the fore. For example, jokes about drunkenness are sparse among Jews and plentiful among Irish. Consult A. J. Chapman and H. C. Foot, eds., *It's A Funny Thing, Humour*; J. Durant and C. J. Miller, eds., *Laughing Matters: A Serious Look at Humor;* and Avner Ziv, ed., *National Styles of Humor*. Of further relevance in a comparative frame of reference is Conrad Hyers, *Zen and the Comic Spirit*. On British humor, consult Amanda-Jane Doran, ed., *The Punch Book of Utterly British Humour*.
2. Schwarzschild, "Aesthetics," p. 1.
3. Berger, *Precarious Vision*, pp. 67–68.
4. Henry D. Spalding, ed., *Encyclopedia of Jewish Humor*, p. xiv (italics added). Jewish humor is nevertheless not free of sexism, as in the stereotypes of the "Jewish American Princess" (JAP) and the "Jewish mother," both of which are male concoctions.
5. Ibid., p. xvi.
6. Chaim Bermant, "humor, Jewish," in Glenda Abramson, ed., *The Blackwell Companion to Jewish Culture: From the Eighteenth Century to the Present* (Oxford: Basil Blackwell, 1989), pp. 361, 362.
7. Cf. Nathan Ausubel, "Why Jews Laugh," in *A Treasury of Jewish Humor*, pp. 21-25; also William Novak and Moshe Waldoks, eds., *The Big Book of Jewish Humor*, pp. xiii–xiv. In the latter source the punch line is cited, "Don't worry. God has protected us from Pharaoh and Haman. He will protect us from the Messiah too."
8. Knox, "Traditional Roots," pp. 153–54, 160–61, 157–59, 164.
9. Peter Steinfels, "Salo W. Baron, 94, Scholar of Jewish History, Dies," *The New York Times* (26 November 1989).
10. See Sarah Blacher Cohen, "Introduction: The Varieties of Jewish Humor," in Cohen, ed., *Jewish Wry*, pp. 1–2.
11. Mark Shechner, "comedy, Jewish," in Abramson, ed., *Blackwell Companion*, p. 141.
12. Cohen, "Introduction," p. 4.
13. Geoffrey H. Hartman, "Imagination," in Cohen and Mendes-Flohr, eds., *Contemporary Jewish Religious Thought*, pp. 464, 465.
14. Novak and Waldoks, eds., *Big Book*, pp. xx–xxi, xv, xvi, xxv. American Jewish humor may be contrasted with Israeli Jewish humor and the latter's satirical, sardonic, and protesting thrusts. Consult Esther Fuchs, "Is There Humor in Israeli Literature and If Not, Why Are We Laughing?" in Cohen, ed., *Jewish Wry*, pp. 216–33; also Carr, ed., *Waiter, There (is) a Fly in My Orange Juice*; and Elliott Oring, *Israeli Humor and Its Oral Tradition* (Albany: State University of New York Press, 1981).
15. "During the fifties and sixties Jewish entertainers no longer kept a low ethnic profile. A belated pride in the founding of the State of Israel, combined with a profound grief for the loss of their fellow-Jews in the Holocaust, prompted them to resurrect their buried Jewish identity and draw upon its wit for many of their routines" (Cohen, "Introduction," p. 8).
16. Periodically, International Conferences on Jewish Humor take place, under the auspices of Tel Aviv University. The first meeting was held in Tel Aviv in 1984, another in New York in 1986, and a third in Tel Aviv in 1989.

17. Novak and Waldoks, eds., *Big Book*, p. xiii. A *schnorrer* is a beggar (with *chutzpah*); consult ibid., pp. 178ff.; also *Leo Rosten's Giant Book*, p. 489; and Spalding, *Encyclopedia*, pp. 27–39.

18. Cf. James Thurber: "There is always a laugh in the utterly familiar" (*Collecting Himself*, p. 218).

19. Mark Shechner, "Dear Mr. Einstein: Jewish Comedy and the Contradictions of Culture," in Cohen, ed., *Jewish Wry*, pp. 142–46.

20. Arthur A. Cohen, *The Natural and the Supernatural Jew: An Historical and Theological Introduction* (New York: Pantheon Books, 1962).

21. Novak and Waldoks, eds., *Big Book*, pp. xiv–xv, xviii, xix.

22. Shechner, "Dear Mr. Einstein," pp. 146–47.

23. Shechner, "comedy, Jewish," pp. 142–43 (italics added). Woody Allen "catches his world as completely and hilariously as Sholom Aleichem caught his. Where Sholom Aleichem dealt with the poor and oppressed, Allen deals with the affluent and depressed. . . . One may almost speak of Allen as the Sholom Aleichem of Manhattan" (Bermant, "humor, Jewish," p. 362).

24. Woody Allen, as cited in Graham McCann, *Woody Allen*, p. 58. To date, McCann's study is the most profound analysis of Allen and his contribution. Allen is seen as primarily a maker of movies. In all his work Allen "is making the important observation that movies have become an important means of enjoying oneself, losing oneself, finding oneself, and knowing oneself. The past lives twice: once in itself, a second time in our reconstruction of it. The past is a multiple of our fantasies; reconstructed, it is not the past that was, but it is what remains of our stardust memories" (p. 218).

25. Richard L. Rubenstein, *After Auschwitz: Radical Theology and Contemporary Judaism* (Indianapolis: Bobbs-Merrill, 1966). However, Rubenstein's views are somewhat altered in Richard L. Rubenstein and John K. Roth, *Approaches to Auschwitz: The Legacy of the Holocaust* (London: SCM Press, 1987); see, for example, pp. 311–12.

26. Shechner, "comedy, Jewish," p. 144.

27. Woody Allen, *Side Effects*, pp. 82–83.

28. Woody Allen, *Without Feathers*, pp. 24–25.

29. As cited in Cohen, "Introduction," p. 11.

30. Woody Allen, *Getting Even*, pp. 52–56.

31. Shechner, "Dear Mr. Einstein," pp. 154–55. Shechner closes his exposition with a comment about the Irish comic tradition, which also arose in a culture where religious authority was central to cultural formation. In both cases the comedy was aggressive and rude and struck with "antinomian force at the heart of the exalted" (p. 155).

32. Jewish humor has not been alone in this. Other equally potent factors include religious pluralism, a democratic social order, and the separation of church and state. The partial Jewish-izing of American food has also been of influence.

33. On the phenomena of *schlemiels* and *shlimazels*, see chap. 12 below, under Sanford Pinsker; also, Spalding, *Encyclopedia*, pp. 51–58. *Sphritzes* are im-

promptu, rapidfire monologues. Consult, further, Rosten's section on "Yinglish" in *Giant Book*, pp. 559–70.

34. McCann, *Woody Allen*, p. 120.
35. Cf. Maurice Samuel: "The question that haunts us historically is, why did they [the Jews] not disintegrate intellectually and morally? How were they able, under hideous oppression and corroding privation, under continuous starvation—the tail of a herring was a dish—to keep alive against a better day the spirit originally breathed into man? The answer lies in the self-mockery by which they rose above their condition to see afar off the hope of the future" (*In Praise of Yiddish* [New York: Cowles, 1971], pp. 210–11).
36. Albert Goldman, "Boy-Man, Schlemiel: The Jewish Element in American Humor," *Explorations* (London: Institute of Contemporary History and Wiener Library, 1967), p. 17.
37. Lionel Blue, *To Heaven With Scribes and Pharisees* (New York: Oxford University Press, 1976), p. 81.
38. Irving Howe, "The Nature of Jewish Laughter," in Cohen, ed., *Jewish Wry*, p. 20.
39. *Essential Lenny Bruce*, pp. 40–41.
40. Redd Foxx, cited in Joseph Boskin, "Beyond *Kvetching* and *Jiving*: The Thrust of Jewish and Black Folkhumor," in Cohen, ed., *Jewish Wry*, p. 60. See also Joseph Boskin, "The Complicity of Humor: The Life and Death of Sambo," in *Philosophy of Laughter and Humor*, John Morreall, ed., pp. 250–63. Boskin shows how, in the white effort at racial superiority and the furtherance of a racist class structure, Sambo appeared as Bergson's comic "machine-person."
41. *Essential Lenny Bruce*, p. 16.
42. Of Lenny Bruce, Joan Rivers says: "He *spoke truth*. He called things as they are." See "Next Time, Dear God, Please Choose Someone Else: Jewish Humour—American Style," *Arena*, BBC Television, 23 February 1990.
43. Alter, "Jewish Humor," p. 36.
44. Viktor E. Frankl, *Man's Search for Meaning: An Introduction to Logotherapy*, trans. Ilse Lasch (London: Hodder and Stoughton, 1964), rev. ed., p. 42. "In Auschwitz, they told the story of a band of slowly freezing Jewish prisoners being marched up and down in the coldest winter. Their guard ... ordered them to repeat after him and call out with military smartness the location they were at. They marched down one path. The guard called out, 'Goering Strasse!' The prisoners replied, calling, 'Goering Strasse!' On the next path, the guard called out, 'Goebbels Allee!' The prisoners replied, 'Goebbels Allee!' They reached the open field where they stood for roll call, and the guard shouted out, 'Hitler Platz!' (meaning square, but also meaning, in Yiddish, 'drop dead!'). The prisoners replied, 'Amen!' " (Irving Greenberg, *The Jewish Way: Living the Holidays* [New York: Summit Books, 1988], p. 256). Of course, there were numerous anti-Nazi jokes in various countries; see, for example, Spalding, *Encyclopedia*, pp. 184–200. Peter L. Berger writes that while the Nazis were surely "the monsters of a nightmarish horror show," they were at the same time "inexorably ridiculous, appearing as figures of a surrealistic farce" (*Precarious Vision*, p. 212). Consult also Yaffa Eliach, *Hasidic Tales of the Holocaust*.

45. Meyer Wiener, "On Sholom Aleichem's Humor," in Cohen, ed., *Jewish Wry*, p. 50.
46. With the reemergence of the State of Israel, the freedom of Jews as a people is resurrected (after more than 1900 years). Yet elements of Jewish tragedy persist: Israel lies in a surround of enemies.
47. Sharon Weinstein, "Jewish Humor: Comedy and Continuity," *American Humor: An Interdisciplinary Newsletter* 3 (Fall 1976): 1.
48. Elie Wiesel, *Four Hasidic Masters*, p. 95.

12

From New York, Tel Aviv, and
Points East and West

Why should some Jewish comic figures be rostered at this juncture rather than in, say, chapter 8 along with other Jewish and non-Jewish funny people? One answer is "Why not?," perhaps an unsatisfactory response (though not an un-Jewish one?). The question and the answer may be related to the problematic yet also identifiable qualities of "Jewish humor" as we have reflected upon them in chapter 11.[1]

Woody Allen

Pasta as an expression of Neo-Realistic starch is well understood by Mario Spinelli, the chef at Fabrizio's. . . . His fettuccine, though wry and puckish in an almost mischievous way, owes a lot to Barzino, whose use of fettuccine as an instrument of social change is known to us all. . . . The linguine, on the other hand, is quite delicious and not at all didactic. True, there is a pervasive Marxist quality to it but this is hidden by the sauce. . . . Robert Craft, writing about Stravinsky, makes an interesting point about Schoenberg's influence on Spinelli's salads and Spinelli's influence on Stravinsky's Concerto in D for Strings. . . . For dessert, we had tortoni, and I was reminded of Leibniz's remarkable pronouncement: "The Monads have no windows." How apropos! Fabrizio's prices, as Hannah Arendt told me once, are "reasonable without being historically inevitable." I agree.[2]

All of literature is a footnote to Faust. I have no idea what I mean by that.

I see that *Commentary* and *Dissent* have merged. The new name is *Dysentary.*

There is a section of Brooklyn known as Flatbush. It is the heart of the old world. The people's values in life are God and carpeting.

The Russian Revolution, which simmered for years, suddenly erupted when the serfs finally realized that the Czar and the Tsar were the same person.

A Jewish woman's son becomes President of the United States.
"You must be so proud," says her friend.
"That's nothing," the mother replies, "my other son's a doctor."

Mr. Berkowitz, leaving a fancy dress ball attired as a moose, is shot, stuffed, and mounted at the New York Athletic Club, which normally is "restricted."

Life is like a concentration camp. You're stuck here and there's no way out. You can only rage impotently at your oppressors.

I believe there's an intelligence to the universe, except for certain parts of New Jersey.

It's not that I'm afraid to die, I just don't want to be there when it happens.

I landed at Orly Airport and discovered my luggage wasn't on the same plane. My bags were finally traced to Israel where they were opened and all my trousers were altered.

Yea, though I walk through the Valley of the Shadow of Death — or on second thought, even better, though I *run* through the Valley of the Shadow of Death — that way I'll get out of it quicker.

I broke with Freud on the concept of penis envy. He felt it should be restricted to women.

The reason puzzled intellectuals can never answer the question "How could the Holocaust possibly happen?" is that it's the wrong question. Given what people are, the question is "Why doesn't it happen more often?"

There is something second-rate about comedy. It's like eating ice cream all the time; after a while you need to take in something more solid.

People in Manhattan are constantly creating . . . unnecessary neurotic problems for themselves because it keeps them from dealing with the terrible, unsolvable problems of the universe.

Maturity has borne out my childhood. I'd always thought death was the sole driving force: I mean that our effort to avoid it is the only thing that gives impetus to our existence.

I like to observe the little idiosyncrasies in people. I understand, I think, what makes people stand alone. I suppose in that way acting has been therapeutic for me. It sort of satisfied some deep protectiveness in my nature. A wish, perhaps, to insulate myself against the hurts I have suffered. Through my screen characters, I have grown a skin over my own skin.[3]

––––––––––––––

Anonymous

Abramovitch, walking down the street in Minsk, is suddenly slapped hard by a stranger.
"So much for you, Rabinowitz!"
Abramovitch retorts, "The joke is on you. My name is not Rabinowitz."

(Here is an instance of what might be called the humor of round-and-round — A.R.E.):

First hasid: Do you know that my Rabbi converses daily with God Himself?
Second hasid: How do you know this?
First hasid: My Rabbi told me.
Second hasid: And suppose he told you a lie?
First hasid: Idiot! Would a man who converses daily with God tell a lie?

May you have a hundred estates, and on every estate a hundred mansions, and in every mansion a hundred rooms, and in every room a hundred beds: and may a malarial fever toss you from bed to bed (a Yiddish curse).[4]

Nathan Ausubel

An old Jew in Lithuania went to the village post office.
"When does the post leave for Gomel?" he inquired.
"Every day."
"Thursday too?"

Perhaps the classic Jewish joke about fools is the one that tells of the small dealer in wheat who went to Minsk to sell his grain. Before leaving, he faithfully promised his wife to send her a telegram if he succeeded in making a profitable transaction. Having, with God's help, closed his deal he went to the telegraph office and sat down to compose his telegram. He wrote:
"Sold wheat profitably return tomorrow embrace lovingly Itzik."
As he was about to hand the text to the clerk he hesitated.
"Now why do I have to write 'profitably'? Certainly, my wife knows that I am no *shmendrik* [simpleton] to sell my wheat at a loss!"
So he crossed out the word "profitably."
Then he went over the telegram more carefully.
"Tsk-tsk! What have I done? Doesn't my wife know already that I went to town to sell my wheat? So why the devil do I write the words 'sold wheat'?"
He crossed out "sold wheat."
Made doubly cautious now by his errors he reread the telegram.

"God in heaven! What am I jabbering about? What makes me write 'return tomorrow'? When then should I return—next month? My wife will suppose I've gone out of my mind and imagine I'm Rothschild!"

Without hesitation he crossed out "return tomorrow."

Then with an eagle eye he went over the telegram once more.

"*Goilem* [numbskull] that I am! Why do I have to write 'embrace lovingly'? How else do I embrace my wife? And why should I embrace her today of all days? Is it her birthday, or Yom Kippur, or something?"

He crossed out "embrace lovingly."

Looking down at the telegram, he noticed that there was only one word left now—"Itzik."

"Nu? What do you say to my cleverness? Why do I have to sign 'Itzik'? Who else would be sending my wife a telegram?"

And he crossed out the word "Itzik."

Now he scanned the telegram, and, finding that he had crossed out every word, a light dawned on him.

"By my *bubba's* [grandmother's] moustache! Do I really have to send this telegram? Money doesn't grow on trees, Itzik!"

So he tore up the telegram and went away rejoicing that by this cleverness he had saved himself fifty kopecks.

The wish to be wiser than everybody else is the biggest foolishness (Sholom Aleichem).

Love your neighbor—even when he plays the trombone.

"It's unfair," President Nasser complained bitterly. "They have 2.3 million Jews on their side but we have none." So he asked Moscow to send the 2.4 million Soviet Jews to Egypt right away.[5]

Lionel Blue

It was announced in Tel Aviv that God was soon to send a tidal wave thirty-feet high over the city because of its sins.

Muslims went to their mosques and prayed for a speedy translation to the paradise of Muhammad.

Christians went to their churches and prayed for the intercession of the saints.

Jews went to their synagogues and prayed, "Lord God, it's going to be very hard living under thirty feet of water."[6]

Joseph Boskin

Two workers in a clothing factory in New York were back together after the weekend and conversed as they worked: one folded the material and passed it to the other who in turn folded again and passed it on to a worker next to him; and so on.

"So, Harry, how was your weekend?" asked Sam as he passed the material. "Fine, fine," replied Harry as he folded the material. "I went hunting."

"What did you hunt?" asked Sam as he passed the material.

"Moose," as he folded the material.

"Moose?" as he passed the material.

"Moose!" as he folded the material.

"So what happened?" asked Sam, as he passed the material.

"What happened?" answered Harry, as he folded the material. "I took my rifle and my toot and I tooted for the moose. Pretty soon, a huge moose came over the hill and I tooted some more. He finally saw me, lowered his head and charged."

"So?" as he passed the material.

"So," as Harry folded the material, "I raised my rifle and pulled the trigger."

"So?" as he passed the material.

"So, nothing," as he folded the material. "The gun didn't go off."

"So, so?" as he passed the material.

"I shot again but nothing happened. The moose kept charging at me and pretty soon it was right on top of me."

"Now wait a minute, Harry," as he passed the material. "You mean to say that you shot at this big moose twice and nothing happened, that he was right on top of you and you're here right now. How come you're not dead?"

"You call this living?!" answered Harry, as he folded the material.[7]

Lenny Bruce

The furst thing I gwine do when I gwine get to Hebbin is fine out what a gwine is.

Dig: I'm Jewish. Count Basie's Jewish. Ray Charles is Jewish. Eddie Cantor's goyish. B'nai B'rith is goyish; Hadassah, Jewish.

If you live in New York or any other big city, you are Jewish. It doesn't matter even if you're Catholic; if you live in New York, you're Jewish. If you live in Butte, Montana, you're going to be goyish even if you're Jewish.

Kool-aid is goyish. Evaporated milk is goyish even if the Jews invented it. Chocolate is Jewish and fudge is goyish. Fruit salad is Jewish. Lime jello is goyish. Lime soda is *very* goyish.

All Drake's Cakes are goyish. Pumpernickel is Jewish and, as you know, white bread is very goyish. Instant potatoes, goyish. Black cherry soda's very Jewish, macaroons are *very* Jewish.

Negroes are all Jews. Italians are all Jews. Irishmen who have rejected their religion are Jews. Mouths are very Jewish. And bosoms. Baton-twirling is very goyish.

Underwear is definitely goyish. Balls are goyish. Titties are Jewish.[8]

Martin Buber

Buber was once asked why the Christian world takes him much more seriously than the Jewish world.

His reply: "Jews are smarter."

Maurice Carr[9]

You can pray if you like, but not too loud. Your neighbor may not be interested in your prayer (Nissim Aloni).

MINISTRY FOR PRODUCTION & DEVELOPMENT
OF MEANINGLESS WORDS

"What will our duties be?" we asked.

He reflected and said: "You will be responsible."

"Responsible for what?" we wondered.

"Responsible! Period. You are senior officials, so you will be responsible."

"But for what?" we persisted.

He was perplexed. Then he asked: "What was your job in your former Ministry?"

"Inspection," we snapped.

His eyes lit up.

"Inspection of what?"

"Inspection!" we cried. "Everybody knows what's behind the concept."

"Settled!" he roared. "Responsibility is like inspection" (A. B. Yehoshua).

How (Not) to Succumb on a Senior Civil Servant's Salary

1. Keep no accounts and stay ignorant of your plight.
2. Remove all mirrors and conceal your woeful appearance from yourself.
3. Take on three moonlighting jobs on the side and send your wife and eldest daughter out to work.
4. By hook or by crook go on an official mission abroad once a year.
5. Discover a rich uncle in America.
6. Pawn all family heirlooms, if not already in hock or sold.
7. Stick on a false beard and eat in the soup-kitchen of a talmudic academy.
8. If the beard comes unstuck, subsist on inexpensive and nourishing food, such as porridge for breakfast, lunch and supper.
9. Dine out at a posh restaurant once a month, to remind yourself who you are.
10. Mid-month, when your salary is running out, spend your last coppers on a bouquet of hardy flowers to keep your spirits up for the rest of the month until pay day (Edwin Samuel).

FIDDLER OFF THE ROOF

Ah, Tevye the milkman himself, aha! Doesn't go by the name of Tevye anymore. Gvinati to you—what else?—which's Hebrew for Big Cheese! A Tnuva Dairy Coop expert, that's what he is. Doesn't milk no more cows nor churn no more butter. All he does with his fair hands is point a finger at one fellow to run and do something here, and a finger at another fellow to run and do something there, and he signs cheques in a huge scrawl. The boss, top salary, lives off the cream of the land. Call him "Tevye!" and he'll knock your block off. . . .

Me? I was an idler always. In Antievka I'd sit on a roof, playing the fiddle. Here roughnecks smashed my fiddle. Anyway, where in Tel Aviv would I find a roof that isn't crowded out with TV antennae? (Ruth Bondy).

What if the people of Israel hadn't been elected the Chosen People?

Some other people would have got it in the neck instead (Dahn Ben-Amotz, in Yehuda Haezrahi and Yitzhak Shimoni, "Repartee").

In the house of a hunchback never mention camels (Shalom Rosenfeld).[10]

Rodney Dangerfield

The first time I played hide and seek they wouldn't look for me.

My psychiatrist told me I was crazy. I told him I wanted a second opinion. He said, "All right, you're ugly too."

I told my doctor there's something wrong with me. Every time I look in the mirror I throw up. He said, "Well, your eyesight is perfect."

Totie Fields

I purchased fifty pairs of stockings at twelve cents a pair, and soon discovered their seams go up the front. At that price, I can learn to walk backwards.[11]

Hillel Halkin

Italian to Israeli: "I read in the newspaper that they were digging not long ago beneath the streets of ancient Rome and found cables. Do you realize what that means? We had electricity!"

Israeli to Italian: "And I read in the paper that they dug beneath the streets of ancient Jerusalem and found nothing. Do you realize what *that* means? We had wireless!"[12]

Alan King

A man died. His three brothers insisted that the rabbi deliver a eulogy. The rabbi said, "Your brother was a knave, a liar, a cheat; he does not deserve a eulogy. I will only say the prescribed prayers." But the three brothers pleaded over and over that the rabbi deliver a eulogy. Finally, the rabbi gave in.

Before the assembled congregation, the rabbi said: "The deceased was a terrible man. He was guilty of unnumbered sins. But compared to his three brothers here, he was an angel."[13]

Steven Lukes and Itzhak Galnoor

Two Jews meet in Warsaw in 1968.

"Rosenberg," says the first, "they tell me that you have lost your job and yet you look well, happy and prosperous. How is this? What are you living on?"

"I'm living by blackmail," the other replies.

"By blackmail? How come?"

"It's very simple. There is a Polish family that hid me during the war against the Nazis."

"So?"

"I'm blackmailing them."

Battle was about to be joined. The Tsarist officer strutted up and down in front of his troops.

"Right, men," he ordered, "fix your bayonets. The fighting will be man-to-man."

"Would you mind showing me now which is my man?" Private Goldberg asked. "Perhaps we can come to some arrangement."[14]

Graham McCann on Woody Allen

Allen's heroes *de*banalize evil; evil exists to them, people are again held responsible for their actions, and little Alvy Singer and Mickey Sachs walk around saying to people, "How on earth could people have done such things [as the Holocaust]?"

Allen is forever trying to transcend dualism: he yearns to find some happy union of mind and body, comedy and tragedy, love and lust, fantasy and reality, the lover and the loved one.

Allen's comic vision has recently acquired the kind of compassion that enables him, at last, to begin, nervously, to trust.

As the character says in *Hannah and Her Sisters*, "Maybe the poets are right. Maybe love is the only answer. . . ."[15]

Hyam Maccoby and kindness to animals

RABBI JUDAH AND THE CALF

Rabbi Judah the Prince suffered for many years from stones in the kidneys, which caused him great pain. This suffering came to him through a certain incident. A calf was being taken to the slaughter. It broke away, hid under the long robe of Rabbi Judah the Prince, and wept.

Said Rabbi Judah the Prince to the calf, "Go, for you were created for this."

Upon this, it was said in Heaven, "Since he does not show pity, suffering will come upon him."

After thirteen years, his sufferings departed. This also happened through an incident. One day, his maidservant was sweeping the house and found some kittens. She was about to throw them out, but he stopped her, saying, "Leave them, for it is written 'His tender mercies are over all his works'(Psalm 145:9)."

Upon this, it was said in Heaven, "Since he is merciful, let mercy be shown to him."

SOME LAWS ON KINDNESS TO ANIMALS

Prevention of suffering to animals is a biblical law, and therefore takes precedence of all rabbinical laws (e.g., rabbinical laws relating to the Sabbath may be broken in order to prevent an animal from suffering).[16]

Groucho Marx

From the moment I picked up your book until I laid it down, I was convulsed with laughter. Someday I intend reading it.

I could dance with you 'til the cows come home. On second thought, I'll dance with the cows and you come home.

Why, I'd horsewhip you if I had a horse.[17]

Steve Mittelman

Like most Jewish men I know, my goal in life is to be mistaken for an Italian.

Jan Murray

A woman arranged to fly to Israel with her dog on El Al Airline. A special carrying case was prepared and placed in the hold of the airplane. Upon arrival at Ben Gurion Airport, the officials could not find the dog. The woman stormed up and down the airport lounge shouting her anger. Finally, two handlers located the case in the baggage room. One looked inside and saw that the dog was dead: "O my God, what do we do now?"

An official came to the rescue: "Look, the dog is an ordinary cocker spaniel. Go next door to the pet shop and buy another one of the same size and color. The woman won't know the difference."

Shortly thereafter the woman was given the case and looked inside: "That's not my dog!"

The official responded, "What do you mean that's not your dog?"

The woman answered: "My dog was dead. I was taking him to Israel to bury him there."[18]

William Novak and Moshe Waldoks

It is said that Cain killed Abel because his brother told him a joke he had known since childhood.

Two rival businessmen meet in the Warsaw train station.

"Where are you going?" says the first man.

"To Minsk," says the second.

"To Minsk, eh? What a nerve you have! I know you're telling me you're going to Minsk because you want me to think that you're really going to Pinsk. But it so happens that I know you really *are* going to Minsk. *So why are you lying to me*?" (Sigmund Freud).

When Yankel met Mendel on the train, he was surprised to find his friend in pain, yelling "Oy" every minute or two.

"What's the matter with you?" asked Yankel.

"It's my feet," replied Mendel. "My feet are killing me. My shoes are too small."

"But that's crazy," replied Yankel. "Then why do you wear them?"

"I'll tell you why. My partner made off with all our profits. My daughter is about to marry a goy. My other daughter is so ugly and unpleasant that she'll never get married. My son is nothing more than a bum. My wife doesn't stop nagging. And bills—every day I come home and there are more bills to be paid. Right now I'm out of work. And so every night I go home, and then I take off these shoes—and Yankel, believe me, I feel like a million dollars!"

Two Jews are sitting silently over a glass of tea.

"You know," says the first man, "life is like a glass of tea with sugar."

"A glass of tea with sugar?" asks his friend. "Why do you say that?"

"How should I know?" replies the first man. "What am I, a philosopher?"

A woman on a train walked up to a distinguished looking gentleman across the aisle. "Excuse me," she said, "but are you Jewish?"

"No," replied the man.

A few minutes later the woman returned. "Excuse me," she said again, "but are you sure you're not Jewish?"

"I'm sure," replied the man.

But the woman was not convinced, and a few minutes later she approached him a third time. "Are you absolutely sure you're not Jewish?" she asked.

"All right, all right," the man said. "You win. I'm Jewish."

"That's funny," said the woman. "You don't *look* Jewish."

Mendelson is dying. "Call the priest," he says to his wife, "and tell him I want to convert."

"But, Max, you've been an Orthodox Jew all your life. What are you talking about, you want to convert?"

"Better one of them should die than one of us."

The afternoon was drawing to a close, and the guests were getting ready to leave. "Mrs. Goldberg," said one of the ladies, "I just wanted to tell you that your cookies were so delicious I ate four of them."

"You ate *five*," replied the hostess. "But who's counting?"

May all your teeth fall out — except one, so you can have a toothache.

It was Yom Kippur, and the cantor was chanting the *Hineni*, the self-deprecatory supplication that begins the Musaf Service. Coming to the end of the prayer, the cantor added his personal cry: "Dear God, Lord of the Universe, I am nothing, nothing, nothing at all!"

Hearing this heartfelt plea, the rabbi added a similar prayer: "I am nothing, Lord, nothing, even less than nothing."

And then a third voice joined in, from the back of the room. It was the *shammas*, the sexton, who had thrown himself on the floor and was proclaiming: "I, too, am nothing, O Lord, nothing at all."

Whereupon the rabbi turned to the cantor with a sniff and whispered, "Look who thinks he's a nothing!"

A sexy young woman walks into a dinner party on the arm of a crusty old man. At dinner, the lady sitting to the woman's right turns to her and says, "My, that's a beautiful diamond you're wearing. In fact, I think it's the most beautiful diamond I've ever seen."

"Thank you," the young woman replies. "This is the Plotnick diamond."

"The Plotnick diamond? Is there a story to it?"

"Oh, yes. This diamond comes with a curse."

"A curse?" asks the lady. "What's the curse?"

"Plotnick," comes the whispered reply.

Do not make a stingy sandwich;
Pile the cold cuts high!
Customers should see salami
Comin' thru the rye (Allan Sherman).[19]

Pinchas Peli

First friend: How are you?
Second friend: Fine.
First friend: How is your wife?
Second friend: Fine.
First friend: How are your children?
Second friend: Fine. Everyone's fine. Everything's fine.
First friend: What do you do for aggravation?

In Israel a Jew from Yemen sat in a tree eating its oranges. The police came and called up to him, "Thou shalt not steal!" He replied: "What a wonderful land this! Where else in the world can you sit in a tree, eat marvelous fruit, and listen to verses from the Bible?"

Sanford Pinsker

When a *shlimazel's* bread falls on the floor, it always lands butter-side down. With a *schlemiel* it is the same — but he has buttered his bread on both sides.

Joan Rivers

On our wedding night, my husband said: "Can I help with the buttons?" I was naked at the time.

A Jewish porno film is made up of one minute of sex and six minutes of guilt.

Marry rich. Buy him a pacemaker, then stand behind him and say boo![20]

You have to be abrasive to be a current comic. If you don't offend somebody, you become pap. . . . Humor is tasteless. These are tasteless times. Everybody is frightened, grabbing out, values gone, losing all restraint. And I've ridden right on that crest.[21]

Leo Rosten

Two brothers wished to give their aging mother a birthday present that would keep her company. They paid $500 for a parrot that spoke Yiddish. They put the bird in an expensive gilded cage and had it sent to the mother. Later they eagerly called home to see how she liked the gift. "Delicious," she replied.

During a dramatic moment in the performance of *King Lear*, in Yiddish, at a Houston Street theater, an actor, at the climax of his great scene, collapsed on stage.
"Doctor!" cried another actor.
"Get a doctor," shouted a stagehand.
"Is there a doctor in the house?"

In the fourth row, a man rose. "I'm a doctor!"' He hurried up the stairs to the stage, bent over the prostrate actor, pried open an eyelid, felt the recumbent's pulse.

From the balcony an old lady shouted, "Give — him — an — enema!"

The doctor leaned over and placed his ear against the fallen one's breast. Not a heartbeat was to be heard.

"Give — him — an — enema!" trumpeted the old lady in the gallery.

The doctor straightened up. "Lady, this man is *dead!* An enema won't help."

"It vouldn't *hoit!*" returned the old lady.

"Yinger mon, ir farshteyt Yiddish?" ("Young man, do you understand Yiddish?")

"Yaw," I answered.

"Vat time is it?"

Mrs. Fishbein's phone rang.

"Hul-lo," a cultivated voice intoned. "I'm telephoning to ask whether you and your husband can come to a tea for Lady Windermere — "

"Oy," cut in Mrs. Fishbein, "have *you* got a wrong number!"[22]

Joey Russell

A visitor to Israel ran over a cat.

"I'm sorry," he told the cat's owner. "Is there anything I can do?"

"Mister," the Israeli replied, without a flicker of expression, "you can catch mice?"

Abraham Shulman

A LECTURE — A CALAMITY

The lecture was a calamity from the very beginning. I arrived by train to this remote town and nobody was waiting at the station as previously arranged. This was in itself aggravating. I called the secretary and his tone was cool and unfriendly. He advised me to get a cab and go to a hotel where the executive committee had reserved a room. He said he would come and pick me up shortly before the lecture.

The hotel was a dilapidated affair. The bellboy was an elderly half-blind and completely deaf gentleman who took me to my sixth-floor room in an antiquated elevator operated by a rope. The room was small. The walls were covered with black wallpaper, and the floor was waxed with some black shiny wax. There were only three pieces of furniture: a black wardrobe, a black rocking chair and a huge bed covered with a black spread.

My mood was already gloomy, and was further depressed by the arrival of the secretary, a silent and irritable man, who didn't even try to suppress his impatience. He took me in his car — a black limousine — to the hall which was half filled with a few dozen elderly people. The chairman introduced me briefly and then sat back, already bored. The subject of my lecture, "The Magic of Jewish Folklore," required a different setting. I must have looked miserable, because the majority of the listeners sat fidgeting in their seats. Before the lecture, which dragged hopelessly, was over, a part of the audience began to sneak out through a back door. One of them was the secretary. After I finished, the chairman waited until everybody had gone. He then put out the lights, led me out through the front door into a completely deserted street, advised me to get a cab and disappeared.

I returned to the hotel room in a black mood, lay down in the black bed (what gave my wife the idea of putting a black pair of pajamas into the suitcase?) and as soon as I closed my eyes, I sank into a series of black nightmares.

It must have been no more than six in the morning when my telephone rang. I grabbed the black receiver. "Genosse Shulman?" "Yes." "This is the chairman." "Yes?" "The chairman of your last night's lecture." "What happened?" "Nothing special. I just wanted to tell you that your lecture was a catastrophe."

"And to tell me this you wake me at six in the morning? You couldn't wait till later?" "I could," he said, "but I wanted to be the first."[23]

Isaac Bashevis Singer

Once a Jewish man went to Vilna and he came back and said to his friend, "The Jews of Vilna are remarkable people. I saw a Jew who studies all day long the Talmud. I saw a Jew who all day long was scheming to get rich. I saw a Jew who's all the time waving the red flag, calling for revolution. I saw a Jew who was running after every woman. I saw a Jew who was an ascetic and avoided women." The other man said, "I don't know why you're so astonished. Vilna is a big city, and there are many Jews, all types." "No," said the first man, "it was the same Jew."[24]

NOTES

1. References in the present chapter are primarily to materials bearing the name of the persons listed or at least from whom the items have been garnered. Ofttimes these persons are utilizing other sources, which, wherever feasible, are identified in parentheses or footnotes.
2. Allen, *Side Effects*, pp. 173–76.
3. The final thirteen items are adapted from McCann, *Woody Allen*, pp. 15, 26, 35, 40, 43, 54, 83, 94, 156, 160, 163, 218, 246.
4. Quoted in Samuel, *World of Sholom Aleichem*, p. 202.
5. Ausubel, *Treasury of Jewish Humor*, pp. 305–6, 414–15, 448, 567, 759.
6. Blue, *To Heaven*, p. 80.
7. Recounted by Arnold Pasternak, June 1966, as quoted by Boskin, "Beyond Kvetching," in *Jewish Wry*, Sarah Blacher Cohen, ed., pp. 66–67.
8. *Essential Lenny Bruce*, p. 33.
9. There follow a few instances of Israeli humor.
10. Carr, ed., *There (is) a Fly*, pp. 52, 79, 95, 163–64, 189, 194.
11. Totie Fields, cited by Sarah Blacher Cohen, "The Unkosher Comediennes," in *Jewish Wry*, Sarah Blacher Cohen, ed., p. 114.
12. Hillel Halkin, *Letters to An American Jewish Friend: A Zionist's Polemic* (Philadelphia: Jewish Publication Society of America, 1977), p. 12.
13. Alan King, in "Next Time, Dear God."
14. Steven Lukes and Itzhak Galnoor, *No Laughing Matter*, pp. 27–28, 161.
15. McCann, *Woody Allen*, pp. 154, 224, 247, 248.
16. Maccoby, *Day God Laughed*, p. 171, citing Bava Metsia, 85a and Shabbat, 128b.
17. As cited in McCann, *Woody Allen*, p. 52.
18. Jan Murray, in "Next Time, Dear God."
19. Novak and Waldoks, eds., *Big Book*, pp. xxiii, 2, 6, 7, 96, 142, 152, 195, 264, 290.
20. Joan Rivers, cited by Cohen, "Unkosher Comediennes," pp. 116, 117, 120.
21. Rivers, in ibid., p. 119.

22. *Leo Rosten's Giant Book*, pp. 435–36, 557, 568.
23. Abraham Shulman, *Adventures of a Yiddish Lecturer,* pp. 64–65.
24. Isaac Bashevis Singer, as cited by Richard Burgin, "Singer Talks . . . ," *The New York Times Magazine* (26 November 1978).

13

Comedy Human, Comedy Divine

God is a comedian playing to an audi-ence that is afraid to laugh.
—Voltaire

Tevye to God: You help complete strangers — why not me?
—Sholom Aleichem

Humor, together with irony, forms a safeguard against idolatry.
—Krister Stendahl

The devil is the spirit of gravity.
—Nietzsche

Thus far I have said little of the province and concerns of theology as such. This book as a whole is not — or is more than — "theological" in any technical or apologetic sense. However, I do have an overall theological orientation that may be alluded to at the present juncture. The orientation is postmodernist.

Harvey Cox writes: "A viable postmodern theology will be created neither by those who have completely withdrawn from the modern world nor by those who have affirmed it unconditionally. It will come from those who have lived within it but have never been fully part of it, like the women in Adrienne Rich's poem who, though they dived into the wreck, have not found their names inscribed within it."[1] The postmodernist stands within the modern world — who can escape that world? — but is never fully *of* that world.

173

Let us see how this general outlook may be explored within the bounds of our subject. Pertinent questions for the present chapter include: How may the concept "theology" be utilized? What is the relation/are the relations between humor and religious faith? Between humor and the affirmation/negation of God? How may the special claims of Christianity be handled at the bar of theological humor? And what may we say of the relation between humor and the problematic of the future (the eschatological question)?

I

Amongst its special historical forms, functions, or applications, "theology" means a human word (*logos*) directed to the realm of God and the sacred.

Three references are apropos. Conrad Hyers notes the major categories shared by religion and comedy; these include creation, celebration, mystery, wonder, finitude, pride, humility, justice, iconoclasm, salvation, hope, and eschatology (the "last things").

Robert Alter asserts that "humor collapses in the face of utter chaos, and the characteristic Jewish humor of shrewd observation especially needs to assume a realm of meaning accessible to intelligence, even if it suspects that whatever meaning it unearths will be perverse, unconsoling."

Marie Collins Swabey links three realities: the life of reason, the religious spirit, and the comic spirit:

> When the religious spirit is compared with the comic spirit, one sees that in different degrees both are metaphysical, that both intimate what the universe is, that it involves a basic coherence overreaching passing incoherences, an order superseding disorder, an enveloping cosmos beyond the semblances of chaotic detail. Yet both include a kind of paradox: the religious consciousness, as Santayana says somewhere, feels that "it is right that things should go wrong, yet it is wrong not to strive to right them," whereas the comic spirit, though it lacks a fervent sense of providential control and moral obligation, is nevertheless torn between delight in the incongruities confronting it everywhere and a sense of challenge to resolve them. In the comic experience as in the religious there is a momentary escape of the prisoner from life; he stands outside as in eternity. Yet while the spirit of the religious man remains submissive, reverential, worshipful of a providential power, that of the comedian remains disobedient, irreverent, and disrespectful. . . . [In] the comic experience . . . the sense of freedom, of liberation got in our droll perception of the

foolishness of mortals, marks the high point of the experience rather than any sense of our subservience to the ultimate.[2]

Contra Swabey: What is to be said and done when an ostensibly divinely-sustained order of things is subjected to the wrecking power of a *Shoah*? Again, the religious person or community is not always submissive. Tevye's rather timorous question to God, "You help complete strangers — why not me?," is joined and then swept ahead by the shattering cry of the psalmist, "My God, my God, why hast thou forsaken me?" (Ps. 22:1). The life of religious faith may itself be suffused by a critical (comic?) spirit that judges God and finds God wanting. This has happened many times within the story of Judaism — a fact that gives a special edge to Lionel Blue's astonishing claim, "the most typical weapon of Jewish spirituality is humor." Mark Shechner has been cited: "Religion subordinates this world to another; it translates upwards, while comedy undercuts the transcendent, criticizes it, subordinates it to the common." A critical theology may do exactly what comedy does.

When the two points are put together — the eventuality of a subjection of order to chaos, and a moral criticism of the transcendent at the hands of comedy — we catch sight of a kinship between comedy and theology. As Irving Kristol puts it, "Jewish humor dances along a knife-edge that separates religious faith from sheer nihilism. It 'knows' that the material world is the only true reality, but it also finds that this world makes no sense in its own terms and is impossible to live in."[3]

In a word, the humor of theology is occasioned, on the one hand, by the ludicrousness that, from a divine "point of view," is invariably present within human theologizing, as within all human endeavors, and, on the other hand, by certain incongruities that surround God and the divine-human relation, incongruities that human beings are able to detect.

II

If religious faith is itself inherently "serious," a life-and-death matter, the expression of an "ultimate concern" (Paul Tillich), and if comedy and humor are in certain important respects "unserious," sometimes even climaxing in frivolous joy, is it possible to relate the two categories?

Reinhold Niebuhr answers this question affirmatively with aid from a phenomenon familiar to us: incongruity.

> The intimate relation between humour and faith is derived from the fact that both deal with the incongruities of our existence. Humour is concerned with the immediate incongruities of life and faith with the ultimate ones. Both humour and faith are expressions of the freedom of the human spirit, of its capacity to stand outside of life, and itself, and view the whole scene. But any view of the whole immediately creates the problem of how the incongruities of life are to be dealt with; for the effort to understand life, and our place in it, confronts us with inconsistencies and incongruities which do not fit into any neat picture of the whole. Laughter is our reaction to immediate incongruities and those which do not affect us essentially. Faith is the only possible response to the ultimate incongruities of existence which threaten the very meaning of our life.

In remembrance of our series of Proto-Jokes (chapter 1) I am inclined to qualify somewhat the terms of Niebuhr's distinction. For is it not the ultimate incongruities of life that make humor possible? I think that Swabey is thus correct that the religious spirit and the comic spirit alike partake of the metaphysical. And Hyers is right that the quality of humor knows no limits; human beings are capable of laughing at the ultimate incongruities as well as the immediate ones.[4]

Furthermore, we have not resolved the question of whether faith is more capable than humor of coming to grips with ultimate incongruousness. Niebuhr contends that faith can indeed do this. His exposition contrasts to some extent with Swabey's exaltation of reason and coherence. For Niebuhr, the irrationalities of existence can never be made amenable to a nice system:

> Philosophers seek to overcome [the basic incongruity of life] by reducing one world to the dimension of the other; or raising one perspective to the height of the other. But neither a purely naturalistic nor a consistently idealistic system of philosophy is ever completely plausible. There are ultimate incongruities of life which can be resolved by faith but not by reason. Reason can look at them only from one standpoint or another, thereby denying the incongruities which it seeks to solve. They are also too profound to be resolved or dealt with by laughter. If laughter seeks to deal with the ultimate issues of life it turns into a bitter humour. This means that it has been overwhelmed by the incongruity. Laughter is thus not merely a vestibule to faith but also a "no-man's land" between faith and despair. We laugh cheerfully at the incongruities on the surface of life; but if we have no other resource but humour to deal with those which reach below the surface, our laughter becomes an expression of our sense of the meaninglessness of life. . . . That is why laughter, when pressed to solve the ultimate issue, turns into a vehicle of bitterness rather than joy. To

laugh at life in the ultimate sense means to scorn it. There is a note of derision in that laughter and an element of despair in that derision.

Again, once we acknowledge the real power of sin, we must see that laughter is incapable of dealing with that problem. "If we continue to laugh after having recognized the depth of [human] evil, our laughter becomes the instrument of irresponsibility. Laughter is thus not only the vestibule of the temple of confession but the no-man's land between cynicism and contrition." And when the issue is that of our own sin, we see that the joy of reconciliation with God, "the fruit of genuine repentance, is a joy which stands beyond laughter though it need not completely exclude laughter."

Niebuhr concludes:

> Our provisional amusement with the irrational and unpredictable fortunes which invade the order and purpose of our life must move either toward bitterness or faith, when we consider not this or that frustration and this or that contingent event, but when we are forced to face the basic incongruity of death. . . .
>
> Faith is . . . the final triumph over incongruity, the final assertion of the meaningfulness of existence. There is no other triumph and will be none, no matter how much human knowledge is enlarged. Faith is the final assertion of the freedom of the human spirit, but also the final acceptance of the weakness of man and the final solution for the problem of life through the disavowal of any final solution in the power of man.
>
> Insofar as the sense of humour is a recognition of incongruity, it is more profound than any philosophy which seeks to devour incongruity in reason. But the sense of humor remains healthy only when it deals with immediate issues and faces the obvious and surface irrationalities. It must move toward faith or sink into despair when the ultimate issues are raised.
>
> That is why there is laughter in the vestibule of the temple, the echo of laughter in the temple itself, but only faith and prayer, and no laughter, in the holy of holies.[5]

For Reinhold Niebuhr, then, a rank order obtains, beginning with the level of philosophic reason, going up to the sense of humor, and then extending upwards to the dimension of faith. I think that this rank ordering is defensible only so long as the evils that religious faith itself tends to produce — intolerance, aggression, violence, tyranny — are subjected successfully to both humor and reason. Niebuhr was himself always aware of these destructive accompaniments of faith, and he fought with them ceaselessly all through his writings and public career. Conrad Hyers puts the issue well:

Much of "man's inhumanity to man" historically is the result of some faith, some vision or ideal, that has been taken absolutely and with absolute serious-ness. When one considers all the "good" that has been done to the human race in the name of one faith or another, faith has considerable incongruities of its own to worry about. If humor without faith is in danger of dissolving into cynicism and despair, faith without humor is in danger of turning into arrogance and intolerance. Faith without humor is itself an incongruity, for it is inevitably the faith of this or that finite and conditioned group of human beings — as the humorist is quick to point out.[6]

So there is faith and there is faith. There is absolutist faith and there is (what else could it be?) relativist faith. Faith serves as an abiding judge of humor, but humor — along with morality — remains a steady judge of faith.

Israel Knox comments fittingly upon the final paragraph from Reinhold Niebuhr that is cited above:

Prayer and faith and awe *are* present in the Jewish Holy of Holies, but it is exactly because there is awe — "Know before Whom you stand" — that Abraham can plead with God: "Shall not the Judge of all the earth do justly." And several millennia later the compassionate Rabbi Levi Yitzchok of Berdichev can dare to engage God in a *din toreh*, in "litigation": *Vos hostu tzu dein folk Yisroel? Vos hostu zich ongezetz af dein folk Yisroel?* ("What have you against your people Israel? Why have you heaped afflictions upon your people Is-rael?") And in Peretz's folktale, *Berl Shneider,* the humble little tailor — with-out the prerogatives of a rabbi — can muster the courage and the impudence to quarrel with God for His indifference to the plight of the poor who are required, like the well-to-do, to abstain scrupulously from dishonesty, but, unlike them, do not always have food for their hungry children.[7]

Knox's *midrash* leads us into the question of humor and the affirmation/negation of God. For Lionel Blue's aphorism has again interjected itself: "The most typical weapon of Jewish spirituality is humor." The remainder of this chapter may itself be viewed as a critical *midrash* upon the Niebuhrian exclusion of laughter from the "holy of holies." Are we perforce required to accept this exclusion? I doubt it.

III

We may begin with Rabbi Blue's further observation: "God has no human form in Jewish theology but He reveals a very human psyche in Jewish jokes. There He enters into the suffering and paradoxes of the world, and experiences the human condition. There He is immanent, if not incarnate, and a gossamer bridge of laughter stretches over the void, linking creatures of flesh and blood to the endlessness of the *Ein Sof,* and the paralysing power of the Lord of hosts."[8] Here, humor fills a role remarkably like unto the Christian teaching of the Incarnation of God in Jesus, a *foolishness* that is "wiser than men" (I Cor. 1:25).

The life of humor may be regarded as a child of the monotheizing impulse (so central within Judaism and Jewish life). "If God alone is Truth and Goodness, is not everything else set free to be really quite comical?"[9] — or at least to be less than wholly serious. Or to use Irving Greenberg's wording: "Ultimately, laughter is a unique reflection of Judaism's conception of life and reality. One of the Torah's central positive teachings is that there is no other God. If one believes in the infinite One God, then everything else is relative. No other deity, no other value source, no other power has the right to claim absolute status." Humor helps to offset and chasten human idolatries by insisting that the structures of this world are not absolute; there is something beyond them.[10] If only God is God, the entire creation of God can be thrown open to laughter; it is the Unconditional that makes possible the humor of the conditional world. The dictum "You shall have no other gods besides Me," by forbidding the idolatrizing of finite reality, thereby authorizes a posture of comedy respecting the finite realm. Contra pantheism, to laugh at and with the world is not to laugh at God. The humor of the Jewish people is realizable in and through the strict monotheism of Judaism. The golden calf of utter seriousness is turned into a joke (cf. Exod. 32:1–35). In a word, the life of humor becomes authoritatively functional within a good creation that is not itself God; the desacralizing of the world is the legitimizing of laughter.[11] (This is not to forget that any religion of monotheism may itself descend into exclusivism and intolerance. One of the persistently, dialectically ironic elements in religion is that while religion helps safeguard the world against fanaticism, it also helps create fanaticism. Not unexpectedly, then, there is an anti-humor tradition in Christianity,[12] as there is, though to a lesser extent, in Judaism.)

Theological attestation may come "from below" or it may come "from above." Let us consider these two possibilities in order.

A. To reason and to act theologically "from below" is to proceed from the standpoint of human experience, human fortune, human dignity.

In chapter 1 the possibility is raised of laughing, not at God, but with God. Yet how can this eventuality be defended, morally speaking, in the presence of such a reality as the *Shoah*? Put differently, in a post-Holocaust world is there divine comedy, or is there only divine tragedy? Put in yet a third way, once self-mockery is seen to suffuse highly moral humor, what is there to exempt God from mockery?

Our scenario is suffused with an accusation, not against the world, but against God. A further word is in order from Levi Yitzchok. Of this man, "called the Compassionate One, it was told that on a certain Day of Atonement, hearing the Jews confess their sins to the Almighty, he became tired of this one-sided demonstration of humility; he suddenly closed the doors of the Ark, turned to the congregation, and cried: 'That's enough now. It's God's turn to confess *His* sins!' "[13]

Elie Wiesel thus describes the genesis of his play, *The Trial of God:* "Inside the Kingdom of Night [the *Shoah*] I witnessed a strange trial. Three rabbis—all erudite and pious men—decided one winter evening to indict God for allowing his children to be massacred. I remember: I was there, and I felt like crying. But there nobody cried." As the play moves on, only a single party is to be found who will agree to serve as defense attorney for God. That party turns out to be none other than the devil.[14]

Within the frame of reference of the *Shoah*, our Third Proto-Joke (The Absence of Any Say in One's Birth) may become almost unbearable. For the Absolute that is the *Shoah*—the Nazi decree that *all* must die— gives that Joke a terrifying visage (unless there is some road away from the Joke). The Jew of the *Shoah* addresses God (= the human being of the Jew addresses God): We could not choose our birth. And we as Jews did not choose to be chosen. And now we are robbed of the ordinary right to die with dignity. *Are you or are you not a fiend?* This is the question of the Holocaust to God, the only question of the Holocaust to God—*not* to other beings, to *God,* for it is God who ultimately bears the responsibility. As Rabbi Eliezer Berkovits of today's Jerusalem declares (strictly in the context of the *Shoah*): "God is responsible for having created a world in which man is free to make history."[15] It is God who is brought to trial, it is God who stands in the prisoner's dock—as never before in the history of the world, for never before was the Absolute Word formulated, "No more Jews." The *Shoah* comprises the ultimate historical (= existential) refutation of the erstwhile religious notion that human beings have no right to question God and the ways of God. On the contrary, to silence that questioning would be an act of sacrilege, for any such silencing constitutes an assault upon human dignity, the *imago dei,* humankind made in the very image of God.[16] Suppose that the trial of God is the one way left to honor God — in the shadow of the *Shoah*?

How, then, may God be redeemed? — if there is to be redemption for God. It is not out of the question that God should seek out human forgiveness. In Wiesel's work *Souls on Fire,* Levi Yitzchok reminds God that he would do well to ask forgiveness for the hardships he has visited upon his children. This is why, so the tale goes, the phrase *Yom Kippur* also appears in the plural, *Yom Kippurim*: "the request for pardon is reciprocal." And yet: Rabbi Berkovits concludes that within the dimension of time and history, the ways of God are unforgivable.[17]

But suppose that human beings — a few at least — resolve to forgive God anyway? Suppose they say, in effect, "What the hell!" Suppose they determine to forgive the unforgivable? Perhaps the most overwhelming fact about Wiesel's *Trial of God* is that the play is set on the Feast of Purim, a day when, as the prosecutor himself observes, "Everything goes." Purim is a time, not alone for children and beggars, but also for fools (cf. chapter 9). In the act of poking fun at everyone, the fool is making merry. And how could God ever be excluded from the party? Irving Greenberg points up the rationale of Purim: "One can only respond with laughter and mockery and put-on, satirizing God and the bitter joke this world threatens to become. . . . But as the hilarity reaches its climax, Jews move beyond bitterness to humor. . . . Through the humor, Jews project themselves into a future redeemed reality that transcends the moment. Thus, hope is kept alive and the Messiah remains possible."[18]

In Elie Wiesel's tale, *The Gates of the Forest,* the dancing and the singing of a certain hasid convey his resolution to tell God: "You don't want me to dance; too bad. I'll dance anyhow. You've taken away every reason for singing, but I shall sing. I shall sing of the deceit that walks by day and the truth that walks by night, yes, and of the silence of dusk as well. You didn't expect my joy, but here it is; yes, my joy will rise up; it will submerge you."[19] We seem here to be impelled back into a humor of defiance (chapter 1). And yet: It is with his very body that the hasid acts out his ironic joy. Is this not to affirm

God after all, the One who created that body, the One who may yet act to redeem that body? Furthermore, on Purim it is fitting to wear a mask. Abraham J. Heschel emphasizes the "overwhelming sympathy with the divine pathos" that the prophet Isaiah developed.[20] "Why do we not just don the mask of Isaiah? The play's the thing: no one will stop us. Contrary to Berish—the prosecutor [in *The Trial of God*]—to be sorry for God and for human beings is never an either/or: the two deeds sustain each other. For me, the penultimate height of faith—not the final height, for that would be salvation, the last reconciliation of humankind and God—the penultimate height of faith is to find oneself genuinely sorry for God (*daath elohim,* sympathy for God)."[21]

But why are human creatures to feel sorry for God? This question thrusts upon us a frightening, ultimate dialectic between faith and humor: The reason we are to feel sorry for God is that God is nothing less than a klutz. In Woody Allen's film, *Love and Death,* Boris Grushenko proposes that the worst thing we can say about God is that he is an Underachiever. From that perspective, God may be counseled to try harder. But what if trying harder only compounds certain mischiefs? No,

> God is, *kiveyakhol,* more a klutz than anything else. Heinz Moshe Graupe identifies the Hebrew term *kiveyakhol* as an appropriate one in Hebrew literature for conveying religious content "that almost seems blasphemous." The term is variously translated as "so to speak," "as if it were possible," and "as one might be allowed to say." The appellation of the divine klutzyness or incompetence will shock many, sounding grotesquely sacrilegious to them. However, such people may only open themselves to a nagging question: How do *you* propose to reconcile the fear of sacrilege with the rightfulness of a transcending human dignity? . . .
>
> God is the ultimate klutz—*kiveyakhol.* God would have to go and make Godself a world. Now God is stuck with it, and with us, and God is left with little choice but to keep on undergoing the agony of it. . . . And by revealing and making normative certain apodictic [absolute] requirements, God opened the way to being held unmercifully to account before the very same requirements—and, of all things, at the hands of that upstart, humankind. The Creator of all the universes made radically assaultable, and under God's very own sponsorship! If this is not the essence of klutzyness, then I do not know what that concept means. . . . However: I think I am prepared to suggest a deal. . . . I am willing to substitute *vulnerability* for klutzyness.[22]

Does God laugh? Does God tell jokes? Does God listen to jokes? In this book the Freudian treatment of humor has been kept rather at arm's length. Freud's assumption that jokes express hidden aggressions remains debatable — at least as an allegedly comprehensive accounting of humor. And yet, we may find it interesting, or at a minimum heuristic, to reflect upon that point of view within a theological frame of reference. The psychiatrist Martin Grotjahn remarks that the successful joke disguises aggression sufficiently to make its utterance allowable. The teller of jokes — the gifted one anyway — "is an artist who commits the sin of expressing the dangerous thought. He is more aggressive than the one who simply laughs at the joke. And that very sin of the creative artist is then *forgiven* with our acceptance of his joke — through our laughter," which frees up or redeems our own aggressive impulses.[23]

How may God receive the "dangerous thoughts" of those intercessors who serve the comic cause, not only upon Purim but throughout the year? I should propose that, ultimately speaking, forgiveness may win the day. The aggression against God — or the counteraggression — in response to the divine aggression is itself eligible for forgiveness. Yet I should submit that in the final reckoning forgiveness is never a purely human achievement. It is a gift from beyond. Thus may forgiveness enter the dialectic of humor and faith, pointing to the beginnings of reconciliation amongst all parties. In the depths of authentic humor everyone stands forgiven.

This last point takes us over into a theological reckoning "from above."

B. To reason theologically "from above" is to proceed, *kiveyakhol,* from the standpoint of God — insofar as such *chutzpah* may be permissible. ("Permissible" or "not permissible" by whose authority?) The brevity of B, in contrast to A, may be received as reflective of a certain apprehensiveness when the venture is made to "think God's thoughts after him."

Emil Fackenheim ends a recent book by referring to a Talmudic ambiguity upon the hiding of God: "Does [God] hide in wrath against, or punishment of, His people? God forbid that He should do so at such a time [as ours]! Does He hide for reasons unknown? God forbid that He should, in this of all times, be a *deus absconditus* [a secretive or obscuring God]!   Then why does He hide?" It is his weeping that he hides. "He hides His weeping in the inner chamber, for just as God is infinite so *His pain is infinite, and this, were it to touch the world, would destroy it . . . . God so loved the world that He hid the infinity of His pain from it lest it be destroyed.* [24]

As Christians ponder these words from Fackenheim, they may be reminded of other words: "God so loved the world that he gave his only Son" (John 3:16). Is the chasm between the Jewish interpretation and a Christian view uncrossable? No, the chasm may be crossed — from both directions. But this is possible only upon the foundation of the love of God: It is in the hiding that the love of God is given; and it is in the giving that the love of God is hidden. Were the infinity of God's pain to touch the world, the world would indeed be destroyed. And so God must act to control Godself, while never ceasing to weep within the inner chamber. This means that, however guilty God may appear to be, God is innocent. God does not willfully sin. Therefore, it is fitting, if astonishing, that in the Elie Wiesel work *Twilight*, Raphael should at the end reject the idea that God could ever be cruel.[25]

In the last resort, we may have but two choices: tragedy or comedy — a tragic God who is subject to Fate, wherein is also dictated human despair; or a comic God who is free to do the best she can (as we are being made free to do the best we can). A destructive God whose laughter is the instrument of judgment, or a redeeming God whose weeping is the instrument of love and laughter. Perhaps we have the makings here of an Eleventh Proto-Joke: Infinite power vis-à-vis klutzyness (the latter necessitated by love) — an exquisitely divine comedy. We could do a lot worse than to attend to the epigram of Voltaire: "God is a comedian playing to an audience that is afraid to laugh."

We are advised that in the shadow of the *Shoah* only tears have meaning. But if the tears are the tears of God, then may human laughter be restored. Tragedy is turned into comedy, in the measure that fate is turned into freedom. Human suffering is repudiated by the human spirit itself, the *imago dei*. Contrary to Reinhold Niebuhr, laughter is restored within the "holy of holies" itself. Graham McCann attests: "After the death camps there are at least six million reasons not to laugh anymore, and at least six million reasons to try and laugh again."[26]

IV

We come to the possible fate or disposition of the Christian message in the presence of a theology of the human/divine comedy.

Through the years, the claim has been made that the Christian faith is a form of gladsome, salvational comedy.[27] I suggest that the tenability of this claim is contingent upon the absence/presence of Christian absolutism.

Religious absolutism — "we have the truth, you do not" — tends to correlate with extreme theological and moral soberness. The absolutist has great difficulty in laughing at himself and sometimes even with God, though he finds it very easy to laugh at the "ignorant," the "unwashed," the "unconverted." This state of affairs already points up the Christian problem as well as intimating a way to its resolution.

Christian imperialism/triumphalism — the assertion that no one is "saved" except through personal faith in Jesus Christ (ostensibly "here and now," though sometimes, it is conceded, in the "hereafter") — involves absolutist ideology. ("Ideology" refers to the utilization of a belief-system and action-system in the furtherance of collective self-interest and self-justification.) Exclusivistic religious claims have a way of plunging a religious community into the fate (tragedy) of denying equal justice for all. The destructive tragedy of a triumphalist or elitist Christian church can begin to be transformed into a human comedy — as also a divine comedy — through the church's potential faithfulness to the God of Israel and to the love of humankind that is sustained by acts of justice. For human beings to make absolutist claims for themselves and their religion is to flout their true condition as mortals. Whereas such absolutism demands total seriousness, the ideal or right state of religious affairs is seen to be nonabsolutist comedy.

Incessantly.through the centuries, the Christian church has afflicted itself with the ideology that its gospel succeeds, indeed supersedes, Judaism. The way of Judaism is treated as a dead end. The Jewish people are deprived of any real future. On the other side of the fence, the American Catholic theologian Michael McGarry identifies Christian supersessionism (vis-à-vis Judaism) as a form of Christian heresy.[28] From this point of view, heresy is consanguine with tragic fatefulness. By contrast, the overcoming of heresy is seen to be a victory over the power of fate, a restoration of human freedom and a rebirth of the Christian comedy. "For at the heart of the comic spirit and perspective is an acceptance of the prophetic warning against idolatry, and against that greatest blasphemy of all, the claim to understand or be God."[29]

In addressing the frequent resort to the Crucifixion/Resurrection of Jesus as a recommended means of coping spiritually with the *Shoah*, Robert E. Willis points out that the "passion of Christ" has become integral to "the very evil it seeks to illuminate."[30] In different terms, culpability for this state of affairs focuses in the very Christian symbolism that is put forward as a remedy. For the theological ideology that Jesus suffered for all humankind (therefore, for Jews too) is turned upon its head in the *Shoah*: Jews are made to suffer for Jesus. In *A Beggar in Jerusalem* Elie Wiesel has the blind hasid Shlomo meeting Yeshua (Jesus) on the day of the Crucifixion. Shlomo says: "You think you are suffering for my sake and my brothers', yet we are the ones who will be made to suffer for you, because of you." A man named Moshe then responds to the tale: "If only you could have made him laugh, things would have been different now."[31] The Christian church always has the choice of joining the Jewish community in the theocentric repudiation of human suffering and in the struggle against suffering, as an alternative to Christocentric, suffering-centered triumphalism, with its temptations to the dirty and cruel jokes of sadism and masochism.[32] For modest aid in this struggle, yet the influence of which cannot be overestimated, we may reminisce over such a figure as Francis of Assisi (1182–1226). St. Francis

had a comic streak. As a boy, he had admired traveling troubadours. Later he called himself and his followers *joculatores Domini* (jesters of the Lord). Many of the stories about them handed down in *The Little Flowers* are strongly reminiscent of the capers attributed to the Russian [Christian] holy fools. Once, for example, Francis is said to have sent Rufinus through the streets to the church to preach clad only in his underwear. On another occasion, the inimitable Brother Juniper cut the adornments and decorations from a church and gave them to poor people so that they could get money to buy food. The famous pilgrimage Francis himself took through the battle lines of the crusading armies to visit the caliph was a classic fool's errand. The reason the Muslims did not kill him is that they also had a certain respect for holy madness.[33]

V

There remains the eschatological dimension.

A caveat is in order: To attest with Reinhold Niebuhr that the ultimate incongruities of human life can be resolved by faith is, at best, to speak ideally or "in principle." And the same may be said concerning the intellectual, moral, and therapeutic values of humor and laughter. Neither faith nor humor can boast ultimate, redeeming power. Incongruity is the precondition of humor (as it is of faith and of tragedy). Within the bounds and bonds of this world, incongruity must and will remain. The end of laughter (as of tears) is possible only within an imagined or projected eschatological condition of ultimate congruity. In our realistic moments we concede that the present dispensation of death and woe can know no happy endings. In accordance with biblical-Jewish-Christian testimony, the reign of God continues to be unrealized, for all the reputed signs of its coming. The human/divine comedy may be so named only by linking it to a fulfillment that is not here, to a domain beyond all jokes and all Proto-Jokes.

By the end of the film *Easy Street,* the underdog Charlie Chaplin has gained the upper hand, "and everything is love and peace and flowers." Yet "the ending is so clean and orderly that we laugh in an amused sense of its absurdity. . . . We know that that is not the way life is, has been, or is ever likely to be." Our alerting to the comic Muse "comes not out of sarcasm or cynicism but out of a humor that lies between fideism and despair." The alerting is administered by, among other things, the preposterousness of the finish. Yet withal, the catharsis of human hope abides. In one sense

it does not matter whether the comic victory is ever achieved in the real world, whether good finally conquers evil, or justice everlastingly prevails over ruthless power, or the meek at last and invincibly inherit the earth. Such is the peculiar mythological requirement of linear views of history which can only justify time and history, flesh and blood, as that which leads to perpetual progress or some final bliss. In the fantasy of comedy, the human dream has already been achieved, and is achieved in every comic ritual — *symbolically.* But it is not achieved in such a way as to freeze life and its ongoing dreams. It permits the game to be played again and again. Its mission is not to annul history or conquer death or obviate suffering but to renew and celebrate life.

The real world remains — as it is "seen in a special way, infused with a special spirit, offering a special grace. It is not paradise. But it is also not the ordinary world as ordinarily perceived. It is a world in which all the winnings and losings, dreams and dreadings, are appropriated comically. It is a world in which comedy has the last word and the last laugh."[34]

The last word and the last laugh combine to witness against tragedy and to oppose suffering. Tragedy may help imbue a sense of human courage, but only comedy can foster a sense of hope.[35] Where there is humor there is hope, where there is hope there is humor. The tragic is the inevitable; the comic is the unforeseeable.[36] In unrelieved tragedy forgiveness is lacking. In the life of comedy, as we have noted, forgiveness enters the fray. We have referred, in a frame of reference of Jewishness and Judaism, to the dichotomy of tragedy/fate and comedy/freedom. The latter especially involves what Peter Berger refers to as liberation from "the bondage of deadly earnestness."[37]

In contrast to an ideology of the "tragic hero" who supposedly ennobles suffering, we have Itzhak, the one who laughs, and the one who will laugh. And we have Sholom Aleichem's Tevye, who acts upon the Yiddish proverb, "burdens are from God, shoulders too," refusing to allow that there is any kind of fulfillment in suffering and refusing to create a mythology out of suffering (in steady contrast to much Christian tradition).

> Jewish humor typically drains the charge of cosmic significance from suffering by grounding it in a world of homey practical realities. "If you want to forget all your troubles," runs another Yiddish proverb, "put on a shoe that's too tight." The point is not only in the "message" of the saying, that a present pain puts others out of mind, but also in its formulation: *Weltschmerz* begins to seem preposterous when one is wincing over crushed bunions. If in the tradition of Jewish humor suffering is understandably imagined as inevitable, it is also conceived as incongruous with dignity.... The perception of incongruity implies the perception of alternate possibilities, humor peeking beyond the beleaguered present toward another kind of man and another kind of time; for the very aura of ridicule suggests that it is not, after all, fitting for a man to be this pitiful creature with a blade of anguish in his heart and both feet entangled in a clanking chain of calamities.[38]

Irving Greenberg's eschatological finding returns us to the Feast of Purim:

> Why on Purim do Jews satirize their own traditions...? The answer is that the ultimate Jewish claims of faith are truly dissonant with the world as humans

know it. Judaism affirms that this is a world in which life will overcome death, yet people die. Judaism affirms that the ultimate truth is justice and human dignity, yet now people perish from hunger and oppression and sickness and neglect. Judaism affirms that God has created a good world, and someday this will be manifest in every aspect of life, yet in this interim there is cancer and persecution and slavery.

Upon what basis are the above affirmations to be made? The answer is twofold: *faith* and *commitment.* "Faith is a vision of a truth that will come into being, backed by a commitment to make it happen." And the most appropriate way to express this faith is by humor—"by simultaneously affirming and admitting the present limitations. True faith is neither oblivious to the facts that contradict nor afraid to affirm that the vision will finally triumph. Humor makes statements of faith credible without being insensitive to present states of suffering. Through humorous affirmation, Jews admit that they follow God not because their hopes have been realized but because they have trust in the Divine." Thus does the laughter of Purim preserve "integrity and sanity together. This is Purim's remarkable role in Jewish history."[39]

At this point the message of Christianity recalls that of Judaism, and insofar as this is the case the church becomes a truthful inheritor of the Jewish *Anschauung.* Peter Berger writes from just such a Christian perspective:

> If . . . the universe is not a mindless machine destroying all within it, if death should turn out to be not the ultimate reality of the human phenomenon, then the clown's magic takes on a strange new dignity. The comic transformation now may suddenly appear as a promise of a reality yet to come. . . . [In] a way strangely parallel to that of the Christian faith, comedy overcomes the tragic perspective. From the Christian point of view one can say that comedy, unlike tragedy, bears within it a great secret. This secret is the promise of redemption. For redemption promises in eternity what comedy gives us in its few moments of precarious liberation—the collapse of the walls of our imprisonment. It would not be surprising if, to the blessed, redemption appears after the terrors of the world as a form of comic relief.

"By laughing at the imprisonment of the human spirit, humor implies that the imprisonment is not final but will be overcome."[40]

A faithful humor escapes at once the cynicism of hopelessness and the utopianism of fancying that there can be perfection in this world. The underdogs, the fools, the jesters, the children keep dancing and singing and making jokes—over against all the incongruities and up against all the mysteries. There is no other ending. There is only an openness to the future.

Pardon me a moment; I have some serious work to do.

The substance of this chapter, together with parts of chapter 1, was presented as the First Maxwell Lecture in the Study and Teaching of the Holocaust, Oxford Centre for Postgraduate Hebrew Studies, 24 April 1990.

NOTES

1. Harvey Cox, *Religion in the Secular City: Toward a Postmodern Theology* (New York: Simon and Schuster, 1984), p. 209.
2. Hyers, *Comic Vision*, p. 18; Alter, "Jewish Humor," p. 35; Swabey, *Comic Laughter*, pp. 240–41.
3. Irving Kristol, "Is Jewish Humor Dead?," in *Mid-Century: An Anthology of Jewish Life and Culture in Our Time*, Harold U. Ribalow, ed. (New York: Beechurst, 1955), p. 436.
4. Hyers, *Comic Vision*, p. 31.
5. Niebuhr, "Humour and Faith," pp. 135, 145, 136–37, 146, 141, 142, 148–49. Niebuhr's essay originally appeared in his *Discerning the Signs of the Times* (New York: Scribner, 1946).
6. Hyers, *Comic Vision*, p. 31.
7. Knox, "Traditional Roots," pp. 159–60.
8. Blue, *To Heaven*, p. 78.
9. A. Roy Eckardt, *For Righteousness' Sake*, pp. 10, 112.
10. Greenberg, *Jewish Way*, pp. 254, 255.
11. Perhaps it is the suspicion that the knowers do not really exist that "can sum up the general state of mind that results from the comic revelation that society is fiction, magic, precariousness. The expertise of all the experts is painfully synthetic, whether they specialize in love or learning, power or . . . faith. Again we would contend that this attitude is not a one-sidedly oppressive one. It also has a liberating side. For while it is rather bad news to hear that the oracles are ghostwritten by nervous little men who copy from each other, there is also some comfort in this news. While it may undermine our civic confidence it may at the same time restore our trust in our own stature. If there are no oracles, there may be something to our own knowledge" (Berger, *Precarious Vision*, p. 84).
12. See Hyers, *Comic Vision*, pp. 15–17; Morreall, *Taking Laughter Seriously*, pp. 125ff.
13. Samuel, *World of Sholom Aleichem*, p. 212.
14. Elie Wiesel, *The Trial of God (as it was held on February 25, 1649 in Shamgorod)*, trans. Marion Wiesel (New York: Random House, 1979).
15. Eliezer Berkovits, "The Hiding God of History," in *The Catastrophe of European Jewry: Antecedents-History-Reflections*, Yisrael Gutman and Livia Rothkirchen, eds. (Jerusalem: Yad Vashem, 1976), p. 704.
16. Eckardt, *For Righteousness' Sake*, p. 317.

17. Wiesel, *Souls on Fire*, p. 107; Eckardt, *For Righteousness' Sake*, p. 321; Berkovits, "Hiding God of History," p. 704.
18. Greenberg, *Jewish Way*, p. 254.
19. Elie Wiesel, *The Gates of the Forest*, p. 196.
20. Abraham J. Heschel, *The Prophets*, vol. I (New York: Harper Colophon Books, 1969), p. 92.
21. Eckardt, *For Righteousness' Sake*, p. 323.
22. Ibid., pp. 10, 324 (slightly edited). The Heinz Moshe Graupe reference is to *The Rise of Modern Judaism: An Intellectual History of German Jewry 1650–1942*, trans. John Robinson (Huntington, N.Y.: Robert E. Krieger, 1978), p. 249.
23. Martin Grotjahn, as cited in Collins, "Joke as Healthy Aggression."
24. Emil L. Fackenheim, *What Is Judaism? An Interpretation for the Present Age* (New York: Summit Books, 1987), p. 291.
25. Elie Wiesel, *Twilight*, trans. Marion Wiesel (New York: Summit Books, 1988), p. 211; A. Roy Eckardt, *Reclaiming the Jesus of History: Christology Today* (Minneapolis: Fortress Press, 1991).
26. McCann, *Woody Allen*, p. 154.
27. Cf. Buechner, *Telling the Truth*, chap. 3, "The Gospel as Comedy."
28. Michael McGarry, "Emil Fackenheim and Christianity After the Holocaust," *American Journal of Theology & Philosophy* 9 (Jan.–May 1988): 131.
29. Hyers, *Comic Vision*, p. 52.
30. Robert E. Willis, "Christian Theology After Auschwitz," *Journal of Ecumenical Studies* 12 (1975): 506.
31. Eckardt, *For Righteousness' Sake*, p. 314; Wiesel, *Beggar in Jerusalem*, pp. 67–68.
32. For a compelling affirmation of a theocentric Christianity, consult Paul F. Knitter, *No Other Name? A Critical Survey of Christian Attitudes Toward the World Religions* (Maryknoll: Orbis, 1985).
33. Harvey Cox, *Many Mansions: A Christian's Encounter with Other Faiths* (Boston: Beacon, 1988), p. 16.
34. Hyers, *Comic Vision*, pp. 158–60, 163.
35. Berger, *Precarious Vision*, p. 213.
36. Buechner, *Telling the Truth*, p. 57. Cf. Buechner's later comment: "From the divine perspective, I suspect that it is the tragic that is seen as not inevitable whereas it is the comic that is bound to happen" (p. 72).
37. Berger, *Precarious Vision*, p. 209.
38. Alter, "Jewish Humor," p. 26.
39. Greenberg, *Jewish Way*, pp. 256–57.
40. Berger, *Precarious Vision*, pp. 213–14; Peter Berger, *A Rumor of Angels: Modern Sociology and the Rediscovery of the Supernatural* (Garden City: Doubleday, 1969), p. 90.

14

Other News from Wollenjoobyland

A. LESS THAN FINAL ESSAYS AND VERSE

SLEEP

Each day I, Mortimer Frackfand, am stabbed awake at 10 AM, following upon a twelve-hour stint in the twisting arms of Morpheus. Breakfast is a tasteless oat-bran nothing. No later than 10:30, I am back between the sheets, already worn out from the shock of (a) "another great new day" and of (b) chewing cold toast. Consequent to a paltry two-hour morning nap, I face the challenge of lunch and the consequent, crying necessity of an afternoon siesta (1:00–4:30 PM). Once again I am up and about, but now tearfully and uncontrollably, for this is my third rude awakening in less than seven hours. Small wonder that after a quick supper, I collapse in a much-needed evening snooze — yet only to have to endure the agony of staggering upstairs at ten in order to get a decent night's rest.

Few things are as exhausting as sleep.

TRAVEL-LOG

The village of Krjaacook-in-the-Mold has a population of 7,023 souls and exactly the same number of bodies.

It is true that a couple of the souls are nonsomatic. This is balanced out, however, by Roundtoit Squoll and Semint Alivy. Each of these men carries two bodies.

193

MORTAL PERIL

The Alcibiades, also known as the Dreaded Sporiopagi, was buzzing around my head. Suddenly he dove in, came out, and made off with the lobe of my middle ear.

TYRANNOSAURUS LINGUAE

Accents can be disconcerting.

English with a German accent
Charms listeners into compliance.

The Queen's English
Is only slightly less captivating.

The North American accent?
Who cares!

GOOD AND PLENTY

Wheatmefiremania?
Certainly.
All because of cornucopia.

TRAVELATION

Infahrt,
Ausfahrt,
The Agony
And the
Ecstasy.

THE VEGETABLE VENDOR

When Sistro Dalln Codvaas was a little boy he dreamed endlessly that one day it would be his vocation to sell vocados. But he never could find any, exactly why I don't know. So there was no way for him to realize his vocation. Following what seemed an eternity of unemployment, Sistro settled, at the age of fifty, for an avocation. He collects avocados.

EDUCATION AT OXFORD,
DISTILLED

> There's a pungent
> Old Scotch named
> Pignose–from–
> Wollage,
> Only obtain–
> Able at
> Brasenose–the–
> College.

WHAT IS GARBAGE?

I concede unreservedly that no garbage need be present in a fresh bottle of ketchup.

The trouble comes later.

Garbage may be defined as the residue that is left between the top of a container and the remainder of the contents. The greater that distance and the longer the time involved, the more powerful and revolting the garbage. Hence it was inevitable that the Wet Queen, Holy Protector of Garbage and Garbologists, should be the one to invent the elongated ketchup bottle. There was nothing phallic about this; it was and remains a strictly anal phenomenon. For only fourteen people in the history of the world have ever succeeded in getting the ketchup to come out.

Some authorities contend that the definition of garbage extends to wipings on one's napkin. It so happens that I am a member of this school. In fact, my own personal creed can be stated in ten words: One wipe of the napkin is enough to create garbage. This accounts for the fact that any napkin of mine quickly becomes a mashed ball. I am doing my best to hide the garbage and get away from it just as soon as I can.

This explains why long dinner parties are such an ordeal. They prevent any early escape from garbage.

ENJOY! ENJOY!

When last week at Grosshhjean's my waiter Enriquexx said to me "Enjoy your soup!" I sensed that disaster lay ahead.

You and I have been afflicted for years by waiters and waitresses urging us, "Enjoy your meal!" But at least they've been decent enough to call a halt at that abstract point. Now that the soup course has been singled out for special attention, I am certain there will be no stopping these conspirators of specificity. Salad, main course, vegetables, dessert, coffee — all these will surely go the way of the soup.

Indeed, a few days ago at Grosshhjean's I had expected the worst and the worst was not long in coming. I noticed that, upon bringing my soup and urging me to enjoy it, Enriquexx had not faded away but lingered on, hovering over me. Each time I raised spoon to mouth, he would reel off: "Enjoy that spoonful! Enjoy that spoonful!" Ad infinitum and ad nauseam. A few moments later I fancied I was seeing light at the bottom of the bowl, but Enriquexx was there ahead of me: "Enjoy that final spoonful!"

My dinner as a whole soon turned into a nightmare. Enriquexx scarcely had time to get out to the kitchen for the different courses, so obsessed had he become with his "Enjoy!"

I single out two episodes from amidst the overall terror.

Enriquexx asked, "Mr. Strennnd, you usually put 188 grains of salt upon your dinner, is it not so?"

"Of course not. I take my meals without a grain of salt."

"No problem! Enjoy that absent grain!"

Second, when the toothpicks were brought I felt a premonition of final doom. I did my best to spirit a toothpick to my teeth without Enriquexx seeing it but, alas, he was too quick for me: "Enjoy your toothpick!"

This was followed by Enriquexx's coup de grâce: "How dare you not inform me which end of the toothpick you are using!"

By this time I had been reduced to a blithering, helpless accomplice of Enriquexx's solicitude. I muttered: "The flat end."

"Eh, bien! Enjoy the flat end of your toothpick!"

What happened next remains a complete blur to me. Apparently, I had lunged straight for Enriquexx's throat, and Grosshhjean's is now advertising for a new waiter. Meanwhile, here at Bellevue they have untied my right arm so that I can eat my supper. I have just reached for the plastic soupspoon, and an orderly named Noescapio is bending over me with a solicitous leer: "Enjoy your soup!"

Yet life still has its blessings: Bellevue does not serve toothpicks.

PARTY INTRODUCTIONS

Aleck: Gerry, have you met Brian?
Gerry: No, I haven't.
Aleck: Tom, have you met Brian?
Tom: No, I haven't.
Aleck: Stu, have you met Brian?
Stu: No, I haven't.
Aleck: Harry, have you met Brian?
Harry: No, I haven't.
Aleck: I'm not surprised. We never did invite him.

TRANSUBSTAN–
TIA–
TION

An evil angel turned my
Studebaker into
Rutabaga, but
It soon spoiled and
Wouldn't start
(Short pause)
Up.

SWEET NEUTRALITY

The Chocolate Redeemer
Came from Switzerland.
All Gody.
"Take, eat, This is
My Body."

Quick! Call the Metamucil Man!

PRONUNCIATION LESSON

Take the word "issue"
(i.e., iss-sue;
or even ish-sue;
or even iss-shoo;
or even ish-shoo).

Promise never to say the word
Without supplying
The world with
All possibilities.

Your family
Will kill you,
Figuratively,
Of course.

What is the issue
(i.e., iss-sue;
or even ish-sue;
or even iss-shoo;
or even ish-shoo)
Here?

B. A PENULTIMATE WORD UPON THE WET-X-QUEEN

There can be no final word upon the Wet-X-Queen; she remains, as ever, beyond finality. But I do yearn to report to you — just who *are* you anyway? — that she and I are finally reconciled. That is to say, over the past thousand centuries now — or is it three fortnights? — I have jogged past her cell window on the Isle of Woman upon no less than 684,000 occasions (the exact number of times, you will recall, that the Wet-X-Queen had sought to go over to the Herzegovinians — minus 683,316), and I am ecstatic to tell you that she has not attacked me a single time, this despite the fact that, under the aegis of her ever-faithful Sir Reginald Damp-Saddle (this name has nothing to do with a damp saddle [except "Reginald," of course; literally, "soaking leather"]

but simply refers to his two inherited family names), repeated ship-
ments of the Wet-X-Queen's choice weapon, the Magnum-Bow, have
been smuggled onto the Island right into her prison compound. (Sorry,
I tried and tried, but there just seemed no way to keep that sentence
going any longer.)

The Wet-X-Queen had wangled a day off from prison. We two
were to meet in the Cyrenasianschloss Park, greatest of all parks on
the Isle of Woman. In our particular city of Wur we have many parks,
and an arch to go with each one—for example, Marble Cake, Cream
Puff, Fallen, and Heroes. However, befitting the occasion the two of
us would be reunited under the Arch Arch. After all, how many times
do X-Queen and Chief meet face to face?

Shortly after rising, the Wet-X-Queen had rushed over to the park
from her modest cell. She had had a quick bowl of cereal—not only
post toasties but also post haste—yet, naturally enough, no peanut
butter. She hadn't even stopped to brush her teedums-weedums-
whoodums-b'doddums, whereas right after breakfast I always brush
my teedums-weedums-whoodums-b'doddums. What do *you* do right
after breakfast? You don't brush your teedums-weedums-whoodums-
b'doddums? I am surprised at you.

It was a tender moment—not the Wet-X-Queen's failure to brush
her teedums-weedums-whoodums-b'doddums, nor my having brushed
my teedums-weedums-whoodums-b'doddums, nor for that matter your
own inability (refusal?) to brush your teedums-weedums-whoodums-
b'doddums, but instead the reunion of the Wet-X-Queen and me under
the Arch Arch.

I had been fully prepared to let bygones be bygones. The Wet-X-
Queen was ready to go a second mile and let byebyegones be
byebyegones. Or was she just oneupswomanshiping me?

I had come in order to be me. Wet-X (as I now intimately call her)
had come primarily to recite her poetry. I knew this would be a particularly trying test for our act of reconciliation, but I had ironed
myself for the task. Following upon a strangely perfunctory "Good
Morning," Wet-X started off with a piece called "The Fate of the Non-
Disabled":

> He is a Nobody —
> A Minister Without Portfolio.

But not because he once had polio.
No, his problem has always been
Scholiolioliolio.

Wet-X looked up at me, anxiously seeking my approval. True, a
tear had been brought to my eye. But the other eye was paying no
attention. Finding no evenly enthusiastic response, Wet-X blinked her
own top eyes (the two strongest and most penetrating of all her many
glims, as I at once vividly recalled from those dear, dead days not
beyond recall, in and around the Rewot fo Nodnol — or was it the
Nodnol fo Rewot?). And from within my right collarbone, even my
left one, I could feel a certain shock — quickly followed by an aftershock.
    She went on: "And now 'Compass Greetings.' I just adore it":

A Flappy Norther to a few,
A Yappy Souther to the rest.
A Sappy Wester to the yew,
A Happy Easter to the dressed.

Then, really warming to her Muse and without even a glance in my
direction, Wet-X let go with "On the Purification of Politics," her very
own favorite:

Do not
Stain.
Abstain.

There was no stopping her now. On and on she raved, until, having
given voice to another forty-three comparable gems, she finally collapsed in a heap at my athlete's feet, panting and exhausted.
    "Do you know something?" I finally blurted out. "You stink!"
    The Wet-X-Queen at once turned moody and withdrawn. At last,
she managed to pull herself erect, weary but resolute. For the first
time, I took the full measure of the woman, her seven feet eleven. I
am, at a minimum, eight feet one. So there could be a match here after
all — *habeas mabeas*. Then suddenly I was made to grasp the full measure of her soul as well:
    "Okay, so I'll never make it as a poet, even a prison poet! Chiefie,

you are right. Tell you what I'll do: I promise to keep you perpetually wet [I was staggered by the sheer grace of the woman, not to mention her sheer lace] if you'll only promise to meep my jet." (In the Friggostonchian tongue-and-tonsils — the linguine franci of the Isle of Woman — "meep" means, literally as well as figuratively, "to make available, though only for local flights.")

The poor, pitiful creature was asking very little actually; no more than an occasional release from the boredom of her 40 X 80 foot cell, complete with UHF, VCR, Muzak, and a thousand-meter deep heated pool (not for swimming, for inhaling).

And, most astonishing of all, instead of being angry at me, Wet-X now simply shrugged her massive shoulders, quietly folded her poems, and tucked them in her sprocket (Frigg. for pocket).

Of a sudden, everything was new and fresh and different. It had been a dull, gray morning, but all at once both of the Isle of Woman's suns broke through in the northern and southern skies, and the clouds fled. (The two suns had been among the byproducts of my seven-inch expansion of the Universe.)

Despite all her past enmity toward me — her trickery, her treasonableness, her reactionary policy respecting the size of the Universe, her cynical refusal to die, her invention of the ketchup bottle — and now her dreadful "poems," I find that I love the Wet-X-Queen. I freely concede that this is not unrelated to the fact that she remains, as always, soaking wet, thereby fulfilling bottomless (or maybe bottomful) urges that are also desperately mine. But I think it is mostly because of herself. She is, after all, my Lady, Wet or Dry. Somehow I am assured that she will never leave my bed and bed board — even though I imagine I'll always think of the Wet-X-Queen as one Big Wet Blanket.

15

Close Out

*It's remarkable how many people are
up and around.*
— James Thurber

To be human is to wish.
— Graham McCann

An old man is nothing but a little boy.
— Isaac Bashevis Singer

In the arena of both everyday life and academic life there is at
present burgeoning interest in the question of human laughter and
comedy. This is illustrated in the holding of international humor conferences.[1]

Perhaps I can bring together a few of the more salient points in
which my little contribution to this current interest has involved itself.
I will add in a few closing observations.

The alternating of chapters between sober analysis and funny business is what makes the book as a whole a contribution to humor, or
perhaps a series of jokes in and of itself, or even a single Joke as such.

In accordance with the assumption that the servant of comic laughter is one who tells of others while talking of himself (chapter 1), the
forms of humor I have especially represented and stressed are linked
to personal disposition.

Has the book come out where I intended? I am not certain how to
answer since from the beginning I have myself wondered where the

whole fabrication would go. Way back in the introduction I expressed doubt whether my effort could realize a definite purpose. Much of the problem of these pages has been to try to make clear to myself, as to the reader, or at least to work with, laughter's place or places in human life. I have learned that it is not easy to do this. A difference remains between what humor *is* (hard to fathom) and what humor *does* (not as hard to fathom). Humor does all sorts of things.

On the other hand, it appears safe to say that comedy remains (along with tragedy) a commentary upon humankind's finitude — upon, in existentialist language, the human condition of "thrownness." "If this is so, then the comic is an objective dimension of man's reality, not just a subjective or psychological reaction to that reality."[2]

One obvious conclusion from our journey together is the great pluralism in interpretations of humor, comedy, and laughter, and indeed in humor, comedy, and laughter in themselves. The interpreters are legion and the phenomena are legion. The conclusions we may tender in our study of humor are numerous and not always easily reconciled. Much depends upon the *situation* involved: the identity of joke-makers, the identity of their audiences, the motivations behind the humor, and the functions that particular instances of humor perform or are supposed to perform.

It does seem to me that the body of Proto-Jokes I suggest in chapter 1 may provide a broader and deeper objective foundation for a working interpretation of humor than would a more restricted understanding of such a foundation. Of course, should these Proto-Jokes be rejected or abandoned as a proper basis of humor and of the study of humor, the broadening and the deepening either would not take place or would have to build from a different foundation. But since it remains a fact, if a truism, that we have nothing to say about our birth into this world (Proto-Joke Three), how convincing would it be to object to our treating things as, in principle, comic? I think the objection would be no more convincing than to object to our treating things as, in principle, tragic. Whatever is, is serious; whatever is, is comical. Although evil is a perversion of good, humor is not a perversion of seriousness but is instead its completion — just as seriousness is a completion of humor.

The personhood of humor discloses itself in the incongruous, the ludicrous, the unexpected, the incommensurate, the unforeseeable, the judging, the celebrative, the juxtapositional, the defiant, the comforting. And yet humor also succeeds in hiding itself within these very same conditions. I still think, accordingly, that laughter is more a question than an answer, more a mystery than anything else. Our world keeps close watch over its many secrets. Since the same generalization of mystery seems to hold for humankind itself, laughter may be viewed as an integral facet or special case of the mystery of humankind. "Human knowledge is a little island in a great ocean of nonknowledge" (Isaac Bashevis Singer). We do not know why human beings laugh — unless it may be said that they were made to laugh and therefore that, in a sense, they all share Itzhak as *Stammvater* and namesake. Laughter keeps us from ever wholly betraying our youth, indeed our childhood.

A most serious, ongoing perplexity centers in what humor can succeed in doing and what it must only fail to do.

Good humor does not harm other people. Thus, sexism and racism in humor is humor gone bad. However, the method by which humor helps people is often by judging them (at least indirectly) for their acts of injustice, their failures to love. Yet humor can never substitute for needed social and political action; when it tries to do so it deteriorates into ideology, in the negative and destructive sense of that form of ideational praxis. As Reinhold Niebuhr puts it, laughter alone never destroys the tyrannies of power.[3] The instrumentalities of humor may serve to sweeten social, cultural, and political life but they are powerless at the point of concrete moral policy. At the latter place, only political action, that is, action involving power and counterpower, can suffice: the ballot, demonstrations, legislative reform, the disposition of wealth, the responsible utilization of police and military force, and so on.

That still today the humor business remains on balance a male monopoly itself testifies to the inability of humor to redeem life. Think of our double standard. The female comedian Pudgy points out that "a male comedian can use four-letter words and be effective. A woman comedian cannot." However, it may well be that women do not *need* humor the way men do, especially in humor's more gross forms. Jonathan Miller writes: "Men don't get on well with each other, they don't have standards of intimacy, so they exchange jokes. There is something about women's minds that means they establish a level of intimacy much more rapidly, without having to go through ritualized conduct. [Women] belong to an oppressed minority and the thing about oppressed minorities is they share the same dilemma." One of the engaging things about women's minds is "they don't seem to require those awful machismo displays of goodwill, good humour, and good chappery."[4]

One healthy recent development is Garrison Keillor's humor of compassion, wherein many women pass before us, all kinds of women, not just women of a single type.[5]

Some of my own contributions to the humor of the present book reflect my participation in injustice; for example, my verse on hauling wood (chapter 4) may be reacted to as hurtful to the millions of people who lack any means to keep themselves warm. Yet comedy is not without its own morality and forms of power. "Real comedy can't be learned; it comes from a need for justice" (Elayne Boosler). Humor can act to make life a mite more just. It blows fresh breezes of consolation and delight. Maurice Charney sees comedy as an effort to master anxiety, and laughter as a defense against the catastrophes that are coming.[6] For James Thurber, humor, like the imagination, is "one of the necessary accessories of fortitude."[7] Therefore, we do not repudiate humor. Because laughter is somehow already there, before we come to it, we are permitted to join up with it and to laugh ourselves: this is the marvelous thing. "Humor bespeaks a sad acceptance of our weakness and frustration. But laughter also means freedom. You must feel free to laugh" (Martin Grotjahn).[8] As Sigmund Freud testifies, humor is a nonvindictive liberation from the wounds of life. In its repudiation of suffering, human laughter is to be numbered amongst the great and historic foes of wrong and anguish.[9] Again, "in laughter we transcend . . . ourselves and our circumstances. We transcend disappointment and suffering. We transcend the jumbled contradictions of our lives. We transcend even the self-imposed requirement that life always make sense, conform to a plan, work out, give us our due, or be equitable and just" (Conrad Hyers).[10]

Laughter is also a gentle yet potent block against idolatry, the ultimate sin. For to laugh at our many idols is to be helped in the quest to journey beyond idolatry. The rutted road of laughter is strewn with demolished gods.

The other side of the coin is just as readable: Laughter's strength in helping us transcend ourselves and our circumstances is a limited one.

It can remove neither disappointment nor suffering nor life's contradictions. How could there ever be salvation in laughter? Humor is not a final solvent of anything. At best, it eases the pain somewhat. Indeed, "they say" that the great comedians, the truly comical ones, are at heart sad people.[11] Joan Rivers speaks of herself as a "walking wound," and acknowledges that her routines "come out of total unhappiness."[12]

Sometimes "they [even] say" that God herself has bouts of sadness, of depression:

> You shall tell them this word:
> "Let my eyes run down with tears night and day,
>   and let them not cease,
> for the virgin daughter of my people
>   is smitten with a great wound,
> with a very grievous blow. . . ." (Jer. 14:17)

Nevertheless: Within the reaches of comedy something *begins* to take shape that just may end in triumph. The children of comedy are the victors, or they will be. Isaac will laugh. From the standpoint of the fate of Everyperson, comedy falls victim to tragedy in the sense of sorrow. Yet it is not impossible that tragedy will finally be taken prisoner by comedy. The human comedy, which appears as no more than a pitiable protest or transitory reflex, may at last be vindicated by the divine comedy. Here and now we are empowered to sit in the earth and laugh because the One who sits in the heavens laughs and will laugh — not, ultimately, against us but with us and for us.

This is a very good world, this is a very bad world; comic laughter has been taught through hard experience these antinomic marks of human fortune. To the goodness, humor responds with celebration; to the badness, humor responds with protest and consolation. To celebrate and to console, to be a child and to be an old person, to be the old person in the child and the child in the old person — here is the redeeming road along which the comic travels. Here is told the life story of laughter.

The Little Boy and the Old Man

Said the little boy, "Sometimes I drop my spoon."
Said the little old man, "I do that too."
The little boy whispered, "I wet my pants."
"I do that too," laughed the little old man.
Said the little boy, "I often cry."
The old man nodded, "So do I."
"But worst of all," said the boy, "it seems
Grown-ups don't pay attention to me."
And he felt the warmth of a wrinkled old hand.
"I know what you mean," said the little old man.[13]

NOTES

1. The eighth such international humor conference took place at Sheffield, England in July/August 1990.
2. Peter Berger, *A Rumor of Angels: Modern Sociology and the Rediscovery of the Supernatural* (Garden City: Doubleday, 1969), p. 90.
3. Niebuhr, "Humour and Faith," p. 138.
4. Jonathan Miller, as cited in Heather Kirby, "Seriously, humour is no joke," *The Times* (London) (21 March 1990).
5. See Garrison Keillor's books: *Lake Wobegon Days; Leaving Home; We Are Still Married.*
6. Maurice Charney, "Stanley Elkin and Jewish Black Humor," in *Jewish Wry,* Sarah Blacher Cohen, ed., p. 194.
7. Thurber, *Collecting Himself,* p. 220.
8. Grotjahn, as cited in Collins, "The Joke as Healthy Aggression."
9. Freud, "Humor," p. 113.
10. Hyers, *Comic Vision,* pp. 58–59.
11. Woody Allen "convinces us that there is more to his anxiety than a bundle of neuroses — that he truly suffers from the terrifying silence of the universe" (Barbara and Leonard Quart, "Woody's Quest," *Midstream* 28 [Jan. 1982]: 49). Barry Took speaks of many comedians as, in their private lives, "monsters of selfishness and ingratitude." If this is so, they redeem us in spite of themselves. Cf. James Thurber: "The closest thing to humor is tragedy" (*Collecting Himself,* p. 217). E. B. White alters the terms of the question: There is some truth in the claim that humorists are very sad people, but the truth "is badly stated. It would be more accurate, I think, to say that there is a deep vein of melancholy running through everyone's life and that the humorist, perhaps more sensible of it than some others, compensates for it actively and positively. Humorists fatten on trouble" (*Second Tree from the Corner,* pp. 173–74).
12. Joan Rivers, in "Next Time, Dear God."
13. Shel Silverstein, *A Light in the Attic.*

For Further Reading

The nonexhaustive listing to follow mirrors several elements of choice: pertinence to this handbook, serendipity, personal predilection, social appeal or significance, scholarly notability, recent vintage (save for a few classics), and a dash of arbitrariness. Asterisked items are particularly germane to this study. One book alone is marked with two asterisks; I shan't say which it is, so that you can locate it for yourself. Two asterisks are the equivalent of a six-star hotel.

Adams, Cecil. *The Straight Dope: A Compendium of Human Knowledge*. Chicago: Chicago Review Press, 1984.

*Aichele, George, Jr. *Theology as Comedy: Critical and Theoretical Implications*. Lanham, Md.: University Press of America, 1980.

Allen, Fred. *Fred Allen's Letters*, ed. Joe McCarthy. New York: Pocket Books, 1966.

*Allen, Steve. *Mark It and Strike It: An Autobiography*. New York: Holt, Rinehart and Winston, 1960.

*Allen, Woody. *Getting Even*. New York: Warner Books, 1972.

*————. *Side Effects*. New York: Ballantine Books, 1981.

*————. *Without Feathers*. London: Sphere Books, 1978.

Apte, Mahadev. *Humor and Laughter: An Anthropological Approach*. Ithaca: Cornell University Press, 1985.

*Ausubel, Nathan. *A Treasury of Jewish Folklore*. New York: Crown, 1948.

*————. *A Treasury of Jewish Humor*. New York: Doubleday, 1967.

Avner, Ziv, ed. *Jewish Humor*. Tel Aviv: Papyrus Publishing House, 1986.

Barnes, Julian. *A History of the World in $10^1/_2$ Chapters*. London: Jonathan Cape, 1989.

Barson, Michael, ed. *Flywheel, Shyster, and Flywheel: The Marx Brothers' Lost Radio Show*. New York: Pantheon Books, 1988.

Benny, Mary Livingstone. *Jack Benny*. New York: Doubleday, 1978.

*Berger, Peter L. *The Precarious Vision: A Sociologist Looks at Social Fictions and Christian Faith*. Garden City: Doubleday, 1961.

*Bermant, Chaim. *What's the Joke? A Study of Jewish Humor Through the Ages*. London: Weidenfeld and Nicolson, 1986.

Bierce, Ambrose. *The Devil's Dictionary*. New York: Dover Publications, 1958.

*Bombeck, Erma. *I Want to Grow Hair, I Want to Grow Up, I Want to go to Boise: Children Surviving Cancer*. New York: Harper & Row, 1989.

Bryson, Bill. *The Lost Continent: Travels in Small Town America*. London: Secker & Warburg, 1989.

*Buechner, Frederick. *Telling the Truth: The Gospel as Tragedy, Comedy, and Fairy Tale*. San Francisco: Harper & Row, 1977.

Caesar, Sid, and Bill Davidson. *Where Have I Been? An Autobiography*. New York: Crown, 1982.

Campbell, Joseph. *The Hero With a Thousand Faces*. New York: Meridian Books, 1956.

*Carr, Maurice, ed. *Waiter There (is) a Fly in my Orange Juice*. Jerusalem: Shikmona Pub. Co., 1975.

*Carroll, Lewis. *Through the Looking-Glass and What Alice Found There*. Philadelphia: J. B. Lippincott, 1929.

Chapman, A. J., and H. C. Foot, eds. *It's a Funny Thing, Humour*. Oxford: Pergamon Press, 1977.

*Cohen, John, ed. *The Essential Lenny Bruce*. New York: Ballantine Books, 1968.

Cohen, Sarah Blacher, ed. *Comic Relief: Humor in Contemporary American Literature*. Urbana: University of Illinois Press, 1978.

————, ed. *From Hester Street to Hollywood: The Jewish-American Stage and Screen*. Bloomington: Indiana University Press, 1983.

*————, ed. *Jewish Wry: Essays on Jewish Humor*. Bloomington: Indiana University Press, 1987.

Coren, Alan, ed. *The Penguin Book of Modern Humour*. London: Penguin Books, 1983.

————. *Seems Like Old Times: A Year in the Life of Alan Coren*. London: Robson Books, 1989.

*Cox, Harvey. *The Feast of Fools: A Theological Essay on Festivity and Fantasy*. Cambridge: Harvard University Press, 1969.

Cuppy, Will. *The Decline and Fall of Practically Everybody.* Boston: David R. Godine, 1984.

*Davies, Christie. *Ethnic Humor Around the World: A Comparative Analysis.* Bloomington: Indiana University Press, 1990.

Doran, Amanda-Jane, ed. *The Punch Book of Utterly British Humour.* London: Grafton Books, 1989.

Dudden, Arthur Power, ed. *American Humor.* New York: Oxford University Press, 1987.

Durant, J., and C. J. Miller, eds. *Laughing Matters: A Serious Look at Humor.* New York: John Wiley, 1988.

*Eckardt, A. Roy. *For Righteousness' Sake: Contemporary Moral Philosophies.* Bloomington: Indiana University Press, 1987.

Edmunds, Lowell. *The Silver Bullet: The Martini in American Civilization.* Westport, Conn.: Greenwood Press, 1981.

Eliach, Yaffa. *Hasidic Tales of the Holocaust.* New York: Avon Books, 1982.

Eliot, T. S. *The Illustrated Old Possum: Old Possum's Book of Practical Cats.* London: Faber and Faber, 1974.

Ellenbogen, Glenn C., ed. *The Directory of Humor Magazines and Humor Organizations in America and Canada.* 2nd edition. New York: Wry-Bred Press, 1988.

Elliott, Bob, and Ray Goulding. *From Approximately Coast to Coast . . . It's the Bob and Ray Show.* New York: Atheneum, 1983.

————. *The New! Improved! Bob & Ray Book.* New York: McGraw-Hill, 1985.

Fowler, Douglas. *S. J. Perelman.* Boston: Twayne, 1983.

*Freud, Sigmund, "Humor," in *The Philosophy of Laughter and Humor,* John Morreall, ed. (q.v.).

*————. *Jokes and Their Relation to the Unconscious,* trans. James Strachey. New York: Norton, 1960.

Fulghum, Robert. *It Was on Fire When I Lay Down on It.* New York: Villard Books, 1989.

God: the Ultimate Autobiography. London: Pan Books, 1988.

Goldman, Albert. *Ladies and Gentlemen—Lenny Bruce!* New York: Random House, 1974.

*Greenberg, Irving. *The Jewish Way: Living the Holidays.* New York: Summit Books, 1988.

Guinness, Alec. *Blessings in Disguise.* New York: Warner Books, 1985.

*Gurewitch, Morton. *Comedy: The Irrational Vision.* Ithaca: Cornell University Press, 1975.

Hall, Rich. *Unexplained Singlets of the Universe.* New York: Collier Books, 1986.

Hein, Piet. *Grooks.* Cambridge: MIT Press, 1966.

*Hirsch, Foster. *Love, Sex, Death, and the Meaning of Life: Woody Allen's Comedy.* New York: McGraw-Hill, 1981.

Holland, N. N. *Laughing: A Psychology of Humor.* Ithaca: Cornell University Press, 1982.

Howe, Irving, and Eliezer Greenberg, eds. *A Treasury of Yiddish Stories.* New York: Schocken Books, 1973.

Huizinga, Johan. *Homo Ludens: A Study of the Play Element in Culture.* Boston: Beacon Press, 1950.

Hyers, Conrad. *And God Created Laughter: The Bible as Divine Comedy.* Atlanta: John Knox Press, 1987.

*———. *The Comic Vision and the Christian Faith.* New York: Pilgrim Press, 1981.

*———, ed. *Holy Laughter.* New York: Seabury Press, 1969.

———. *Zen and the Comic Spirit.* Philadelphia: Westminster, 1974.

Iskander, Fazil. *The Gospel According to Chegem,* trans. Susan Brownsberger. New York: Vintage Books, 1984.

Jónsson, Jakob. *Humour and Irony in the New Testament: Illuminated by Parallels in Talmud and Midrash.* Reykjavík: Bókaútgáfa Menningarsjóds, 1965.

Keillor, Garrison. *Lake Wobegon Days.* New York: Viking, 1985.

———. *Leaving Home.* New York: Penguin Books, 1987.

*———. *We Are Still Married: Stories & Letters.* New York: Viking, 1989.

Keller, Charles, compiler. *Laughing.* Englewood Cliffs, N.J.: Prentice-Hall, 1977.

Kishon, Ephraim. *New York Ain't America.* New York: Bantam Books, 1982.

Kundera, Milan. *The Book of Laughter and Forgetting,* trans. Michael Henry Heim. New York: Penguin Books, 1981.

*Lear, Edward. *The Nonsense Books of Edward Lear.* New York: New American Library, 1964.

Lebowitz, Fran. *Social Studies.* New York: Pocket Books, 1982.

Legman, G. *The Limerick: 1700 Examples, with Notes, Variants and Index.* New York: Bell Publishing Company, 1964.

Lewis, C. S. *The Screwtape Letters.* Glasgow: Collins, 1977.

Liben, Meyer. *New York Street Games and Other Stories and Sketches.* New York: Schocken Books, 1984.

Lukes, Steven, and Itzhak Galnoor. *No Laughing Matter: A Collection of Political Jokes.* London: Penguin, 1987.

*McCann, Graham. *Woody Allen: New Yorker.* Cambridge: Polity Press/ Basil Blackwell, 1990.

Maccoby, Hyam, ed. and trans. *The Day God Laughed: Sayings, Fables, and Entertainments of the Jewish Sages.* New York: St. Martin's Press, 1979.

*McKnight, Gerald. *Woody Allen: Joking Aside.* New York: W. H. Allen, 1983.

Manguel, Alberto, and Gianni Guadalupi. *The Dictionary of Imaginary Places,* expanded edition. San Diego: Harcourt Brace Jovanovich, 1987.

Markfield, Wallace. *You Could Live If They'd Let You.* New York: Knopf, 1974.

*Marx, Groucho. *Groucho and Me.* New York: Woodhill Press, 1978.

*————. *Memoirs of a Mangy Lover.* New York: Woodhill Press, 1978.

*Marx, Groucho, and Richard J. Anobile. *The Marx Brothers Scrapbook.* London: W. H. Allen, 1976.

Metz, Johan Baptist, and Jean-Pierre Jossua, eds. *Fundamental Theology: "You have sorrow now, but your hearts will rejoice."* London: Concilium, 1974.

*Milne, A. A. *Winnie-the-Pooh.* New York: E. P. Dutton, 1950.

*Morreall, John, ed. *The Philosophy of Laughter and Humor.* Albany: State University of New York Press, 1987.

*————. *Taking Laughter Seriously.* Albany: State University of New York Press, 1983.

*Muir, Frank, ed. *The Oxford Book of Humorous Prose: William Caxton to P. G. Wodehouse.* Oxford: Oxford University Press, 1990.

*Nash, Ogden. *The Ogden Nash Pocket Book,* intro. Louis Untermeyer. New York: Pocket Books, 1944.

Novak, Michael. *The Joy of Sports: End Zones, Bases, Baskets, Balls and the Consecration of the American Spirit.* Lanham, Md.: University Press of America, 1988.

*Novak, William, and Moshe Waldoks, eds. *The Big Book of Jewish Humor.* New York: Harper & Row, 1981.

Oring, Elliott. *Israeli Humor and Its Oral Tradition.* Albany: State University of New York Press, 1981.

*———. *The Jokes of Sigmund Freud: A Study in Humor and Jewish Identity.* Philadelphia: University of Pennsylvania Press, 1984.

O'Sullivan, Sean, ed. and trans. *Folk Tales of Ireland.* Chicago: University of Chicago Press, 1968.

*Palmer, Miles. *Woody Allen: An Illustrated Biography.* New York: Scribner, 1980.

*Perelman, S. J. *The Best of S. J. Perelman.* New York: Modern Library, 1947.

*———. *The Most of S. J. Perelman.* New York: Simon and Schuster, 1963.

Polhemus, Robert M. *Comic Faith: The Great Tradition from Austen to Joyce.* Chicago: University of Chicago Press, 1981.

*Pollack, Pamela. *The Random House Book of Humor for Children.* New York: Random House, 1988.

*Richler, Mordecai, ed. *The Best of Modern Humour.* London: Penguin Books, 1984.

Rivers, Joan. *The Life and Times of Heidi Abromowitz.* New York: Delacorte, 1984.

Rogers, Will. *The Autobiography of Will Rogers,* ed. Donald Day. Boston: Houghton Mifflin, 1949.

*Rosten, Leo. *Leo Rosten's Giant Book of Laughter.* New York: Bonanza Books, 1989.

*Rosten, Norman. *Neighborhood Tales.* New York: George Braziller, 1986.

*Samuel, Maurice. *The World of Sholom Aleichem.* New York: Schocken Books, 1965.

Satan: The Hiss and Tell Memoirs. London: Pan Books, 1989.

Sayward, John. *Perfect Fools: Folly for Christ's Sake in Catholic and Orthodox Spirituality.* New York: Oxford University Press, 1980.

Shulman, Abraham. *Adventures of a Yiddish Lecturer.* New York: Pilgrim Press, 1980.

*Silverstein, Shel. *A Light in the Attic.* New York: Harper & Row, 1981.

*———. *Where the Sidewalk Ends.* New York: Harper & Row, 1974.

*Smith, R. L. *The Stars of Stand-Up Comedy: A Biographical Encyclopedia.* New York-London: Garland, 1986.

*Spalding, Henry E., comp. and ed. *Encyclopedia of Jewish Humor:*

From Biblical Times to the Modern Age. New York: Jonathan David, 1969.

*Swabey, Marie Collins. *Comic Laughter: A Philosophical Essay.* Hamden, Conn.: Archon Books, 1970.

Thurber, James. *Selected Letters of James Thurber,* ed. Helen Thurber and Edward Weeks. Oxford: Oxford University Press, 1990.

————. *The Beast in Me and Other Animals,* abridged. New York: Avon Books, 1948.

*————. *Collecting Himself: James Thurber on Writing and Writers, Humor and Himself,* ed. Michael J. Rosen. London: Hamish Hamilton, 1989.

*Took, Barry. *Comedy Greats: A Celebration of Comic Genius Past and Present.* Wellingborough, Northamptonshire: Thorsons Publishing Group, 1989.

Via, Dan O., Jr. *Kerygma and Comedy in the New Testament.* Philadelphia: Fortress, 1975.

Walmsley, Jane. *Brit-Think, Ameri-Think,* rev. ed. New York: Viking Penguin, 1987.

**White, E. B. *The Second Tree from the Corner.* New York: Harper & Row Perennial Library, 1989.

*Wiesel, Elie. *A Beggar in Jerusalem,* trans. Lily Edelman and author. New York: Random House, 1970.

*————. *Four Hasidic Masters and Their Struggle against Melancholy.* Notre Dame: University of Notre Dame Press, 1978.

*————. *The Gates of the Forest,* trans. Frances Frenage. New York: Avon Books, 1967.

*————. *Messengers of God: Biblical Portraits and Legends,* trans. Marion Wiesel. New York: Random House, 1976.

*————. *Souls on Fire: Portraits and Legends of Hasidic Masters,* trans. Marion Wiesel. New York: Random House, 1972.

*————. *The Testament,* trans. Marion Wiesel. New York: Summit Books, 1981.

Wilde, Larry. *More of The Official Jewish/Irish Joke Book.* New York: Pinnacle Books, 1979.

————. *The Official Jewish/Irish Joke Book.* New York: Pinnacle Books, 1974.

Willimon, William W., compiler. *And the Laugh Shall Be First: A Treasury of Religious Humor.* Nashville: Abingdon, 1986.

————. compiler. *Last Laugh*. Nashville: Abingdon, 1991.

Wilmut, Roger. *From Fringe to Flying Circus*. London: Methuen, 1980.

*Wolfenstein, Martha. *Children's Humor*. Glencoe: Free Press, 1954.

*Yacowar, Maurice. *The Comic Art of Mel Brooks*. New York: St. Martin's Press, 1981.

*————. *Loser Take All: The Comic Art of Woody Allen*. New York: Ungar, 1979.

Zangwill, Israel. *The King of Schnorrers*. New York: Dover Publications, 1965.

Ziv, Avner, ed. *National Styles of Humor*. New York: Greenwood Press, 1988.

Index

India's Persistent Dilemma

India's Persistent Dilemma

The Political Economy of Agrarian Reform

F. Tomasson Jannuzi

Westview Press

BOULDER • SAN FRANCISCO • OXFORD

Copyright © 1994 by Westview Press, Inc.

Published in 1994 in the United States of America by Westview Press, Inc., 5500 Central Avenue, Boulder, Colorado 80301-2877, and in the United Kingdom by Westview Press, 36 Lonsdale Road, Summertown, Oxford OX2 7EW

Library of Congress Cataloging-in-Publication Data
Jannuzi, F. Tomasson, 1934–
  India's persistent dilemma : the political economy of agrarian
reform / F. Tomasson Jannuzi.
    p.   cm.
  Includes bibliographical references and index.
  ISBN 0-8133-8835-X
  1. Land reform—India.   I. Title.
HD1333.I4J36   1994
333.3'154—dc20
                                                             94-538
                                                             CIP

Printed and bound in the United States of America

The paper used in this publication meets the requirements
⊗ of the American National Standard for Permanence of Paper
for Printed Library Materials Z39.48-1984.

10   9   8   7   6   5   4   3   2   1

For
Surendra Mohan
my friend and brother

Contents

Preface

The Government of India in 1950 established within the context of the Directive Principles of State Policy in *The Constitution of India* a grand vision of socioeconomic change and a commitment to promote the general welfare of the mass of the people. Those who then constituted the Government of India following independence promised to promote the general welfare of the mass of the people, including the weakest and poorest sections of the citizenry in rural areas. This promise was to be fulfilled by means of state-led policies and programs designed to transform India's political economy. The promise was to ensure that the ownership and control of material resources were distributed in a fashion likely to contribute to the well-being of all citizens, providing thereby the basis for a new social order in which justice -- social, economic and political -- would be infused in the institutions of the new republic. It was intrinsic within the frame of the Directive Principles of State Policy that India's economic development agenda would require a commitment from those who governed to promote simultaneously both economic growth and social justice. Moreover, because the great majority of the people lived and worked in the agrarian sector of the economy -- a sector characterized by gross inequalities in the distribution of income, economic assets (notably land) and political power -- it was also intrinsic within the frame of the Directive Principles that the Government of India would undertake to promote the establishment of an economic system characterized by the empowerment of the people and, where necessary, by the redistribution of economic assets so as to limit sharply "the concentration of wealth and means of production to the common detriment."[1] Agrarian reform, defined amorphously and variously by those who governed, was to become a principal means by which the commitments of the Directive Principles were to be made tangible in rural India.

---

1. India, Ministry of Law, *The Constitution of India,* As modified up to the 1st May 1965, (Delhi: Manager of Publications, 1965), Part IV, Directive Principles of State Policy, p. 25.

Unfortunately, the Government of India has been unable to design, implement or promote the policies and programs of agrarian reform necessary to the fulfillment of its own articulated commitment to transform the political economy of rural India so as to ensure an improved distribution of economic assets, an improved environment for entrepreneurial opportunity for small farmers and an improved socioeconomic context where peoples' rights and opportunities are not constrained economically and politically within what I have elsewhere called "the traditional hierarchy of interests in land."

This book is an account of the failure of the Government of India to establish a coherent national program for agrarian reform in modern India -- a program, if implemented, that might have enabled India to emerge out of the shadow of British colonialism after 1947 to establish a new political economy based on new principles of public policy and democratic governance. It exposes the views on agrarian reform (and land reform) among those in India who, following independence, shaped public policy and proclaimed commitment in documents of state to the transformation of India's political economy to ensure that there would be created in time a new social order based not only on political freedom but also on economic justice. This new social order, suggested those who governed, would be designed to affect the well-being of the mass of the people in rural areas and would result from systemic changes in historical land systems. Such systemic changes would transform the conditions of production and distribution in rural India, helping thereby to ensure that the attainment of political freedom would not be an end in itself -- devoid of economic substance for the mass of the people.

This work is, also, an account of the failure of those who governed to translate pre-independence visions of agrarian reform and land reform into implementable post-independence programs capable of producing a more productive and just political economy. It shows how various post-independence visions of agrarian reform and rural economic development in India were conditioned by British colonial legacies (both legal and procedural), were articulated by Indians and others and then were either transformed, diluted and denied or, in some instances, slavishly adhered to in the period since India gained political freedom.

However, this book does not tell a story of venal leaders who sought consciously either to dismiss visions of a new political economy or to subvert plans for socioeconomic transformation of the Indian countryside. Neither is it the story of a conspiracy -- capitalist, socialist or some other -- to deny to the "tillers of the soil" in India their opportunity to live more secure and productive lives. It is, instead, a record of failure derived from a process, for the most part open and democratic, by which some people sought to introduce change in the political economy of rural India while others opposed change. It is the story of the mediation of opposing views by those who governed -- producing new visions and definitions of agrarian reform that ultimately would please neither those pressing for radical transformation of existing agrarian structures nor those who would have preferred no change at all in those structures. It is an account of a failure derived from a political process that, on the one hand, guaranteed India's landholding elites strong and continuous representation in the shaping of such agrarian reforms as were legislated and partially implemented, and, on the other, gave no meaningful voice to the people in the countryside who were to be the beneficiaries of agrarian reform: gave them no systematic means of ensuring that such reforms as were envisioned and enacted into law by the powerful would be designed to meet their needs, the needs of the powerless.

As a result of the Government of India's failure and the failure of most Indian states to enact into law and implement agrarian reform measures designed to transform its historic land systems so as to confer new rights and economic opportunities on actual cultivators, India now faces an uncertain future. India's existing political economy is one that denies generally its rural majority the socioeconomic changes long ago promised by India's Founding Fathers and made explicit in the Directive Principles. The existing political economy in rural India is shaped mainly, as it was prior to independence, by the interests of a minority of landholders whose political and economic power are derived from secure rights in land. This political economy works to deny both the socioeconomic changes promised by India's Founding Fathers and to thwart the needs and interests of the rural majority who lack secure rights in land. Such a political economy, where the economic power of a minority is used to deny the interests of a majority, cannot long persist in a society committed to democratic principles of governance -- a society within which even the weakest sections of the peasantry increasingly confirm by their daily behavior and their participation in general elections that they are capable of giving expression to their needs. In the days ahead, the functional meaning of India's democratic society will be tested as the people at the base of her agrarian economy gain in their ability, both within and outside of the institutionalized political process, to press for change in existing conditions.

F. Tomasson Jannuzi

Acknowledgments

The ideas that inform this work have been in gestation for many years. They have been shaped by experience and field work in India since the 1950s, as well as by my teaching and research in the fields of South Asian Studies and economics at The University of Texas at Austin and, since 1986, at The University of Oxford in the United Kingdom. I want to thank The Ford Foundation, New York, for supporting my initial field work in India in the 1950s and my more recent work in India and in the United Kingdom beginning in 1989.

I am particularly indebted to Roger Louis and Prosser Gifford, the organizers of a series of international conferences on the theme "India: the First Decade" -- conferences held in India in January of 1990, in Oxford in June of 1990 and at The University of Texas at Austin in the Fall of 1990. The theme of this book grew out of a paper that I presented at those conferences and my interactions with conference participants, most particularly S. Gopal, Upendra Baxi and Robert Frykenberg.

The production of this work has been facilitated by numerous persons in India, in the United Kingdom and the United States, not all of whom can be mentioned here. I want to recognize the support I have received from Ravinder Kumar, Director of the Nehru Museum and Library, New Delhi, who accorded me access as a visiting scholar to that library's resources in the Spring of 1989 when I was on sabbatical leave to carry out research in India. I want to thank Robert Cassen, Director of the International Development Centre, The University of Oxford, for ensuring that I had affiliated status, periodically in recent years, as a Fellow of the International Development Centre.

Within India, with respect to the content of this book, I must thank Tarlok Singh for his friendship and patient answering of all my questions, even those imbedded with implicit criticism of his own way of conceptualizing agrarian reform during his days in the Planning Commission. I would like to recognize also the contribution to my work in India in 1989 of Amit Kumar Gupta, at that time a Fellow of the Nehru Museum and Library, whose insights concerning peasant agitations in East India in the pre-independence period helped to shape my thought and writing on that theme.

The book's perspective and whatever insights I have derived from a virtual lifetime of work in Indian Studies owe most to two persons, separated in time and context: the late Vera Anstey of the London School of Economics, who set me on course, and Surendra Mohan, my mentor and friend in India.

Finally, in the production of this work, the probing questions of my wife, Barbara Gallagher Jannuzi, and our endless discussion of relevant themes have been fundamental to the whole creative process.

F.T.J.

1

Pre-Independence Visions
of Agrarian Reform
and Rural Development

The Colonial Impact of the British

A Constrained Definition of
Rural Economic Development

From the days of the East India Company in the eighteenth century, the agrarian policy of the British in India was not focused mainly on transforming traditional agriculture. In some areas of India, some investments in irrigation were made by the East India Company early in the nineteenth century and more substantial investments in irrigation were made by the government after 1866.[1] These investments were of obvious importance to agricultural production. However, these investments were regionally delimited and cannot be considered, by

---

1. The record shows that the East India Company took steps early in the nineteenth century to repair the Ganges and Jumma Canals and the Grand Anicut on the Cauvery River. And, as Vera Anstey has observed, "A new impetus to Government construction came after 1866 when -- in connection with the famine policy of the time -- a big scheme for Government irrigation works financed by loans was launched. After this date much larger works were projected, whilst in the nineties and at the beginning of the twentieth century canal colonization was carried out in the Punjab. Immense new areas, previously desert, were turned by the latter into flourishing and fertile wheat-and cotton-producing districts." [Vera Anstey, *The Economic Development of India,* Fourth Edition, (London: Longmans, Green and Co., 1957), p. 161.]

themselves, to be transforming of traditional agriculture. The primary thrust of British agrarian policy was directed toward ensuring that the East India Company and, later, the British Government of India, would receive reliable payments of land revenue. In effect, the British in India implemented an agrarian policy that included only a constrained definition of rural economic development: a definition that tended to ignore the interests of the actual tillers of the soil.

In East India, for example, instead of focusing on the needs and interests of actual tillers -- tillers who generally, prior to the advent of British power in the subcontinent, had enjoyed security of tenure on lands tilled by them, as distinct from absolute ownership of those lands -- the British were prepared, as in the Permanent Settlement of 1793, to establish a modus vivendi with a peculiar set of landholders who had earlier been appointed by Mogul authorities to collect tribute in the form of land revenue from actual cultivators. These landholders of the Mogul legacy were called zamindars or landlords.[2] These landlords were neither absolute owners of the land nor were they engaged in agricultural operations. Functionally, they were revenue farmers acting as intermediaries between established authority and the tillers of the soil. Nonetheless, the British treated the zamindars as if they were not only absolute owners of the lands in their Mogul-designated estates, but also were capable of being induced to engage in agricultural activities akin to those performed by British landlords.[3]

Belatedly, in the nineteenth century the British realized that an absolute property right in land, equivalent to ownership of land in the

---

2. Zamin means land in Persian. "The suffix -dar implies a degree of control, or attachment, but not necessarily ownership." [Tapan Raychaudhuri and Irfan Habib, editors, *The Cambridge Economic History of India,* (Cambridge: Cambridge University Press, 1982), Volume 1, p. 244.]

3. The British assumed "that because the revenue payers of a district were classed as zamindars owning 'estates' graded according to their revenue, these somehow corresponded with units of agricultural production. This was far from the case. The 'estate', or mahal, was in origin no more than a unit of account in the revenue records and brought under one head the lands for which a particular person or group had revenue responsibility. .... In contrast, the actual unit of production, or agricultural farm in the Western sense, was the cultivating holding, and was usually limited to the land that could be cultivated by a single family using its own and a certain amount of additional labour." [Raychaudhuri and Habib, editors, *The Cambridge Economic History of India,* Volume 1, p. 53.]

West, had not generally existed within the customary terms of reference that were applicable to the indigenous land systems of the subcontinent. It became apparent over time that the indigenous land systems had been characterized by a hierarchy of interests in land in which the rights and prerogatives of various categories of landholders had been recognized.[4] Accordingly, steps were taken periodically by the British to qualify and curtail the rights of landholding zamindars and to establish anew and protect the rights of those cultivating peasants whose rights in land had been subordinated to those non-cultivating zamindars. Thus, for example, in what is today the eastern region of India, the British sought in the nineteenth century to prevent the zamindars from levying illegal cesses (taxes) on the cultivating peasantry (classified in a de jure sense in colonial India as tenants of the zamindars). The British also sought to make compulsory the signing of written leases governing all tenancies. However, these British initiatives were difficult to enforce and did little to preserve or enhance any residual rights of actual cultivators of land tilled within zamindars' estates. Finally, by way of illustration, the British, by means of the *Bengal Tenancy Act of 1885,* gave de jure recognition to the rights in land of others besides the zamindars in the agrarian hierarchy. This legislation, though never rigorously enforced in British India, has symbolic historical significance. It marked the beginning of a British interest in establishing agrarian policies that would be conducive to broader participation among cultivating peasants in the transformation of India's traditional agriculture.

By 1903, the agrarian policy of the British was modified to include investment in agricultural research and experimentation as a means of promoting scientific agriculture. Thus, during Lord Curzon's Viceroyalty (1899-1905), the Imperial Institute of Agriculture was established at Pusa in the Darbhanga District of Bihar. This action marks the inception of a new British commitment to foster their own version of rural economic development in India: a version rooted in scientific research and experimentation.

The agrarian policy of the British in India had an evolving definition of purpose: consistently emphasizing the reliable extraction of land revenue; sometimes (for example the irrigation works in the Punjab

---

4. For example, in a district of the Bengal Presidency in British India, there were as many as 64 tiers of intermediaries between the cultivator and the state.

late in the nineteenth and early in the twentieth century) emphasizing the provision of physical infrastructure; sometimes focusing on the promotion of scientific agriculture; and, in the late nineteenth century and early twentieth century, occasionally recognizing the need for limited tenurial reforms. They never fully conceptualized a program of rural economic development that would combine, simultaneously, emphases on investment in rural infrastructure, scientific agriculture, and the transformation of the traditional hierarchy of interests in land so as to enable actual tillers of the soil to adopt new methods of production and, at the same time, to enhance their own well-being.

British agrarian policy in India, in its essence, was characterized by a constrained and uncertain definition of rural development and how best to achieve it: a definition that was made explicit in the twentieth century by the Royal Commission on Agriculture in India, 1928.

The Royal Commission on Agriculture in India, 1928

The Terms of Reference. The terms of reference of the Royal Commission on Agriculture in India, 1928, were as follows:

> To examine and report on the present conditions of agriculture and rural economy in British India and to make recommendations for the improvement of agriculture and the promotion of the welfare and prosperity of the rural population; in particular to investigate (a) the measures .... being taken for the promotion of agricultural and veterinary research, experiment, demonstration and education for the compilation of agricultural statistics, for the introduction of new and better crops and for improvement in agricultural practice, dairy farming and the breeding of stock; (b) the existing methods of transport and marketing of agricultural produce and stock; (c) the methods by which agricultural operations [were] financed and credit afforded to agriculturists; (d) the main factors affecting rural prosperity and the welfare of the agricultural population; and to make recommendations.
>
> It will not be within the scope of the Commission's duties to make recommendations regarding the existing system of land ownership and tenancy or of the assessment of land revenue and irrigation charges, or the existing division of functions between the Government of India and the local Governments.[5]

---

5. *Royal Commission on Agriculture in India, 1928,* (London: His Majesty's Stationery Office, 1928), Volume 1, Part 3, p. iii.

The Exclusion of Agrarian Reform. Clearly, these terms of reference not only specified the commission's scope of work in a fashion emphasizing technical agronomic issues, but also placed explicit constraints on the commission's mission in India. In effect, the terms of reference of the Royal Commission on Agriculture in India, 1928, hereafter RCAI-1928, were designed explicitly to ensure that the commission did not deal systematically with agrarian structural issues pertaining either to the distribution of rights in land in rural India or the government's claim to land revenue. Issues such as these, it seems, were excluded from the terms of reference both to insulate the commission from political controversy and to ensure that the commission's work did nothing to threaten the British Government of India's working relationships with members of the landholding elite, particularly those entrusted to act as intermediaries of the state in the collection of land revenue -- at the time, the primary source of revenue for the colonial government.

Moreover, the terms of reference notably denied any linkage between changes in the distribution of rights in land in India and the fostering of an economic environment conducive to rural economic development and to an improvement in peoples' welfare, even though the commission had been asked to make recommendations for both "the improvement of agriculture and the promotion of the welfare and prosperity of the rural population."[6] Thus, the commission's charge precluded any attempt by its members to ascertain whether agrarian reform might have an important role in the context of a strategy for rural economic development in British India. In effect, the commission's terms of reference made plain to its members that agrarian reform, however defined, would not be a topic worthy even of discussion in the context of an effort designed to take stock of conditions in rural India and to make recommendations concerning how best to improve agricultural production and to promote the general welfare of the rural population.

A Biased Commitment to Cooperative Institutions. While the terms of reference of the RCAI-1928 removed agrarian reform from any subsequent strategies by which the British in India would seek to promote rural economic development, nothing in the commission's charge limited its enthusiasm for cooperative institutions of all kinds,

---

6. Ibid.

and especially cooperative credit societies. Indeed, it is difficult to read the commission's findings and eventual recommendations without perceiving what appears to be a collective bias in favor of cooperative institutions: a bias held even in the face of solicited testimony from persons who argued variously against the prospect of promoting effective cooperative institutions in rural India. The commission's systematic bias in favor of cooperative institutions is time and again made evident, especially in its manner of posing questions to its respondents. The following questions are illustrative of this imbedded bias.

What steps do you think should be taken to encourage the growth of the cooperative movement -- (i) by Government (ii) by non-official agencies ...?

Where cooperative schemes for joint improvement, such as cooperative irrigation or cooperative fencing or cooperative consolidation of holdings, cannot be given effect to owing to the unwillingness of a small minority to join, do you think legislation should be introduced in order to compel such persons to join for the common benefit of all?[7]

These are clearly leading questions, questions that suggest that a cooperative "movement" already existed in India, was worthy of being promoted either by government or by non-official agencies, and had efficacy as a means of ensuring rural development, even if the movement's presumed momentum might have to be reinforced by compulsive public policy.

As noted earlier, the cooperative institutions most clearly favored by the commission were cooperative credit societies, though other forms of cooperation, including joint cooperative farming, were sometimes lauded, even in the face of evidence suggesting that cultivators were so wedded to individual rights in land that they might resist engaging in joint farming activities. As one member suggested,

No doubt it is a very difficult task to bring the cultivators to agree to joint farming, but a few successful cases will open the eyes of the cultivators to the advantage of joint farming. .... I think that by joint farming alone the produce will be increased by twenty-five percent.[8]

7. Ibid., p. xii.
8. Ibid., Volume 13, p. 167.

What is most striking about this endorsement of cooperative joint farming activity is that no data were presented to the commission that could be construed as confirming its presumed productivity effects. Moreover, no data were presented to the commission that could be construed even as confirming the feasibility of cooperative joint farming in rural India.

The commission's record does confirm that many of its respondents were highly skeptical about the promotion of cooperative institutions of any kind in regions other than the northwest of the country, and particularly in the Punjab. The most skeptical testimony came from East India: for example, a suggestion by a member of the Indian Civil Service in Bihar, that the villagers were not at all inclined to cooperation and that the future of cooperative institutions in the region would depend on government exercising close paternal control over the movement. And, even when the commission heard testimony favoring the promotion of cooperative institutions in eastern India, the quality and significance of the testimony were questionable. For example, a Bihari zamindar told the Commission, initially, that the region's "agricultural salvation" would rest on the continued promotion of cooperative institutions, and then, when asked to amplify his testimony, admitted that he not only had no personal connection with the cooperative movement in his region, but also had only tenuous links to agriculture. He explained that his only connection to agriculture came from his having written books on agriculture, one thousand of which were then stored in his almirah, there being no demand for them, as few people in his region, according to him, took any interest in agriculture.[9]

Finally, the commission's own record suggests that its most favorable data concerning the potential of cooperative institutions came from the Punjab, where cooperative credit societies, in particular, had seemed to be successful institutions, providing large numbers of cultivators with non-usurious sources of credit and thereby undercutting the power of local moneylenders. Regrettably, this favorable evidence from one region of India was used by the commission, ultimately, to make generalizations concerning the feasibility of promoting cooperative institutions everywhere in India: generalizations that were clearly unwarranted in the light of the relative failure of cooperative

---

9. Ibid., p. 456.

institutions in other regions of the subcontinent (as was made quite evident to members of the commission).[10]

The evident bias of the RCAI-1928 favoring the development of cooperative institutions in India was no doubt reinforced by the writings and testimony before the commission of Malcolm Darling, one of the truly outstanding historical figures of the Indian Civil Service, who had worked assiduously in the Punjab to establish cooperative credit institutions as a means of promoting rural development and curtailing the economic power of traditional moneylenders or mahajans in that province. Darling's widely read and influential book, *Punjab Peasant in Prosperity and Debt*, detailing the success of his own approach to rural development, had been published by Oxford University Press in 1925. It provided both a first-hand description of the feasibility of creating cooperative institutions in the Punjab and a vision of their potential as a means of fostering rural development elsewhere in the subcontinent. Given the paucity of first-hand accounts of how the Indian countryside could be transformed, it is not surprising that Darling's classic account of his work in the Punjab would contribute to the commission's own sense of the feasibility and appropriateness of cooperative institutions in rural India.[11] Certainly,

---

10. While cooperative credit societies were appropriately perceived by the commission to be less difficult to promote in the Punjab than some other forms of cooperation (e.g., joint farming cooperatives), the testimony gathered by the commission indicated that even cooperative credit societies were difficult to establish in other regions of India. This was especially evident in eastern India where, notwithstanding government efforts to promote cooperative credit societies, there were in 1925, among thirty-eight million people, only 177,136 members of such societies. On the basis of such data and the testimony of government officials before the commission, the commission itself could conclude only that rural credit in that region continued to be made available to cultivators mainly through local moneylenders, and that the region's cooperative credit societies were obviously insufficient in number to "make an effective impression on the mahajans monopoly." [Ibid., p. xxix.]

11. In fairness to Darling, it must be said that his own enthusiasm for cooperatives was deeply rooted in his field work as a District Officer in one region of undivided India, the Punjab. While his enthusiasm for cooperative institutions was, in a sense, unbounded, he was circumspect about extrapolating from his virtual life-time of experience in the Punjab to make generalizations concerning how easily cooperative institutions could be

(continued...)

the record suggests that the commission's enthusiasm for cooperatives drew on Darling's description of his work in the Punjab, but exaggerated his vision of the potential of cooperative institutions as instruments of social and economic change in rural areas outside of the Punjab.

In sum, however the commission's bias in favor of cooperative institutions is explained, the commission, ignoring the testimony of skeptics, made cooperatives a virtual panacea for rural development and promoted the notion that a cooperative movement already existed and was gaining momentum in rural India. No subject allied to agriculture was more frequently mentioned in the commission's final report than cooperation. And, that report linked the importance of cooperative institutions "with other activities and, in particular, in their relation to agricultural improvement, to education, to irrigation, in fact to anything which affects the cultivator."[12]

A Limited Definition of Structural Change. As earlier emphasized, the commission's terms of reference specifically separated the work of the commission from any concern about the possible need to transform the agrarian structure of India by means of agrarian reform. The terms of reference made plain that the commission's scope of work did not include even the gathering of data, or opinion, concerning the possible relationship between the distribution of rights in land in India and the fostering of an economic environment conducive to rural economic development and to an improvement in the peoples' welfare. The imposed limits on the commission's mission in India

---

11.(...continued)
developed in other regions of India. When I had substantive discussions on this theme with then Sir Malcolm Darling in London in 1957, I was impressed by his scholarly demeanor and his unwillingness at that time to suggest that cooperative institutions could be a panacea for rural development in India as a whole. While his testimony before the RCAI-1928 did include some observations clearly intended to apply to rural development in the whole of India, if there was extrapolation from Darling's testimony concerning his "Punjab model" and its appropriateness for the rest of India, that extrapolation was carried out independent of Darling by the members of the Royal Commission on Agriculture in India, 1928, and later by many proponents of cooperative institutions in independent India.

12. *Royal Commission on Agriculture in India, Abridged Report,* (London: His Majesty's Stationery Office, 1928), p. 51.

notwithstanding, it is not surprising that one agrarian structural issue was considered by the commission to be salient to agricultural development in India. That issue pertained to the on-going process by which agricultural holdings were, as a result of population growth and the operative laws of inheritance, becoming subdivided into smaller units of production. This process was alarming to the commission, it being assumed at the time, without empirical evidence, that small, fragmented landholdings were inherently inefficient whereas large, consolidated holdings were inherently likely to promote economic efficiency. Given this negative perception of small, fragmented units of agricultural production, the commission, from the outset of its assignment, was prone to endorse the efficacy of "Consolidation of Holdings." In fact, consolidation of holdings ultimately became the only agrarian (structural) reform that the commission considered worthy of consideration or endorsement within its limited terms of reference.[13]

There was a persistent emphasis throughout the RCAI-1928 report on the need to promote large scale farming and, therefore, to take steps that restricted the fragmentation or subdivision of landholdings or that ensured the consolidation of small holdings into larger units of production. As noted earlier, it was assumed that small units of production would be inefficient and unproductive, whereas large units of production would support economies of scale and, inherently, would be efficient and productive.

As in its support of cooperative institutions, the commission often betrayed its imbedded bias in favor of large units of production and its propensity to derive generalizations for the whole of India out of testimony focused on one region, the Punjab. The commission's own historical record of its hearings in India is permeated with its members' negative attitudes toward the fragmentation of landholdings

13. The imposed distance of the commission from a wide range of agrarian (structural) reform issues can be made more explicit here by listing the headings actually used by the commission as it framed the questionnaire it used in taking testimony in India: "research, agricultural education, demonstration and propaganda, administration, finance, agricultural indebtedness, fragmentation of holdings, irrigation, soils, fertilizers, crops, cultivation, crop protection, implements, veterinary, animal husbandry, agricultural industries, agricultural labor, forests, marketing, tariffs and sea freights, cooperation, statistics." [*Royal Commission on Agriculture in India, 1928,* Volume 1, Part 3, p. iii.]

and its favorable view of consolidation of holdings. The favorable view of consolidation was based largely, it appears, on evidence pertaining to successful consolidation operations carried out in the Punjab. Thus, for example, we find a member of the commission asking Malcolm Darling, giving testimony based on his experience in the Punjab, whether Darling would "agree that, in India, it is the minute subdivision of holdings which is the greatest difficulty in the way of introducing any changes in agricultural improvement?"[14] And, we find Darling answering in the affirmative, having earlier suggested that "It is useless to think of real enduring agricultural progress without consolidation. That is absolutely vital."[15]

In presenting its recommendations favoring consolidation as a means of promoting rural development in India, the commission seems to have devalued or ignored testimony, given elsewhere in India, that questioned the feasibility of consolidating holdings under conditions perceived to be less favorable to consolidation than those found in the Punjab. In particular, the testimony of respondents in the eastern region of India was sharply negative concerning the prospects for promoting consolidation of holdings along lines established in the Punjab. Even respondents in eastern India who were inclined to favor the goal of consolidation, made plain that they could not envision successful initiatives by the government in their region that would lead to the consolidation of small, fragmented landholdings into larger units of production. Thus, the Assistant Director of Agriculture for Bengal, when asked whether the prospects for consolidation in Bengal were hopeless or just a matter of time, said that the situation was very nearly hopeless. And, he went on to suggest that, though he had personally investigated successful consolidation efforts in the Punjab, he saw no way of applying the Punjab experience in Bengal. He added that the obstacles to successful programs of consolidation in Bengal were rooted in the differences in the land systems of the two regions. When asked to elaborate, he dared to go beyond the terms of reference of the commission to suggest that differences in the land tenure systems of the Punjab and Bengal constituted the prime obstacle to consolidation in Bengal.[16]

14. Ibid., Volume 2, Part 2, p. 634.
15. Ibid., p. 629.
16. Ibid., p. 53.

A number of additional obstacles to the consolidation of landholdings were cited by persons giving testimony before the commission. Among these obstacles were the following:

1. the existence of different classes of land in a village and cultivators' obvious interest in maintaining holdings representative of those diverse classes of land,[17] rather than to be forced, as a result of consolidation, to have possibly a single landholding comprised of only one class, or category, of land;
2. the hostility of landlords to consolidation of holdings;
3. legal difficulties in effecting consolidation;
4. the conservatism of cultivators;
5. the laws of inheritance and the constant traffic in part holdings;
6. the lack of popular interest in land consolidation,[18] together with the lack of any public concern that there were economic costs associated with the fragmentation of holdings; and

---

17. The cultivators often sought to maintain different kinds of holdings, representative of differences in the quality of land in their locality. They feared that consolidation would deny them diversity in the quality of their holdings. To have diverse holdings was favored by many, in circumstances where the quality of land was not homogeneous, as a way of ensuring, for example, that it would be possible to plant different crops in different seasons on land (either wet or dry, above the flood plain or below it) that would ensure a variety of foods, seasonally differentiated. This was a rational means by which cultivators could seek to maximize their economic security. The commission, neglecting such cultivators' reasoning, tended to assume that the fragmentation of rural landholdings was in no way linked to rational decision-making and resulted only from the working of inheritance laws (by which landholdings were customarily divided among sons on the death of the father) and the rapid growth of population on the land. Apparently, the commission also tended, ultimately, to assume that the settings within which consolidation of holdings would be fostered in India were ones likely to be characterized by homogeneous conditions applicable both to the quality of the land and the nature of the soil in a locality. This assumption was to a substantial degree appropriate to the Punjab, but was clearly inappropriate for many regions of India, including the eastern region of the subcontinent.

18. Illustrating this obstacle to consolidation, the Director of Land Records and Surveys in Bihar told the commission that enacting legislation for the consolidation of holdings would be premature "until there is some desire for consolidation." [*Royal Commission on Agriculture in India, 1928,* Volume 13, p. 284.]

7. the distrust between peasant cultivators (raiyats) and landlords, between landlords and landlords, and between raiyats and raiyats.

The above listed obstacles to consolidation notwithstanding, the report of the RCAI-1928, not only endorsed consolidation of holdings as an agrarian reform critical to agricultural development, but also embraced the recommendations of those respondents who suggested that compulsion should be used, if necessary, to overcome cultivators' resistance and, thereby, to secure speedy consolidation of landholdings.[19]

An Interest in Landlords' Entrepreneurial Potential. At least from the days of Lord Cornwallis in the eighteenth century, the British had hoped that the persons perceived by them to be landlords in India could be induced to take a direct, personal interest in agricultural operations and, in general, to behave as enterprising farmers on the land held by them. The British seemed, initially, to be puzzled when Indian landlords, and particularly the zamindars of East India, failed to behave according to the norms that the British hoped to see established. When it became apparent that the traditional landlords were non-cultivating holders of land, persons not engaged in agricultural operations, the British in India sought to alter the landlords' traditional behavior and to encourage them to take an active interest in improving agricultural practices on their landholdings. The British assumed that they could alter the landlords' traditional behavior by offering them new incentives. They hoped to encourage the landlords to become personally involved in agricultural operations and, even, to invest in the transformation of traditional agriculture. From this perspective, the decision of Lord Cornwallis to establish the Permanent Settlement of 1793 with the zamindars (landlords) of eastern India could be interpreted as an attempt to transform non-cultivating landholders into landholders who would take an entrepreneurial interest

19. See, for example, the testimony of Mr. F.L. Brayne, ICS, in *Royal Commission on Agriculture in India, 1928,* Volume 2, Part 2, pp. 57-102. Brayne's pre-independence work in rural development in the area around Gurgaon (a virtual suburb of contemporary New Delhi) was later of instrumental importance to the development of the idiom and concepts of rural community development projects in India in the 1950s and 1960s.

in their landholdings.[20] This settlement, by fixing an unalterable revenue demand payable by the zamindars to the British authority, permitted the zamindars the right to fix their own terms with actual tillers of the soil, classified inappropriately within the frame of the permanent settlement as tenants of the zamindars. In principle, then, the settlement could have provided an incentive for the zamindars to become engaged directly in agricultural operations on their holdings, taking steps to foster increases in agricultural production, without having to worry subsequently about increases in revenue demand payable to the British. In effect, within the frame of the settlement, the zamindars could have invested in the land, engaged in agricultural innovation, and increased their own income from the land. And, they could have taxed the cultivators on their (the zamindars') landholdings at progressively higher rates, reflecting increases in productivity, while making payments of land revenue to the British at low rates fixed in 1793 in perpetuity.

Whatever the expectations of the British, the historical record confirms that the zamindars were not induced to perform new functions by the working of the Permanent Settlement of 1793. They failed to behave either as entrepreneurial farmers or as facsimiles of British landlords of the same era. Their behavior might have been anticipated had the British not been confused by the existing system of rights in land in the territory over which they had established authority. As earlier noted, Cornwallis and his officers of the East India Company assumed that the zamindars were in fact owners of the land held by them. This was not the case. Under the existing land system, even the zamindars' rights in land were qualified and were, in no sense, absolute. The zamindars had been appointed by Mogul authorities to hold land under that authority for the purpose of collecting land revenue from the actual cultivators. It was understood that the zamindars would not be directly engaged themselves in agricultural operations. Instead, the zamindars would be, in a functional sense, revenue farmers whose interests would be utterly different from those

---

20. Of course, the primary goal of the permanent settlement, as has been emphasized earlier in the text, was to ensure that the British received regular payments of land revenue. The collection of land revenue clearly superceded any other goal of British colonial agrarian policy. The settlement made plain that the zamindars would act as intermediaries between the East India Company and the actual tillers of the soil in the regular collection of land revenue.

below them in the agrarian hierarchy who actually labored on the land. The British clearly erred in treating the zamindars as if they were absolute owners of the land who could be induced, by one means or another, to take a direct interest in agricultural operations.

Over time, the British understood that the indigenous land systems of India had not vested in any landholder an absolute property right in land. Instead, they came to appreciate that the traditional land systems were defined by a hierarchy of interests in land. Accordingly, the British took steps to specify the rights and obligations of those landholders in the agrarian hierarchy of interests. And, recognizing belatedly that the zamindars in eastern India were, in general, separated absolutely from labor on the land and investment in it, the British sought progressively not only to alter the zamindars' traditional behavior, but also, by means of tenancy legislation, to protect the actual cultivators from the zamindars' abuses of power. At the same time, however, as is made evident in the report of the RCAI-1928, the British repeatedly assumed that the best means of effecting change in agricultural operations in rural India would be by working from the top down -- using large landholders, including traditional landlords, as presumed agents of change.

This vacillation in British expectations concerning the roles that were played, or might be played, by Indian landlords in promoting rural economic development was amply demonstrated in the testimony before the RCAI-1928 of Mr. W.B. Heycock, ICS, the Commissioner of Patna Division. On the one hand, Heycock was explicit in stating that the zamindars in his region were primarily rent collectors, direct cultivation by landlords being virtually unknown in the province of Bihar. Said Heycock, the landlords "do not farm or cultivate their private lands themselves."[21] Instead, suggested Heycock, they give out their lands to subordinate tenants and sharecroppers for purposes of cultivation. Moreover, Heycock said that he saw "little prospect .... of the big zamindars taking a practical interest in farming."[22] On the other, however, Heycock suggested that much could be done to transform agriculture in Bihar "if zamindars could be induced to cultivate their own private lands .... and to take an interest in farming."[23] In this fashion, Heycock and many other British colonial

---

21. *Royal Commission on Agriculture in India,* Volume 13, p. 218.
22. Ibid.
23. Ibid.

officers before and after him considered landlords to be simultaneously responsible for the perpetuation of an inefficient, backward system of traditional agriculture and capable of transforming that traditional system, if only the right means could be found to change landlords' traditional behavior.

There were, of course, some British colonial officers who did not accept the mainstream views of their colleagues concerning how best to transform traditional agriculture, and who dared, also, to argue that they could see no means by which the traditional system of agriculture in India could be altered unless the existing system of rights in land was, itself, transformed. One such person was Mr. A.D. Tuckey, ICS, the Director of Land Records and Surveys in Bihar at the time of the Royal Commission's survey. Challenging the commission's limited terms of reference and focus of enquiry in his opening statement, Mr. Tuckey said that he felt compelled to detail the relationship, as he saw it, between the existing system of landholdings and tenancy and the problem of agricultural development. In effect, he told the commission that he had discovered no panacea by which agricultural development could be promoted in eastern India. He could not rely on zamindars to become agents of change. Indeed, he denounced the behavior of the zamindars of Bihar, Bengal and Orissa, suggesting that they exercised ruthless power over the cultivating peasantry. The zamindars, said Tuckey, indulged in practices that were in clear violation of existing laws designed to prevent rack-renting, in practices that denied permanent occupancy rights in land to cultivators who had earned such rights, and in practices by which they turned free men who had incurred debt into bonded laborers.

Having begun his testimony by stating that he felt compelled to comment on the relationship between the existing land system and the problem of agricultural development,[24] Tuckey made his opening remarks more explicit by stating that the existing system of relationships of people to the land (the product of the historical land system in his region) was inimical to economic progress in agriculture. In blunt language, Tuckey argued that the commission should not ignore the relationship between landholding and tenancy, on the one hand, and, on the other, the persistence of an inefficient, backward system of agriculture. Said Tuckey:

---

24. Ibid., p. 277.

The superior intelligence and education of those in power on the land is devoted in the main to obtaining, as rent, as much as possible of the profit accruing from the existing system of cultivation, and of keeping the cultivators in a state of dependence rather than to improving the out turn from the soil. An interesting example of this is the tremendous keenness of proprietors in partition cases to obtain within the estate allotted as many low caste and as few high caste tenants as possible. The failure to grant rent receipts, particularly for land held in produce rent, the exaction of illegal dues in addition to the legal rent and cess, the denial of legal rights of occupancy in land held on produce rent and in .... land which has been at some time in the direct possession of the landlord and has then been leased, are the main breaches of the tenancy law in common vogue among private landlords in the province. Obtaining labor at less than the market rate from tenants and from debtors, binding debtors to work as serfs in payment of the interest on debts which they are never given the opportunity to repay, and the deliberate ruining of refractory tenants by means of litigation criminal and evil, often supported by forged documents and false evidence, are common and every-day practices also of those in power on the land, and it is hard for the actual cultivators of the soil to gain that security, freedom and economic independence which are so necessary for improvements in husbandry.[25]

Tuckey also told the commission that the zamindars in his region were interested in maintaining their dominance and found "objection to anything which would make the tenant more independent."[26] He said that the zamindars denied cultivators proper receipts for rent, denied them permanent occupancy rights to land in contravention of law, and, using what Tuckey called "the power of the purse," held sway over the cultivators, if challenged by them, in the courts.[27]

Tuckey argued, in essence, that the existing system of rights in land and tenancy relationships was an obvious impediment to economic progress in agriculture, especially in eastern India. When asked the obvious question at the end of his testimony, whether he would consider the relations existing between zamindars and tenants in the eastern region to be a serious obstacle to agricultural improvement, Tuckey said simply, "Yes, I should."[28]

---

25. Ibid., pp. 280-281.
26. Ibid., p. 290.
27. Ibid., pp. 290-292.
28. Ibid., p. 292.

Another British civil servant, Mr. A.C. Dobbs, Director of Agriculture in Bihar when the commission took testimony in Bihar, also dared to associate rural poverty and agricultural backwardness with the historical land system in his region of East India. In his testimony before the commission, Dobbs described the land system as one by which rural assets were mortgaged to urban absentees.[29] Having touched on what was for the commission a proscribed theme, Mr. Dobbs quickly added that he understood that the laws of property could not be easily altered. However, before concluding his testimony, Dobbs asserted that he would favor the elimination of the traditional system of land revenue and its replacement with "a special tax on income secured by law on contracts."[30] Dobbs also stated that the existing system of agriculture in his region was one within which peasant cultivators lived "in a state of perpetual fear."[31] They were afraid, he said, of natural and supernatural phenomena; they were afraid of their priests, of the police, of governmental officials, of the zamindars and moneylenders (or mahajans); indeed, they were afraid of "almost anybody and anything."[32] However, even Dobbs, when giving his advice to the commission concerning how best to improve agricultural conditions in the countryside, reverted ultimately to the safe ground of suggesting that improved agricultural practices and new technology in agriculture could best be introduced in rural areas by targeting zamindars and other large landholders who, having already "won the confidence of the people .... will pass on the knowledge to the small cultivators ...".[33]

The boldness of much of Dobbs' testimony notwithstanding, it was Tuckey whose testimony was in stark contrast to the mainstream of testimony before the Royal Commission. It was Tuckey, perhaps more than any other officer, who told the commission neither what it expected nor, possibly, wanted to hear. As the commission's own record of its field surveys in India makes evident, Tuckey was among a limited number of colonial officers at the time whose perceptions of what would be needed to ensure agricultural development focused mainly on agrarian structural issues, rooted in the historical land

---

29. Ibid., p. 48.
30. Ibid., p. 49.
31. Ibid., p. 56.
32. Ibid.
33. Ibid.

system of his region, that shaped the relations between those having superior rights in land (the zamindars) and those with inferior rights (the actual tillers of the soil).   And, it was Tuckey who would not permit his testimony before the commission to be constrained by the commission's terms of reference.   I believe that it is fair to deduce from the historical record that men like Tuckey were in short supply in British India.   Few members of the British colonial services saw the need to change historical land and tenancy systems in order to reduce their inhibiting effects on rural development.   Few saw such change as a prerequisite for promoting rural development by other means, including the promotion of cooperative institutions and the consolidation of landholdings.   Indeed, Tuckey stands virtually alone among those who gave testimony to the commission in associating the backwardness of agriculture in his region with the perverse effects of a historical land system in which non-cultivating landholders exercised capricious authority over actual tillers lacking secure rights in land.

While the commission carefully recorded Tuckey's observations, no evidence suggests that his testimony was persuasive to its members. After all, the commission heard testimony from many others (including Dobbs in the end) whose views, possibly shaped by different experience, were supportive of the proposition that the best means of transforming traditional agriculture in India would be to rely on the landholding elites to be both the primary agents of change and the primary beneficiaries of government initiatives to promote the transformation of agricultural practices.   Thus, however much evidence they themselves amassed concerning the unwillingness of traditional landholders, including zamindars of East India and landlords in other regions, to become engaged directly in agricultural operations, the Royal Commission's findings ultimately rested on the notion that India's landholding elites could become effective agents of rural transformation.   And, in harmony with these findings, the British Government of India stubbornly persisted in the belief that traditional landholders, including non-cultivating landlords who were not disposed to engage in agricultural operations themselves, would somehow, someday, transform traditional agriculture in India.

The historical record of the British in India supports this generalization: British agrarian policy in India, even when it was gradually transformed late in the nineteenth century and early in the twentieth century to focus not only on the collection of land revenue, but also on how best to transform traditional agriculture and to promote rural economic development, relied inordinately on those landholders who were at the apex of the hierarchy of interests in land to be the agents of change. In the process, the British tended to concentrate their efforts on non-cultivating landholders having superior rights in land to the persistent neglect of the interests of actual cultivators having tenuous rights in land.

The British erred, ultimately, in assuming that non-cultivating landlords had common attributes and could be induced to behave as entrepreneurs with respect to the land in their possession. It would be equally inappropriate today to assume that Indian landlords could be lumped together and described as a homogeneous group having common behavioral traits everywhere in India.[34] Landlords were (and are) heterogeneous in character and behavior. Moreover, landlords operate, even in the modern era, within the frame of different historical land systems and regionally differentiated laws governing rights in land. For these reasons, all generalizations concerning the character and behavior of landholders occupying different positions in what I call the hierarchy of interests in land in India are inherently dangerous. Thus, for example, while it is appropriate to suggest that large numbers of landlords in East India during the British period could be classified as holders of land who did not reside in villages contiguous with their holdings, who did not cultivate themselves the land held by them, and who acted mainly as rent collecting intermediaries of the state in the collection of land revenue, it is also the case that some landlords in East India did in fact periodically take some interest in agricultural operations. Some were involved in ensuring that minor irrigation works on lands held by them were maintained.[35] Others were primary sources of agricultural credit, though at rates that would usually be considered to be usurious.

Negligible Interest in Kisans and Agricultural Laborers. The focus of the RCAI-1928 was seldom on small farmers or kisans. And, when

---

34. Like the British in India, some Marxists err in this direction when they fit landlords into the Procrustean Bed of class analysis. I believe, like the late Eric Stokes, that attempts to impose class structure and, therefore, class analysis on India are unwarranted and lead to analysis of complex socioeconomic relations that is both simplifying and distorting of reality.

35. In East India, zamindars often made investments in the construction of irrigation works and supervised their maintenance. [See: Dharma Kumar, editor, *The Cambridge Economic History of India,* (Cambridge: Cambridge University Press, 1983), Volume 2, p. 125.]

the commission did focus on small farmers, the obvious emphasis was on landholders who had permanent, de jure rights to the land in their cultivating possession. Within the hierarchy of interests in land in India, such persons were cultivators of high status. Nonetheless, their rights in land, like landlords' rights in land, were qualified, and in no sense absolute. Some kisans had the characteristics of individual proprietors with respect to the land in their cultivating possession. Such as these might till the land themselves, using family members, or they might behave as small landlords, giving out land seasonally to other cultivators, acting as sharecroppers.[36] Other kisans could be classified under law as tenants of zamindars.[37] Such as these enjoyed their secure rights in land only so long as they were timely in their payments of rent to their zamindars, who acted as intermediaries of the state in the collection of land revenue. Given the complexity of the hierarchy of interests in land throughout India and the restrictive terms of reference under which the commission operated, it is no wonder that the commission gave little attention to kisans, however defined. The commission's record in India confirms that it not only gave negligible attention to kisans as it gathered testimony, but also neglected generally whole categories of actual cultivators whose rights in land were more tenuous than those of kisans. That is to say, the commission did not even purport to take testimony that pertained to actual cultivators below the kisans in the agrarian hierarchy, cultivators who under law were classified as having non-occupancy rights in land. Nor did the commission take testimony that would have illuminated the condition of legions of actual cultivators who had no rights whatsoever in land excepting those rights acquired seasonally from superior landholders, usually on the basis of oral, sharecropping agreements.

The commission's negligible focus on kisans was no doubt related to the fact that the kisans, not to mention other categories of cultivators, were at the time not well organized in advocacy groups in most regions of India. However, in Bihar, where the kisans were organized in a

---

36. The usual sharecropping arrangement was based on the batai system, where the crop was divided fifty-fifty between the sharecropper and the superior landholder. A more pernicious system of sharecropping in some regions was the danabandi system, where the sharecropper was expected to provide the superior landholder 50 percent or more of the value of the estimated crop in cash in advance.

37. Such tenants of zamindars were generally classified in a de jure sense as "permanent occupancy raiyats."

group called the Bihar Kisan Sabha, the commission did solicit testimony from a representative of the group. The most striking aspect of this testimony was the kisan sabha representative's description of himself as a cultivator having a considerable area of tenancy lands tilled by his tenants and sharecroppers. Under questioning, the kisan sabha representative went on to explain that he, while classified as a kisan, was not himself a tiller of the soil, that he was a Brahmin who had never touched the plow, and that his most recent activity as a cultivator had been to supervise "some fifty bighas of cultivation."[38] Such illustrative testimony from a self-described kisan, together with the commission's general neglect of testimony from others who legitimately might be classified as actual tillers of the soil, exemplifies, in my view, the commission's distance from actual cultivators as it took testimony in India concerning how best to promote rural prosperity and the welfare of the agricultural population.

The commission obviously also had difficulty gathering from its respondents meaningful data concerning landless agricultural laborers in India. There are, nonetheless, moments in the commission's record when it focused briefly on the condition of agricultural laborers, and even on the existence of bonded labor in some regions of the country. Not surprisingly, given the persistence of bonded labor in the same area in contemporary India, this testimony dealt with bonded labor in the districts of Palamau and Hazaribagh (regions within the contemporary Indian State of Bihar). The commission heard that there was a tendency for landless agricultural laborers, when unable to pay back a loan taken from a superior landholder, to become permanently attached to that landholder -- bound to perform whatever menial services that might be required of them for so long as they lived. It was unlikely that they would either be permitted or otherwise would ever again have the capacity to regain the status of free laborers.[39]

Even though the commission heard testimony concerning the existence of bonded labor, and was alerted also to conditions in rural

38. *Royal Commission on Agriculture in India, 1928,* Volume 13, p. 277.

39. A striking fact of life in contemporary India is that, should testimony be taken today concerning the condition of agricultural labor, there could be evidence presented of forms of bonded labor, virtual slavery such as kamauti or kamia, from the same region wherein it was reported to the Royal Commission on Agriculture in India in 1928. [Ibid., p. xxviii.]

areas where there was said to be a problem of terrorism[40] resulting from the actions of landlords on those below them in the hierarchy of interests in land, the RCAI-1928 made no attempt ultimately to link its recommendations concerning rural economic development to programs designed specifically to lessen cultivators' and laborers' dependence on landlords, to address rural terrorism, to eliminate bonded labor, or to prevent illegal taxes (cesses and abwabs). Regrettably, such highly charged issues had, in effect, been excluded from the purview of the commission at the outset, even before it began to take testimony on agricultural conditions in India, by the commission's carefully delineated terms of reference.

A Governance System Inimical to Rural Economic Development

In general, British agrarian policy in India, as exemplified by the work of the RCAI-1928, was conditioned by a constrained and uncertain definition of rural development: a definition which did not include linkage between agricultural development and changes in the traditional land systems. Similarly, the British colonial system of governance in rural India was rooted in an implicit definition of rural development which excluded any encouragement of change in the way people related to the land: a definition of development which emphasized the maintenance of the status quo with regard to historical land systems.

Night Watchman Functions Linked to the Maintenance of Law, Order and Political Stability. The British colonial system of governance in India was designed, above all, to ensure the maintenance of British power in the countryside. The system was designed to ensure a stable rural environment: an environment where British authority was respected or feared; where law and order was assured; and where the collection of land revenue was regularized. The goal was to ensure stability. The system of governance was geared, therefore, to the maintenance of conditions in the countryside as they were, and not to their transformation. And, there is no way of

---

40. Ibid., p. 66.

defining rural economic development that does not endorse change over stability.

More specifically, the British in India were more prepared to work within the institutional arrangements that conditioned India's historical land systems than to invest in their transformation. They were more willing, for example, to maintain the zamindari system in East India, using it as a means of extracting land revenue, than to transform or abolish it. They were more willing to establish working relations with powerful, non-cultivating landholders in rural areas than to take steps, meaningfully, to empower actual cultivators. In general, the British did not attempt to transform the traditional land systems of India by investing in agrarian structural change. While they did pass legislation periodically to limit the abuses of power of traditional landholders in various regions of India, no systematic attempt was made to initiate programs of agrarian reform that would have restructured India's historical land systems. Indeed, the only variant of agrarian reform that they were, belatedly, prepared to introduce was that having to do with the consolidation of landholdings. Consolidation of landholdings, as earlier emphasized, was promoted on grounds that raise questions about its significance as a means of contributing meaningfully to the transformation of traditional agriculture in India. Moreover, consolidation of landholdings, as supported by the British, was not designed to affect significantly the traditional land systems.

Administrative Procedures Disassociated from the Transformation of Existing Rural Conditions. The British system of governance developed and adopted elaborate rules and procedures that were disassociated from any goal to transform existing rural conditions in India. For example, they took steps periodically to conduct Survey and Settlement Operations in rural areas by means carefully delineated in manuals of procedure. These operations, requiring painstaking, time-consuming, cadastral surveys and the checking of village records, took years to complete and were seldom up-to-date. Moreover, the Survey and Settlement Operations were conducted by revenue officers of the government -- confirming the orientation and purpose of the activity. The procedures were in no way associated with the gathering of data for purposes that could be related to the transformation of the existing hierarchy of interests in land. Instead, the procedures were designed, elaborately, only to record the existing hierarchy of interests, and, incidentally, to confirm revenue demand. Indeed, had such Survey and Settlement procedures been geared, in any way, to the transformation of traditional agriculture in India, it would have been logical to assign their implementation to agricultural ministries instead of to revenue ministries.

Functional Dichotomy Maintained Between the Revenue and Agricultural Ministries. A striking feature of the British colonial system of governance in India, as it pertains to rural economic development, is that it established and maintained a functional dichotomy between revenue and agricultural ministries. This functional dichotomy separated revenue collection from investment in agriculture. As noted above, this functional dichotomy separated the definition of goals for agricultural development, a function of the agricultural ministries, from the maintenance of up-to-date records of rights in land, a function of revenue ministries. In addition, the functional dichotomy between these ministries meant that any legislation during the British period affecting rights in land was drafted and made ready for legislative action by revenue ministries, not by agricultural ministries. In essence, the functional dichotomy meant that the revenue ministries focused actively only on rural issues pertinent to the maintenance of revenue collection within the existing hierarchy of interests in land. Meanwhile, the agricultural ministries of British India focused only on technical agronomic issues, issues separated absolutely (as in the terms of reference applicable to the RCAI-1928) from the traditional systems of relationships of people to the land. The functional, administrative separation of agricultural and revenue ministries was clearly inimical to rural economic development in British India, if rural economic development is defined to suggest a need not only to change agricultural practices, but also to transform peoples' relationships to the land.

The Uncertain Policies of the Left

The Policies of the Communist Party of India

In the pre-independence period, the Communist Party of India (CPI) never established a coherent, unified position within its ranks concerning whether its own interests, or the interests of the people of India, should be linked to the promotion of agrarian reform, however defined. Created in the 1920s by the Comintern and relying for many years on guidance from Moscow through Comintern agents, the Communist Party of India lacked roots in the soil of India: it lacked an indigenous will to shape its policies to meet conditions in India, generally, and particularly in the agrarian sector of the Indian economy. At the outset, the leadership of the Indian Communists was comprised of a small band of urban-based intellectuals.[41] These leaders had difficulty in articulating distinctive indigenous positions on political and economic questions, especially on questions pertaining to agrarian reform and the role of peasant cultivators in the future of India's political economy.

The CPI's inability to conceptualize and articulate an indigenous vision for agrarian reform in India was associated, in part, with its dependence on the advice of persons located outside of India for ideologically correct positions on political and economic issues. Men like R. Palme Dutt, a principal advisor to the Indian Communists prior to independence, were peculiarly unsuited by background and experience to provide advice and counsel to Indian Communists. Dutt, born of an Indian father and a Swedish mother and raised entirely in Britain, was a Comintern agent based in London. He visited India for the first time in 1946. Thus, his pre-independence advice to the CPI cannot be said to have been rooted in the soil and culture of India. Instead, his ideas were rooted in the dogma of the Communist International. Like Karl Marx, who, in the 1850s had made authoritative seeming statements about India without ever having been there,[42] Dutt showed no inhibitions about advising Indian Communists on matters about which he could have had little feel or in-depth understanding. Indeed, citing Marx as his authority, Dutt arrived at conclusions about India that were derived from distorted perceptions of conditions in the region prior to the advent of British rule. In the process, Dutt elaborated a history of the Indian subcontinent that was both romanticized and separated, utterly, from any negative images of the indigenous culture and context. Within the frame of Dutt's reconstruction of Indian history, ideal, cohesive village communities had indeed existed in India until destroyed by the force of British

---

41. Bhabani Sen Gupta, *Communism in Indian Politics,* (New York and London: Columbia University Press, 1972), p. 9.

42. In the 1950s, Marx wrote some 23 articles on India for *The New York Daily Tribune.*

imperialism.[43]   This line, embellished with Comintern dogma, was received and readily accepted by many Indian intellectuals, both Marxists within the CPI and non-Marxists, in the years leading up to independence. While there could have been few Indian intellectuals as divorced from actual conditions in the Indian countryside as R. Palme Dutt, there was a widespread tendency among intellectuals, including non-Marxists associated with the Independence Movement, to underestimate peasant cultivators as potential agents of change and as rational people who knew best the conditions in rural India that constituted obstacles to economic progress.

The capacity of the CPI to establish its own coherent and effective line on any issue of political economy was also limited by debate and division within the Comintern in the 1920s as to the role of Communists in colonial territories.   Whereas Lenin argued that Communists should assist national liberation ("bourgeois-democratic") movements, such as the Congress Movement in India, M.N. Roy, an Indian national and Comintern agent, wanted the Comintern to assist in the development of the Communist Party of India as an exclusive force devoted "to the organization of the broad popular masses for the struggle for the class interests of the working people."[44] When Roy, on behalf of the Comintern, gave advice to the Communist Party of India in its formative years, he continued to object to the Comintern line for India: namely, that "the Communists should try to take over the nationalist movement by capturing the Congress faction from within."[45]   In any event, the CPI continued in the pre-independence period to exist at the margin of Indian politics. And, as a party, it did not articulate ideas having indigenous meaning and cogency.

One could not have expected from such an institution a consistent line on any issue, let alone a set of coherent ideas on agrarian reform. Not until the eve of independence, in 1945, did the CPI adopt a position on agrarian reform, including land reform, in its election manifesto. That manifesto enabled the party to join, belatedly, what was by then virtually an Indian nationalist chorus proposing the abolition of landlordism. Even then the CPI's vision of agrarian

---

43. R. Palme Dutt, *India Today,* (Bombay: People's Publishing House Ltd., 1949).

44. *The Second Congress of the Communist International: Proceedings,* Moscow, 1920, p. 478.

45. Bhahani Sen Gupta, *Communism in Indian Politics,* p. 10.

reform and land reform was in no sense radical or designed to appeal beyond its generally high caste, urban, intellectual base: it was not designed to appeal to actual cultivators, including sharecroppers and others lacking secure rights in land, in the Indian countryside. The 1945 manifesto of the CPI suggested that landlords, when abolished after independence, should be permitted to retain maximum holdings of one hundred acres, a substantial landholding given man-to-land ratios in that era, to say the least. Moreover, the manifesto made plain that the CPI's vision of agrarian reform was one within which the "middle and rich peasant would prosper more than the poor peasant."[46] Thus, the CPI, prior to independence, was in no sense an institution committed to a well-delineated program of agrarian reform. It was prepared only to join belatedly with Indian nationalists in arguing amorphously for non-radical, mildly reformist policies with respect to agrarian reform and land reform. The Party's message on land policy remained uncertain and equivocating.

The Activities of Kisan Sabhas and the Congress Socialists

Prior to independence, small farmers or kisans were, in general, subservient to those above them in the agrarian hierarchy. As individual landholders, they could not easily challenge the rights and prerogatives of large landholders. Moreover, because of their heterogeneity, they found it difficult to coalesce and to establish a common agenda for action on agrarian issues, including issues of agrarian reform or land reform.

Kisans were not homogeneous in character. Some had attributes of landlords: such as these tended to be detached personally from agricultural operations; they often tilled their lands by giving them out to others for purposes of cultivation, usually under sharecropping arrangements governed by oral leases. Other kisans had attributes of small farmers: cultivators who might be classified by some as "individual proprietors" who themselves, with family labor, tilled the land in their possession. In some regions of India, such as these could be classified in a de jure sense as occupancy raiyats, cultivators with a

---

46. Gene D. Overstreet and Marshall Windmiller, *Communism in India,* (Berkeley: University of California Press, 1959), p. 230.

permanent right to their land so long as they made regular payments of rent to superior landholders. In other regions of India, the term kisans could be applied to persons lacking de jure occupancy rights to the land in their possession: such as these could function as sharecroppers whose rights to land were temporary and tenuous. Given this elastic description of kisans, it is obvious that kisans' interests in agrarian issues, including agrarian reform, would be as heterogeneous as their own characteristics. Common perceptions of common needs were difficult, therefore, for kisans to establish.

Prior to independence, the kisans who did organize for collective action in their own behalf were more likely to have attributes of non-cultivating landlords than the attributes of small farmers and sharecroppers, as described above. This notwithstanding, organizations of kisans became conspicuous in some parts of rural India in the 1930s. These organizations, or kisan sabhas, were, at the outset, separate in inspiration and orientation from the Non-Cooperation Movement of the Indian National Congress. The kisans were more narrowly focused on problems of rural economic development and their own rights in land, than on broader issues of national liberation. Thus, when the kisans agitated in rural areas to promote their interests, their demonstrations were rightly perceived initially to be spontaneous and local in character, not dictated by larger, all-India organizations, such as the Indian National Congress, or other political parties.

The kisans' capacity for independent action in their own behalf made evident to superior landholders that those below them in the agrarian hierarchy were increasingly capable of forms of collective action and could not be dismissed as if they were dispirited and powerless. Moreover, the kisans' agitations quickly attracted the independent support of a number of recognized nationalist leaders who were already concerned about agrarian issues, including the plight of poor peasants. Among these leaders were Professor N.G. Ranga, Indulal Yajnik, Swami Sahajanand, and Kalka Prasad. These men were geographically removed from one another, and, according to Amit Kumar Gupta,[47] were sometimes hampered in their activities by the then Government of India, and even by colleagues in the Independence Movement who did not share their concern about

---

47. Amit Kumar Gupta, "The Leftists and the Rural Poor in India, 1934-39," (Draft Manuscript). I am indebted to Mr. Gupta for sharing this manuscript with me in New Delhi, India in 1989.

agrarian issues and the problem of rural poverty. Nonetheless, the activities of these relatively independent leaders of opinion for the welfare of the kisans enhanced the national visibility of the kisan organizations.

While the interests of the kisans were not homogeneous, individual leaders within the kisan sabhas began to articulate their own visions of agrarian reform and land reform. Some leaders demanded the abolition of specific categories of landlords, notably zamindars and taluqdars. Others advocated state proprietorship over all landholdings, together with the redistribution of such landholdings, in economically viable units for purposes of cultivation, among small farmers. And, some of the kisan leaders called for the revocation of all irregular levies by landlords and the liquidation of arrears of rent and debt.

Meanwhile, in 1934, the Congress Socialist Party (CSP), organized within the Indian National Congress, became a militant exponent of land reform, defined to include the confiscation of private property. What is more, the Congress Socialists soon established their own nexus with the kisan sabhas, providing the diverse kisan groups a common platform and an opportunity to foster their own agendas for action within the frame of the agrarian reform programs of the Congress Socialists. Association with the Congress Socialists gave the kisan sabhas a leftist patina. Together, the kisan sabhas and the Congress Socialists seemed, increasingly, to be committed to radical, if still amorphous, measures of agrarian reform.

Landholding interests within the Indian National Congress were alarmed at the prospect that the kisan sabhas and the Congress Socialists would press jointly for agrarian reforms, including programs designed to abolish landlords and to redistribute rights in land. Accordingly, the Congress Working Committee acted in June of 1934 to reassure landholders within the Congress Movement by condemning what it called loose talk about the confiscation of private property. At the same time, even the British-led Government of India, which had earlier welcomed the emergence of the Congress Socialists, now referred to them as an organization of political gangsters seeking to "promote class war and confiscate property or, seize power and acquire wealth by robbing others."[48]

---

48. Amit Kumar Gupta, "The Leftists and the Rural Poor in India, 1934-39," (Draft Manuscript), citing India, Home Poll., File No. 39/23/34 of 1934, National Archives of India.

By 1936, the Congress Socialists had decided to work systematically to organize the peasants of India, drawing on the work already accomplished in that direction by N.G. Ranga, who had initiated the Andhra Provincial Ryots[49] Association in 1928, and Swami Sahajanand, who had set up the Bihar Provincial Kisan Sabha in 1929. Toward this end, the Congress Socialist Party now considered it useful to establish effective linkages among disparate kisan-oriented organizations.[50] Accordingly, using Jaya Prakash Narayan and N.G. Ranga as conveners, the Congress Socialist Party invited the various kisan leaders to meet in Lucknow on April 11, 1936, at a time coincident with an already scheduled meeting of the Indian National Congress. At the Lucknow meeting an All India Kisan Congress was established, a group soon be referred to, officially, as the All India Kisan Sabha. As an umbrella organization, the All India Kisan Sabha (AIKS) was supposed to represent a broad spectrum of peasant interests. However, the leaders of the AIKS[51] clearly sought to lay stress on the causes of the rural poor, including those cultivators near the base of the agrarian hierarchy who had intermittent and tenuous rights in land as well as sharecroppers and landless agricultural laborers.

As the thematic focus of the All India Kisan Sabha took shape, and as its program evolved in practice, leaders within the Indian National Congress were both attracted and repelled by AIKS's agenda for action. On the one hand, the All India Kisan Sabha no doubt

---

49. The word "ryot" (often spelled "raiyat"), a rough equivalent of kisan in this context, means "peasant cultivator or small farmer."

50. I refer here to "kisan-oriented" organizations, rather than to "peasant-based" organizations -- a phrase frequently used in India to describe the same groups. The former phrase is used consciously by me to suggest that the leadership of these organizations was not drawn in the main from peasants, however defined. Instead, it was drawn from educated, usually urban-based, persons who showed varying degrees of empathy for people in rural areas whose rights in land and economic status placed them in weak positions in the agrarian hierarchy.

51. As a synthetic organization, the combination of the Congress Socialist Party and the All India Kisan Sabha (CSP-AIKS) contained a peculiar amalgam of leaders. Some could be classified loosely as ideological leftists. Others could not be so labeled. As S. Gopal has observed, the leadership "was comprised of a motley crowd of Marxists, Fabians, Gandhians and orthodox Hindus." [S. Gopal, *Jawaharlal Nehru: A Biography, 1889-1947*, (Delhi: Oxford University Press, 1981), Volume 1, p. 188.]

influenced favorably the views of Congress leaders who were already disposed to give attention to rural land policy issues. On the other hand, the AIKS's focus and program worried a broad spectrum of powerful Congress leaders, including Mohandas K. Gandhi and Jawaharlal Nehru as well as the ideological conservatives Rajendra Prasad and Sardar Patel. Such leaders as these were not prepared to accept the possibility that the Congress Movement might be induced by the AIKS to adopt a radical, divisive approach to rural economic development, an approach rooted in the proposition that India's historical land systems would have to be transformed by means of agrarian reform and land reform when India gained freedom from Britain.

Accordingly, Nehru contrived to put distance between the Congress and the All India Kisan Sabha. At the annual meeting of the Indian National Congress in 1936, he established the principle that the members of the AIKS could be full members of the Congress only if they joined as individuals, rather than as representatives of organized groups having interests which, if forcibly expressed within the Congress, might disturb the unity of the movement. By enforcing this principle, the Congress denied the AIKS both organizational affiliation and group identity with the Indian National Congress. By establishing and enforcing this principle, Nehru had achieved a tactical victory over the AIKS. He had taken action both to limit the growth of a separate faction within the Congress and he had placated the interests of Congressmen who were threatened at the prospect that the Indian National Congress might be forced some day by the AIKS to commit itself to a radical agenda for action involving variants of agrarian reform. Thereafter, the Indian National Congress could be free, when necessary, both to embrace the rhetoric of agrarian reform and land reform and to reassure its most conservative members, including zamindars and other large landholders, that its agrarian policies would be reasonable, protective of their vital interests, and not too disruptive of traditional rights in land.

In practice, the Congress sought to avoid any direct involvement in disputes involving large landholders and peasant cultivators. As a movement struggling to develop and maintain a broad-based coalition of disparate interests against the British, the Congress clearly wanted to avoid the appearance of siding openly with the weaker sections of the peasantry against the large landholders. The Congress also wanted to avoid the appearance of favoring the interests of the large landholders. This avoidance strategy was clearly derived from assessment of the divisive effect of some Congress actions in the past, as when the Congress interposed itself between the landlords and a section of the cultivating peasantry in Bihar. In that instance, the Congress ultimately pleased neither the Bihari zamindars nor the peasant agitators led by the Bihar Kisan Sabha. In what became widely known in the 1930s as the Bakasht Movement of Bihar, peasant cultivators, led by the local kisan sabha, had sought to claim permanent occupancy rights to land that they had "taken-in" for purposes of cultivation from landlords on terms governed by oral agreements.[52] The Indian National Congress sought to mediate the dispute, naming Rajendra Prasad, himself a zamindar, as the mediating authority. In the end, however, neither the zamindars, who anticipated vigorous action by Rajendra Prasad in their behalf, nor the Bihar Kisan Sabha, who accused Prasad of collaborating with the zamindars and flouting the interests of the peasant cultivators, was comfortable with the Congress's involvement in the dispute. Thereafter, the Congress would be reluctant both to take positions on agrarian issues involving disputes over rights in land and, especially, to become identified with prescriptive policies promising variants of agrarian reform that might alienate members of the landholding elite within the Congress.

The historical record suggests, then, that the pre-independence activities of the disparate kisan sabhas, the All India Kisan Sabha, and the Congress Socialists were not productive of a consensus within the Congress Movement concerning the place of agrarian reform or land reform in any rural development strategy that might be pursued when India became free of British rule. If anything, the activities of the All India Kisan Sabha and the Congress Socialists were so threatening of profound change in the traditional systems of rights in land in rural India that they caused persons within the Congress coalition, who otherwise had given lip service to amorphous variants of agrarian reform, to retreat from commitment to any reform measures. This applied especially if those measures were couched in language that seemed to be radical or militant. Thus, the pressures for radical measures of agrarian reform threatened the fragile unity of those seeking to lead India to freedom.

---

52. Within the context of the Bakasht Movement, the Bihar Kisan Sabha sought to use provisions of the *Bengal Tenancy Act of 1885* to establish a de jure basis by which the kisans of Bihar might claim permanent occupancy rights in land.

The Conflicting Visions
Within the Congress Party

The Ambivalence of Mohandas K. Gandhi

While Mohandas K. Gandhi is appropriately perceived as a leader of the Independence Movement who identified with the needs and interests of people in India who were low in social and economic status, there is no evidence to suggest that Gandhi fully understood the relationship between the plight of such people in rural areas and their low position in the hierarchy of interests in land. His empathy for the broad concerns of the peasantry was evident. His willingness, as in Awadh in 1921, to lend his support to peasant agitations was demonstrated. However, there is no evidence in his writings to suggest that he was a sophisticated student of India's historical land systems and the customary arrangements, peculiar to those systems, governing peoples' relations to one another and to the land. Gandhi did not seek to change conditions in rural India by means of agrarian reform.

Gandhi's capacity to contribute to any debate concerning land policy in India was somewhat diminished by his belief that there had existed in antiquity isolated, self-sufficient village republics, and that one of the goals of independent India should be the restoration of these "village communities." Without making particular reference to the views of Gandhi, Peter Robb has challenged this notion that there ever existed, as many Indian nationalists have averred, such isolated, self-sufficient village republics. Drawing on the scholarship of the late Eric Stokes, Robb suggests that "The old notion of isolated village republics was patently wrong."[53] Robb also argues for a "deconstruction of the notion of the village community. It was not unchanging or passive, ... nor was it inevitably transformed by capital or colonialism. It was not isolated, ... nor was it integrated. It had elements in which it was autonomous or resilient, but it was not homogeneous."[54]

---

53. See Peter Robb's article entitled "Ideas in Agrarian History: Some Observations on the British and Nineteenth-Century Bihar," *Journal of the Royal Asiatic Society*, No. 1, 1990, pp. 17-43.

54. Ibid., p. 22.

Whether or not Gandhi's idealized historical perception of Indian villages was wholly wrong, it seems clear from what we know about Gandhi's thinking on the subject that he, like many Indian nationalists, actually believed that conditions in village India had been altered adversely by British colonialism. Therefore, the emphasis of an independent India should be, from his perspective, on re-establishing the idealized villages of the past. He could not, or would not, recognize that factors other than the influence of British colonialism contributed to adverse conditions in the countryside. That is to say, he could not accept the notion that Indian villages, whether adversely affected by British colonialism or not, were hierarchical, inegalitarian, faction-ridden agglomerations of people.[55] And, clearly, Gandhi could not accept the idea that such agglomerations of people were arranged in a socioeconomic hierarchy reflecting mainly the existing distribution of rights in land. Understandably, working within his frame of reference, Gandhi could more easily imagine recreating idealized village communities of antiquity than focus on actual conditions in village India in his own era. Had he been willing to recognize conditions as they were, without assigning blame for them exclusively to the British colonialists, Gandhi could have placed himself in a position to think conceptually about how precisely those conditions could be transformed in his time by variants of agrarian reform. However, Gandhi never put himself in such a position to adopt the role of an agrarian reformer.

Moreover, in his role as political leader, Gandhi's obvious overriding interest was in promoting a broad-based coalition of interests (urban and rural, rich and poor, landlords and peasants, educated and illiterate) that would lead India to freedom from British colonialism. To do this, he could not alienate his movement's urban-based wealthy patrons, many of whom were also large landholders, by becoming a committed exponent of particular variants of agrarian reform or land reform. Had he done so, Gandhi would have shaken or destroyed the fragile unity of the Indian National Congress. As a

---

55. Gandhi's perception of village India was quite unlike that of his great contemporary, B.R. Ambedkar, who suggested that the Indian village was no more than "a sink of localism, a den of ignorance, narrow-mindedness and communalism." [B.R. Ambedkar, as quoted in Upendra Baxi, *The Crisis of the Indian Legal System,* (New Delhi: Vikas Publishing House, Ltd., 1982), p. 295.

political leader, Gandhi needed to find a means by which he could demonstrate his empathy for those, including both landlords and peasants, whom he sought to unite in common struggle against British authority.[56]

Accordingly, instead of promoting agrarian reform or land reform as a means of addressing the needs of the poorest and weakest sections of the peasantry, Gandhi offered his followers his Doctrine of Trusteeship. The message imbedded in this doctrine, whether calculated or not, gave precedence to the preservation of national unity in opposition to British rule. That is to say, the message made plain that landlords and industrialists, peasants and workers, should find common cause in the struggle for freedom -- that they should not become engaged in divisive struggle among themselves.

Within the Doctrine of Trusteeship, therefore, Gandhi preached the importance of mutual forbearance and tolerance. Thus, even in the context of the peasant movement in Awadh in February, 1921, Gandhi instructed the peasants to bear in mind "that we want to turn zamindars into friends."[57] At Awadh he instructed the peasants to cease engaging in acts of violence directed at landlords, to carry out all government orders, and not to withhold rent from landlords.[58] On other occasions, he argued that peasants and workers, whatever their grievances, should not withhold rent or go on strikes, and that landlords and industrialists, as "trustees" of the assets in their hands, should provide their peasants or workers good living and working conditions, should take only a "just" amount in rent from tenant cultivators, and should pay "fair" wages to workers.

Clearly, the Doctrine of Trusteeship, as expounded by Gandhi and made applicable to rural India, was utterly disassociated from programs of agrarian reform or land reform. Under this doctrine, there was no call for transformation of India's historical land systems, no call for changes in the existing hierarchy of interests in land, and no call for changes in land tenure that would confirm actual tillers' rights to land.

---

56. Tarlok Singh has emphasized that, prior to Independence, Gandhi was behaving as a sagacious political leader who did not want to rule out the involvement in the Independence Movement of any segment of the Indian population. [Tarlok Singh, Interview, New Delhi, February 21, 1989.]

57. Mohandas K. Gandhi, *Collected Works of Mahatma Gandhi*, (Ahmedabad: Government of Gujarat, 1966), Volume 19, pp. 419-420.

58. Ibid.

Under this doctrine the landlords would have lost nothing and the cultivating peasants who lacked secure rights in land would have gained nothing.[59]

Finally, while the historical record does seem to confirm that, in the pre-independence period, Gandhi was not a strong proponent of agrarian reform or land reform, it has been suggested that Gandhi's attitude toward agrarian reform was changing in the last phase of his life. An oft-cited interview with Louis Fischer in 1942 can be used to suggest that Gandhi then believed that Indian peasants, following independence, might simply "take" the land in their cultivating possession, and thereby effect their own land reform by means of direct action in their own behalf. In any event, however Gandhi's behavior and message are interpreted, his was no clarion call for agrarian reform or land reform. And, because he was assassinated in February of 1948, this great leader of India's struggle for freedom never had a substantive role in defining or influencing post-independence land policy.

The Pragmatism of Jawaharlal Nehru

Prior to independence, when Jawaharlal Nehru made statements concerning agrarian reform or land reform, he spoke amorphously and ambiguously. His goals were vague and his means uncertain. Sometimes, in public addresses, he would speak assertively in favor of cooperative or collective farming as a means of transforming India's archaic land systems. In the next breath, he would suggest that cooperatives or collectives would be extremely difficult to introduce in India unless, first, the historical land systems were abolished. And then, as if reflecting on the magnitude of such an undertaking, he would retreat from his assertive opening to muse aloud that abolishing the traditional land systems would not be "such an easy matter."[60]

---

59. F. Tomasson Jannuzi, *India in Transition: Issues of Political Economy in a Plural Society,* (Boulder, San Francisco, and London: Westview Press, 1989), p. 82.

60. India, Ministry of Information and Broadcasting, *Jawaharlal Nehru's Speeches,* Fourth Edition, (Delhi: Director, Publications Division, May, 1983), Volume 1, p. 116.

Nehru readily admitted that he was intellectually and emotionally removed from the needs and interests of peasant farmers. An urbanized, Kashmiri Brahmin who had been educated at Harrow and Cambridge in the United Kingdom, he described himself as having been cut adrift from the outlook of peasants. He considered their ways of thought, custom and religion alien to him.[61] And, when he thought about how best to achieve economic progress, Nehru said that his propensity was to think in terms of industrialization, rather than in terms linked to the transformation of peasant agriculture. By his own account, Nehru tended to depreciate the peasantry and to consider their viewpoints reactionary.[62]

Moreover, except for his brief involvement in the pre-independence kisan agitations in the United Provinces,[63] Nehru's experience had not equipped him to have much understanding of the complexity of India's various land systems together with the socioeconomic conditions associated with them. "He had made no study of economic and land problems and he had no clear ideas about peasant participation."[64]

What is more, to the extent that Nehru accepted the need to transform traditional agriculture in India, he did not see agrarian reform as being integral to that process. For him, transforming traditional agriculture mainly meant ensuring that modern science and technology would be applied to agriculture. When Nehru did speak of agrarian reform -- for example, when he won provincial elections in 1937 while promising agrarian reform and later, in his first broadcast to the nation following independence,[65] when he spoke of the need to transform radically India's traditional land systems[66] -- he considered that agrarian reform and land reform offered mainly a means by which historical inequities concerning rights in land could be ended and social

---

61. Jawaharlal Nehru, *Mahatma Gandhi,* (Calcutta: Signet Press, January 1949), p. 71.

62. Ibid.

63. The territory of contemporary Uttar Pradesh is, essentially, that of the former United Provinces prior to independence.

64. S. Gopal, *Jawaharlal Nehru: A Biography,* (A Project of the Jawaharlal Nehru Memorial Fund), (New Delhi: Orient Longman, Ltd., 1972), Volume 1, p. 42.

65. Michael Brecher, *Nehru, A Political Biography,* (London: Oxford University Press, 1959), p. 358.

66. Ibid. p. 597.

justice conferred on long-denigrated sections of the peasantry. In effect, Nehru separated the goals of agricultural development (perceived by him as a process by which modern technology and science could ensure self-sufficiency in foodgrains for the country) from the process of agrarian reform (perceived by him as a process by which historical inequities in the countryside could be ameliorated or ended). Concerned as he was about the need to provide ever increasing quantities of food for India's growing population and having established this conceptual dichotomy between agricultural development and agrarian reform, Nehru's highest priority was always assigned to agricultural development. For example, it was characteristic of him, when addressing the Constituent Assembly in February of 1948 on rural development issues, to give primacy to increases in agricultural production and to say that "everything that we do should be judged from the point of view of production first of all."[67] And, later on, he made plain in writing to all Pradesh Congress Presidents that, while he might favor efforts to implement land reform, such efforts should be carried out in a fashion ensuring that production increases were not thwarted.[68] In effect, having separated agricultural development conceptually from agrarian reform or land reform, Nehru persistently devalued the need for agrarian reform and land reform relative to the need for increases in food production.

Nehru's pre-independence lack of specificity concerning the variants of agrarian reform that he favored reflects not only his intellectual distance from village India and his lack of detailed knowledge of India's historical land systems, but also his adeptness as a pragmatic politician dealing with a volatile, divisive issue. By choosing not to delineate his own agenda for action in the sphere of agrarian reform, while remaining exhortative and broad-gauged in his public statements concerning the need to transform traditional agriculture in India, Nehru could minimize the political costs of his general, but opaque, advocacy of reform measures. He could verbalize his democratic socialist ideals without translating those ideals into implementable policies and programs. At the same time, he could defend his lack of specificity by

---

67. India, Ministry of Information and Broadcasting, *Jawaharlal Nehru's Speeches,* Volume 1, p. 108.

68. In this context, see Nehru's letter to all Pradesh Congress Presidents dated May 26, 1954, in the Congress Party *AICC Economic Review,* (New Delhi, June 15, 1954), Whole No. 101, Volume 6, No. 4, pp. 3-5.

arguing both that he wanted to avoid dogmatic, narrowly ideological prescriptions for the resolution of complex problems, and that he needed to ensure that the Congress Movement took consensus positions on tough issues -- positions fully representative of the views of every element in the body politic.[69] In this way, Nehru took on the mantle of a pragmatic politician and avoided, for the most part, being perceived as a threatening social or economic reformer.

The Radicalism of K.T. Shah

Prior to independence, the most radical vision of agrarian reform was articulated by the National Planning Committee, a committee constituted toward the end of 1938 to chart the preferred course of economic policy to be followed when the Indian National Congress was in a position to form a government and to assume responsibility for governing.[70] The National Planning Committee was divided into twenty-six sub-committees focusing on many facets of economic

---

69. Tarlok Singh, who worked closely with Nehru for many years, has suggested that "Nehru's socialism consisted of human and social values ...". At the same time, Singh has said that Nehru's "ideas on economic and social development did not amount to a complete and fully worked out system and, given the correct direction, he was willing to leave a great deal to evolve out of future experience." [Tarlok Singh, *Towards an Integrated Society: Reflections on Planning, Social Policy and Rural Institutions,* (Calcutta: Orient Longman Ltd., 1969), p. 356.]

70. The National Planning Committee met first in Bombay on December 17, 1938, under the Chairmanship of Jawaharlal Nehru with Subhas Chandra Bose, then President of the Congress, inaugurating the proceedings. Though the work of the committee was interrupted by World War II and the arrest by British authorities of many of the committee's members, twenty-six volumes of sub-committee reports were eventually completed. All of these reports were edited by Professor K.T. Shah and, it seems to me, are flavored by what might be called in context his radical, democratic socialist idealism. This judgement applies especially to the Report of the Sub-Committee on Land Policy, Agricultural Labour and Insurance -- a sub-committee chaired by K.T. Shah himself. The National Planning Committee was dissolved on March 26, 1949, when it submitted its final report, at Nehru's suggestion, to the Congress Working Committee. [See: K.T. Shah, editor, *Report, National Planning Committee,* (Bombay: Vora and Co. Publishers Ltd., June, 1949).]

policy. Of these, the Sub-Committee on Land Policy, Agricultural Labour and Insurance was chaired by Professor K.T. Shah. Ultimately, Shah's sub-committee presented a detailed set of policy recommendations designed to reform India's historical land systems in a fashion perceived by Shah, in particular, to be consistent with the "Resolution on Agrarian Programme" passed by the Indian National Congress at its annual meeting in April, 1936. The resolution set an agenda for action that included the following elements.

This Congress is of (the) opinion that the most important and urgent problem of the country is the appalling poverty, unemployment and indebtedness of the peasantry .... due to (the) antiquated and repressive land tenure and revenue systems and intensified in recent years by the great slump in prices of agricultural produce. The final solution of this problem inevitably involves the removal of British imperialistic exploitation, a thorough change of the land tenure and revenue systems and a recognition by the state of its duty to provide work for the rural unemployed masses.

In view, however, of the fact that agrarian conditions and land tenure and revenue systems differ in the various Provinces, it is desirable to consult the Provincial Congress Committees and such peasant organizations as the Working Committee considers fit, in the drawing up of a full All India Agrarian Programme as well as a program for each Province. This Congress, therefore, calls upon each Provincial Congress Committee to make recommendations in detail to the Working Committee by August 31, 1936, for being considered and placed before (the) All-India Congress Committee having particular regard to the following matters --

1. Freedom of organization of agricultural labourers and peasants.
2. Safeguarding of the interests of peasants where there are intermediaries between the State and themselves.
3. Just and fair relief of agricultural indebtedness, including arrears of rent and revenue.
4. Emancipation of the peasants from feudal and semi-feudal levies.
5. Substantial reduction in respect of rent and revenue demands.
6. A just allotment of the State expenditure for the social, economic and cultural amenities of villages.
7. Protection against harassing restrictions on the utilization of local natural facilities for their domestic and agricultural needs.

8. Freedom from oppression and harassment at the hands of Government officials and landlords.
9. Fostering industries for relieving rural unemployment.[71]

The resolution outlined above was one of the Indian National Congress policy pronouncements to be considered by the National Planning Committee as the committee pursued its task of delineating future policies for the Congress. However, as the National Planning Committee organized to begin its work, it established an organizational dichotomy that bifurcated consideration of agricultural policy issues: a dichotomy that would influence the way in which the planning committee delineated future agricultural policies for the Congress. That is to say, in organizing its sub-committees, the committee established several sub-committees designed to focus on agricultural production issues[72] and one sub-committee, to be chaired by K.T. Shah, to deal with issues pertaining to agrarian reform. Thus, with regard to agrarian policy, the National Planning Committee established the same sort of dichotomy as had been set earlier by the Royal Commission on Agriculture in India, 1928. The commission's rationale for its dichotomous treatment of agrarian policy issues was made explicit in its terms of reference, as earlier discussed. Without offering its own rationale, the National Planning Committee maintained the same dichotomy between agricultural production issues and agrarian reform. This bifurcation of agricultural production issues and issues of agrarian reform not only affected the subsequent recommendations of the National Planning Committee, but also became a persistent feature of thinking and discourse on agrarian policy long after India gained freedom from Britain. This bifurcation not only limited subsequent thought and discourse within the committee on the need for an integrative agrarian policy -- a policy that might recognize, for example, that the attainment of productivity goals in agriculture might actually be enhanced if agrarian reforms were effected in ways that would give new incentives and opportunities to long-neglected

---

71. K.T. Shah, editor, *Report, National Planning Committee,* (Bombay: Vora and Co. Publishers Ltd., June, 1949), pp. 29-30.
72. Among these production-oriented sub-committees were those dealing with the planning and production of crops and on animal husbandry and dairying.

sections of the cultivating peasantry -- but also limited the scope of work of the Shah Sub-Committee.

Working within the restrictions imposed by the committee's dichotomy between agricultural production issues and agrarian reform, K.T. Shah's sub-committee on land policy did its utmost to deal with agrarian reform issues in as holistic a fashion as possible. Specifically, the Shah Sub-Committee dealt with the following items:

1. the use and ownership of land and their effects on cultivation and social stratification;
2. measures to be suggested for agrarian reform with a view toward bringing about an equitable distribution of land resources and their effective utilization for the maximum benefit of the country;
3. land policy and supporting legislation designed to facilitate the establishment of economic units of production;
4. land revenue issues, including legislation affecting land tenure, agricultural rent, and the alienation of agricultural land by sale to non-agriculturists;
5. the supply of cheap power for agricultural purposes;
6. the establishment of a strategy by which culturable waste lands might be brought under cultivation;
7. the potential of cooperative institutions in rural areas;
8. the problem of rural indebtedness;
9. the role of legislation designed in various ways to affect positively the life and activities of agriculturists;
10. the conditions affecting agricultural labor (defined to include landless laborers, "partial owners", and "tenants" and "sub-tenants" working on the land), including wages, hours of work, conditions of employment, etc.; and
11. agricultural insurance, including issues pertaining to the effects of famines, floods, the loss of crops due to particular pests.

Within the frame of this broad scope of work, the Shah Sub-Committee eventually made the following observations and sweeping recommendations for agrarian reform. First, the sub-committee said that the ownership of all forms of natural wealth, including land, must belong to and vest absolutely and collectively in the people of India. While this recommendation was not necessarily consistent with the view of some scholars that, historically, the state or the ruling authority had been the super-landlord at the apex of the hierarchy of interests in land,[73] at least one member of the sub-committee, Professor Radhakamal Mukherjee, saw this recommendation as threatening individual rights in land or what he called "peasant proprietorship."[74] Second, the sub-committee said that all produce from land, mines, and forests must also vest absolutely in the people of India collectively. Third, the sub-committee suggested that all forms of "Natural Wealth" (including land) should be distributed for cultivation, exploitation and management among such associations and organizations, including collectives or cooperatives, within the terms and conditions of what it called "fundamental land law." And, in this context, the sub-committee made plain that such collective or cooperative associations should be organized and established in every part of the country on a compulsory basis. Fourth, the sub-committee recommended that rights of inheritance applying to land and other forms of "Natural Wealth" be abolished. Fifth, the sub-committee recommended establishing under law what it called "a minimum scale of living" for the people in rural areas who would work the land collectively or cooperatively. Sixth, the sub-committee recommended that any surplus derived from agriculture, after the basic needs of the people in the countryside had been met, be taken by the state to meet the requirements of a pre-determined national plan. Seventh, the sub-committee advised abolishing all those landholders (including zamindars, taluqdars, malguzars, lease-holders, farming contractors, etc.) in India who could be classified as "intermediary parasites"[75] between the state and the

---

73. See Daniel Thorner's defence of this proposition in his *The Agrarian Prospect in India,* (Delhi: Delhi University Press, 1956).

74. Mukherjee wrote a sharp note of dissent on this subject, a note published in the sub-committee's final report. In his dissent, Mukherjee took exception especially to the sub-committee's recommendation in favor of collective or cooperative farming and argued that the reinforcement of individual rights in land would be preferable as a means both of ensuring "social peace" and of giving cultivators economic incentives to transform traditional agriculture.

75. The sub-committee's use of the word "parasites" to describe the behavior of such landholders who were to be "abolished" after independence is indicative of the radical tone of its recommendations. Nonetheless, such large landholders, acting as intermediaries of the state in the collection of land revenue, had earlier been similarly castigated for their behavior by the relatively conservative British economist, Vera Anstey, and described by her

(continued...)

actual tiller of the soil. This recommendation specified that such landholders should have all of their traditional rights and privileges pertaining to their landholdings taken away from them under terms and conditions prescribed in a "National Land Law" (to be enacted when an independent India came into being). Eighth, the sub-committee endorsed the need for the consolidation of landholdings into "standard units that can be efficiently operated." And, it suggested that, once consolidated, agricultural land should not be subdivided in future as a result of the application of laws of inheritance or as a result of decisions made to mortgage land. This stipulation could be understood in the context of a later stipulation in the sub-committee's report that all private property rights in land should, in any event, be abolished. Finally, the Shah Sub-Committee recommended that all of these changes in the traditional system of rights in land in India should be effected, as noted above, by means of a "Fundamental Land Law" having all-India efficacy.[76]

Whether the Shah Sub-Committee's recommendations could have been effectively implemented by means of national legislation was never tested. After independence, land policy was made a state subject, rather than a central responsibility, under the Indian constitution. It would become painfully evident in the years ahead among those who favored agrarian reform that such reforms could be thwarted easily if instituted by means of legislation in the states of India without a national land law and without the threat of coercive power being exercised, under law, by the central Government of India.

The Generic Views of Intellectuals

In the years immediately preceding India's independence, few intellectuals within or outside India were as separated from actual conditions in the Indian countryside as was R. Palme Dutt, the

---

75.(...continued)
as "mere parasites, who batten on the product of the cultivators." [Vera Anstey, *The Economic Development of India,* (London: Longmans, Green and Co., 1929), p. 99.]

76. K.T. Shah, *Land Policy, Agricultural Labour & Insurance,* Report of the Sub-Committee of the National Planning Committee Series, (Bombay: Vora and Co. Publishers Ltd., 1948), pp. 48-61.

Comintern leader based in London. This notwithstanding, there was a widespread tendency among indigenous intellectuals associated with the Independence Movement to be distant from peasant cultivators and their needs. Indeed, even intellectuals who sought to transform India's land systems by means of agrarian reform were not disposed to define the content of agrarian reform in interaction with actual tillers of the soil in the countryside. The goal of the intellectuals was to confer the benefits of socioeconomic change on the people in rural areas -- not to establish goals in concert with those people. The imbedded assumption in the minds of the intellectual elite, whatever their ideological propensities or commitments, was that the people in rural areas (particularly those lacking either secure rights in land or any land at all) were not equipped to give expression to their own needs and interests. Above all, I believe, it was assumed by India's intellectual elite that the peasantry, however defined, were not rational people who knew better than anyone else the actual conditions in rural India that inhibited economic progress and that, therefore, would have to be changed if economic transformation was to become a broad-based phenomenon. The intellectuals, even those concerned about the backwardness of traditional agriculture, assumed that the peasantry -- poor, illiterate and powerless as the peasants seemed to be -- could not be expected either to have ideas of their own or to be capable of action in their own behalf. Thus, the prevailing view within and outside of the Congress Movement was both indulgent of peasants' needs, as defined by urban-based intellectuals, and patronizing of peasants' abilities to specify the means (including variants of agrarian reform) by which those needs might best be addressed.[77]

This propensity among intellectuals to underestimate peasants has been imbedded to some degree in the attitudes of all post-Marxist social scientists, whether they identify with the left or the right of the ideological spectrum. And, I believe that this propensity to underestimate peasants has contributed to persistent misperceptions of peasants' capacities to play innovative roles in the transformation of

---

77. This pejorative view of peasants' capacities to act in their own interests was made evident, for example, when the Indian National Congress in 1936, while articulating its agrarian program, made plain that it saw little scope for the implementation of its program if the initiative for change "rests exclusively with the cultivator, who is usually illiterate and unable to see his own advantage ..." in such programs. [K.T. Shah, editor, *Report, National Planning Committee,* p. 24.]

traditional agrarian societies. Thus, it was virtually the "conventional wisdom" among opinion leaders of the pre-independence period in India that rural people, amorphously classified as peasants, if they were to be made modern and productive, would have to be exhorted, organized, taught, or even compelled by "outsiders" not only to articulate their "felt" needs, but also to work harder, to employ new techniques of production and, in general, to shed habits of mind perceived by others to be impediments to sustained economic progress in rural areas. With such views deeply rooted in the minds of India's intellectuals, it is no wonder that even those who favored variants of agrarian reform were ill-equipped to conceptualize and promote changes in the traditional system of rights in land that would have resonated with the actual tillers of the soil.

The Resistance Strategies of Landholders

While, prior to independence, the Shah Sub-Committee was calling for radical programs of agrarian reform and giving specificity to its recommendations, the view that certain kinds of landholders should be abolished was gaining currency. Moreover, for some nationalists, it became an article of belief that the British had introduced the landlord system in India to solidify their rule. While this idea is ahistorical, it exemplifies the need of some Indian nationalists to blame the British for having created the conditions in the Indian countryside that were adverse to economic progress. This nationalist paradigm, though widely held, was rooted in Marxist-oriented interpretations of British colonialism. R. Palme Dutt, for example, gave explicit expression to the popular view when he said (with respect to the British East India Company's Permanent Settlement of 1793) that "The purpose of the permanent Zamindari settlement was to create a new class of landlords after the English models as the social buttress of English rule."[78] If one accepted this premise, one could go on to argue that conditions inimical to economic progress in the Indian countryside could be transformed at once if landlords were abolished. From this simplified perspective, the favorable, pre-British colonial period, status quo ante would be restored and the cultivating peasantry emancipated when the landlords created by the British ceased to exist.

---

78. R. Palme Dutt, *India Today,* p. 217.

As this idea became popular, almost a nationalist credo, it was threatening to some members of the Congress coalition, especially ideological conservatives, including Rajendra Prasad and Sardar Patel who were themselves powerful leaders of the Independence Movement. And, it was especially threatening to large landholders, including zamindars and taluqdars, who had been drawn into the Congress in the common struggle against British rule. Fearing that agrarian reform, however defined, would reduce their economic dominance and political authority, such landholders evolved strategies (especially in the 1930s in response to agitations inspired by the kisan sabhas) to protect their interests in land.

For example, in the 1930s large landholders of Bengal (jotedars) progressively denied actual tillers (usually sharecroppers or bargadars) secure rights in the land tilled by them by obtaining court orders declaring that any land claimed by such actual cultivators was in fact the landholders' khas land (land to which the superior landholder held an exclusive right under existing law). Because land use contracts between superior and inferior landholders (that is, between a jotedar and his tenant or sharecropper) were usually oral and the records of payment of rent were kept by the superior landholder or his agent, the actual tiller had little chance of defending himself in a civil suit, especially when the court, revenue officials and the local police were likely to side with the superior landholder in any dispute over rights in land. The relative powerlessness of the inferior landholder or sharecropper was no doubt reinforced by his poverty and his inability, generally, to produce records that would confirm his own claim to land.[79] Thus, actual tillers could be denied acquisition of secure rights in land and evicted from lands tilled by them. And, within the frame of existing law, superior landholders' rights in land could be maintained even in circumstances where those rights were challenged. Incidentally, when a superior landholder succeeded in evicting a cultivating peasant from a disputed plot of land, that landholder was in a position to negotiate a new contract with another tiller at an

---

79. As noted in the text, it was likely that the superior landholder or his agent would have sole possession of land records, including records of rent payments. Such records could be contrived to suit the purposes of the superior landholder and legalized by obtaining the thumb print of the inferior landholder. Often illiterate, inferior landholders were thus bound to the terms of documents they could not read.

increased salami (charge for the new contract) and an additional payment (nazrana) to the landlord.

In the United Provinces, now Uttar Pradesh, zamindars and taluqdars refined strategies by which they could deny their tenants permanent rights in land. Using existing law, the zamindars were entitled to a permanent occupancy right (as distinct from absolute ownership) to their sir and khudkasht lands. The sir lands were, nominally, those lands cultivated by the superior landholders themselves, or with the help of hired labor. If a superior landholder permitted an inferior landholder (a tenant farmer or sharecropper) to "take in" some sir land for purposes of cultivation, it was understood (at least by the superior landholder) that the tiller of the sir land remained a "tenant-at-will perpetually under the threat of ejectment."[80] That is to say, the inferior landholder who tilled a piece of sir land could not acquire under law a permanent occupancy right to it. Whatever his arrangement with the superior landholder, he remained a "tenant-at-will" and, therefore, subject to removal from the land as a trespasser. In order to deny a tenant-at-will any prospect of acquiring a permanent right to the land being tilled by him, the superior landholder would, first, keep no record of the name of the tenant-at-will and, second, use existing law (for example, the *Agra Tenancy Act of 1926*) to register a trespassing case against the tenant-at-will. Under the relevant law, this could be done within three years of the initial agreement by which the inferior landholder took in the sir land for purposes of cultivation. By this means, a superior landholder could recycle his "tenants-at-will" every three years by de jure means and even claim damages from the evicted tenant at four times the rental value of the land.[81]

Superior landholders in the United Provinces used the same de jure means to thwart tillers' claims to their khudkasht lands when such lands were given out to others for purposes of cultivation. Having given out such lands to landless agricultural laborers or sharecroppers for purposes of cultivation, superior landholders would prefer charges

---

80. Amit Kumar Gupta, "The Leftists and the Rural Poor in India, 1934-39," (Draft Manuscript).

81. Amit Kumar Gupta, "The Leftists and the Rural Poor in India, 1934-39," (Draft Manuscript), citing United Provinces, Revenue Department, "Legal Expert to Revenue Secretary," August 10, 1938, File No. 475/38 at the United Provinces State Archives, Lucknow.

against them for trying to take "forcible possession" of the khudkasht lands they tilled. The tillers would then be ejected from those lands as stipulated in a court order.

Similarly, in Bihar, superior landholders in the 1930s (classified legally as zamindars or tenure-holders) exercised direct control over their so-called bakasht lands. When they gave out bakasht lands for purposes of cultivation to landless laborers or sharecroppers (called bataidars in Bihar), the superior landholders knew that existing law (the *Bengal Tenancy Act of 1885*) could enable the tiller to acquire a permanent occupancy right to that land if he tilled the same holding for at least twelve consecutive years. Needless to say, the zamindars and tenure-holders, if threatened by the prospect that a sharecropper might claim a permanent right to bakasht land, could thwart the working of the law simply by ensuring that sharecroppers were shifted from plot to plot and denied any opportunity to meet the de jure terms of permanent occupancy.

In Bihar, the threat of agrarian reform to superior landholders took shape long before independence. In 1936, in Monghhyr, Gaya, Patna, Shahabad, and Saran Districts, sections of the peasantry were mobilized to protest their eviction from bakasht lands and even to claim in some instances occupancy rights to the land in dispute within the terms of the *Bengal Tenancy Act of 1885*. Using mainly non-violent, Gandhian means of protest at the outset, the agitators dared to place their demands, sometimes by squatting on the lands from which they had been ejected. A crisis atmosphere quickly developed, and the Congress Party in Bihar decided to intervene. However, the Party faced a dilemma derived from the composition of its membership in Bihar. That membership was dominated by superior landholders (zamindars and tenure-holders) who were disposed to defend their own interests against the demands of cultivators below them in the agrarian hierarchy. At the same time, the Congress in Bihar could not easily turn its back on Party resolutions emphasizing the need for agrarian reform and the importance of addressing the needs of poor peasants.

To resolve the crisis, referred to popularly as the Bihar Bakasht Movement, the Congress appointed a committee of enquiry chaired by the respected Bihari leader, Rajendrda Prasad.[82]   The Prasad

---

82. Rajendra Prasad would in due course become the first President of India following independence and an ardent supporter of landholders who opposed variants of agrarian reform.

Committee attempted to establish the status quo ante by suggesting that the conditions concerning rights in land should be restored in the countryside to those existing before 1936 when the Bakasht Movement began. That is to say, the committee sought to placate the interests of cultivating peasants by restoring their right to till lands occupied by them, but claimed subsequently as bakasht by zamindars. At the same time, however, the Prasad Committee upheld the zamindars' right to select the plot to be given to an inferior landholder and to specify the terms under which the land would be tilled. This meant that the zamindars were given renewed license by the Prasad Committee to shift tillers from plot to plot and to deny tillers "rent receipts"; they were given renewed license to use the already conventional means by which superior landholders could prevent actual tillers any prospect of acquiring a permanent right to the land in their cultivating possession.[83] In effect, then, the Prasad Committee's mediating effort ultimately pleased neither the zamindars nor the inferior landholders. By 1938, the confrontation between the superior and inferior landholders had become violent. In actions strikingly reminiscent of the violence in contemporary Bihar, the zamindars and tenure-holders sent their men on raids to intimidate those below them in the agrarian hierarchy who dared to confront them. In retaliation, a zamindar was waylaid and killed.[84]

As clashes continued between zamindars and peasant cultivators in Bihar, tensions within the local Congress Movement escalated. The primary leader of the peasant agitations, Sahajanand, was removed from the Congress Working Committee; the Provincial Congress issued a directive that its members should not speak at kisan sabha meetings; and, the Congress actually established its own "Kisan Branch" as a countervailing force against the local kisan sabha. However, when the Congress's own "Kisan Branch" attempted to negotiate accords

---

83. Within the frame of the *Bengal Tenancy Act of 1885*, a permanent right to the land would have been established, as noted earlier in the text, when a tiller cultivated the same plot for twelve consecutive years. At such point, under law, the tiller could have been classified as a permanent occupancy raiyat and would be considered in principle, if seldom in fact, the virtual "owner" of the land in his possession.

84. Amit Kumar Gupta, "The Leftists and the Rural Poor in India, 1934-39," (Draft Manuscript), citing India, Home Poll., "Fortnightly Report for First half of November, 1937," File No. 18/11/27, National Archives of India.

between the zamindars and sections of the cultivating peasantry, the local kisan sabha accused the Congress of "collaborating with the zamindars by flouting the interests of the cultivators."[85] This accusation was not without foundation. Amit Kumar Gupta has suggested that the local Congress had in fact entered into a secret agreement with the zamindars on December 13, 1937, following prolonged negotiation and the intervention of the Congress troubleshooter and strong man, Sardar Patel.

The Bakasht Movement continued, and violent confrontations became more evident in 1939. There were forcible crop cuttings on zamindars' lands by cultivators in February followed by a zamindari attack on cultivators in March. In April, cultivators armed with lathis (wooden clubs) dared to confront the police. And, in July in Gaya, Bihar, there was armed conflict between superior landholders and cultivating peasants.

The local Congress Ministry now broke with the Bihar Kisan Sabha and decided to invoke what it called a policy of "the carrot and the stick." The carrot was represented by local arbitration committees; the stick involved the deployment of large numbers of policemen, including mounted military police and armed reserve police.[86] By September of 1939, the cultivators' agitations had diminished in intensity. However, neither the policy of the carrot nor the threat of the stick can be said to have ended the Bakasht Movement in Bihar. The ending of the movement can be attributed mainly to the decision of the local Congress Ministry to cease cooperation with the British with the advent of World War II and to resign. When the Congress Ministry resigned in 1939, the movement petered out.

In the 1930s, peasant agitations sent a message to superior landholders that sections of the peasantry who lacked secure rights in land could be mobilized in direct action in their own behalf. Agitations made plain that variants of agrarian reform would be pursued by peasants in the years ahead, particularly if India gained freedom from Britain. Superior landholders, including those who had established leadership positions in the Congress Independence

---

85. Amit Kumar Gupta, "The Leftists and the Rural Poor in India, 1934-39," (Draft Manuscript), p. 109.

86. Amit Kumar Gupta has argued that the mustered force included Gurkha soldiers who were ordered to break up stubborn resistance. [Ibid., p. 118.]

Movement, understood the message and its implicit threat to their own economic position. Men such as Rajendra Prasad and Sardar Patel were led to differentiate themselves from the agrarian reformers within and outside of the Congress coalition. Indeed, the peasant agitations together with the landholders' response to them, foreshadowed the difficulties that would be encountered after independence when the Congress-led Government of India would consider promoting agrarian reform. In post-independence India, as in pre-independence India, the Congress Party would have difficulty in establishing a consensus within its divided ranks as to the efficacy of agrarian reform.

2

Post-Independence Perspectives
on Agrarian Reform
and Rural Development

The Colonial Legacy of the British

The British colonial legacy in India was deep, pervasive and continuing in its impact on land policy in the first years following independence. The colonial legacy included British scholarly interpretations of the historical land systems of India.[1] It also incorporated the work and recommendations of special commissions (for example, the Royal Commission on Agriculture in India, 1928) that ultimately helped to shape the development agenda for independent India. In its essence, the colonial legacy included all of the laws enacted during British rule that had bearing on rights in land; it included all of the administrative procedures and rules pertaining to rights in land, even those related to the gathering of data concerning rights in land; and it included all of the rural development policies articulated or invoked by British authority, especially in the twentieth century when rural economic development became one of the goals of the British in India. That legacy continues to influence the process by which India today addresses rural development and agrarian reform issues.

Instead of defining agrarian reform in new ways shaped by nationalist visions concerning how the agrarian structure of India might be reshaped, even radical exponents of agrarian reform in India supported reform that would involve mainly the modification or amendment of established acts

---

1. See, for example, some of the writings of B.H. Baden-Powell, especially *Land Revenue and Tenure in British India,* Second Edition, (Oxford: The Clarendon Press, 1913).

pertaining to rights in land. That is to say, the leaders of independent India invoked the need for change in traditional land systems within an ideational and legislative frame defined, ironically, by their erstwhile colonial rulers.

When independent India, within the context of Congress Party leadership, articulated the need for radical restructuring of historical rights in land by calling for the abolishment of the zamindari land system, it appears that the only conceptual means considered to implement zamindari abolition was rooted in colonial era procedures.   More specifically, the Congress leaders followed colonial precedent to assign revenue ministries the responsibility both to update land records, using time-consuming British-written manuals of procedure, and to write amendments to colonial law. There was no discernible inclination within the Congress "High Command" to call for new methods and procedures by which such agrarian reform could be effected. There was no attempt made, for example, either to repeal British laws as a means of transforming the zamindari land system or to repudiate British colonial methods and procedures by which land policy in India had been shaped. In other words, there was no obvious attempt to effect agrarian reform, including zamindari abolition, by new means reflecting the grand visions of change invoked in India's own documents of state, including the constitution and the various five year plans.

When agrarian reform was invoked after independence by the Government of India, it took for granted, apparently, that such reform would be implemented by means of legislation within the frame of British colonial law.[2] Working within the ideational legislative frame of the British, the Government of India permitted colonial legacy laws defining rights in land either to remain in force, or to be amended incrementally, thereby minimizing significant change in the historical land systems of the country.

As one reflects on what transpired with respect to agrarian reform after India gained freedom from Britain, the dominant impression is of

---

2. Upendra Baxi, India's distinguished legal scholar and educator, castigated independent India's reliance on colonial era precedents in law. Baxi suggested that the Indian legal system has, virtually, regarded "the attainment of political independence as immaterial or irrelevant ...". This has resulted, says Baxi, in what amounts to "juristic dependencia" (a phrase borrowed consciously by him from Latin American "dependencia theory"). [See: Upendra Baxi, *The Crisis of the Indian Legal System,* (New Delhi: Vikas Publishing House Ltd., 1982), pp. 41-43.

continuity with the past rather than change -- even when the rhetoric of reform was radical in tone. The historical record confirms that independent India's land policy has been defined and constrained by the laws, by the administrative practices, and by the policy recommendations of the British in India. Instead of a demonstrably indigenous agenda for agrarian reform sharply divergent from the British legacy in this sphere, the record of independent India has been one mainly of endorsement and reiteration of British colonial ideas, recommendations, procedures and policies concerning peoples' rights in land.

In the last days of the Raj, the British had associated the improvement of the welfare and prosperity of the rural population mainly with the promotion of programs emphasizing agricultural research leading to the introduction of new and better crops, the development of improved agricultural practices, the promotion of veterinary science, and the development of improved means of providing agricultural credit. Excepting only one variant of agrarian reform (the consolidation of small units of production into larger productive units), the British in India did not associate the promotion of agrarian reform with the improvement of the welfare and prosperity of the rural population in India. This kind of dichotomous thinking was reflected in the administrative systems established by the British to deal with issues of rural development. Thus, agricultural ministries dealt with issues pertaining to the welfare and prosperity of the rural population. Meanwhile, revenue ministries focused on issues pertaining to the hierarchy of interests in land in rural India -- including issues related to agrarian reform, land reform, revenue collection, and the maintenance of records concerning rights in land. In this way, both conceptually and procedurally, the British tended to ignore agrarian reform as a means of promoting the welfare and prosperity of the rural population and contributing to rural economic development.

Sadly, independent India reiterated the British colonial dichotomy by which agricultural development was separated conceptually and procedurally from agrarian reform issues -- thereby inhibiting the development in modern India of synthetic policies of rural economic development: policies confirming the necessary linkages between programs of agricultural development and agrarian reform so as to promote simultaneously increases in productivity in rural areas and the general welfare of the rural population. Instead of new thinking about rural economic development, the leaders of independent India behaved as if they were still constrained by the advice and counsel of the British Raj. Thus, even the draft outline of India's First Five Year Plan, and all subsequent plans, continued to make functional, elemental distinctions between programs designed to promote agrarian reform and those designed to promote agricultural development. In this way, the agrarian policy recommendations of independent India continued to separate agrarian reform from agricultural development issues. Wittingly or unwittingly, independent India behaved with respect to agrarian reform and agricultural development issues as if those who governed were themselves constrained by the politically invoked "terms of reference" established by the United Kingdom for the Royal Commission on Agriculture in India, 1928 (RCAI-1928).

Agrarian Reform Recommendations[3]
of the Congress Party

If the decision-making elites of the Congress Party ever came close to establishing a consensus concerning land policy (agrarian reform) issues following independence, they did so within the context of the deliberations of the Congress Agrarian Reforms Committee under the leadership of its Chairman, J.C. Kumarappa.[4] Nonetheless, the final report of what became known as the Kumarappa Committee contained, in addition to its principal recommendations pertaining to agrarian reform, sharp notes of dissent by two members of the committee, N.G. Ranga and O.P. Ramaswamy Reddiar. These dissenting notes foreshadowed what

---

3. I refer here to the recommendations of what became known popularly as the "Report of the Kumarappa Committee." The full citation is: J.C. Kumarappa, Chairman, *Report of the Congress Agrarian Reforms Committee,* (New Delhi: The All-India Congress Committee, 1949).

4. In addition to J.C. Kumarappa, the committee was comprised of M.L. Dantwala, then Reader in Agricultural Economics at Bombay University School of Economics; Shri S. Das Gupta, Secretary of the Board of Revenue of the Government of West Bengal; Shri T.V. Raghavulu, Representative, Agricultural Labour; Shri O.P. Ramaswamy Reddiar, Ex-Premier, Government of Madras; Shri N.G. Ranga, President, All-India Kisan Congress; Shri Ameer Raza, Secretary of the Zamindari Abolition Committee of the Government of Uttar Pradesh; Shri Phulan Prasad Varma, Member of the Damodar Valley Corporation; and Shri K. Mitra, Secretary of the Economic and Political Research Department of the All-India Congress Committee. The last named, Mitra, was the Member Secretary for the committee; he was assisted by H.D. Malaviya who subsequently wrote on agrarian reform issues from a leftist polemical perspective.

would be a continuing debate on land policy within the Congress: a debate of such divisive intensity, ultimately, that the Congress never did reach what might be called an all-India consensus concerning precisely how the hierarchy of interests in land in the countryside could be reshaped by means of agrarian reform to meet the modernization goals of independent India.[5]

The Congress Agrarian Reforms Committee met for the first time on February 23, 1948, with Rajendra Prasad presiding.[6] Its charge was to survey actual conditions in rural areas of India and thereafter to make recommendations about agrarian reforms arising out of the abolition of the zamindari system in the light of conditions prevailing in the different provinces. In addition, the committee was asked to consider and report on cooperative farming and methods of improving agricultural production and to report on the status of landholders having small holdings, sub-tenants and landless agricultural laborers.[7] In response to its charge, the committee travelled more than fourteen thousand miles around India gathering documents concerning the hierarchy of interests in land and interviewing a great number and variety of persons.

---

5. Kumarappa was clearly distressed that Ranga and Reddiar found it necessary to criticize the formal recommendations of the Congress Agrarian Reforms Committee; his distress was made evident when he transmitted the final report to the then President of the Indian National Congress with the observation that those who had written notes of dissent were inclined to be rather academic. Earlier, Kumarappa had suggested that the dissenting notes were written by persons who had not served adequately and consistently on the committee and, therefore, had been deprived of access to data that might have enabled them to clarify their views (that is, to join with other members of the committee in supporting without reservation the committee's recommendations).

6. While I have found no evidence to suggest that Rajendra Prasad shaped or influenced the deliberations of the committee, his commitment to agrarian reform, especially zamindari abolition, was at least highly qualified. Tarlok Singh, a key member of the Planning Commission and the person directly responsible for writing the draft outline to the First Five Year Plan, has said that Rajendra Prasad, then President of the Republic, had once summoned him for a discussion on land policy. According to Singh, "The President asked a variety of questions and seemed to be of the view that we might be going too far in our recommendations for agrarian reform. He was, after all, a rather conservative person." [Tarlok Singh, Interview, New Delhi, January 23, 1989.]

7. J.C. Kumarappa, *Report of the Congress Agrarian Reforms Committee*, pp. 3-4.

The activities of the Kumarappa Committee can be summarized briefly: it recommended the elimination of intermediaries between the state and the tiller; it sought to establish national guidelines concerning the size of landholdings; it specified a need for cooperative joint farming; it endorsed collective farming on reclaimed land; it specified community rights in land; and it failed to provide a framework for agrarian reform. These committee activities are discussed in greater detail below.

Recommending the Elimination of Intermediaries

In its final report, published in 1949, the Congress Agrarian Reforms Committee gave primacy to the "elimination of all intermediaries between the State and the tiller."[8] In general, these intermediaries were the revenue farmers of British India -- landholders who enjoyed permanent occupancy rights to the land in their possession so long as they acted to collect the state's land revenue. Such intermediaries had been widely condemned during the Independence Movement as non-cultivating parasites who should be abolished when the colonial era was ended.

The committee's recommendation for the abolition of intermediaries was made in spite of the fact that, because the Congress Party derived strong support from such landholding intermediaries, the abolition of intermediary interests would become a difficult task involving political costs not easily entertained by Jawaharlal Nehru and the governing elite. Nevertheless, the Kumarappa Committee's majority view was uncompromising concerning the need to abolish all intermediary landholders between the state and the actual cultivator. The committee stated that in the agrarian economy of an independent India there should be "no place for intermediaries and land must belong to the tiller ...".[9] With this in mind, the committee recommended that the subletting of land (for purposes of cultivation) should be prohibited "except in the case of widows, minors and other disabled persons."[10] It envisaged a transition period before subletting would be prohibited and, in this context, also recommended that actual cultivators who had tilled the same land (including land "taken in" from a superior landholder for purposes of

----

8. Ibid., p. 7.
9. Ibid.
10. Ibid.

cultivation) for six consecutive years should receive a permanent occupancy right to that land, the rough equivalency in India of ownership.[11]

By recommending against the subletting of land and by suggesting that actual tillers should have a clear means of acquiring a permanent right to the land they tilled, the Kumarappa Committee sought to attack the common practice by which landholders derived income from the land while separating themselves and their families either from labor on it or investment in its improvement. Regrettably, even as the committee set forth these recommendations, it also was sending a contradictory signal: namely that, following the enactment of agrarian reforms, landholders who had given out land to others for cultivation should be permitted to resume that land for their own personal cultivation. The committee did specify that "personal cultivation" should be defined so as to require the landholder to labor, himself, on the land and to be directly participatory in agricultural operations. Later, such a stringent definition of personal cultivation by a landholder was omitted in land reform legislation enacted in the Indian states. As a result, even after the enactment of land reform legislation in the states, superior landholders (including ex-zamindars) could resume land for personal cultivation even if this meant evicting actual cultivators and tilling the resumed land "personally" by utilizing servants, agricultural laborers, and sharecroppers.

The Kumarappa Committee also recommended that actual cultivators who lacked secure rights in land should be able to purchase such rights "at a reasonable price to be determined by Regional Land Tribunals."[12] Anticipating that the threat of land reform might cause landholders to evict "tenants" who had a de jure claim to occupancy rights in land, the committee emphasized the need to ensure that up-to-date records of rights in land were prepared.[13] The committee also suggested that steps be taken to protect cultivators from rack-renting and illegal exactions.

---

11. By contrast, for example, the *Bengal Tenancy Act of 1885* had specified that a tiller could acquire a permanent occupancy right to land tilled by him only after twelve years. However, while the Kumarappa Committee's recommendation concerning the means by which a cultivator could acquire an occupancy right to land was a departure from the colonial era standard, it clearly represented an incremental change within the frame of British legacy law, rather than a new way of thinking about how permanent occupancy rights in land could be conferred to actual tillers.

12. Kumarappa, *Report of the Congress Agrarian Reforms Committee*, p. 7.

13. Ibid., p. 8.

According to the committee, the ideal means by which the rights and interests of actual tillers might be protected in the context of agrarian reform would be local "Land Tribunals" invested with the power to make regionally differentiated decisions on the spot.

Specifying the Size of Landholdings

The Kumarappa Committee recognized three distinct kinds of landholdings: basic, economic and optimum. Basic holdings were defined as holdings so small in size as to be uneconomic, too small to afford a reasonable standard of living for a cultivator. The committee recognized that there were vast numbers of such small, fragmented, and apparently uneconomic holdings in rural India. The committee indicated that such holdings could not be ignored. At the same time, the committee suggested that it would be extremely difficult to transform such landholdings into viable, productive economic units. Accordingly, the committee asserted that such basic holdings would have to be addressed by new approaches -- approaches that might be beyond the organizational capacity of the state.[14] In effect, the Kumarappa Committee adopted in this context the same negative view of small, fragmented landholdings in India as had the RCAI-1928. Such small units of production were perceived by the committee as an integral part of the problem of traditional agriculture. Basic holdings would require a different approach and treatment than economic or optimum holdings. Nonetheless, the committee, judging from the content of its final report, did not realize that its own emphasis on conferring rights in land to actual tillers would, if implemented, lead to the proliferation of the "basic" landholdings it considered too small to afford a reasonable standard of living for cultivators. In fact, the committee saw no discrepancy between its emphasis on "land to the tiller" and its disparagement of small landholdings.

The committee considered an economic holding to be one that would afford a reasonable standard of living to a cultivator; but, it made the definition of an economic holding opaque by stating that such a holding would vary in size in accordance with agronomic conditions in different regions of the country.[15]

---

14. Ibid., pp. 8-9.
15. Ibid., p. 8.

The term optimum holding was used by the committee to suggest that "there should be a ceiling to the size of holdings which any one farmer should own and cultivate."[16] In this context, the recommendation was that the optimum size of a landholding should be three times the size of an economic holding. Thus, the idea of ceilings on the size of holdings was introduced within a vague frame of reference -- especially when the committee had accepted the notion that economic holdings would be regionally differentiated in size. Further complicating its reference to the need for ceilings on the size of landholdings, the committee also suggested that variations in ceiling size might be allowed "in cases of joint families and charitable institutions."[17]

Thus, the Kumarappa Committee, as it sought to establish national guidelines concerning the size of landholdings (basic, economic and optimum), put forward vague and indeterminate standards that would make it quite difficult for the Indian states, within their own legislative chambers, subsequently to reach consensus concerning whether and how they should regulate the size of landholdings.

Specifying the Need for Joint Farming

The committee invoked the need for what it called cooperative joint farms to be established by amalgamating small, basic landholdings into larger units of production. The explicit rationale for such cooperative joint farms was that they were necessary to an efficient agriculture. The obvious concern was to establish economies of scale in agricultural production. In effect, the committee withdrew its absolute commitment (as earlier enunciated in its report) to a definition of land reform based on "land to the tiller" and made plain again, as had the RCAI-1928, that it did not equate a modern and efficient agriculture with peasant proprietorship on small units of production. In this context, the Congress Agrarian Reforms Committee went on to specify that cultivators of small, non-economic landholdings would have to cultivate their farms jointly with other such landholders.[18] The tone and content of this recommendation were instrumental in the decision of one member of the committee, Professor N.G. Ranga, to reject the committee's final report

---

16. Ibid., p. 9.
17. Ibid.
18. Ibid., p. 10.

and to introduce a dissenting note. Then President of the All India Kisan Congress, Ranga said that he was "unable to agree to making the actual cultivation of land a cooperative process through compulsion ...".[19] He said that he favored the perpetuation of small landholdings under individual proprietors. Nonetheless, Ranga made plain that he had no objection to the development of cooperative institutions designed to provide inputs and credit to such small farmers. Indeed, he said that, if small farmers were provided inputs and credit, there "need be no limit to the smallness of the holding of any cultivator ...".[20] Ranga, therefore, said that he saw no need to use coercion to bring about cooperative joint farming in India.[21]

Ranga's dissent notwithstanding, the committee insisted on recommending joint cooperative farming -- suggesting as it did so that such joint farming would have to be introduced gradually in the wake of what it called intelligent propaganda, liberal state-aid, and specially trained persons to "reduce the psychological hesitation of the farmer to take to the cooperative patterns recommended by the committee."[22] Yet, having thereby recognized cultivators' inhibitions to come together in joint farming cooperatives, the Kumarappa Committee also argued, paradoxically, that the agrarian traditions of India actually favored the introduction of cooperative joint farming.

Endorsing Collective Farming on Reclaimed Land

The Kumarappa Committee, recognizing briefly the existence of what it referred to as "land hunger" among India's landless agricultural laborers, suggested that the landless should be settled on collective farms derived from reclaimed lands. It suggested that such collective farms, in addition to being a palliative for land hunger, would offer the state an opportunity to test the economics of mechanized farming.[23] In this way, the committee also specified that its earlier endorsement of the slogan "land to the tiller" did not necessarily apply to agriculturists who were

---

19. Ibid., p. 193.
20. Ibid.
21. Ibid., p. 194.
22. Ibid., p. 10.
23. Ibid.

already landless agricultural laborers. It stated quite explicitly that "individual settlements should on no account be allowed on newly reclaimed lands."[24]

Specifying Community Rights in Land

The committee also reviewed briefly the history of India's various land systems and argued that, prior to the advent of British rule, all land in India had been held in common: that there was no historical tradition of individual rights in land. The committee specifically rejected the historical analysis of scholars, including B.H. Baden-Powell, who had argued that the term "village communities" could not be used historically to suggest that land in India had been held in common. Instead, the majority report of the committee cited ancient texts, including the *Purva Mimansa*, and argued that land had indeed been held in common. The report argued that one of the committee's missions was to make recommendations for agrarian reform that would reinstate the village community in India.[25] In this fashion, the committee once again modified and seemed to contradict its own commitment to the goal of "land to the tiller" by stating that it favored dividing rights in land between the cultivator and the village community. It said, amorphously, that the rights in land to be vested in the village community were "the rights which the peasants would enjoy in their group personality ...".[26] Such assertions, rooted in a particular interpretation of India's historical land systems, would seem to be associated with the committee's endorsement of joint cooperative farming and collective farming. Yet, even that endorsement of communal or collective farming was subsequently qualified when the committee also stated formally that there would be difficulties in instituting cooperative farming. The most fundamental of the difficulties, according to the committee, was the "lack of cooperative spirit in the village life."[27]

---

24. Ibid.

25. I have always considered it likely that this section of the committee's report was influenced mainly by Chairman J.C. Kumarappa. Kumarappa's ideological bent was a peculiar mix of leftist and Gandhian thought.

26. Kumarappa, *Report of the Congress Agrarian Reforms Committee*, p. 36.

27. Ibid., p. 51.

Lacking a Framework
for Agrarian Reform

The Kumarappa Committee failed to provide a solid, analytical, factual base for agrarian reform and land reform. Its recommendations, quite apart from the notes of dissent written by Ranga and Reddiar, reflected nationalist polemics (the notion that intermediaries should be abolished), golden age myths (village communities could be reinstated by means of agrarian reform), the misinterpretation of economic precepts (the belief, without adequate evidence, that small landholdings would be economically inefficient), and ideological dogma (the notion that joint cooperative and collective farms could be easily instituted in Indian conditions). Instead of providing a solid frame for the implementation of agrarian reform in independent India, the Kumarappa Committee above all ensured that agrarian reform would be attempted within an informational vacuum regarding its economic purposes and possibilities.

The committee's final report offered a muddled message to those who would, in due course, assume responsibility for legislating agrarian reform in the Indian states. Indeed, the report offered a Pandora's Box of options to those in the central government and in the states who, eventually, were charged with defining and implementing agrarian reform. Some would fasten on the idea that agrarian reform would be achieved when the zamindars of the permanent settlement had been abolished. Some would focus on the need to ensure a land reform that was based on "land to the tiller" and the concept of individual rights in land (that is, the idea of peasant proprietorship). Still others would reject the idea of peasant proprietorship, believing that such an idea would serve only to perpetuate small, uneconomic, inefficient units of production. Such as these would argue, instead, that the primary purpose of agrarian reform should be to reduce drastically the number of small, fragmented landholdings in the country by consolidating landholdings so as to achieve large units of production: large units perceived, without adequate factual evidence, to be more efficient economically than small units of production.[28]

---

28. It will be recalled that this fixation on consolidation of landholdings had been a major preoccupation of the British and had been the only variant of agrarian reform championed by the Royal Commission on Agriculture in India, 1928. In this context, the American economist Erven J. Long has argued that

(continued...)

Finally, the Kumarappa Committee's recommendations could be interpreted as lending support to those who, in the absence of evidence derived from analysis of conditions in rural India, believed that joint cooperative farming or collective farming could be introduced either permissively within a tradition linked to communal landholdings or compulsively, if that communal tradition had been eclipsed by the effects of British tampering with historical land systems. Thus, the committee's recommendations, even if they seemed at the time to represent consensus positions on issues pertaining to agrarian reform, reinforced conflicting images concerning how the traditional agrarian structure of India might be transformed. And, sadly, the committee's recommendations were so poorly grounded in evidence drawn from actual conditions in rural India that they substituted surmise for evidence and, therefore, preconception for judgement.

The Directive Principals of
the Indian Constitution

While the Indian constitution did not offer an explicit vision of the relationship between agrarian reform, however defined, and the transformation of India's traditional political economy, its overarching message was one emphasizing the kinds of social and economic change one might find consistent with the promotion of an agrarian reform that redistributed rights in land and transformed the traditional hierarchy of interests in land. In particular, the Directive Principles of State Policy[29]

28.(...continued)
the Indian debate on agrarian reform, having assumed that economic efficiency required large units of production, neglected evidence of a "very decided inverse relationship between the size of farm and output per acre." Citing field work in Bihar which showed a "quite constant inverse relationship between the size of farm and gross productivity per acre ...," Long suggested that agrarian reform in India should have emphasized small scale, owner operated farms. [Tara Shukla, editor, *Economics of Underdeveloped Agriculture,* (Bombay: Vora and Co., 1969), p. 288.]

29. While the Directive Principles of State Policy were not designed to be enforceable by any court, they were, at the same time, said to be fundamental in the governance of the country. Moreover, Part IV, Article 37, of the constitution made plain that it would be the duty of the state to apply the Directive Principles when enacting the laws of the land.

in the constitution committed the independent Government of India to the promotion of a new social order "in which justice, social, economic and political" would inform "all the institutions of the national life."[30] These Directive Principles delineated a vision of a modern Indian state within which the people, men and women equally, would not only enjoy political freedom, but also could expect the state to promote a just economic order. Such an order was defined as one within which the ownership and control of material resources, including land, would subserve the common good and within which the state would strive to promote the economic welfare of all, ensuring in this process that everyone (including all workers, agricultural and industrial) would have a living wage and conditions of work that would permit a decent standard of living. By articulating such sweeping goals, even before state planning for economic development had been instituted, the Founding Fathers laid a foundation for political and economic transformation: transformation that could have been addressed in rural areas through the implementation of agrarian reform and land reform. Indeed, when Tarlok Singh came to write the draft outline to the First Five Year Plan, he obviously drew on the constitution's mandate for political and economic reform as he shaped recommendations for agrarian reform in the plan.

Draft Outline Specifications for the First Five Year Plan

The draft outline to the First Five Year Plan, coming at the beginning of the process by which India hoped to transform its political economy by means of state planning, established the functional parameters and working goals for agrarian reform from the perspective of the central government. Regarding agrarian reform, the draft outline also sought to provide guidelines for action that would be capable of implementation.

The draft outline appeared in 1951 after the constitution (1950) had specified that agriculture and, therefore, agrarian reform would be a state subject, as specified in the Seventh Schedule, Article 246, Sections 14 and 18. Understandably, then, the vision of agrarian reform in the draft outline is qualified both to reflect the fact that the central government in New Delhi would be in an advisory role to the states concerning the legislation and implementation of agrarian reform, and to confirm that the

---

30. *The Constitution of India,* Part IV, Article 30.

legislation would vary from state to state in accordance with differences in historical land systems. While those responsible for promoting agrarian reform at the center may not have recognized it when the draft outline was written, the constitutional stipulation that agriculture would be a state subject ensured that the central government's role in agrarian reform would be, essentially, exhortative rather than guiding or coercive.

Delineating the "Land Problem"

The draft outline suggested that India's land problem overshadowed all other problems facing the new republic. What was clearly needed to address that problem, said the draft outline, was a strategy for rural development that would change the character of Indian agriculture from subsistence farming on small uneconomic holdings to economic farming on units of production that would benefit from economies of scale and yield a marketable surplus to meet the needs of a growing population. This vision of the land problem was linked implicitly to the British colonial vision earlier articulated within the frame of the Royal Commission on Agriculture in India, 1928. The vision was based on the assumption that the bulk of India's agriculturists were tied to small, fragmented units of production; and, because they lived at the margin of subsistence, such agriculturists were assumed to be unable to invest in the improvement of the land in their possession. It was further assumed, within the frame of this vision of India's land problem, that the central goal of agricultural policy should be to transform such uneconomic units of production into economically efficient units by increasing the size of operational holdings.

Regrettably, this vision of India's land problem, and how to address it, could not be supported by comprehensive statistics confirming the size-distribution of agricultural holdings in India and the proportion of agricultural producers who had permanent occupancy rights to land and cultivated uneconomic landholdings.[31] In other words, even as the draft outline strove to define India's land problem, the central government had a shortage of useful data on which to base its own assessment of the actual dimensions of that problem. As Tarlok Singh, the principal author of the draft outline, later suggested, the dominant feature of his effort to

_____

31. India, Planning Commission, *First Five Year Plan (Draft Outline)*, (New Delhi: Manager of Publications, 1951), p. 94.

define the land problem was that it had to be done with a dearth of up-to-date information concerning the then existing distribution of rights in land within the different regions and among the historical land systems of India.[32]   In such circumstances, it was virtually inevitable that the land problem would be delineated in a fashion consistent with the already established value premises of the RCAI-1928.   Though I have found no evidence to confirm that the independent Government of India consciously adopted those value premises, those value premises, clearly, were the conventional wisdom of the time.

Striving as best he could to specify the nature and extent of the land problem with a limited amount of useful data, Tarlok Singh did try to incorporate in his analysis such data on Indian landholdings as were then available.   Accordingly, he relied on a number of studies drawn from different regions of India.   These studies seemed to confirm the conventional wisdom that the bulk of landholdings were small and uneconomic.   A comprehensive inquiry in the undivided Punjab, for example, had indicated that about 81 percent of its landholdings were below 10 acres in size and that about 64 percent were below 5 acres.[33] Similarly, data gathered in Uttar Pradesh by that state's Zamindari Abolition Committee indicated that 94 percent of its landholdings were below 10 acres in size and 81 percent were below 5 acres.[34] While such fragmentary data were better than no data at all, the fact remains that Tarlok Singh had virtually no regionally differentiated, country encompassing data on the actual distribution of rights in land and no reliable data on land concentration in India. This held especially for what is today referred to as the eastern zone of the country: the region of the British Permanent Settlement of 1793 comprised of the contemporary states of Bihar, West Bengal, and parts of Orissa. For that zone, the Government of India, in 1951, had no up-to-date and reliable land records at all. Such records as did then exist were in the hands of the dominant landholders of the permanent settlement region, the very intermediaries between the actual tillers and the state who, it was assumed, were to be among the primary targets of independent India's program of agrarian reform. Thus, the functional parameters of India's land problem and the working goals of agrarian reform were set forth by Singh in broad outline within what amounted to a statistical vacuum.

---

32. Tarlok Singh, Interview, New Delhi, February 21, 1989.
33. India, Planning Commission, *First Five Year Plan (Draft Outline)*, p. 94.
34. Ibid.

Providing a Definition
of Agrarian Reform

The draft outline sought to provide a working definition of agrarian reform: a definition derived not only from pre-independence and post-independence visions of agrarian reform that had enjoyed support within the Congress Movement, but also from the actual content of legislation already enacted, or then being enacted, in the Indian states. In effect, the draft outline, while recognizing that the legislation for agrarian reform could not be uniform and would ultimately reflect differences in regional conditions, strove to identify the commonalities that might be expected in the national approach to agrarian reform.

These commonalities were, in effect, the goals of agrarian reform that were endorsed within the frame of the draft outline of the First Five Year Plan:

1. the abolition of all intermediaries between the state and cultivators and, under appropriate conditions, the conferment of permanent occupancy rights to land to some of the occupancy tenants;[35] (landholders below the intermediaries in the agrarian hierarchy whose rights to the land in their possession were variable) of the intermediaries;
2. the protection of tenants-at-will; and
3. the determination of a ceiling on future acquisition of land by individuals.[36]

Having stated these general goals of agrarian reform, the draft outline sought to provide guidelines for the legislation of agrarian reform.[37] The

---

35. Tarlok Singh, in the draft outline, referred to the conferment of "rights of proprietorship upon occupancy tenants." Within the frame of Indian law, I believe that it is more appropriate, as in the text above, to refer to a process by which landholders who were subordinate to intermediaries might have conferred on them "permanent occupancy rights" in land, instead of "rights of proprietorship." With either phrase, the meaning is essentially the same: the conferment of a right to land that is the rough equivalent of "ownership."

36. India, Planning Commission, *First Five Year Plan (Draft Outline)*, p. 95.

37. Regarding the means by which agrarian reform would be promoted, I have discovered no evidence to suggest that the proponents of such reform

(continued...)

draft outline suggested that steps should be taken at an early date to pass the necessary legislation in the states to abolish all intermediary interests, including zamindari and jagirdari. The outline referred favorably to the *Bombay Tenancy and Agricultural Lands Act of 1948,* an act designed to give some protection from eviction to tenants-at-will: that is to say, to tenants who, because their rights to land (based generally on oral agreements between superior and inferior landholders) were tenuous and uncertain, were extremely vulnerable to eviction from the land by superior landholders. Indeed, using the Bombay legislation as a prototype, the draft outline suggested that there were strong social and economic grounds for taking similar steps around the country to protect tenants-at-will in raiyatwari areas and to protect the similarly vulnerable sub-tenants in zamindari areas.[38]

In similar vein, the draft outline offered the following additional advice to those in the states who would be responsible for drafting and enacting into law programs of agrarian reform. It was suggested that steps be taken to protect actual cultivators from ejectment from lands tilled by them, especially if such cultivators had tilled that land for the same landlord for a period of time. This suggestion merely reiterated a principle in law already established in the nineteenth century by the British. In this same context, the draft outline stated that, where tenants-at-will were given secure rights to land, their landlord should be permitted to retain an indeterminate amount of land for personal cultivation. In making this recommendation, the draft outline neglected to make plain either what would constitute "personal cultivation" or what might be the limit of land retained by a landlord for personal cultivation. It is noteworthy that, subsequently, the agrarian reform legislation passed in many of the states contained specific phraseology designed to enable superior landholders to retain land for personal cultivation, defined liberally to permit them to hold virtually all of their traditional holdings. Thus, when the draft outline did not define personal cultivation, it opened

---

37.(...continued)

contemplated invoking means other than legislation. Independent India sought to effect changes in land systems and peoples' rights in land by the same statutory means employed formerly by the British. One would have thought that the new Indian government, if intent on transforming the traditional agrarian structure of India, would have contemplated more decisive means, in addition to or instead of legislation, by which agrarian reform could be accomplished.

38. India, Planning Commission, *First Five Year Plan (Draft Outline),* p. 95.

the door for what was to become a classic provision in laws effecting changes in the historical land systems. By claiming land for personal cultivation, whether or not they tilled it themselves, landlords would establish de jure means by which they could either evict their subordinate landholders or encourage what became known popularly as "voluntary surrenders of land."

Recognizing that there had already been instances in the states where landlords had ejected long established tenants as a means of preventing them from establishing a legal basis for secure rights in land, the draft outline recommended only that the legislation enacted in the states should include provisions by which claims and counterclaims to land could be retrospectively reviewed. This limp recommendation (in the face of clear evidence that superior landholders, anticipating agrarian reform, were ejecting long established cultivators from lands customarily tilled by them) illustrates the weakness of the central government's constitutional authority to promote an agrarian reform in the states that would both preserve the rights of some traditional landholders and, at the same time, protect the rights of actual cultivators in a context where the power of the former clearly superceded the power of the latter.

The draft outline recommended that tenants who had made improvements on the land and who were subsequently evicted from it should receive compensation for such improvements "before termination of the lease."[39] This recommendation was predicated on the assumption that a certain number of actual tillers (classified as tenants of superior landholders, including the intermediaries to be abolished) would indeed be evicted in accordance with the law from lands customarily tilled by them. One can see clearly, in retrospect, that such a recommendation could be used casually in some states to ensure that landlords' evictions of their tenants were carried out in a fashion consistent with the letter of the law, if not in accordance with the high principles imbedded in the concept of agrarian reform.

It was suggested in the draft outline that the states enact legislation stipulating that leases of land should be for a minimum of five years and that rents should be regulated. Recognizing that rents in much of the country were set customarily by landlords at one-half of the produce, the draft outline recommended that agrarian reform legislation be enacted to ensure that such rents (rooted in the institution of sharecropping) be reduced. Specifically, the draft outline suggested that the drafters of

---

39. Ibid., p. 96.

legislation in the states consider rents exceeding one-third of the value of the produce of unirrigated land and one-fourth of the value of the produce from irrigated land to be excessive. However, the thrust of this recommendation was diluted when the draft outline subsequently observed that the actual structure of rents in a given state would have to be based on a careful examination of existing rents and the various factors that accounted for those rents. Again, the permissive quality of this central government guidance is evident. The recommendations concerning rents do not have the ring of authority, the tone of command. The language is mild. The substance is virtually Gandhian in character; that is to say, it is in keeping with his Doctrine of Trusteeship including the injunction that, of course, rents must be paid. There is no explicit recognition here that existing rents, augmented by illegal exactions, might be exploitive or in other ways detrimental to the promotion of a modern agrarian sector infused with new opportunity for actual tillers who labor as sharecroppers. Moreover, the suggestion in the draft outline, that the actual structure of rents in a given state would have to be examined before any changes were made, absolved the states of the need to make significant changes in existing rents if they could find a way of accounting for or justifying those rents.

The draft outline suggested that the states establish under law the means by which some cultivators could purchase permanent occupancy rights in land, with prices to be determined, in the absence of mutual agreement between superior and inferior landholders, by revenue courts invested with powers of Agricultural Land Tribunals.[40] The means suggested here by which disputes over the price of land could quickly be adjudicated by revenue courts is appropriate to circumstances where, in the absence of mutual agreement concerning the price of land, the matter might otherwise be relegated for resolution to the civil courts -- thereby delaying or, ultimately, denying the purchase.

The draft outline advised the states to legislate ceilings on the amount of land that could be acquired "in future" by landholders. It commended Bombay for having already set a ceiling for future acquisitions of land at 50 acres, and Uttar Pradesh for having set a 30 acre ceiling on future acquisitions. However, by focusing its ceilings recommendation on future acquisitions, by stressing that the ceilings need not affect existing properties in land,[41] and by failing to specify whether a ceiling would

---

40. Ibid., pp. 96-97.
41. Ibid.

apply to an individual or a family landholding, the draft outline's counsel to the states remained vague and indeterminate as to the central government's conceptualization of ceilings legislation within a preferred program of agrarian reform.

The draft outline specified the need for what it called agricultural reorganization in order to "increase production and to make cultivation more profitable by reducing unit costs and increasing yields at the same time" and to "reduce the number of workers engaged in the ordinary operations of farming."[42] This advice made plain that rural development in independent India would be defined at the outset of state planning within a neoclassical paradigm; it would be measured in terms of output per unit of labor; and, if the central government's counsel were heeded, it would be promoted by applying capital to agriculture in a fashion that reduced the need for labor. There was no sensitivity in this advice to the particular circumstances that then pertained to agriculture in India where so many persons were dependent on agriculture for income and survival and where so few non-agricultural jobs could be conjured up in the short run to absorb labor displaced from agriculture.

Moreover, the draft outline, alluding to agrarian policy needs in a time of food shortages in the new republic, offered advice that would serve, ultimately, only to de-emphasize the importance of agrarian reform. Specifically, the draft outline suggested that agrarian policy would have to be structured in the states so as to strike a proper balance between three different objectives:

1. meeting the need to maintain and increase total (food) production;
2. meeting the need to ensure economic efficiency in agriculture; and
3. meeting the need to promote social justice in the countryside.[43]

In order to address these objectives, the draft outline then made plain that changes in the traditional land systems of India should not be effected to meet only the needs of sectional interests. It defined "sectional interests" explicitly to mean the interests of either cultivators having permanent occupancy rights in land (referred to in the draft outline as peasant owners), or tenants-at-will or landless laborers.[44] Instead, it was suggested that agrarian policy should be designed to meet the needs of the

---

42. Ibid.
43. Ibid.
44. Ibid.

community as a whole. This meant that any changes that were to be effected by means of agrarian reform should not be carried out if they might result in a "loss of production which the community as a whole cannot afford."[45] In this way, the draft outline established a rationale for emphasizing the first two objectives of agrarian policy, as noted above, to the relative neglect of the objective of social justice, an objective not obviously linked to the productivity and economic efficiency goals of agrarian policy as conceptualized by Tarlok Singh, Jawaharlal Nehru and many others at the time. Whether intended or not, this rationale for agrarian policy provided whatever scope was needed in the states to establish and maintain their own dichotomy between the productivity goals of agrarian policy and the goals of social and distributive justice: a dichotomy that could only limit the implementation of agrarian reform.

Enlarging the Unit of Cultivation

Next, the draft outline, echoing a primary recommendation of the Royal Commission on Agriculture in India, 1928, suggested that Indian agriculture could not be developed as an efficient industry unless the unit of management was made larger. Thus, a clear bias against small farms was articulated. "Economies which are not available to small farms are available to large ones."[46] And, four lines of action by which economies of scale in agriculture might be promoted were enunciated. First, it was suggested that land in India could be nationalized and made available to cultivators for collective cultivation. Within the context of this recommendation, there was no recognition of the then established view of scholars[47] that the Indian land systems differed fundamentally from land systems in the West, that absolute property in the land was vested in no one in the countryside, and that, in such circumstances, the state could already be classified as the ultimate landholder, the "owner" of the land. Moreover, within the context of this endorsement of collective cultivation on economic rather than ideological grounds, there was no questioning of the feasibility of implementing such a program under Indian conditions.

---

45. Ibid.

46. Ibid., p. 98.

47. See, Vera Anstey, *The Economic Development of India,* Fourth Edition, (London: Longmans, Green and Company Ltd., 1957), pp. 97-103.

There was no stated concern as to whether the legions of cultivators of small farms in India would respond to the call for collective cultivation by abandoning willingly their small units of cultivation or whether they might have to be compelled to do so by the state. Second, it was suggested, as an alternative to the nationalization of the land, that steps could be taken to put a ceiling on the size of existing landholdings and to utilize land in excess of the ceiling to establish large units of cultivation farmed cooperatively by landless agricultural laborers. Within the context of this recommendation, it was in no way made explicit whether the intent of the Planning Commission was to confer on the landless "individual rights" to land which could be pooled and farmed jointly or cooperatively with others, or whether the preferred approach was to encourage the landless to till the land jointly without being accorded individual rights in land. Third, the draft outline suggested that another possible means of establishing large units of cultivation would be to offer unspecified "inducements to small farmers to become members of cooperative farming societies."[48] Among the four suggestions in the draft outline by which larger units of farm management and cultivation might be achieved, this was the one most obviously favored at the time by Tarlok Singh. Finally, the draft outline observed that the goal of enlarging the unit of cultivation might also be achieved if whole villages were treated as single farms under cooperative management.[49] Of course, none of these recommendations was enunciated in the draft outline in sufficient detail to provide actual guidance to the states concerning precisely how they might proceed to enlarge units of cultivation in order to achieve economies of scale and to establish an efficient, modern system of agriculture. It would appear that the Planning Commission was content in this instance, as in others pertaining to agrarian reform, to enunciate general principles and to give the states enormous latitude concerning whether and how those principles would be legislated and put into effect.

Establishing a System of Cooperative Village Management

In a fashion quite consistent with Tarlok Singh's personal valuations, the draft outline went on to recommend that the broad aim of state policy

---

48. India, Planning Commission, *First Five Year Plan (Draft Outline)*, p. 98.
49. Ibid.

within the sphere of rural development should be to establish a system of cooperative village management. The draft outline suggested that such a system could be achieved by means of democratic persuasion and education,[50] even if peasants were reluctant initially to embrace the cooperative ideal and to function within cooperative institutions. This faith in the universal and compelling appeal of cooperative institutions, so typical of Tarlok Singh, was widely shared at the time by his contemporaries, British as well as Indian, irrespective of their ideological predilections. That is to say, some supporters of cooperative institutions in India, including cooperative farming societies, were economic conservatives. Other proponents of cooperative institutions saw such institutions as a valuable means of fostering a socialistic pattern of society. Nonetheless, those who favored using cooperative institutions to foster rural development in India, from the days of the Royal Commission on Agriculture in India, 1928, through the first decade of state planning following independence, seem in retrospect to have insulated themselves from evidence that might have shaken their faith in a development paradigm based on the assumption that the peoples of rural India, torn by socioeconomic, caste and religious differences, could be permissively induced to become cohesive supporters of community-linked activities.

Addressing the Needs of Agricultural Workers

The draft outline now turned its attention to the plight of agricultural workers in India. It noted that the initial spate of legislation for agrarian reform in independent India had not been designed to any significant extent to address the problems of workers occupying a low status in the agrarian hierarchy.[51] While recognizing that the agricultural workers constituted about one-third of the rural population at the time, the draft outline nevertheless suggested that there was insufficient data concerning the condition of this segment of the rural population to make possible the formulation of policies that might appropriately address their needs.[52] The draft outline made obvious, nonetheless, its disinclination to promote an agrarian reform program that would provide individual landholdings

---

50. Ibid., p. 102.
51. Ibid., p. 106.
52. Ibid.

for agricultural workers.[53] Such a reform would have added to the already large numbers of small units of cultivation in India -- a result not to be countenanced by those responsible for the draft outline, given their stated bias in favor of large units of cultivation farmed within the framework of cooperative institutions. In other words, the draft outline made plain that it would not favor any program of agrarian reform that would provide land to the landless as individual proprietors or as raiyats having a permanent occupancy right to the land. Instead, the draft outline proposed that agricultural workers might be given opportunity to till reclaimed land if they could be persuaded to accept the land within the framework of cooperative or collective institutions, not as individual holdings.[54]

These recommendations concerning how the needs of agricultural workers might be addressed by means of agrarian reform were plainly inadequate to meet the requirements of so large a number of agriculturists at the base of the agrarian hierarchy, most of them members of scheduled and backward castes. Moreover, what is significant here is what was not recommended. There was no reiteration of old slogans like "land to the tiller" to address the needs of India's landless agricultural laborers. In this context, there was, no doubt, the implicit fear that there would be insufficient land that could be made available to meet the needs of all potential claimants, even assuming rigorous implementation of ceilings on the size of agricultural holdings. There was also extreme reluctance to foster agrarian reforms that would have added to the already large numbers of small landholdings. As noted above, at the time of the writing of the draft outline, small units of cultivation were considered to be inimical to the modernization of Indian agriculture. Thus, the draft outline identified the problem of agricultural workers at the base of the agrarian hierarchy, but refrained from offering to the states any bold program of reform that would have meaningfully addressed the needs of so large a segment of India's rural population.

---

53. The draft outline did not offer a clear definition of "agricultural workers." In context, I believe that the term agricultural workers was meant to apply to persons who might also be described as landless agricultural laborers, persons lacking all rights in land whose primary source of income came from performing labor on the land of others.

54. India, Planning Commission, *First Five Year Plan (Draft Outline)*, p. 107.

The Prevailing Views
of Development Economists

The process of defining the nature and extent of India's post-independence commitment to agrarian reform took place at a time when India was embarking on its quest for economic development by means of state planning. At that time, especially in the first decade of India's Independence, what Albert O. Hirschman has called the "subdiscipline" of development economics was young and, in many respects, filled with hubris. Though the subdiscipline's economic theory did not evolve generally from explicit knowledge of actual conditions in developing countries, the mainstream of thought was in no way hesitant to proclaim the means by which developing countries, including newly independent states like India, could quickly transform their societies and economies to ensure sustained economic growth. Within this intellectual frame, economic growth was widely believed to be synonymous with economic development. Early thinking about development and underdevelopment was not only accepting of the notion that economic growth could be attained without reference to persistent inequality in developing countries, but also ignoring of the need for policies (including agrarian reform and land reform) that would associate economic progress with social justice. Moreover, the then fashionable mainstream visions of economic progress[55] emphasized industrialization and rapid capital accumulation, while neglecting the need for directly productive investment in agriculture. Emphasizing the importance of industry, particularly of heavy industry,[56]

---

55. See, for example:

Paul Rosenstein-Rodan, "Problems of Industrialization in Eastern and South-eastern Europe," *Economic Journal,* 53, 1943, pp. 202-11;

Hans W. Singer, "The Mechanics of Economic Development," *Indian Economic Review,* 1952 as reprinted in A.N. Agarwala and A.P. Singh, editors, *The Economics of Underdevelopment,* (London: Oxford University Press, 1958);

Ragnar Nurkse, *Problems of Capital Formation in Underdeveloped Countries,* (Oxford: Basil Blackwell Publisher Ltd., 1953);

W.A. Lewis, "Economic Development with Unlimited Supplies of Labour," *Manchester School,* 22, 1954, pp. 139-91; and

W.A. Lewis, *The Theory of Economic Growth,* (Homewood, Illinois: Irwin, 1955).

56. Sukhamoy Chakravarty, *Development Planning: The Indian Experience,* (Oxford: Clarendon Press, 1987), pp. 10-11.

mainstream economists of a conservative bent, as well as left-oriented P.C. Mahalanobis,[57] tended to ignore the need for investment in agriculture as a critical means of ensuring economic progress in developing countries.

Indeed, few of the scholars credited with being seminal contributors to the theory and practice of economic development after World War II can be said to have given meaningful attention to agrarian reform as a means of fostering social and economic change in developing countries. Among a great number of such scholars (including Colin Clark, Albert O. Hirschman, W.A. Lewis, Hla Myint, Gunnar Myrdal, Raul Prebisch, Paul N. Rosenstein-Rodan, Walt W. Rostow, H.W. Singer, and Jan Tinbergen) one can find few who accorded a prominent place to agrarian reform or land reform in their writings in the 1950s and 1960s. Years later, reflecting on the past, some of these scholars did mention agrarian reform. One finds, for example, three references to land reform or agrarian reform among the contributions of those named above to the book *Pioneers in Development*,[58] published in 1984: one by Gunnar Myrdal, one by Sir Arthur Lewis, and one by Hla Myint in a comment on Myrdal's essay. Myrdal, writing for publication in 1984, suggested the need for radical institutional reforms as a prerequisite for economic development and accused the Government of India of not carrying out or truncating such reforms.[59] Myrdal, however, was making no such pointed observations with respect to Indian agrarian policy in the 1950s.[60] Lewis' 1984 reference to land reform was somewhat defensive to the charge that he and many of his associates had not recognized the importance of investment in agriculture (and agrarian reform) in the 1950s. He said that "Economists on the whole ..." were "not to blame for this. Nothing was more popular with us in the 1950s than land reform, on grounds of equity

---

57. P.C. Mahalanobis, a primary architect of state planning in India, is generally considered to have been a man of the ideological left. Mahalanobis' thinking about economic growth and development seems, at least, to have been influenced by the Soviet economist, G.A. Feldman. [See: Sukhamoy Chakravarty, *Development Planning: The Indian Experience,* p. 13.]

58. Gerald M. Meier and Dudley Seers, editors, *Pioneers in Development,* (New York: Oxford University Press, 1984).

59. Ibid., p. 158.

60. In 1968, Myrdal did make reference to the need for action to implement institutional reforms in the agricultural sector. [See: Gunnar Myrdal, *Asian Drama: An Inquiry into the Poverty of Nations,* (New York: Random House, 1968).]

and of expected effect on output. .... The Third World's failure with agriculture has been mainly at the political level, in systems where the small cultivator carries little political weight."[61]   And, Myint's 1984 reference to land reform was mainly one that took Myrdal to task for not specifying sufficiently what the radical institutional reforms might be that would benefit less developed countries (LDCs).   Myint alleged that Myrdal himself had accepted the notion that it was not feasible for "India to redistribute land, since there were so many landless people relative to the available land."[62]   Myint's criticism of Myrdal mainly exposed Myint's own uncertain definition of land reform.   That is to say, his criticism of Myrdal assumed that land reform necessarily meant giving land to all who might want it, including the landless.   In fact, as Myint might have recognized, land reform can be defined variously in ways that would not require redistributing land to all possible claimants.

In any event, it is arguable that most of the internationally recognized scholars who contributed to the literature on development in the years immediately after India gained freedom from Britain gave scant attention to agrarian reform and land reform.   Notwithstanding Sir Arthur Lewis' observation, noted above, there were very few economists who recommended to the Government of India during the 1950s that agrarian reform and land reform should be prominent instruments of public policy. Indeed, there were few scholars who would have suggested the need, even, for directly productive investment in agriculture to foster rural economic development.   After all, there were few economists in the 1950s whose views, theoretical or practical, were derived in substantial measure from conversations with illiterate peasants in the countryside, as was the case with two conspicuous advocates of agrarian reform, Wolf Ladejinsky and Daniel Thorner.[63]

Moreover, it was not until the 1970s that powerful institutions providing economic and technical assistance to India -- including the United States Agency for International Development (USAID) and the International Bank for Reconstruction and Development (IBRD) -- formerly endorsed agrarian reform (including land reform) as one means

---

61. Gerald M. Meier and Dudley Seers, editors, *Pioneers in Development,* p. 128.

62. Ibid., p. 170.

63. Needless to say, men like Ladejinsky and Thorner are seldom listed among "pioneers in development."

of fostering rural economic development.[64] At that time, it was possible for the IBRD to suggest, as it had not done before, that "Land reform, although equity oriented, can be consistent with all the goals of economic development: raising productivity, increasing employment and providing wider equity. In the long run, land reform need not lead to a reduction in marketed output or savings. Tenancy reforms can redistribute incomes and, by providing security of tenure, can encourage increased on-farm investment."[65] The IBRD suggested that land reform could contribute simultaneously to increases in productivity and employment and to social justice. Indeed, the IBRD made plain in 1974 that land reform could "be consistent with these objectives and, in some situations, may well be a necessary condition for their realization."[66] Nonetheless, the critical observation here is that such endorsements of land reform (and agrarian reform) as goals of public policy were not in evidence either when India gained freedom from Britain or in the two decades that followed India's independence. Like the mainstream development economists noted above, international aid-giving institutions in the 1950s (when India was attempting to shape its agrarian reform and land reform programs) tended both to ignore the potential importance of agrarian reform and land reform as means of addressing the goals of productivity growth and social justice and to underemphasize the need for directly productive investment in agriculture, while emphasizing industrialization and capital formation.

Distracting Political Events
in the Nehruvian Era

While our focus is on the political economy of agrarian reform in India, our perspective on what was or was not accomplished in this

---

64. See, for example, the Country Papers presented at USAID's Spring Review of Land Reform, 1970, including my own contribution to the review process entitled "Land Reform in Bihar, India: The Agrarian Structure in Bihar," in United States Agency for International Development, *Spring Review of Land Reform, June 1970,* Volume 1, Second Edition, (Washington: USAID, 1970). Also, see World Bank (IBRD), *Land Reform. A Policy Statement of the International Bank for Reconstruction and Development,* (Washington, D.C.: IBRD, 1974).

65. World Bank (IBRD), *Land Reform. A Policy Statement of the International Bank for Reconstruction and Development,* p. 37.

66. Ibid., p. 38.

sphere of public policy should be shaped, in part, by understanding that agrarian reform and land reform were not all-consuming objects of state policy following independence. Rather, it must be said that agrarian reform and land reform were domestic policy goals easily subordinated, if not entirely set aside, to other pressing needs in the new republic.

Following independence, the new Government of India had to deal with issues associated with the partition and its aftermath, including conflict with Pakistan (1947-48). Within India, the government had to deal with the settlement of millions of refugees (1948-49), with the incorporation into India of the Princely States (1947-49), with drought and food shortages, with the making of the constitution (1949-50), and with redrawing the political-administrative boundaries of the Indian states (commonly referred to as the linguistic reorganization of states, 1956).

In the same period, the new government was busy articulating and projecting globally its policy of non-alignment and, simultaneously, becoming involved variously in a range of international crises growing out of events in Korea, Hungary, and Suez. Independent India, particularly in the person of Prime Minister Jawaharlal Nehru, became a major player in world affairs at a time coincident with its need to establish and to begin implementing its domestic policy goals, including those linked to agrarian reform and rural economic development. Moreover, Nehru's often consuming interest in foreign affairs inevitably limited the time he had available to cope with other pressing issues of state. While he clearly wanted to play a decisive role in the shaping of India's economic development strategy and programs, including agrarian reform and land reform, Nehru's restless energy was frequently diverted from domestic issues of political economy to foreign affairs. Thus, while the historical record makes evident that Nehru, as Chairman of the Planning Commission, wanted to be at the center of domestic policy formation, it was often the case, given the press of other business, that Nehru knew little of what the Planning Commission was doing.[67] Clearly, then, agrarian reform and land reform issues, however important to the long-term restructuring and development of the Indian economy, were easily displaced by other time-consuming issues -- what may be called political distractions, especially in the sphere of foreign affairs. This condition applied especially in the Nehruvian era (1947-64), a decisive period in the formulation of policies for agrarian reform in India.

---

67. S. Gopal, *Jawaharlal Nehru: A Biography, 1947-1956,* (Delhi: Oxford University Press, 1979), Volume 2, p. 198.

Competing Development Paradigms
in the Nehruvian Era

Following independence, agrarian reform and land reform were often subordinated as objects of state policy to four competing development-oriented paradigms: the commitment to foster the growth of heavy industries; the commitment to multi-purpose irrigation and hydro-electric projects; the commitment to community development; and the commitment to new technology in agriculture. Each of these competing paradigms is reviewed in succeeding paragraphs.

The Commitment to
Promote Heavy Industries

While many economists in the 1950s argued that promoting industrialization was the best means of fostering economic development, P.C. Mahalanobis, the distinguished Indian statistician and physicist, was the primary conceptualizer of India's emphasis on the importance of heavy industrialization to the country's economic progress. Elaborating a model of industrialization similar to one that had originated in the Soviet Union in 1928,[68] Mahalanobis had a most influential, perhaps decisive, voice in the formation of economic policy during the first decade after India's independence.

Mahalanobis' influence on state planning in India can be traced back to 1940 when he first discussed planning for development with Jawaharlal Nehru. At the time, Nehru wanted Mahalanobis to provide a statistical commentary on the work of the National Planning Committee (NPC) which had been set up in 1938 with Nehru as Chairman. Mahalanobis began working as the honorary Statistical Adviser to the Cabinet from February, 1949, when a Central Statistical Unit was started in Delhi at his initiative.

It is clear that Mahalanobis was favorably influenced by what he perceived to be the phenomenal success of economic planning in the

---

68. It has been suggested that Mahalanobis' approach to economic modelling was independent of the work of the Soviet economist G.A. Feldman who produced a similar model in 1928. [See: P.K. Bose and M. Mukherjee, editors, *P.C. Mahalanobis Papers on Planning,* (Calcutta: Statistical Publishing Society, 1985), p. xvii.]

Soviet Union after the October Revolution. And, consistent with that favorable perception of Soviet planning, Mahalanobis elaborated a government directed, growth-centered vision of economic development: a vision based primarily on the notion that development could best be fostered by employing real capital (in the form of machinery driven by steam or electricity) as a substitute for human or animal labor in order to increase the per capita production of the nation. Toward this end, he suggested that it was necessary to establish in India basic engineering and power industries to facilitate the manufacture of both consumer and capital goods in the country.

Mahalanobis' emphasis on heavy industries was, of course, entirely consistent with the views of India's first Prime Minister and Chairman of the Planning Commission. Even prior to independence, on March 3, 1947, Nehru said that "The whole policy of the Government, in so far as I can speak for the Government, is to encourage (the) industrialization of India ...".[69]

Mahalanobis' emphasis on the need for investment in heavy industries contained an implicit bias against directly productive investment in agriculture, a bias shared by many development economists in the 1950s. Tarlok Singh, a contemporary of Mahalanobis, has suggested that Mahalanobis was not overtly hostile to programs of agricultural development, including agrarian reform and land reform.[70] However, Mahalanobis believed that agrarian reform and land reform conferred benefits to a society mainly in the short-run, whereas basic improvements in agriculture over the long-run could be brought about "only through the use of more fertilizers, more irrigation, and better methods of cultivation, all of which would have to depend on large scale industrial development."[71]

With heavy industrialization perceived by Mahalanobis and Nehru as the best means of ensuring rapid economic growth in India, it is not surprising that attention was drawn away from the need in India to transform traditional agriculture -- and especially away from the need to transform it by restructuring traditional rights in land by means of agrarian reform and land reform.

---

69. Jawaharlal Nehru, *Selected Works of Jawaharlal Nehru,* Second Series, Volume 2, (New Delhi: Jawaharlal Nehru Memorial Fund, 1984), p. 580.

70. Tarlok Singh, Interview, New Delhi, February, 1989.

71. P.C. Mahalanobis, "Science and National Planning," in *Sankhya,* Volume 20, Parts 1 & 2, September, 1958, p. 82.

Imbedded in the Mahalanobis approach to economic development was a definition of economic progress measured in aggregate growth rates. Mahalanobis' focus on productivity growth was shared by Nehru who, on many occasions, made plain that he gave primacy to productivity increases, even if this worked against distributive justice, which he also favored, in the short-run.[72] This emphasis was also consistent with the state of the art of development economics at the time. It was much later that economists began to question whether economic growth and economic development should be perceived as synonymous in meaning. This notwithstanding, I still remember being astonished when Mahalanobis suggested to me in 1957 that, in order to maximize the rate of economic growth in India, it would be necessary both to pursue his industrialization strategy and "to write-off two or three generations of peasants ..." in the process.[73]

The Commitment to
Multi-purpose Projects

During the first decade after independence, Nehru became enamored with large-scale, multi-purpose projects involving the construction of dams to provide irrigation and hydro-electric power. He endorsed such projects with enthusiasm and, when inaugurating the Bhakra-Nangal canal system, referred to them as the "New Temples of Worship" in modern India. As such large scale and costly projects were sanctioned by the Government of India and enthusiastically endorsed by Nehru, it was apparent to some, even at the time, that the projects diverted attention and resources from the needs of the mass of the people living in rural areas, especially from the needs of small farmers who might be the beneficiaries of agrarian reform or land reform but who probably would not be the beneficiaries of large hydro-electric projects. S.N. Agarwal, for example, writing from within the Congress establishment in the All India Congress Committee's *AICC Economic Review,* argued in 1954 for a different kind of development strategy, one with a rural focus emphasizing the application of scientific methods of farming on small units of production, intensively farmed. He saw the development of small farms as a means

---

72. Jawaharlal Nehru, *Selected Works of Jawaharlal Nehru,* Vol. 2, p. 583.

73. P.C. Mahalanobis, Interview at the Indian Statistical Institute, Calcutta, February 17, 1957.

of simultaneously addressing both employment and productivity goals in rural India. He questioned the need for large scale capital intensive projects, such as those then being favored by the Government of India. Agarwal argued that such projects, even when they conferred benefits on agriculturists, provided benefits mainly on rich agriculturists and thereby perpetuated what he called "the economic exploitation of the masses."[74] Unfortunately, the concerns expressed by men like Agarwal were entirely offset by the powerful images of the massive hydro-electric and irrigation projects that were so fashionable in the 1950s and 1960s in India. Such projects obviously diverted government resources and attention from seemingly less dramatic programs, including programs of agrarian reform and land reform, that had the potential of restructuring the political economy of rural India.

The Commitment to Community Development

The principal Indian and American proponents of Community Development in India believed that a multi-faceted Community Development program would establish the means by which the people of India in rural areas could be mobilized to work in their own behalf to meet common needs. Unfortunately, the conceptualizers of Community Development assumed that Indian villagers were free agents who could reach consensus easily on common objectives, rather than people who were constrained by the socioeconomic environments within which they lived and worked. Community Development proponents failed to recognize that the needs, the interests and, therefore, the options for action of people in India's rural areas would be determined and might be limited by their places in the existing agrarian hierarchy. Regrettably, the possible need to change the socioeconomic environment in rural areas was not an essential consideration for those who advocated and planned the Community Development program in India. As a result, the movement for Community Development, launched by the Government of India in 1952, was utterly divorced from pregnant issues of land policy, including agrarian reform and land reform.

---

74. Congress Party, *AICC Economic Review,* Volume VI, Nos. 6-7, (New Delhi, July 24, 1954), Whole Nos. 103-104.

One of the primary proponents of the Indian government sponsored movement and program for Community Development was an American, Albert Mayer. An urban architect by training and experience, Mayer's knowledge of rural India was negligible. Indeed, Mayer's initial contact with India was accidental, the result of his military posting as an Army engineer charged with building a number of camps in eastern India during World War II.[75] His role as a conceptualizer of Community Development was derived from a remarkable friendship that he developed with Jawaharlal Nehru, whose own knowledge of conditions in rural India was, at least, questionable. There is little on record to explain why it was that Nehru was drawn to Mayer and, in effect, entrusted him with so much responsibility to design and carry out plans for what was referred to popularly as the reconstruction of rural India.[76] It has been suggested, however, that

---

75. His limited experience in rural India did not prevent Albert Mayer from expounding on the means by which rural India could be transformed. In the process, he instructed Indian villagers how to perform tasks that they themselves had performed without external guidance for millennia. For example, he set forth, as if in a manual of instruction, how villagers might be taught to build mud walls for traditional housing. Said Mayer, "The mud for walls is hard clay softened by mixing with a small amount of water so that it is workable but still pasty and not too wet. Water and clay are thoroughly mixed and worked, and then left for eight hours to become hard. .... Cow dung is then added, and water; also wheat or barley straw not more than one inch long." [Albert Mayer with McKim Marriott and Richard Park, Foreword by Pandit Govind Ballabh Pant, *Pilot Project India: The Story of Rural Development at Etawah, Uttar Pradesh,* (Berkeley: University of California Press, 1958), p. 170.]

76. It remains a sore point with contemporary persons who have served India in various capacities that the Government of India, after independence, sought the advice of foreign experts to perform rural development functions in independent India -- foreign experts, including Albert Mayer, who lacked in-depth experience in India and who were ill equipped to perform tasks that might have been more appropriately performed by well-trained indigenous persons. This was made clear to the author in discussions in 1989, both by J.D. Sethi (subsequently a Member of the Planning Commission in the Janata Government of India) and by Jagat Mehta (a former Foreign Secretary of the Government of India). [J.D. Sethi and Jagat Mehta, Joint Interview, New Delhi, February 2, 1989.]

Mayer was a man of enormous intellectual vitality and humanity. He was the sort of person who would welcome late night, wide-ranging discussions on all sorts of issues with a man like Nehru. Nehru, never a Gandhian, was looking for a way of doing something in the countryside -- of gaining time. Nehru was looking for breathing space -- a symbolic way of showing concern for the needs of the mass of the people in the Indian countryside. He didn't necessarily see Mayer as a man who would produce final solutions to rural problems, but he was prepared to let him try.[77]

Whatever the explanation of Nehru's relationship with Albert Mayer, it is clear that Nehru worked assiduously to ensure that Mayer was given opportunity to work in India in the field of rural development. In 1947, long before Community Development was formally initiated as a government program, Nehru lobbied Govind Ballabh Pant, then the Chief Minister of the United Provinces (U.P.), to employ Mayer as a rural development specialist in that Province. Nehru's initiative with Pant had been prompted by Mayer who, as early as December, 1946, had prepared for consideration in India a "Preliminary Outline for Village Planning and Reconstruction." Months later, in correspondence with Nehru, Mayer showed frustration that he had received no response concerning his draft proposal for rural reconstruction. Addressing Mayer's concerns, Nehru wrote to Govind Ballabh Pant on May 18, 1947.

It would be a pity to lose Mayer not only because he seems to me eminently suited for expert work in India but also because of the experience he has gained. We should not waste all this. Whatever the future may hold, we shall have to work hard to rebuild and reconstruct everything, and I have no doubt that Mayer would be of great assistance. As matter of fact, we can easily employ him on behalf of the Government of India. .... Personally I would rather he concentrate his energies on the U.P. Later, when he comes, we could use him for other purposes also if necessary, and if he has the time to spare from U.P. In any event, I hope you will come to an early decision and inform him so that he can fix his program accordingly.[78]

---

77. These are the words of Alice Thorner, scholar and observer of India since the early 1950s and the spouse of the distinguished student of rural India, the late Daniel Thorner. [Alice Thorner, Interview, New Delhi, January 26, 1989.]

78. Jawaharlal Nehru, *Selected Works of Jawaharlal Nehru*, Volume 2, pp. 591-592.

Govind Ballabh Pant responded affirmatively to Nehru's lobbying. And, what was called a "pilot" rural development project was initiated with the assistance of Albert Mayer in Etawah District of Uttar Pradesh in October of 1948.[79]   In a sense, Mayer's still evolving concept of community development had come to India; it was, after all, the Etawah project from which the national model for Community Development and National Extension Services was subsequently extrapolated.[80]

In its essence, the national program for rural Community Development embraced the assumption, noted above, that the people in rural areas, living in heterogeneous agglomerations, could be energized as a community to work together to meet common needs. This assumption was often associated with suggestions that, but for the advent of colonial domination, the villages of India would have maintained the characteristics of village republics, and that, when colonial domination was eliminated, the villages would again be capable of cohesive action and ordered self-sufficiency. At the same time, the program evolved after 1952 as if with purposeful ignorance as to how the existing distribution of economic assets in the countryside, and especially of rights in land, would condition and qualify the peoples' capacity to work together for the common good. Beginning with the premise that "The life of villagers has been stagnant for many decades,"[81] the proponents of the program saw no connection between that alleged stagnation and the regionally variegated man-to-land relationships of rural India. There was no attempt made, therefore, to associate Community Development conceptually and in practice with initiatives that would transform the

79. For a glowing evaluation of the development of the Etawah Project, see Albert Mayer with McKim Marriott and Richard Park, *Pilot Project India: The Story of Rural Development at Etawah, Uttar Pradesh.*

80.   While Albert Mayer is appropriately identified here as a primary proponent of Community Development, the program, as it evolved, also derived inspiration from the work of the British colonial officer F.L. Brayne (author of *Village Uplift in India,* 1927), and the program received process-oriented counsel from others (for example, Douglas Ensminger of The Ford Foundation, New Delhi) who were familiar with agricultural extension operations in the United States. And, of course, Community Development was introduced within the frame of Mahatma Gandhi's idealization of the Indian village.

81.   Carl C. Taylor, (Ford Foundation Consultant on Community Development), *A Critical Analysis of India's Community Development Programme,* (New Delhi: The Community Development Administration, 1956), p. 56.

existing agrarian structure of India by means of agrarian reform or land reform. Indeed, the separation of agrarian reform conceptually from Community Development seems to have been absolute in the official literature and propaganda of the program. Even in retrospect, it is astonishing that Community Development could have been endorsed and promoted by the Government of India, as well as by foreign aid institutions both public[82] and private,[83] as a program for rural reconstruction divorced from land policy issues being debated at the time by proponents and opponents of agrarian reform and land reform. It is even more astonishing that so few persons at the time saw clearly that the goals of Community Development would not be fulfilled as outlined unless rural reconstruction was defined around successful agrarian reform.

One person who understood the conceptual emptiness of promoting rural reconstruction in India without also sponsoring agrarian reform was Carl C. Taylor, a Consultant to The Ford Foundation, New Delhi, in the 1950s. Writing a formal appraisal of Community Development for the Government of India in 1956, when the program had been extended to one hundred thousand villages, Taylor said:

> The existence of a land reform climate in India will probably make the major difference between the success of a Community Development Programme in India and the success of Community Development programmes in at least seven other countries which I have had the opportunity to study in some detail during the last fifteen years. Locally developed, competent, self-reliant local communities constitute the foundation of an economic, social and political democratic order. In such a social order, democracy is indivisible. It is useless to attempt to have democratic thinking and practices at the top unless there is also democracy at the bottom, and it is impossible successfully to develop democracy at the bottom if feudalism exists at the top. Those countries which are attempting to promise local Community Development but whose Parliaments are dominated by .... landlords will not remove, by land reform legislation, one of the most forbidding conditions to successful Community Development.[84]

---

82. I refer here, for example, to the Technical Cooperation Mission of the Government of the United States.

83. I refer here primarily to The Ford Foundation.

84. Carl C. Taylor, *A Critical Analysis of India's Community Development Programme*, p. 60.

Taylor went on to suggest that land reform was a primary means of ensuring conditions in rural areas that were fully conducive to the implementation of Community Development. And, he concluded his statement with the warning that, where such favorable conditions did not exist, he wondered "how far local Community Development will be created."[85] Taylor's warning was prescient, but buried in the epilogue to his report instead of being incorporated in the main body of his critical analysis and recommendations to the Government of India.

Regrettably, until its eclipse in the 1960s following the death of Jawaharlal Nehru, Community Development continued to evolve as a program separated conceptually and administratively from programs of agrarian reform and land reform as defined and legislated in the Indian states. And, whatever benefits Community Development conferred on the people in targeted villages were distributed mainly in a fashion that reflected and reinforced existing inequalities in the distribution of economic assets, especially of land.[86] The program never became a peoples' program assisted by the government; it remained a government program to be developed with the assistance of people in rural areas, people whose benefits from the program corresponded with their status in the agrarian hierarchy.

The Commitment to New Technology in Agriculture

By the late 1960s, India's commitment to rural economic development was increasingly being defined almost exclusively in technological terms. That is to say, the emphasis in public policy was on how best to achieve increases in agricultural yields by employing a synchronized package of

---

85. Ibid.

86. The Planning Commission of the Government of India, itself, recognized that the Community Development program benefitted mainly cultivators having secure rights in land. In an evaluation published in 1958, its Programme Evaluation Organization noted that the whole program's activity was "concentrated on cultivation, and in as much as Harijans and the backward classes are either landless labourers or rely upon other occupations, they have not participated in the benefits of the programme." [India, The Planning Commission, Programme Evaluation Organization, *The Fifth Evaluation Report on Working of Community Development and National Extension Service Blocks,* (New Delhi: Manager of Publications, May, 1958), pp. 6-7.]

inputs -- improved varieties of plants, synthetic fertilizers, assured irrigation, and pesticides. What was referred to popularly as the new strategy in agriculture[87] promised to enable India to meet its long-established goal of self-sufficiency in the production of food grains and to do this within the existing system of rights in land -- obviating the need for the Government of India to press the states to implement already legislated or new programs of agrarian reform and land reform.[88]

Clearly, the new strategy in agriculture was congenial to the interests of India's landholding elites, not only because it offered the promise of increasing yields but also because it suggested an approach to rural economic development that accepted as datum the existing hierarchy of interests in land. Indeed, the new strategy in agriculture made no reference whatsoever to issues of agrarian structure -- issues deeply imbedded in the internal debate concerning the place of agrarian reform and land reform in India's program for rural economic development. Instead, the new strategy offered a means of meeting food production goals while escaping the difficult political and economic choices encapsulated within any attempt to transform the existing structure of rights in land in rural India.

The new strategy's distance from India's internal debate concerning the role of agrarian reform and land reform in a production and distribution-oriented strategy for rural development resulted from the fact that its origins were in agricultural science, separated absolutely from analysis of socioeconomic conditions that might facilitate or impede the introduction of the new technology. Indeed, the original proponents of the new strategy within the Rockefeller Foundation had been agricultural scientists (a plant pathologist, a plant breeder, and a soils scientist) whose approach to the problem of rural economic development was, understandably, productivity-centered and circumscribed by their academic disciplines.[89]

---

87. For observations on how the "new strategy in agriculture" was introduced in India, see C. Subramaniam, *The New Strategy in Indian Agriculture,* (New Delhi: Vikas Publishing House Private Ltd., 1979). Subramaniam, as Minister for Food and Agriculture and Community Development from 1964 to 1967, was instrumental in ensuring that the new strategy would be acceptable to critics within the Government of India.

88. The new strategy in agriculture was credited by its exponents as providing the basis for a productivity-oriented "Green Revolution" in India.

89. These scholar-practitioners associated with the Rockefeller Foundation were, respectively, Elvin Stakman, Paul Mangelsdorf, and Richard Bradfield.

(continued...)

Their bias suffused the foundation's work in Mexico, where the new technology in wheat was pioneered, and, after 1956, in India, where the foundation sought to contribute to the transformation of traditional agricultural practices in the country by employing agricultural science. This productivity-centered bias became so deeply rooted in the Rockefeller Foundation's conceptualization of how best to promote rural development that it obscured the need to give attention to questions of distribution. The implicit assumption of this approach was that rural economic development could be equated with productivity growth alone. If one embraced this assumption, one could ignore the conditions in the Indian countryside -- especially the hierarchy of interests in land and the inegalitarian distribution of economic assets, especially land -- that would ensure that the primary benefits of the new technology in agriculture would be conferred on cultivators with secure rights in land who "gained relative to tenants and laborers from the adoption of the higher yielding varieties of grain."[90]

As growth-centered, technology driven development policy gained acceptance in India in the late 1960s and early 1970s, it was encouraged by a variety of international institutions, including The Ford Foundation and the United States Agency for International Development (USAID). These institutions, even when warned by analysis suggesting that the new technology was contributing to widening income inequality in the countryside,[91] did not become active exponents of agrarian reform or land reform.[92] They continued to offer an approach to rural development that

---

89.(...continued)
One cannot blame them for working within their disciplines. One can wish, after the fact, that their work had been complemented by the insights of language and area scholars -- not to mention persons indigenous to India -- knowledgeable of the socioeconomic context within which the new technology in agriculture would subsequently be applied.

90. Vernon W. Ruttan, "The Green Revolution: Seven Generalizations," *International Development Review,* December, 1977, pp. 16-22.

91. See, for example, Francine Frankel, *India's Green Revolution,* (Princeton: Princeton University Press, 1971).

92. Indeed, the United States Agency for International Development was not convinced at the time that land reform should have an important place in a strategy for rural economic development in India. Typical of USAID's attitude to land reform in the late 1960s and early 1970s is the following statement: "If land reforms are needed at all, they are needed only in some areas and then

(continued...)

was divorced from notions of agrarian structural change: an approach, whether calculated or not, that "coincided with the interests of substantial sections of India's ruling elite who clearly hoped that economic progress might be achieved somewhat painlessly in rural areas, in a fashion not threatening the dominant status of landholding elites."[93] The approach focused on effecting rapid increases in aggregate food production, it being implicit that if the productivity growth was achieved that its benefits would, in time, accrue to the mass of the people. Existing inequalities in the distribution of economic assets, including land, in rural areas were not perceived generally to be impediments to the process by which food, when produced, would be distributed. Moreover, the positive relationship between land reform and the need to foster increases in productivity was generally not acknowledged by those promoting the dissemination of new technology in agriculture.[94] It was not sufficiently recognized by India's post-independence policy makers that land reform, when effectively implemented, can be a means not only of encouraging increases in output because it provides new options (including what Amartya Sen has called a food entitlement) and incentives to the cultivators who receive secure rights in land, but also of ensuring improved distribution of foodgrains.[95]

Whether the costs of emphasizing new technology in agriculture in India will outweigh the benefits in the long-run or not, it must be admitted that the new technology's productivity effects have been important, if regionally differentiated.[96] The rudiments of the approach

---

92.(...continued)
primarily for their impact on inequities rather than on productivity and employment." [Ronald Ridker, *Land Reform and Rural Poverty in India*, (Washington, D.C.: Agency for International Development, June, 1970).]

93. F. Tomasson Jannuzi, *India In Transition: Issues of Political Economy in a Plural Society*, (Boulder, Colorado: Westview Press, 1989), pp. 83-84.

94. The notion that agrarian reform and land reform could be designed to complement the implementation of food production and distribution programs was recognized rhetorically, if not substantively, at the Chief Ministers' Conferences on Land Reform in New Delhi in 1969 and 1970.

95. It has long been established in theory and practice that land reform can simultaneously contribute to productivity growth and to improved distribution of what is produced. See, for example, Peter Dorner, *Land Reform and Economic Development*, (Middlesex, England: Penguin Books, 1972).

96. The productivity gains associated with the introduction of the new technology in agriculture permitted India by the mid-1980s to claim virtual self-
(continued...)

are neither inherently good nor bad. However, what is incontrovertible in India is that, when the new technology was introduced in regions of great inequality in the distribution of rights in land, the spread effects of the new technology were limited and were distributed in a way that reflected and reinforced existing inequalities. In other words, though applied policy may separate technological inputs from agrarian reform, "the implementation of technological approaches to rural development is both affected by and affects the existing hierarchy of interests in land."[97] Thus, as a competing paradigm to agrarian reform and land reform, the new technology in agriculture exacerbated problems already deeply imbedded in the socioeconomic structures of rural India.

96.(...continued)
sufficiency in the production of food and fiber. The gains in production (particularly in wheat production) were concentrated in the Punjab, Haryana and western Uttar Pradesh.

97. F. Tomasson Jannuzi, *India in Transition: Issues of Political Economy in a Plural Society,* p. 90.

3

Post-Independence Implementation
of Agrarian Reform

The Constrained Role
of the Central Government

The Constraints Imposed
by the Constitution

Having struggled to define the goals of agrarian reform and land reform and to determine the priority to be accorded such reforms in the context of a national strategy for economic development, the independent Government of India was constrained in its capacity to shape the content of agrarian reform and land reform in the states and to ensure that such reforms as were enacted in law were implemented. That is to say, the central government in New Delhi lacked ultimate authority to delineate the content of agrarian reform and land reform in the Indian states. Moreover, the central government arguably, notwithstanding emergency provisions in the constitution permitting the President of India "to assume to himself all or any of the functions of the Government of the State,"[1] lacked coercive power under law both to legislate and implement agrarian reform. Ironically, the central government's lack of authority and coercive power in this sphere of public policy was by design. The Founding Fathers had specified that agriculture would be a state subject under the constitution. Given such a stipulation, there was no constitutional means by which the central government or its instruments, including the Planning Commission in New Delhi, could instruct the state

---

1. *The Constitution of India,* Part XVIII, Emergency Provisions, Article 356.

governments concerning precisely how agrarian reform should be legislated and implemented. In effect, then, it should be understood that India's governing elite, whatever its motivations concerning the importance of agrarian reform, had no intention of imposing on the states a national plan for agrarian reform. Instead, it was made explicit in law that the states themselves would have the primary responsibility and authority for designing and implementing such reforms as they considered appropriate in their circumstances. Given the complexity of India's regionally diverse historical land systems, it would become extremely difficult for the central government even to monitor and to assess the progress of agrarian reform in the states.

Lacking authority and coercive power, the central government was also constrained at the outset by a dearth of up-to-date and relevant data necessary even for making permissive recommendations to the states concerning the kinds of specific reform measures that might be applicable to their circumstances.

The Constraints Imposed by Gaps in Data

Even had the Government of India established an internal consensus concerning the proposed scope and content of agrarian reform and land reform following independence, its ability to set forth explicit, regionally differentiated guidelines for action would have been limited by profound gaps in data concerning the hierarchy of interests in land in the country. In the first decade after independence, at a time when a general commitment to agrarian reform and land reform was most evident and politically acceptable, there was no single person who could be said to have had an all-India grasp of the country's diverse land systems, together with their regional nuances.[2] In such circumstances, it was inevitable that the central government's guidance to the states would be general and, ultimately, would not include either detailed, regionally specific, instructions concerning the content of agrarian reform or an over-all vision concerning what such reform should be designed to accomplish within the frame of India's national approach to economic development.[3] Though a Central Committee on Land Reform was established within the

---

2. Tarlok Singh, Interview, New Delhi, February 19, 1992.
3. Ibid.

Planning Commission to provide advice to the states and to coordinate efforts, this committee clearly lacked both the data and authority to carry out meaningfully its mandated role.

The Constraints Imposed
by Opponents of Agrarian Reform

Even prior to independence, India's landholding elite took steps to protect their interests in land in anticipation of agrarian reform. To nullify the anticipated effects of agrarian reform, those enjoying secure, de jure rights in land demonstrated ingenuity in protecting their interests. They took steps to deny their tenants' de jure claims to land. This could be accomplished easily in some regions in accordance with law. For example, a superior landholder could ensure that no tenant tilled the same land for more than a year or two -- thereby denying the tenant any prospect of securing a permanent occupancy right to that land. Anticipating legislation that would place a ceiling on the size of agricultural holdings, landholders partitioned joint family holdings. This had the effect of disguising the size of family holdings, especially when landholders engaged in benami (fictitious) transfers of land. By such means, the record of rights in land could be obscured -- making it difficult for those who would subsequently legislate agrarian reform to implement the reform provisions. Anticipating agrarian reform, landholders also purchased capital equipment (for example, tractors) as a means of documenting their commitment to agricultural modernity -- hoping thereby to demonstrate that they tilled the land efficiently and in a fashion warranting exemption from any legislation that might limit the size of their landholdings. Finally, anticipating agrarian reform, landholders transformed their holdings technically into registered cooperatives, joint stock companies, or corporations in the hope that such holdings would be exempted from agrarian reform legislation. Clearly, then, landholders in India who considered it likely that they might be the objects of agrarian reform or land reform legislation did not wait until legislation had been enacted in the states to take steps to protect their interests. Indeed, one can discover few evasive techniques following the enactment of agrarian reform legislation in the states that were not pioneered well in advance of such legislation. Moreover, the landholders' anticipatory actions to evade agrarian reform were, at once, regionally differentiated and all-India in scope.

The Primary Role
of State Revenue Ministries

When the Indian constitution made agriculture a state subject, it also made plain that the primary responsibility for effecting agrarian reform would rest with the states -- thereby reducing the central government's power to define the content of reform and to compel it. Within the imposed constitutional division of labor, whatever the central government's general directives in five year plans or other documents of state concerning agrarian reform and land reform, there would be implicative diversity of response in the states -- reflecting differences in the states' historical land systems and different perceptions among the governing elites in the states concerning what would constitute agrarian reform in their contexts, and what would be feasible of implementation.

Formulating Draft Bills

The initial responsibility in the states for drafting legislation for agrarian reform and land reform was assigned, as it had been in the colonial era, to civil servants in the states' revenue ministries -- as distinct from other ministries, including agriculture, having functional responsibility for rural economic development. This confirmed an administrative dichotomy in the states between agrarian reform, or land reform, and agricultural development. The decision to assign administrative primacy for agrarian reform to revenue ministries also ensured that "the most meaningful segments of the legislation initially passed in India after Independence in the name of 'land reform' should be characterized instead as 'revenue reform' -- a means of rationalizing and defending within the framework of the Constitution the states' right to act as 'super-landlords' in the direct collection of land revenue."[4] Thus, what was popularly heralded at the outset as legislation, above all, to effect the abolition of intermediaries, or landlords, was in fact legislation designed mainly to deny those landlords, especially those classified as revenue collecting intermediaries of the state, their long-established right to act for the state in the collection of land revenue. It is surely not surprising, in retrospect, that such agrarian reform

---

4. F. Tomasson Jannuzi, *India in Transition: Issues of Political Economy in a Plural Society,* (Boulder, Colorado: Westview Press, 1989), p. 75.

legislation as was drafted by revenue ministries would prove to be more protective, initially, of the states' revenue demand than destructive of the landholding intermediaries' rights in land. Thus, even had there been no political opposition to agrarian reform and land reform in the states, the institutional biases of revenue ministries would probably have ensured that the resultant legislation would have been separated conceptually from agricultural development goals and divorced from principles of land reform that could have led to a substantial redistribution of rights in land among actual tillers in rural India.[5]

Maintaining Land Records

In addition to the revenue ministries' responsibility for producing the initial drafts of legislation for land reform, these ministries also had responsibility in the states for the maintenance and updating of records of rights in land. By means of what were called Survey and Settlement Operations, carried out within the frame of time-consuming procedures set by colonial-era administrators, these ministries had the responsibility for providing the data concerning the actual distribution of rights in land in rural India. Having such records would be essential to the process by which regionally appropriate agrarian reform legislation could be drafted.

Regrettably, when the time came for agrarian reform legislation to be drafted in the states, there was, in the general case, a lack of adequate and up-to-date information concerning the actual distribution of rights in land in rural India. Indeed, it was not until 1954, after the first spate of agrarian reform legislation had been enacted in the states, that the states

---

5. The phrase "abolition of intermediaries" in the text had particular meaning in regions where the zamindari system prevailed. In such areas, the intermediaries acted as agents of the state, the super-landlord in the collection of land revenue from cultivators who enjoyed de jure rights in land (classified as tenants). Such intermediaries could appropriately be classified as landlords or zamindars. Outside of zamindari regions, landlords were not charged with the responsibility of acting as intermediaries of the state in the collection of land revenue. In raiyatwari regions, for example, there were no intermediaries between the state and actual cultivators. However, there were landlords in raiyatwari areas, and their actual behaviors toward those below them in the agrarian hierarchy were not markedly different than the behaviors of landlords in zamindari areas toward their tenants.

were advised by the central government to take steps to update land records by means of a land census. And, when the states learned that they would not receive financial subsidies to carry out such a census, the states were not enthused to comply with the center's advice.[6] When they did,[7] the data were generally not comparable, and did not provide an adequate set of national records for agrarian reform or land reform purposes.[8] Notwithstanding this effort, the dearth of up-to-date records concerning rights in land would continue to be cited for decades thereafter to explain, and sometimes even to justify, delays in the implementation of such agrarian reform laws as were enacted in the states. Indeed, the historical record makes evident that the states' revenue ministries have never worked with anything like "all deliberate speed" to provide an adequate data base for agrarian reform or land reform in modern India.

Implementing Reform Legislation

The states' revenue ministries were also responsible for implementing such agrarian and land reform as was drafted and enacted into law. The tasks of implementation varied from state to state. In some states, notably those most conspicuously lacking up-to-date land records, the tasks were formidable, and were complicated by the failure of landholders (particularly landholding intermediaries in East India) to provide the government documents detailing their rights in land. In many instances, the landholding intermediaries withheld, or did not have available, rent rolls pertaining to their holdings. In such circumstances, a revenue

---

6. Daniel Thorner, *The Agrarian Prospect in India,* (Delhi: Delhi University Press, 1956), p. 68.

7. Eventually, during the First Five Year Plan, a census of landholdings was carried out in twenty-two states -- of which only ten conducted complete enumeration surveys, as distinct from sample surveys. The census involved only sample surveys in Bihar, Uttar Pradesh, Rajasthan and Travancore-Cochin (now part of Kerala). [See: India, Planning Commission, *Review of the First Five Year Plan,* (New Delhi: Manager of Publications, 1957), p. 324.]

8. As perceived by the Planning Commission, the land census was encouraged by the central government with a view toward collecting data, in particular, for the fixation of ceilings on the size of landholdings. The scope and nature of the census are described in: India, Planning Commission, *Five Year Plan Progress Report for 1954-55,* (New Delhi: Planning Commission, May, 1956), p. 99.

ministry needed not only to reconstruct records of rights in land, but also to establish an entirely new administrative machinery capable of coping with expanded responsibilities associated with the direct collection of land revenue without the assistance of the intermediaries.[9]

Early Critiques of
Agrarian Reform Measures

Ladejinsky's Critique

Wolf Ladejinsky, the American architect of far-reaching agrarian reform in post-War Japan, was brought to India from Japan in 1952 to assess India's progress in agrarian reform and land reform.[10] While Ladejinsky's visit was at the initiative of Chester Bowles, the American Ambassador to India at the time, Ladejinsky's report on his findings was submitted directly to the Planning Commission of the Government of India.

Ladejinsky's observations were based on quick visits to villages in the Punjab, Madras, and Kashmir. A striking omission from his itinerary in India was a visit to East India, the permanent settlement region of the subcontinent, a region characterized by the most exploitive landlord-tenant-sharecropper relations in the country -- a region where zamindars had become negative symbols of the pre-independence period who were worthy, said some politicians, of abolition. This notwithstanding, Ladejinsky, in his inimitable dynamic style (maximizing face-to-face interactions with peasant cultivators), demonstrated the keenness of his powers of observation and his sensitivity to the needs and interests of

---

9. For a detailed account of the administrative reforms that had to be introduced in Bihar, following the abolition of intermediaries, to enable the state itself to collect land revenue from liable landholders, see: V.K. N. Menon, "The New Anchal Adhikari System in Bihar," *Indian Journal of Public Administration,* 2, No. 2, April-June, 1956.

10. At the time, Ladejinsky was attached to the United States Embassy in Japan. The Embassy, responding to a request initiated by the United States Embassy in India, permitted Ladejinsky to spend ninety days in India from October through December of 1952.

actual tillers of the soil, people at the base of the rural hierarchy of interests in land, in the areas that he did visit.

His field observations from the Punjab were explicit and direct. Reflecting on the immediate effects of the *Punjab Tenants (Security of Tenure Act), 1950,* as amended on December 27, 1951, Ladejinsky said that the act, as thus far implemented, had not conferred security of tenure on cultivators classified as tenants-at-will (a category of cultivators who then tilled thirty to forty percent of the land in the Punjab) -- even though the provision of security of tenure to such cultivators had been a primary object of the Punjab legislation.[11] Moreover, Ladejinsky suggested that the Punjab legislation had produced an environment in the Punjab where landlords' ejectments of tenants were apparent. And, based on his own observations in the countryside, he said that it seemed likely that the number of peasant cultivators ejected from lands customarily tilled by them was greater than the number of tenants-at-will whose security of tenure might have been enhanced as a result of the legislation. Ladejinsky also said that the legislation had led to the displacement of large numbers of tenants through the working of provisions in the Punjab act that permitted landlords to reclaim land for self-cultivation. The landlords who had resumed land for self-cultivation, he reported, were not, generally, tilling the land themselves. Instead, they were substituting hired labor for the former tenants. What is more, he added, this meant that the landlords often were employing their former tenants, now diminished in status, as hired labor. In effect then, the Punjab legislation, argued Ladejinsky, had not only failed to confer security of tenure on tenants-at-will, but also had caused many tillers so classified to be diminished in status. That is to say, tenants-at-will in the Punjab were in many instances losing even their traditional, tenuous claims to land and being compelled to join the ranks of landless agricultural laborers (tilling, in some instances, the same land that they had earlier cultivated as tenant farmers).[12]

Ladejinsky questioned provisions in the Punjab legislation that seemed to permit tenant cultivators to purchase land, suggesting that that right seemed to be extremely restricted. He anticipated, therefore, that few tenants would benefit from that provision in the legislation. And, he

11. Louis J. Walinsky, editor, *Agrarian Reform as Unfinished Business: The Selected Works of Wolf Ladejinsky,* (London: Oxford University Press, 1977), p. 156.

12. Ibid., p. 158.

concluded that the legislation as a whole was not only deficient in its provisions, but also was devoid of meaningful enforcement mechanisms.

Turning his attention to conditions in Madras, Ladejinsky minced no words in reporting his findings. He said that he had found in Madras (essentially, the contemporary states of Tamilnadu and Andhra) "no trace of village activities by the Congress Party on behalf of the underprivileged."[13] And, he contrasted the absence of Congress involvement at the village level with the conspicuousness of the Communist influence. At the time of his visit (1952), Ladejinsky said that the tenant cultivators that he had interviewed had made plain, especially in Tanjore, that the Communists were active in the countryside -- working to address the needs and interests of tenant cultivators and others at the base of the hierarchy of interests in land. Reporting on this phenomenon, Ladejinsky, though he was himself a deeply committed anti-Communist, showed his understanding of the potency of the line, under existing conditions, that the Communists were using in the countryside. He said that, throughout Madras, the actual cultivator "should become the owner of the land he tills."[14] This was a characteristic recommendation of Ladejinsky. He always bridled at the notion that "land to the tiller" should be widely perceived as a Communist slogan. It was his own slogan: a slogan derived from his own deeply held belief that economic progress and social justice in agrarian societies required, above all, the development of a system of agriculture where the person who labored on the land, and assumed the primary risks of production, was also its owner.

Ladejinsky was struck by the rich potential of the agricultural setting in Tanjore. However, he noted that he found extreme poverty there, especially among sections of the peasantry who lacked either secure rights in land (tenants-at-will and sharecroppers) or any land at all (permanent and casual laborers). He was skeptical about the working of a new ordinance in Madras that was designed to regulate the division of produce between the landlord and sharecropper -- an ordinance, if enforced, that would provide the landlord sixty percent and the cultivator forty percent of the produce from the land. Talking to sharecroppers in the countryside, he had found that the customary division of produce was one that accorded the landlord seventy-five percent of the produce and the sharecropper only twenty-five percent. This notwithstanding, Ladejinsky

---

13. Ibid., p. 163.
14. Ibid.

noted that the sharecroppers were quite aware of the new ordinance and its stipulation that the landlords' share should be reduced. Moreover, the discrepancy between the rental shares prescribed by the ordinance and shares prescribed by custom fueled anger in the countryside among the sharecroppers, said Ladejinsky. Ignoring the anger in the countryside, the landlords of Madras, according to Ladejinsky, and especially those described by him as the "landed aristocracy" of Tanjore, were bent on thwarting existing or projected land reforms by evicting their tenants, by dismissing their permanent (pannaiyal) labor,[15] and by replacing both with casual laborers (those having the least prospect under existing or projected land reform measures of claiming rights in land from superior landholders).

In sum, Ladejinsky raised an early warning concerning progress in agrarian reform and land reform, based on his quick and rough observations in selected regions of India. However, even though his critical observations and concerns were submitted in writing directly to the Planning Commission, there is no evidence that his views swayed opinion in the Government of India in 1952 or, for that matter, years later when he returned to India to work as a consultant to The Ford Foundation and, later still, as a Resident Representative of The World Bank in the 1970s.[16]

---

15. In 1952, according to Ladejinsky, the pannaiyal laborers worked about nine months per annum. By custom they received about twenty rupees per month, had one-third of an acre of land for personal use, and lived in a hut owned by their landlord.

16. One of Ladejinsky's great regrets in life was that he was unable to persuade the Government of India to heed his various calls for vigorous implementation of agrarian reform and land reform. He frequently expressed privately his anguish at his failure to convince important elements within the Indian bureaucracy of the importance of agrarian reform to the future development of the country. Indicative of his frame of mind in his last years is the following excerpt from his correspondence with me, following the publication of my *Agrarian Crisis in India: The Case of Bihar*. Said Ladejinsky, in a letter dated May 30, 1974: "Your final chapter interested me above all for obvious reasons, and, without flattering you, I couldn't think of a better summary or sounder recommendations. My only trouble with them is who in the devil is going to bother implementing them. This is not to say that you shouldn't have made them, but for an old time watcher of the agricultural scheme I despair of anything being done of so sensible an approach as yours. .... Generally speaking, for the immediate future I have no faith in any

(continued...)

Government of India Claims

As early as 1954, the Government of India provided the international community an encouraging, if somewhat simplified, account of its progress in specifying the goals of agrarian reform and land reform in India and in enacting legislation to address those goals. The government's vehicle for communicating its goals and incipient achievements in this sphere of public policy was its response to a United Nations questionnaire: part of a United Nations effort, carried out by its Department of Economic Affairs, to gather data from member nations concerning progress in effecting land reform. Significantly, the government's response to the UN questionnaire preceded systematic attempts by the central government to review progress in agrarian reform and land reform at the end of the First Five Year Plan (1957).

In its response to the UN questionnaire, the Government of India said that the cardinal principle imbedded in India's legislation for land reform was the abolition of landlordism in all of its variants.[17] To do this, suggested the Government of India, required a large and complex body of legislation reflecting the wide divergence of tenurial conditions in the Indian states. Pointing out that, under the Indian constitution, land reform was the responsibility of the states, the Government of India emphasized that the basic principles of the legislation for land reform were, nonetheless, laid down by the central government.[18]

The Government of India, responding to the UN questionnaire, went on to specify its policy objectives as follows: (i) augmentation of

---

16.(...continued)
revolutionary changes and nor am I too sanguine of any evolutionary changes either."

17. Whether calculated or not, this was a disingenuous statement. The Government of India was not intent on abolishing landlords or landlordism; at most, it was intent on denying landholders classified as intermediaries between actual cultivators and the state the right to continue to act for the state in the collection of land revenue.

18. The clear intent here seems to have been to confirm internationally that it was the central government that was establishing the basic principles for land reform in India. As noted earlier in the text, the central government did establish general guidelines for agrarian reform and land reform. However, the states were in control of the scope and content of the legislation and, as we know with the wisdom of hindsight, could deviate from whatever principles, hard or soft, the central government set forth.

agricultural production by a better system of land management; (ii) reduction of inequalities in opportunities and income; (iii) provision of security for tenants including opportunities for them to become owners of the land they cultivate; (iv) improvement of the position of agricultural workers; and (v) in general, the raising of living standards in rural areas.

The Government of India also said that its land reform measures (as legislated in the states) addressed the interests of five categories of rural interests: landholding intermediaries between cultivators and the states; large landholders classified as owners of land (permanent occupancy raiyats); small and middle sized landholders classified as owners of land (permanent occupancy raiyats); tenants-at-will (temporary holders of land who lacked permanent occupancy rights to that land); and landless agricultural workers.[19] Having specified the five categories listed above, the government briefly outlined its policy objectives with respect to each.

Without elaboration, it suggested that the policy regarding the elimination of intermediary rights between the occupier of land and the state had been accepted in all of the Indian states. However, in this context, the government did not go on to explain that the rights of intermediaries that were to be abolished were only those rights pertaining to the collection of land revenue in behalf of some of the Indian states. The impression was left in the response to the UN questionnaire that intermediaries' rights in land were to be abolished, when this was no where the intent of legislation in the Indian states.

With respect to large landholders, the government stated that such landholders had rights in land that fell into two categories: land cultivated by tenants-at-will and land under the direct management of landholders. The policy of the Government of India was to recommend that such landholders could resume land for personal cultivation from their tenants-at-will up to a certain limit. Similarly, it was the policy of the government to recommend that a ceiling be placed on the absolute amount of land that a landholder could retain under his direct management. In reporting to the UN its recommendation to the states that a limit should be set on the size of landholdings, the Government of India stated that it made a distinction between landholdings considered to be so efficiently

---

19. The parenthetical explanations of these five categories of rural interests are my own. In its response to the United Nations, the Government of India provided no definitional frame for the categories listed.

managed that their breakup might lead to a fall in production and landholdings that did not meet such a test.[20]

In response to the United Nations questionnaire, the Government of India suggested that its policy directives to the Indian states -- policy directives that were applicable to landholders having small and middle-sized holdings -- emphasized the need to restructure such holdings into larger units that could be farmed cooperatively. This recommendation, as reported to the United Nations, illustrated the well-established bias in India, dating from the British colonial period, against small units of production.

With respect to tenants-at-will, the Government of India made plain in its report to the United Nations that it had no intention of proposing legislation that would give such persons a permanent right to the land in their temporary possession. Indeed, the government suggested that the most that such persons could expect would be a secure tenancy for a specified period, possibly from five to ten years. The government also indicated that, as a matter of policy, such tenants-at-will could be denied all access to land in their temporary possession if a superior landholder wanted to resume the land for personal cultivation.

Regarding policies applicable to landless agricultural laborers, the Government of India stated that it had no intention of recommending land reform legislation that would provide them land. Instead, the government said that it was recommending to the states the implementation of minimum wages acts, and hoping also that some land might be made available to the landless from waste land reclaimed by government in the states and from land donated by landholders to the Bhoodan (land gift) movement. Furthermore, the government stated that such land as might accrue to the landless should not be given to them as individual proprietors, but instead should be settled with them in groups and tilled along cooperative lines.[21]

---

20. In this context, the Government of India's response to the United Nations questionnaire was not as complete as it could have been. The central government's guidelines to the states of India concerning ceilings on landholdings also gave the states scope to set limits that were highly variable in accordance with criteria set by the states, and even to exempt from ceilings holdings tilled by mechanized means.

21. The substance above concerning progress in agrarian reform and land reform, as reported to the United Nations by the Government of India, comes from the following source: United Nations, Department of Economic Affairs,

(continued...)

Thorner's Critique

A most prescient analysis of the Government of India's attempt to promote agrarian reform and land reform was presented toward the end of the First Plan by the expatriate American scholar, Daniel Thorner. Thorner's review of progress in agrarian reform and land reform, delivered in a series of lectures at the Delhi School of Economics, was published in Delhi in 1956 as a book entitled *The Agrarian Prospect in India*. In those lectures, Thorner made observations concerning India's historical land systems, and how they might appropriately be transformed, that are as relevant in the 1990s as they were in the 1950s. And, his critique of the legislation for agrarian reform and land reform already then enacted into law in the Indian states was remarkable for its sensitivity to existing conditions in rural areas and its balanced appraisal of what would and would not work to transform the agrarian structure of India and the relations of the people in rural areas to the land.

The strength of Thorner's analysis derived in substantial measure from his methodology. Thorner, working in the tradition of the most enlightened of British colonial officers, like Harold Mann, believed in gathering his own data in face-to-face interactions with villagers in rural areas. Visiting some seventy-five to one hundred villages to gather material for his lectures at Delhi University, Thorner developed an empathetic understanding of the needs and interests of actual tillers in the countryside and an acute awareness of the difference between enacting a law to effect change and actually effecting change in the hierarchy of interests in land in rural India. Thorner knew that the existing conditions that he observed in rural areas were defined both by custom and by law. Accordingly, he had a sense of the limits of law as applied by the British in the nineteenth and twentieth centuries to regulate the relations of landlords and tenants, and to alter traditional agrarian structures. He said that attempts to change the agrarian structure by means of new law almost always fell "short of their goals or had effects other than those intended."[22] Regrettably, this cardinal observation by Thorner, uttered in an academic setting, by itself was insufficient to encourage members of

---

21.(...continued)
Progress in Land Reform (Analysis of replies by governments to a United Nations questionnaire), (New York: United Nations Publication, January 12, 1954), pp. 20-23.
  22. Daniel Thorner, *The Agrarian Prospect in India,* p. 2.

the governing elite in India to modify the already established means by which they, like their colonial predecessors, were bent on transforming India's traditional hierarchy of interests in land.

Thorner also understood that the hierarchy of interests in land in India was reinforced by economic inequality and sanctioned by the caste structure of rural society, and therefore was not amenable to change by legislation alone. This held especially, he believed, for legislative attempts to transform the agrarian structure of India that were tied to British precedents in law. Such legislative attempts were likely to fail, he knew, because they did not address underlying questions of rural hierarchy. Indeed, Thorner saw the new legislation of independent India as deficient at the outset precisely because it was rooted in the British practice of accepting the agrarian hierarchy as it was, and attempting only to regulate the behavior of landlords and to protect tenants within that existing hierarchy.

Thorner sensed that agrarian reform and land reform might founder in India if the enactment of legislation and its implementation were tied to British legacy rules and procedures. In his lectures at Delhi University, and later in his book, he showed clearly how time-consuming procedures by which legislation for agrarian reform and land reform was introduced, debated, enacted into law, subjected to judicial review, and given to revenue ministries for implementation, themselves, could thwart the original intent of the legislation. He certainly accepted earlier than most observers the maxim that land reform that is delayed is land reform that, inevitably, will be denied.

Thorner's field investigations made him aware of the techniques employed by legislators to produce laws that would enable landlords to remain on the scene.[23] Like the Planning Commission's Committee on Tenancy Reform, Thorner was also well aware of how laws designed to permit landholders to resume land for personal cultivation would be used repeatedly to thwart efforts to ensure that land reform might mean "land to the actual tiller." He reported in this context on the practice in Uttar Pradesh of permitting "a person who hires agricultural labor either permanently or casually for the performance of all or some manual tasks .... to be regarded as a tiller of the soil ...".[24] As a result of this practice, Thorner observed that the abolished landlords (zamindars) of Uttar Pradesh became bhumidars permitted to retain their home farms.

---

23. Ibid., p. 19.
24. Ibid., pp. 20-21.

And such erstwhile zamindars, now bhumidars, were given absolute security of tenure; they could not be evicted for any reason within the frame of new legislation, said Thorner.

Citing the history of land reform legislation in Bombay, Thorner argued that the legislation was designed clearly to preserve the traditional agrarian hierarchy of interests in land. Specifically, the *Bombay Tenancy Act of 1948* had included a permissive definition of what it meant for a landholder to cultivate his own land. A landholder could be a personal cultivator if he tilled his land with his own labor, or with the labor of any member of his family, or with servants, or with hired labor supervised by the landholder or a member of his family.[25] Thorner concluded that the Bombay act's definitional frame ensured that the traditional hierarchy -- landlords, permanent tenants, protected tenants, ordinary tenants, sharecroppers and landless agricultural laborers -- would persist.

Thorner argued that landlordism in India knew no bounds. He suggested, for example, that there was little difference in the actual behavior of landlords in raiyatwari and zamindari regions of the country. The only difference between the two kinds of landlords was that the raiyatwari landlords generally "did not enjoy comparable positions of social dominance."[26] In any event, Thorner suggested that the prevailing model of post-independence agrarian reform was not designed to abolish either category of landlord (the popular rhetoric notwithstanding), but to reinforce the old British tradition of legislating to improve conditions for their tenants.[27]

Finally, in sharp criticism of legislation enacted in India up to 1956, Thorner said that land reform laws, ostensibly passed for the benefit of the underprivileged, had not altered substantially India's village structure or the hierarchy of interests in land. The rural oligarchs, he said, had had wit and resource enough to get around the reform laws -- laws in which, in any event, the loopholes[28] were so large as to give them ample

---

25. Ibid., p. 27.

26. Ibid., p. 26.

27. Ibid.

28. Thorner's use of the word "loopholes" is understandable, but inappropriate. As Upendra Baxi, the distinguished legal scholar and Vice Chancellor of Delhi University, has made plain in discussions with me in Delhi in 1990 and again at Oxford University in 1991, the land reform laws of India contained provisions precisely designed to protect the interests of the landholding elite. Such precisely crafted provisions in law, as Baxi rightly observes, should not be classified as "loopholes."

maneuvering ground. "By passing themselves off, whether legally or illegally, as tillers and cultivators," said Thorner, "the village oligarchs have gone on running India's rural life."[29] Added Thorner, the only reform that seemed then credible to him was one that would leave the land alone and redistribute proprietors. That is to say, Thorner suggested that the primary goal of land reform in India should be one aimed at providing secure rights in land to the actual tillers (the people who could actually be observed working on the land) -- thereby depriving all others who held land, but did not themselves till it, of permanent occupancy rights in land.

Planning Commission Evaluation
of Agrarian Reform Progress

Introduction

Notwithstanding the central government's problems already identified in defining the purposes of agrarian reform and giving direction to them, the Indian states proceeded in the 1950s and 1960s to enact into law all kinds of measures, classified as agrarian reform or land reform, designed ostensibly to transform the agrarian structure of the country. Indeed, it is probably accurate to suggest that the Indian states together enacted more legislation for agrarian reform and land reform in the 1950s and 1960s than has been enacted into law in any country before or since. The volume and complexity of the legislation, reflecting differences in the country's historical land systems and differences in the willingness of states' legislators to initiate changes in the countryside that would affect the traditional hierarchy of relationships of people to the land, only added to the difficulty at the center of evaluating the progress of agrarian reform and land reform. Nonetheless, in 1957, as the First Five Year Plan was concluded, the Planning Commission made its own formal assessment of what had, thus far, been accomplished.

The commission's evaluation of the progress of agrarian reform made plain at the outset that the central government's role had been a limited one associated only with the setting of broad principles and directions of policy. It was understood, therefore, suggested the commission, that the

---

29. Daniel Thorner, *The Agrarian Prospect in India,* p. 79.

cumulative record of reform would mainly reflect differences in the states' responses to the center's general guidelines as finally incorporated in the First Five Year Plan.[30] This generalization notwithstanding, the Planning Commission made the overriding judgement that the progress of agrarian reform had been constrained by delays in initiating legislation, and by frequent changes in the detail and content of the legislation that had been enacted in the states. The effects of these delays and changes in the legislation, said the Planning Commission, had "tended to some extent to defeat the objects of land reform."[31]

Success Claimed for
Abolition of Intermediaries

It was estimated by the Planning Commission that about 50 percent of India's agricultural area had been held under the system of "intermediary rights" when India gained freedom from Britain. These intermediaries (loosely referred to as zamindars) had been interposed between actual cultivators and the state, and it was one of the primary objects of land reform, suggested the Planning Commission, that the intermediaries be abolished.[32] Toward this end, some states took action to abolish intermediary interests before central government guidelines were in place. In Bihar, for example, steps were first taken to abolish intermediaries in 1947 when the Bihar Abolition of Zamindari Bill was passed and, in accordance with the then operative provisions of the *Government of India Act of 1935,* reserved for the consideration of the Governor General of India. And, in Madras similar legislation was enacted and partly implemented between 1948 and 1951. However, in most of the areas where intermediaries existed, decisions were made to enact and implement legislation for their abolishment within the period of the First Plan (1952-57).

---

30. India, Planning Commission, *Review of the First Five Year Plan,* p. 314.
31. Ibid., p. 320.
32. The emphasis here on abolishing intermediary interests, including zamindars' intermediary interests, reflected, at least with regard to rhetoric, the broadest area of consensus concerning land policy among the governing elites both prior to and immediately after independence. To suggest that the zamindari system should be abolished became a popular political slogan: regrettably, a slogan that tended to substitute for any comprehensive approach to agrarian reform and land reform.

The progress of legislation to abolish intermediary interests was delayed by challenges by intermediaries in the courts. This process is best illustrated by what happened in the state of Bihar.[33] As soon as Bihar had passed its landmark legislation to abolish its intermediaries, secured the approval of the Governor General on June 6, 1949, and published the act (*Bihar Act XVIII of 1949*), the constitutionality of the legislation was challenged" and the courts issued injunctions restraining the State Government from implementing the scheme."[34] In due course, the legislation was repealed and superceded by a new bill, the Bihar Land Reforms Bill, 1949. This bill was passed by the state legislature in 1950 and transferred for review by the President of India.[35] It received the assent of the President of India and was published as an act, the *Bihar Land Reforms Act, 1950.* This act, however, was again challenged in the courts, and the Patna High Court declared that the act contravened Article 14 of the constitution.[36] Whereupon, the central government introduced and the central legislature passed the *Constitution (First Amendment) Act,* which validated the *Bihar Land Reforms Act, 1950.* This first amendment to the constitution, Article 31A, specified that "no law providing for -- (a) the acquisition by the State of any estate[37] or of any rights therein or

---

33. For a detailed exposition of the record of agrarian reform, including zamindari abolition legislation, in Bihar, see: F. Tomasson Jannuzi, *Agrarian Crisis in India: The Case of Bihar,* (Austin, Texas: The University of Texas Press, 1974).

34. H.D. Malaviya, *Land Reforms in India,* Second Edition, (New Delhi: All India Congress Committee, 1955), p. 205.

35. This was done in accordance with Article 31, Clause 4 of the Indian constitution: "If any Bill pending at the commencement of this Constitution in the Legislature of a State has, after it has been passed by such Legislature, been reserved for the consideration of the President and has received his assent, then notwithstanding anything in this Constitution, the law so assented to shall not be called in question in any Court ...". [India, Ministry of Law, *The Constitution of India,* As modified up to the 1st May, 1965, (Delhi: Manager of Publications, 1965), p. 17.]

36. Article 14 states, "The State shall not deny to any person equality before the law or the equal protection of the laws within the territory of India." [India, Ministry of Law, *The Constitution of India,* As modified up to the 1st May, 1965, p. 8.]

37. Estate in this context does not refer to an operational landholding; it refers to the aggregate of landholdings over which an intermediary or zamindar could claim de jure rights in land.

the extinguishment or modification of any such rights .... shall be deemed to be void on the ground that it is inconsistent with or takes away or abridges any of the rights conferred by Article 14, Article 19 or Article 31."[38] Responding to the amendment of the constitution, zamindari interests in Bihar challenged the constitutionality of Article 31A in a suit brought before the Supreme Court of India. But the court unanimously held that the constitutional amendment was valid. At which, legal proceedings designed to test the constitutionality of the *Bihar Land Reforms Act, 1950,* were once more initiated by interested Bihari zamindars and the matter eventually reached the Supreme Court of India. In 1952, the Supreme Court of India finally upheld the validity of the *Bihar Land Reforms Act, 1950.* Steps could now be taken at the state level to implement the act. However, five years had elapsed from the time of the passage of the Bihar Abolition of Zamindari Bill in 1947 to the final validation of the *Bihar Land Reorms Act, 1950* -- time enough for the Bihar zamindars to take whatever steps they could, outside of the courts, to protect their interests, thereby thwarting the intent of the new law.

The events in Bihar notwithstanding, the Planning Commission claimed that by the end of 1954-1955 the program to abolish intermediaries had been "completed in Andhra, Bombay, Madras, Madhya Pradesh, Punjab, Uttar Pradesh, Madhya Bharat, Saurashtra, Bhopal and Vidhya Pradesh."[39] The commission indicated that initiatives to abolish intermediaries had not been completed at that time in Assam, Bihar, Orissa and Rajasthan.[40] In general, then, from the perspective of the Planning Commission, it could be said at the end of the First Five Year Plan that, except for a few pockets where action was still needed, intermediaries had been "abolished almost entirely throughout the country."[41] While this judgement considerably exaggerated what had been accomplished, it became fashionable at the time, and for some years thereafter, to suggest that the abolishment of intermediaries had been a signal accomplishment of the post-independence Government of India. In fact, what had been accomplished could have been described more

---

38. India, Ministry of Law, *The Constitution of India,* As modified up to the 1st May, 1965, pp. 18-19.

39. India, Planning Commission, *Review of the First Five Year Plan,* p. 315.

40. Ibid.

41. Ibid.

appropriately as land reform by definitional obfuscation,[42] as I shall make plain in due course.

Praise Qualified for
Tenancy Legislation

The Planning Commission's evaluation of the progress in agrarian reform suggested that attempts had been made during the First Plan period (within the sphere of "tenancy legislation") to regulate relations between landlords and tenants.[43] Toward this end, the plan mainly had envisaged legislation limiting the size of agricultural holdings, including the amount of land that a landlord could retain for personal cultivation after ejecting tenants who lacked a de jure claim to land, and legislation designed to regulate and to reduce rents.[44]

As the Planning Commission's evaluation made obvious, the tenancy legislation enacted in the states in the First Plan period was, for the most part, in the tradition of the British Raj. Earlier, beginning in the nineteenth century, the British had enacted legislation designed to address the same general goal -- that of regulating relations between landlords and tenants. Accordingly, the British had passed legislation to provide some landholders enhanced security of tenure on lands tilled by them and to regulate rents. In this context, they had more often taken steps to protect the rights in land of superior landholders, including non-cultivating intermediaries, than inferior landholders, including actual tillers classified as tenants, sub-tenants of intermediaries, and tenants-at-will, whose rights to land were qualified and tenuous. As the Planning Commission

---

42. The phrase "land reform by definitional obfuscation" can be attributed, I believe, to the late Daniel Thorner.

43. The term "tenants" was used widely, as in this instance, without definitional specificity. Thus, some actual tillers whose interests in land were subordinate to "landlords" were perceived to be "tenants" and therefore potential beneficiaries of tenancy legislation, while other tillers who were subordinate to superior landholders were perceived to be "sharecroppers," tillers not recognized in a de jure sense as "tenants" and, therefore, not intended to be the beneficiaries of tenancy legislation. This lack of definitional clarity in the use of the word "tenants" persists today.

44. The projected reform goals in this sphere were minimalist; there was no scope in the plan for redistributive reforms rooted, for example, in the concept of "land to the tiller."

observed, "On the eve of the First Five Year Plan, with some exceptions, tenants of land owners in the raiyatwari areas[45] and sub-tenants of intermediaries in other areas enjoyed very limited protection indeed."[46]

Briefly stated, this is the background against which a considerable volume of "tenancy" legislation was enacted during the First Five Year Plan. For example, in Bombay, Punjab, and Hyderabad changes were made in existing, pre-independence tenancy laws. Meanwhile, Uttar Pradesh included tenancy reforms within the frame of other legislation enacted in 1950 and 1954.[47] West Bengal included tenancy provisions in its *Estates Abolition Act of 1953* and its *Land Reforms Act of 1955*. In Rajasthan, the commission reported that comprehensive tenancy laws were enacted in 1955 and amended in 1956.[48] These laws were enacted after landlords' ejectments of tenants from lands tilled by them had been an issue in Rajasthan as early as 1949.

As a result of the spate of tenancy legislation enacted during the First Plan period, the Planning Commission reported that tenants in many states had been granted secure, permanent occupancy rights in land. There can be no denying that some tenants were indeed beneficiaries of reform measures that made them "permanent occupancy raiyats," virtual owners of the land in their cultivating possession. However, there is ample evidence to suggest that tens of thousands, possibly millions, of tenant cultivators were, at the same time, denied permanent occupancy rights in land. Other tenant cultivators (as in Bombay, Punjab, Rajasthan and Himachal Pradesh)[49] who had assumed that they had a de jure claim to the land they tilled, lost those lands when the new legislation accorded superior landholders the right to resume land from their tenants for personal cultivation. The land that a superior landholder, or landlord, could resume for personal cultivation varied from state to state. In Assam, he could resume for personal cultivation up to thirty-three and one-third acres. In Bihar, erstwhile intermediaries or zamindars could

---

45. Raiyatwari areas were areas within which cultivators, for revenue paying purposes, were in a direct relationship with the state.

46. India, Planning Commission, *Review of the First Five Year Plan,* p. 318.

47. See, in this context, Walter C. Neale's classic study of land tenure and reform in Uttar Pradesh. [Walter C. Neale, *Economic Change in Rural India: Land Tenure and Reform in Uttar Pradesh, 1800-1955,* (New Haven: Yale University Press, 1962).]

48. India, Planning Commission, *Review of the First Five Year Plan,* p. 318.

49. Ibid., pp. 318-319.

retain vast holdings legally -- evicting their tenants in the process and ignoring whatever incipient rights to land might have been accorded to sharecroppers (bataidars) within the frame of colonial era tenancy legislation. Even after the intermediaries or zamindars of Bihar had been legally abolished (their intermediary interests or estates having been vested in the state), Bihari landlords could retain (in addition to some other lands, buildings and structures) all lands in their khas possession, defined in law to include all lands cultivated personally by a landlord or by his own stock and servants or by hired labor and hired stock. In Bihar, this broad definition of possession allowed the ex-intermediary or zamindar to claim land that he did not, in a literal sense, cultivate himself prior to the enactment of zamindari abolition legislation; this was true even when that land was in the personal, cultivating possession of another cultivator (tenant or sub-tenant), so long as that cultivator did not possess the means, monetary or documentary, of establishing his right of permanent occupancy. The tenancy legislation of other states contained similar provisions allowing superior landholders to resume land for personal cultivation, variously defined. And, as the Planning Commission observed, "it would appear that considerable resumption of lands took place."[50] This resumption of land, ostensibly for personal cultivation, involved not only the de jure ejectment of tenant farmers, but also the encouragement of tenants' so-called "voluntary surrenders of land" to superior landholders. Clearly, suggested the commission, "the security of the tenant remained incomplete..." in rural India at the end of the First Five Year Plan.[51] Such understatement neglected evidence from many states of the wholesale ejectment of tenants by landlords and of tenants' voluntary surrenders of land on a grand scale. Indeed, it is quite likely that, by 1957, more tenants of landlords had lost de jure rights in land as a consequence of tenancy legislation in the First Plan period than had received permanent occupancy rights in land.

In 1957, as the Planning Commission assessed progress made in conferring what it referred to as "ownership rights"[52] to erstwhile tenants

---

50. Ibid., p. 320.

51. Ibid.

52. Within the context of Indian law, it would have been more appropriate here for the Planning Commission to have referred to progress made in conferring "permanent occupancy rights" in land, rather than "ownership rights." While permanent occupancy rights are roughly equivalent to ownership rights,

(continued...)

of superior landholders, it noted that the legislation enacted in many states conferred on tenants the opportunity to acquire such rights if the tenants paid compensation to their landlords. However, a tenant who wished to purchase the land that he had "taken-in" for purposes of cultivation from a superior landholder might find that the landholder wanted to exploit provisions in the law that would permit him to resume that land for personal cultivation. In this way, legislation designed both to give tenants an opportunity to acquire a permanent right to land and to permit landlords to retain land earlier given out to tenants, engendered disputes over land between superior and inferior landholders. Needless to say, such disputes over rights in land were resolved generally in favor of superior landholders. While the Planning Commission did not formally recognize this problem resulting from competing claims to the same land, its review of progress at the end of the First Five Year Plan did recognize that the new legislation had not produced significant results, if judged by the number of tenants who had actually exercised their right under law to acquire "ownership" rights to land. Explaining this phenomenon, the commission said that many tenants, apparently, were reluctant to purchase rights in land, even if permitted to do so -- especially if the purchase of rights in land meant accepting the dual burden of making payments of compensation to their erstwhile landlords and payments of revenue to the state to meet the state's customary revenue demand (a demand made applicable when the erstwhile tenant was registered as a permanent occupancy raiyat holding land in a direct relationship with the state).

Praise Withdrawn for
Tenancy Legislation

Within two years of its review of progress in agrarian reform at the end of the First Five Year Plan, the Planning Commission provided additional critical evaluation of agrarian reform, particularly in the sphere of tenancy legislation. This critical evaluation was contained in the report of the Committee on Tenancy Reform (one of several review committees

---

52.(...continued)
there is a subtle distinction that can be made between the two. Permanent occupancy rights are less absolute -- confirming, at least implicitly, that the state or ruling authority is the ultimate owner of the land.

established by the commission's Panel on Land Reforms).[53] Noting that
the First Plan had recommended (a) that security of tenure be conferred
on tenants, subject to the landlord's right to resume a limited area for
personal cultivation, (b) that the tenants' rents payable to landlords be
reduced, and (c) that tenants be given a right to purchase ownership
(permanent occupancy) rights to holdings customarily tilled by them, The
Committee on Tenancy Reform said that this package of recommendations
had "been implemented effectively only in a few States."[54] Moreover, the
committee indicated that the intended reforms had not been initiated in
some states, and in others, where some effort had been made to legislate
the reform package, the legislation had not produced the benefits to
tenants that had been recommended by the central government in the
national plan.

Adding specificity to its summary review, the committee bluntly stated
that tenants in Andhra remained without security of tenure, that tenancies
in Madras had, in the general case, not been regulated, and that the
ejectment of tenants (by landlords) had only recently been stayed in that
state. The committee noted that sharecroppers were not yet classified as
tenants in some states, notably Travancore-Cochin (the contemporary
State of Kerala). And, in such circumstances, the sharecroppers were
still paying heavy rents -- often exceeding fifty percent of the gross
produce. In Orissa, said the committee, there was reason to believe that
landlords were demanding and getting at least half of the gross produce
from their tenants -- even though the law specified that the landlords'
share should be no more than one-fourth. In the Punjab, the committee
found that landlords were systematically ejecting tenants from the land,
notwithstanding the fact that legal steps had been taken to stay
ejectments.[55] In Bihar and West Bengal, the committee reported that
sharecroppers (lacking de jure status as tenants) were being ejected from
lands customarily tilled by them by their landlords. In Bombay, the
committee noted that the number of protected tenants had been reduced
by 20 percent[56] in the period from 1948 to 1951, suggesting that large

---

53. India, Planning Commission, Panel on Land Reforms, *Reports of the
Committees of the Panel on Land Reforms,* (Delhi: The Manager of Publications,
1959), pp. 1-93.

54. Ibid., p. 36.

55. Ibid.

56. Ibid.

scale ejectments of such tenants had taken place.[57] And, the committee reported similar evidence of ejectments of protected tenants in Hyderabad (now part of the State of Andhra Pradesh), where the number of registered tenants had declined by fifty-seven percent in five years (1951-1955). The striking feature of these ejectments was that, "in the large majority of cases," they had been achieved by the well-established process (confirming the coercive power of superior landholders throughout rural India) of so-called voluntary surrenders.[58] Subsequently, the committee reported that it had gathered evidence indicating that large scale evictions of tenants had occurred during the First Plan period under the guise of voluntary surrenders. "Such surrenders," observed the committee, "have taken place even in cases where the tenant was aware of his rights granted under law ...".[59]

Reflecting on such evidence of the failure of tenancy reforms, the committee said that new laws designed to protect tenants were not being enforced -- that tenancies continued to be governed by local custom, rather than by law. Moreover, suggested the committee, "in the absence of a clear conception about the final goal of our land reform measures,"[60] the threat and demonstration of rapid changes in law (e.g., the lowering of limits in the Punjab for the resumption of land by landlords from their tenants for personal cultivation from 100 acres in 1951, to fifty acres in 1952, and thirty acres in 1953) was contributing to instability in landlord/tenant relations and the widespread denial even of tenants' rights previously recognized in law. Without making the point categorically, the committee made plain that the spate of land reform legislation in the

---

57. I am assuming here that the committee's reference to "protected tenants" refers to tenants who had previously been classified as "occupancy raiyats" -- persons who should have enjoyed security of tenure on the land tilled by them. Their reported reduction in number suggests a process, which I have observed elsewhere in India, by which protected tenants or occupancy raiyats have been ejected from land tilled by them by landlords employing, generally, extra-legal means to resume land (allegedly) for personal cultivation. At the same time, "concealed tenancies" (where landlords' tenants are denied de jure recognition) have continued to proliferate. For an additional perspective on this theme, see: Kripa Shankar, *Status of Land Reforms,* (Allahabad: Govind Ballabh Pant Social Science Institute, 1988).

58. India, Planning Commission, Panel on Land Reforms, *Reports of the Committees of the Panel on Land Reforms,* p. 36.

59. Ibid., p. 38.

60. Ibid., p. 37.

states was producing the converse of what had been intended by the proponents of tenancy reform in the central government.[61]

The committee castigated provisions in the states' land reform laws that permitted landlords to eject tenants legally by resuming land for personal cultivation. It noted that the intent of the law had been to permit bona fide cultivators to return to the land; the intent had not been to give absentee landlords living in distant towns the right to resume land from their tenants for personal cultivation and then to cultivate that land using sharecroppers and hired labor.[62] In further criticism of laws permitting landlords to resume land for personal cultivation, the committee said that, even when some states had placed restrictions on the amount of land that could be resumed by landlords by ejecting tenants,

no distinction was made for the demarcation of the resumable area as distinct from the non-resumable area. Thus, though the landlord's right of resumption was limited in extent, he was able to exercise an undue influence over all tenants, which added to his bargaining power and rendered the law ineffective. He could even extort money by threatening to resume land. Similarly a tenant's right of purchase either applies to the non-resumable area or is operative pari passu with the landlord's right to resume land. In the absence of demarcation of the non-resumable area, if a tenant tries to assert his right to purchase any plot of land, the landlord can render it ineffective by saying that he would resume that plot of land for personal cultivation. In some cases, the landlords have sold out or partitioned the land which they personally cultivated and having thus brought their holdings below the permissible limit, proceeded to evict the tenants to resume further areas.[63]

---

61. This kind of evidence raises an obvious question. If land reform, in the early judgement of the Planning Commission of the Government of India, was doing more harm than good, why did the Government of India continue to promote it? The brief but obvious answer for proponents of land reform in India at the time was that failure to promote land reform would mean accepting existing conditions as they were -- conditions that were widely perceived at the time to be adverse to the interests of the people struggling for subsistence at the base of the agrarian hierarchy. In general, those who remained advocates of land reform in India were more prepared to accept the risks of failed reforms than to accept the risks of doing nothing to ameliorate (demonstrably bad) existing conditions.

62. India, Planning Commission, Panel on Land Reforms, *Reports of the Committees of the Panel on Land Reforms,* p. 37.

63. Ibid.

The Committee on Tenancy Reform took note of the difficulty tenants were having in understanding and using the laws, even where laws had been enacted to delineate their rights and protect their interests. The tenants, said the committee, were in a weak position relative to landlords in the countryside. Moreover, the tenants' position in the agrarian hierarchy made them both economically and socially dependent on those above them in that hierarchy, the landlords. That is to say, suggested the committee, tenants relied on their landlords (who were often moneylenders and tradesmen) to provide them credit and to meet other needs. And, tenants, because they often belonged to the "scheduled castes and backward classes," were so low in the social hierarchy as to make it difficult for them to exercise new rights conferred on them by law. In these circumstances, the committee argued that tenancy reform laws would not support tenants' interests unless action was taken to establish administrative machinery "within easy reach of tenants" -- machinery capable of acting as a countervailing power to that exercised traditionally by superior landholders in their dealings with persons below them in the agrarian hierarchy.[64]

The committee showed how a tenant's claim to land could be thwarted by a lack of up-to-date village land records. Such records either did not exist in many parts of the country or were maintained by landlords. And, even when a tenant had documentary evidence of his interest in land, he had difficulty defending that interest (especially in a court of law) where his adversary was more affluent and powerful than he. "Finally," suggested the committee, "the attitude of the revenue officers may be at times unconsciously against him."[65] On this theme, the committee indicated that it had found that the rights and privileges of the actual cultivator were "not yet fully comprehended ..." by those charged with enforcing tenancy reform laws. "The unconscious resistance of revenue officers to liberal ideas can, therefore, be easily understood. In the case of conflicting evidence, there is a greater tendency to believe the landlord than the tenant, the position being that a poor man is more likely to speak untruth with a view to obtain some land than the rich landlord who, having already enough land, may not be under immediate pressure to do so."[66]

---

64. Ibid., p. 38.
65. Ibid.
66. Ibid.

In conclusion, the committee said that the attempt thus far made to regulate the tenant-landlord relationship had failed. And, the committee saw no clear prospect of change in existing conditions unless steps were taken to interpose the state between the tenant and the landlord.[67] Such forthright and critical analysis of the failure of new laws to effect change in the agrarian structure of India made few waves in the India of the 1950s. The spate of agrarian reform and land reform legislation continued, almost unabated, giving the impression that change in existing conditions was at hand. At the end of the First Plan, it was easy for many in government and out simply to equate legislative action with actual elimination of conditions in the Indian countryside adverse both to economic progress and social justice. Moreover, this tendency to equate legislative action with the elimination of adverse conditions in the Indian countryside became virtually institutionalized through successive five year plans.

Recognition Accorded for Cooperative Farming

Reflecting the long-term bias in India, dating from the British colonial period, in favor of cooperative institutions, the First Five Year Plan had considered cooperative farming as a method by which tillers of small landholdings could be encouraged to bring into existence sizeable farm units considered to be essential to the introduction of modern, scientific farming.[68] With this in mind, the central government had encouraged the states to enact legislation that would encourage cultivators to group themselves voluntarily into cooperative farming societies. "While the practical response from state governments in the form of proposals to be

---

67. Ibid., p. 39.

68. It has been assumed that the emphasis on cooperatives in the First Plan reflected, in some measure, the influence of Tarlok Singh on the planning process. Indeed, it has been suggested that Singh's book, *Poverty and Social Change,* published in 1945, had more influence than did the Shah Sub-Committee's report on land policy in delineating the central government's vision of agrarian reform. Within this vision, cooperative village management of land and cooperative farming became stated objectives of agrarian reform during the First, Second and Third Five Year Plans. See: Carl C. Taylor, Douglas Ensminger, Helen W. Johnson, and Jean Joyce, *India's Roots of Democracy,* (Bombay, Calcutta, Madras and New Delhi: Orient Longmans, 1965), p. 293.

implemented was relatively small, almost every state government drew up its rules and bye-laws for cooperative farming societies and issued executive instructions."[69]

Reviewing the national achievement in establishing cooperative farming societies in 1957, the Planning Commission said that one thousand three hundred and ninety-seven such societies had been established during the First Plan (1952-1957). The largest numbers of cooperative farms were registered in five states -- Bombay (three hundred forty-two), Punjab (two hundred eighty-nine), Uttar Pradesh (one hundred sixty-eight), Rajasthan (seventy-six), and West Bengal (seventy-five). These seemingly favorable results notwithstanding, the Planning Commission had to admit that only "a fair proportion of these cooperative farming societies were genuine and were composed of persons who, given the necessary guidance and help in the solution of new and difficult problems, could achieve a measure of success."[70] "There were others," said the commission, "in which the main object of those who got together into cooperatives was to escape the incidence of tenancy legislation."[71] This qualified recognition by the central planners that some cooperative farming societies were formed during the First Plan to thwart the objects of agrarian reform (tenancy) legislation seems, in retrospect, highly appropriate. My own observations at the time, especially in Uttar Pradesh and Bihar, led me to conclude that the vast majority of such newly registered cooperative farming societies were bogus -- landlords' instruments designed to maintain their traditional landholdings and to disguise the acreage of those holdings in anticipation of legislation imposing ceilings on the size of agricultural holdings.

Evaluation Avoided on
Ceilings Legislation

During the First Plan, the central government had suggested to the states that there be agrarian reform legislation enacted to place a ceiling on the size of agricultural holdings. The central government cautioned the states not to impose ceilings on efficiently managed farms in a fashion

---

69. India, Planning Commission, *Review of the First Five Year Plan,* pp. 327-328.

70. Ibid., p. 328.

71. Ibid.

that would lead to a fall in production on these efficient agricultural holdings. At the same time, the central planners had urged the states to review the size distribution of agricultural holdings and to establish variable ceilings on the size of landholdings. In other words, the planners at the center hoped that ceilings on the size of holdings could be implemented in the states in a fashion that would serve often conflicting goals: both the generation of a surplus of land above the ceilings that could be acquired by the states and used to provide land to the landless, and the maintenance of economically efficient, substantial, consolidated units of agricultural production.

The task of establishing ceilings on the size of agricultural holdings proved to be a formidable one for the states. Their legislative efforts got bogged down in endless debate: debate concerning whether ceilings should be set on the size of individual holdings or on the size of family holdings; debate about whether the ceilings should be variable in accordance with the quality of the land (wet or dry, highly productive or not); and debate on whether mechanized farms should be exempted from the scope of such legislation. Predictably then, there was no uniformity in the ceilings laws that were enacted in the states. Moreover, some states failed to enact ceilings legislation during the plan period. Bihar, for example, having introduced a bill providing for variable ceilings (twenty-five to seventy-five acres), was unable to pass a ceilings act during the First Five Year Plan. With such results, the Planning Commission's review of progress concerning the enactment of ceilings legislation was cautious and lacking in specificity. Indeed, the commission's review made plain that sufficient time had not passed following the enactment of ceilings in some states to assess properly the benefits or costs of changes in the agrarian structure and relations that had resulted, or would result, from the application of limits on the size of agricultural holdings.[72] Finally, the commission's review abjured mentioning what was already conspicuous at the time: namely that, acting in anticipation of legislation, landlords were seeking to avoid the effects of ceilings by dividing their holdings into small units and transferring titles to others. By means of these fictitious or benami transfers of land, large landholders could and did systematically thwart the intent of ceilings legislation -- legislation enacted in the states during the First Plan period and thereafter.

---

72. Ibid., p. 326.

Recognition Given to
the Bhoodan Movement

During the First Plan, the Planning Commission had not sought to promote a land reform that would provide significant amounts of land to landless agricultural laborers. This notwithstanding, the commission hoped that some land would become available (possibly as a derivative of legislation establishing ceilings on the size of landholdings and of land reclamation projects) for settlement with landless agricultural laborers. Accordingly, it was recommended by the commission that such land as did become available for distribution to the landless be tilled along cooperative lines. At the time, there was an obvious preference in the Planning Commission (especially in the person of Tarlok Singh) against providing land to the landless as individual landholders. It was assumed that such a distribution of land would serve only to proliferate the number of small, uneconomic units of production -- this at a time when it was widely perceived that small units of production were inherently uneconomic and already the bane of Indian agriculture.[73]

As it turned out, very little land was acquired by the states that could be distributed among the landless. As the Planning Commission observed in its 1957 review of progress, "Taking the plan period as a whole, it must be admitted that the expectations in the First Five Year Plan in regard to resettlement schemes for landless labourers were not fulfilled."[74] Nonetheless, some hope was expressed by the commission that a contemporary non-governmental effort, the Bhoodan (land gift) movement, would be capable of securing land in substantial amounts for the landless in the Indian countryside. Indeed, the commission reported that Vinobha Bhave, the leader of Bhoodan, had already received in private donations about four million acres of land during the plan period. And, the commission indicated that the potential of the Bhoodan movement to address meaningfully the needs of the landless needed to be studied.[75]

The Bhoodan (land gift) movement had been initiated in 1951 by Vinobha Bhave, a follower of Mahatma Gandhi. The movement was begun in reaction to a Communist-led effort to mobilize sections of the peasantry in Telangana in guerrilla warfare against established authority

---

73. Tarlok Singh, Interview, New Delhi, January 23, 1989.
74. India, Planning Commission, *Review of the First Five Year Plan,* p. 330.
75. Ibid.

in a region within the former Princely State of Hyderabad in southern India. In the midst of this Communist-inspired, neo-Maoist insurrection, Bhave secured his first gift from an established landholder of land for the landless. Extrapolating from this first land gift, Bhave suggested that he had found a means of resolving India's land problem: a way of demonstrating that land could be made available to the landless by peaceful means without resorting to class struggle and guerrilla warfare.

> While it cannot be said that Bhave's demonstration of the efficacy of his nonviolent approach to land reform was a primary factor in limiting the potency of guerrilla warfare in Telangana, the fact that his movement originated in confrontation with a segment of the Communist Party of India led some observers to view the movement as a deterrent to the Communist Party in India and contributed to Bhoodan's popularity in the West.[76]

At the same time, Bhave's Bhoodan movement enjoyed a high profile in India and captured the patronage of leaders of the Congress Party, including Jawaharlal Nehru, during the first decade of India's independence.

While the Bhoodan movement's inception and growth were more spontaneous than planned, it soon attracted followers from all walks of life, including the widely revered socialist leader, Jaya Prakash Narayan.[77] Narayan tried to give the movement a substantive plan for action[78] and sought the advice of distinguished economists, including M.L. Dantwala and the late Raj Krishna, and pragmatic politicians (for example, Acharya Kripalani) in shaping his vision of a Utopian social order where all

---

76. F. Tomasson Jannuzi, *Agrarian Crisis in India: The Case of Bihar,* pp.93-94.

77. Narayan, a Bihari, was widely regarded in the 1950s as a possible successor to Jawaharlal Nehru, then India's Prime Minister. However, Narayan became disillusioned with politics and joined Vinobha Bhave, suggesting as he did so that he was committed to the resolution of the land problem in his own state, as well as in India, and to the establishment with Bhave of a new social order based on popular power (loka-shakti) vested in village republics, rather than in a central government in New Delhi "that could not muster enough intelligence to govern India's numberless villages well and wisely." [Jaya Prakash Narayan, Interview, Patna, Bihar, December, 1956.]

78. Jaya Prakash Narayan, *Planning for Sarvodaya (Draft Plan),* (New Delhi: Ananda Press, 1957), pp. 16-17.

wealth, including land, would be considered common property to be used for the good of every person.

What is striking about the movement, in retrospect, is the degree to which it was, for a time, accorded respect as a means by which landholders could be persuaded voluntarily to donate land for distribution among the landless. As noted above, the Planning Commission's review of the First Plan gave recognition to Bhoodan and accepted the movement's claim to have received donations totalling more than four million acres of land. Moreover, the Congress Party's "High Command" repeatedly conferred legitimacy on the movement, consorting with Vinobha Bhave and his followers in numerous public meetings in the 1950s (for example, at Bodh Gaya in Bihar and at Yelwal in Mysore). At Bodh Gaya, in 1954, the movement's annual conference was graced by the presence of the President, the Prime Minister, the Vice President of India and large numbers of ministers from the central government and the states, plus ordinary members of the Congress Party and the opposition Praja Socialist Party. And, the All India Congress Committee's *AICC Economic Review*, reporting on the Bodh Gaya event, suggested that Bhave had become the symbol of a great economic revolution.[79] Later, at Yelwal, Nehru and others (including Tarlok Singh of the Planning Commission) had serious conversations with Bhave concerning how the government's Community Development programs could be linked productively to Bhave's movement.[80]

Of course, it is tempting to suggest that India's governing elite was only paying homage (doing darshan) to Bhave as a spiritual leader in the Gandhian tradition. However, my own observations of the Bhoodan movement in Bihar, and numerous conversations with the late Jaya Prakash Narayan (beginning in 1956 and extending to June of 1975), lead me to conclude that the movement enjoyed credibility among India's ruling elite in the 1950s, especially when Bhave promised publicly to remain in Bihar until the land problem was solved in that state. Toward that end, he estimated that he and his followers would have to collect 3.2 million acres of land.

By June 30, 1956, Bhave claimed to have received 2.1 million acres, more than a million acres short of his stated goal. This record notwithstanding, Bhave then left Bihar to carry his message elsewhere.

---

79. Congress Party, *AICC Economic Review,* Volume VI No. 1, May 1, 1954, Whole No. 98.

80. Tarlok Singh, Interview, New Delhi, January 23, 1989.

In Bhave's absence, the movement in Bihar gradually lost whatever momentum it had gained during his presence. The number of active workers in Bihar dwindled until it could be said that the movement scarcely existed. Indeed, almost all activity ceased except on those occasions when Jaya Prakash Narayan returned to his home in Patna. By March 31, 1966, the movement had to admit officially that its acreage totals for land collections in Bihar had not increased; instead, they had decreased from approximately 2.1 million acres in 1956 to around 1.1 million acres in 1966. At the same time, in March of 1966, the movement claimed to have distributed only 311,037 acres of land to previously landless families of Bihar.[81]

Bhoodan's failure to resolve the land problem of Bihar within the frame of its own terms of reference is not, of course, the whole story of the movement's failure in that state and in India generally. The movement had been disingenuous in reporting its record of achievement in Bihar, and elsewhere. Its accounting of donations of land had been inflated. Many donors had given land to the movement that was not theirs to give, legally contested land and government land, for example. Some donors had given permanently fallow, waste land. The Maharajah of Ramgarh told me with evident glee that he had given the movement thousands of acres of land belonging to the State of Bihar.

Notwithstanding the movement's increasingly questionable record of performance, the Bhoodan movement continued to receive formal recognition in documents of the Government of India. The Third Five Year Plan suggested that the movement had helped "to create a favourable atmosphere for implementing progressive measures of land reform."[82] In the same document, the planners said that the movement confirmed "the potentialities which reside in voluntary action stimulated by high idealism and missionary zeal."[83] Nor was official support confined to words alone; the movement was accorded statutory recognition in some states.[84] And, the movement received direct subsidies from the central government amounting to millions of rupees. Nonetheless, by 1970, even Jaya Prakash Narayan was thoroughly disillusioned with the Bhoodan movement. Meeting with me on August 13, 1970, at his temporary

---

81. F. Tomasson Jannuzi, *Agrarian Crisis in India,* p. 100.

82. India, Planning Commission, *Third Five Year Plan,* (Delhi: Manager of Publications, 1962), p. 221.

83. Ibid., p. 293.

84. See, for example, the *Bihar Bhoodan Yagna Act of 1954.*

headquarters in Musahari Block, Muzaffarpur District, Bihar, Narayan admitted ruefully that the movement's successes had been greatly exaggerated. What Narayan belatedly recognized was already well known in India. By the mid-1970s, the movement lacked credibility[85] and was increasingly seen as irrelevant as a means of promoting agrarian reform or land reform.[86]

Kerala's Implementation of Agrarian Reform Measures

While most Indian states failed dismally to promote their own variants of agrarian reform and land reform, one state, more than any other, is usually credited with having carried out what Ronald Herring has called "serious and successful reforms."[87] Ironically, the agrarian reforms in Kerala did not bear the imprint either of the Government of India or the Congress Party. Instead, they were, essentially, the work of the Communist Party of India.

The Communists first came to power in Kerala in 1957, winning an electoral victory over the Congress by establishing themselves as the

---

85. Nonetheless, even the Seventh Five Year Plan of the Government of India (1985-90) continued to report in its review of performance of land reform that "About 4.2 million acres of land were received in Bhoodan, but so far only about 1.3 million acres have been distributed." [India, Planning Commission, *Seventh Five Year Plan (1985-90)*, (New Delhi: Manager of Publications, 1985), Volume II, p. 63.]

86. So far as I know, Jaya Prakash Narayan never broke publicly with Vinobha Bhave. However, the break between Narayan and Bhave was complete in 1975 when Narayan, having re-entered politics, led a populist movement against the administration of then Prime Minister Indira Gandhi. He was incarcerated without trial when Mrs. Gandhi suspended constitutional governance and proclaimed a "State of Emergency." At that time, Vinobha Bhave supported Mrs. Gandhi and the Government of India against Narayan and the dissidents he had mobilized.

87. Ronald J. Herring, "Explaining Anomalies in Agrarian Reform: Lessons from South India," in Roy L. Prosterman, Mary N. Temple and Timothy M. Hanstad, editors, *Agrarian Reform and Grassroots Development: Ten Case Studies*, (Boulder, Colorado: Lynne Rienner Publishers, 1990), p. 50. Also see Ronald J. Herring, *Land to the Tiller: The Political Economy of Agrarian Reform in South Asia*, (New Haven: Yale University Press, 1983).

group most likely to put into effect the radical promises and programs that the Congress dominated central government had been unable, or unwilling, to implement. And, while Kerala's Communist-led government was dismissed by the central government in 1959, the Communists were subsequently returned to power through democratic elections -- confirming thereby that the Party's electoral roots in the countryside were deep and that the people who supported the Communists truly believed that the Communists were more likely than the Congress to implement meaningful agrarian reforms.

The agrarian reforms of Kerala, like those elsewhere in India, were instituted by means of legislation and came into effect on January 1, 1970. The reforms were sweeping in content and were based, loosely, on the principle of "land to the tiller" -- a principle earlier endorsed, but subsequently abandoned by the nationalist elites who had shaped the early rhetoric of the Independence Movement. The Kerala reforms sought nothing less than to abolish the landlord tenant system and to enforce the principle that all actual tillers would have secure rights in land, the equivalency of ownership. The legislation also sought to establish the principle that there could be no ownership of land apart from the tilling of it.

The Kerala reforms of 1970 included provisions establishing ceilings on the size of landholdings.[88] However, the ceilings, even if vigorously enforced, were not designed to produce sufficient amounts of surplus land to provide viable landholdings for a majority of potential claimants (tenant farmers and landless agricultural laborers). Moreover, because more than a decade elapsed between the government's first attempt at ceilings legislation in 1959 and the legislation of 1970, landholders had sufficient time and motivation to disguise the size of their holdings and, thereby, to limit further the redistributive potential of the Kerala ceilings legislation. Thus, if agrarian reform is considered successful in Kerala, its success does not rest on the ceilings provisions of the reform legislation. As Ronald Herring has emphasized, "The core of the reform was thus the abolition of tenancy, vesting land in the cultivators, affecting about 43 percent of the nonplantation land in the state."[89]

---

88. The ceilings ranged from five standard acres per adult to twenty ordinary acres for a large family.

89. Ronald J. Herring, "Explaining Anomolies in Agrarian Reform: Lessons from South India," in *Agrarian Reform and Grassroots Development: Ten Case Studies,* p. 60.

While, as noted above, the Kerala reforms were not expected to provide land in economically viable units to even a majority of landless claimants, the reforms included provisions by which a substantial minority of landless agricultural laborers (271,000 of about 2.2 million) received small holdings useful as kitchen gardens.[90] Such kitchen gardens had symbolic value, especially for the erstwhile landless agricultural laborers who received them. They also served the nutritional and economic needs of those families.

The implementation of the Kerala reforms was not without struggle. There were legislative delays; there were mass demonstrations; there were bureaucratic obstacles to be surmounted. But, what gave dynamism to the process of implementation in Kerala, fortuitously, was the competition in the state (from 1964) between the so-called right and left Communists. The right Communists (the Communist Party of India) led a coalition government; meanwhile, the left Communists (the Communist Party of India-Marxists) were the primary opposition. And, it was the left Communists, according to Herring, who mobilized interest groups and maintained the pressures that helped to ensure the implementation of the Kerala reforms. Otherwise, suggests Herring, whatever the merits of the legislated reforms in Kerala, it is likely that they would have been as ineffectively implemented as in other regions of the country.[91]

If the mobilization of interest groups, including landless agricultural laborers favoring agrarian reform, was critical to the implementation of reform measures in Kerala, it must be observed also that conditions applied in Kerala that did not apply (at the time) in any other region of India. The pressures from below, generated in the countryside, were sustainable in part because Kerala was a state inhabited by a mainly literate, politically conscious citizenry whose attitudes were shaped daily by the news media and by effective grassroots organizations (including peasant associations and unions of landless laborers). Had these conditions not applied, it seems likely that Kerala, like other Indian states, would have had its reform legislation weakened by amendments in the legislature, delayed in the courts, and possibly denied by the actions of revenue ministry implementors and the landlords themselves.

The Kerala success story must be further qualified. The generally successful implementation of the Kerala reforms can obscure limitations in the reforms as conceptualized and legislated. The reforms were not as

---

90. Ibid.
91. Ibid., p. 61.

sweeping or as radical in character as they appeared to be. The reforms were designed not to apply to twenty percent of the net cultivated area of the state (in 1987). That is to say, the reforms exempted the lands of the state's plantation economy. The logic behind this exemption rested on the need (reiterated from the British colonial era) to preserve economies of scale in tea, coffee and rubber plantations.[92] This exemption of plantation lands from the working of ceilings legislation limited further the prospect of giving viable economic holdings to larger numbers of tenant farmers and landless agricultural laborers.

Moreover, the conceptualizers of Kerala's reform legislation, while emphasizing "land to the tiller" as an operative principle, defined tillers as those only who assumed the risks of cultivation by providing the cash costs of production. By this definition, agriculturists who only labored directly in the fields -- who plowed, planted, weeded, and harvested crops -- were not classified as tillers of the soil worthy of receiving secure rights in land, if land became available. "This curious conceptualization had clear political-tactical roots, as tenants were the core of the local leadership cadres, but it contributed to the fracturing of leftist unity after land reform."[93]

Thus, even the successful agrarian and land reforms of Kerala can be perceived as being flawed in some critical respects. Nonetheless, the reforms were profoundly disturbing of the old hierarchy of interests in land: for example, transforming the Brahmin landholders of Palghat District from unquestioned wielders of socioeconomic power over those below them in the agrarian hierarchy to petitioners for relief as a depressed class.[94] It can be argued, then, that the traditional hierarchy of interests in land in Kerala was, in fact, transformed by means of the legislation enacted and implemented in that state. Today, the old landlords no longer hold sway. "Laborers remain largely dependent on others for access to the means of production, but agrestic slavery, serfdom, acute social humiliation, and oppression have been obliterated

---

92. The economies of scale logic was accepted even by the Communists. However, as Ronald Herring has pointed out, there was also a Marxist rationale for exempting the plantations from agrarian reform legislation. The Communists' primary goal in Kerala was to eradicate vestiges of feudalism; capitalist farmers in the plantation sector of the economy were therefore not targets of reform legislation. [Ibid., p. 64.]

93. Ibid., p. 64.

94. Ibid., p. 69.

or dramatically reduced by social processes of which the land reforms were a central part."[95]

In sum, if one agrees with Herring, "The broad complex of distributive and redistributive measures undertaken in Kerala have effectively abolished a system of absentee landlordism characterized by extreme exploitation and oppression. In the process of breaking the back of landlordism through mobilization of the rural poor, the conditions for genuine democracy and protection of human rights at the local level have been firmly established."[96] Moreover, the changes in the agrarian hierarchy of interests in land in Kerala were effected within the frame of a liberal constitution and by democratic means.

Nonetheless, even Ronald Herring has recognized that the Kerala reforms created no Utopia in that state. Even when effectively implemented, Kerala's reforms probably accorded rights in land too liberally to families that had other primary sources of income and who, therefore, only engaged in agricultural operations in a perfunctory supervisory manner. Indeed, such beneficiaries of land reform were seldom working farmers who themselves labored on the land in their possession.

Finally, it must be noted that the Kerala reforms were not associated with a revolution in agricultural production. The reforms gave precedence to redistribution over production, and Kerala remains a food deficit state in contemporary India where the paddy land under cultivation has steadily been declining. Even in Kerala, then, land reforms were neither easy nor costless, nor were they a panacea for successful rural development, if rural development is defined to emphasize the need both to increase agricultural production and to promote distributive justice.

---

95. Ibid.
96. Ibid., pp. 72-73.

4

The Repeating Cycle
of Agrarian Reform
and Rural Unrest

Rural Tensions Increased

The forces of custom and tradition still reigned supreme in the Indian countryside for many years after India gained freedom from the United Kingdom. Notwithstanding the flood of legislation for agrarian reform and land reform, particularly in the 1950s and 1960s, the traditional hierarchy of interests in land was not significantly altered. Those who enjoyed secure rights in land, including the traditional landholding elites, continued to exercise the prerogatives of socioeconomic power and status that accompanied control of land, that most primary of resources in an agrarian society. Those with tenuous rights in land, especially persons classified as tenants-at-will and sharecroppers, enjoyed few prerogatives of status or power, except in relation to those persons (for example, landless agricultural laborers) who were below them in the agrarian hierarchy.

The powers and prerogatives of the landholding elite within the various land systems of rural India continued to be recognized by those over whom they exercised traditional authority. And, the relationships between superior and inferior landholders, harsh and exploitive as perceived by outsiders, were conditioned in some degree by feelings of mutual obligation and mutual dependence. Those who were low in the agrarian hierarchy had no alternative, generally, but to continue to perform their primary agricultural functions, expecting to give up a share of their produce in cash or in kind to non-tilling landholders who were above them in the hierarchy. Meanwhile, superior landholders, while taking whatever steps they could to preserve and protect their traditional rights in land, continued periodically to perform functions for those below them in status: providing loans at varying rates of interest, providing protection against the claims of other landholders, and performing ritual services on ceremonial occasions.

Legislation for agrarian reform and land reform, even legislation designed specifically not to alter significantly the existing hierarchy of interests in land, gradually disrupted whatever equilibrium of mutual obligation and dependence that had existed among members of India's rural hierarchy. Paradoxically, agrarian reform and land reform did not have to be implemented to effect changes in existing conditions in the countryside. The mere threat of reform measures was sufficient to cause superior landholders to take steps to disguise the size of their landholdings, to alter land records, to evict tenants from the land, to encourage voluntary surrenders of land, to register bogus cooperative farming societies, and, generally, to take whatever steps they could to delay and deny whatever reforms might subsequently be enacted into law. And, this process gradually produced a great awakening among the peasantry. That is to say, profound attitudinal change occurred among sections of the peasantry whose subserviency to authority and malleability under pressure had been assumed to be constants by the landholding elite.

In this context, the general elections of 1967 provided striking evidence that long-subservient sections of the peasantry were prepared to think and act independently of those above them in the rural hierarchies. The shattering of Congress Party dominance in those elections showed for the first time after independence that previously subordinated groups were beginning to act in their own interests by voting along lines not anticipated by the landholding elite. By contrast, ten years earlier, in the general elections of 1957, it had been assumed by traditional landholders that those below them in the agrarian hierarchy would vote as they were told. And, as I observed at that time, people at the base of the rural hierarchy, if they voted at all, voted along lines dictated to them by superior landholders. However, in the wake of the 1967 elections, it seemed clear that increasing numbers of persons near the bottom of the rural hierarchy were prepared to articulate the need for change in the traditional systems of relationships of people to the land and, in some regions of the country, to become agents of change.

By 1968 in East India, especially in Bihar and parts of West Bengal, one could not move about in the countryside without hearing people at or near the base of the rural hierarchy expressing their frustration concerning their status and economic vulnerability. The inarticulate were becoming articulate. Many in the countryside who earlier had referred to the immutability of their condition now dared to cry out in protest against the circumstances that denied them the ability to provide the barest necessities for their children. It seemed only a matter of time before local leadership would emerge to give focus to the newly articulated feelings of anger among people who were increasingly prepared to take action against traditional landholders in support of their own interests.

Indeed, as the 1960s drew to a close, in many regions of India tensions between persons near the base of the agrarian hierarchy and those above them in that hierarchy were evident. What the Government of India called "agrarian unrest" began to be reported with some frequency in the late 1960s in a great number of states including Andhra Pradesh, Tamil Nadu, Kerala, Assam, Bihar, West Bengal, Orissa, Tripura, Manipur, Gujarat, Punjab, Rajasthan, and Uttar Pradesh.[1] And, while it cannot be said that this unrest could be attributed only to either the slow pace of agrarian reform or the growing expectations of people at the base of the agrarian hierarchy that change in existing conditions was necessary to their well-being, the Home Ministry of the Government of India, itself, said that the unrest was associated with "the persistence of serious social and economic inequalities"[2] in the Indian countryside.

Among the cases of unrest reported at this time were many involving peasant cultivators in land-grab activities.[3] In Bihar, for example, roving bands of peasants had forcibly harvested standing crops in separate incidents in Purnea, Bhagalpur, Santhal Parganas, and Darbhanga districts. During January-February of 1968 two hundred persons had tried to encroach upon government land in Champaran District. And, there were repeated demonstrations in Bihar in which landless peasants were said to have demanded land from officials of government.

During the same period in the neighboring state of West Bengal, there were frequent, often violent, outbreaks of agrarian unrest. For a time in 1967, the most militant expressions of this unrest were localized around Naxalbari in West Bengal. By August of 1969 there had been 346 separate incidents of forcible occupation of land in West Bengal alone,

---

1. Government of India, Ministry of Home Affairs, Research and Policy Division, "The Causes and Nature of Current Agrarian Tensions," (Unpublished report, 1969), Annexure I.

2. Ibid., p. 4.

3. Though based in New Delhi from 1965 to 1968, I travelled widely throughout India in this period, gathering data and impressions concerning the unrest in the countryside.

and the peasant agitators, now widely referred to as Naxalites (after Naxalbari) were perceived by the Government of India to pose a serious threat to the state.

By 1969, following careful assessment of evidence concerning all types of peasant agitations in various states, the Ministry of Home Affairs had concluded that steps would have to be taken both by the central government and by the states to reduce tensions in rural areas. This could best be achieved, it seemed, by meeting some of the immediate needs of the landless, the sharecroppers, and the tenants lacking secure rights in land. The Home Ministry warned that a failure to meet these needs, or even to address them seriously, would leave the field to 'certain political parties.' These parties, the Ministry noted, had already succeeded in organizing dissident groups of peasants by appealing to their hunger for land and their yearning for better standards of living. While they had not demonstrated 'capacity for launching sustained agitations' and might be organizationally weak, these parties (together with their peasant political organs) were considered by the Home Ministry to be capable of continuing to exploit the rural tensions produced by a 'widening gap between the relatively few affluent farmers and the large body of small landholders and landless agricultural workers.'

The Ministry recognized that twenty-two years of planned rural development had not transformed the agrarian structure in much of India. Land reforms, generally, had not benefited the actual tiller. Superior rights in land were concentrated in the hands of a few. Much of the land was still cultivated by sharecroppers lacking security of tenure and forced to pay exorbitant rents. The Home Ministry report emphasized the fact that '... the programmes so far implemented are still more favourable to the larger owner-farmer than to the smaller tenant-farmer. As for the sharecropper and the landless labourer, they have been more often than not left out in the cold. In consequence .... disparities have widened, accentuating social tensions...' and producing a situation requiring urgent actions by responsible authorities.[4]

---

4. F. Tomasson Jannuzi, *Agrarian Crisis in India: The Case of Bihar,* (Austin and London: The University of Texas Press, 1974), pp.134-135. The quotations within this excerpt are from pages 4-10 of the earlier cited Home Ministry Report, "The Causes and Nature of Current Agrarian Tensions", an unpublished report made available to me and other scholars shortly after it was completed in 1969.

Government Action Proposed

The seriousness of the tensions growing in rural areas were recognized by the then Prime Minister of India, Indira Gandhi. Accordingly, on August 18, 1969, Mrs. Gandhi sent a message to all state chief ministers, a message in which she indicated that an effective agricultural development strategy for India would "require not only organization and inputs but also the removal of existing institutional and social impediments to production."[5] She suggested that small farmers, including tenants and laborers, had not been sharing meaningfully in whatever progress had been generated by means of rural development programs, including agrarian reform. And, alluding to the apparent growth of agrarian tensions, Mrs. Gandhi said that it was apparent that "landless labourers have been dissatisfied about not getting their due share,"[6] even in circumstances where agricultural production increases had been achieved.

In her message to the chief ministers, Mrs. Gandhi urged them to take steps to ensure that programs were implemented in the states that would benefit the rural have-nots, reduce social tensions, and produce an environment that was conducive to rural development. She asked specifically that a "fair share of fertilizer, seeds and irrigation facilities" be guaranteed to cultivators tilling small holdings. She appealed for the implementation of measures that would confer security of tenure on tillers threatened with eviction by superior landholders. She asked for the quick implementation of ceilings on the size of landholdings so that land above the ceilings could be acquired by the states and distributed among landless laborers -- a recommendation which, if followed, might contribute to the proliferation of small units of cultivation.[7] On the other hand, following a long established precedent, she urged the consolidation of fragmented

---

5. India, Ministry of Food, Agriculture, Community Development and Cooperation, "Chief Ministers' Conference on Land Reform -- Notes on Agenda," (New Delhi: Department of Agriculture, November 28-29, 1969), Annexure C, p. C1.

6. Ibid.

7. Mrs. Gandhi did not specify, with regard to this plea for the distribution of land to the landless, whether land should be distributed in small units to individuals or distributed only to those who were willing to farm larger units of land cooperatively. Her recommendation was made at a time when it was no longer fashionable in India to suggest that the landless should be encouraged (or compelled) to till whatever land they might receive jointly in cooperative farms.

landholdings within a specified period of time.[8] Finally, Mrs. Gandhi called for the expansion of employment opportunities outside of agriculture for segments of the peasantry, and particularly the landless. Such opportunities, she indicated, would reduce the pressure of population on available land resources.[9]

The Indian Prime Minister concluded her message to the chief ministers by stressing that the implementation of her recommendations was important both to ensure social justice in the countryside and to facilitate the widespread dissemination of new technology in agriculture,[10] even among small landholders, including sharecroppers, who had been slow to adopt new practices because existing land and tenurial systems gave them insufficient incentive. Mrs. Gandhi "left implicit the argument that state action on her various recommendations was important to the preservation of political stability ..."[11] in the countryside.

The recommendations of the central government, as transmitted to the states' chief ministers by the Indian Prime Minister, were followed by the convening of a "Chief Ministers' Conference on Land Reform" held in Vigyan Bhavan, New Delhi, over two days, November 28-29, 1969. At this conference, an effort was made to review progress in agrarian reform and land reform, to identify gaps in the then existing legislation that might be closed by subsequent legislation, to discuss problems impeding the implementation of existing legislation, to establish conceptual links between land policy and the introduction of new technology in agriculture, and to address the needs of landless agricultural laborers. The conference was an obvious attempt by the central government, twenty-two years after independence, to encourage a national consensus concerning the importance of agrarian reform and land reform

---

8. Once again, we see the persistence after independence of the colonial era fixation on the need for consolidation of landholdings as a prerequisite for agricultural progress. As noted earlier in the text, this fixation was a primary feature of the report of the Royal Commission on Agriculture in India, 1928.

9. Mrs. Gandhi's recommendations, as outlined in the text, have been paraphrased, except when quoted, from her letter to the chief ministers. [India, Ministry of Food, Agriculture, Community Development and Cooperation, "Chief Ministers' Conference on Land Reform -- Notes on Agenda," Annexure C pp. C1-C2.]

10. This was at a time when a decision had been made to introduce new technology in agriculture in India, the package of inputs associated with the so-called "Green Revolution."

11. F.T. Jannuzi, *Agrarian Crisis in India: The Case of Bihar,* p. 137.

both to political stability and economic progress. The conference was held, after all, in the midst of agrarian unrest and at a time when an attempt was being made to introduce a new strategy for rural development linked to the widespread dissemination of a new package of inputs (comprised of high yielding varieties of seeds, especially of wheat, assured irrigation, fertilizer and pesticides). The substance of the Chief Ministers' Conference on Land Reform, 1969 is presented and critically assessed in succeeding sections. Readers will note that the conference judgments and recommendations concerning agrarian reform and land reform often reiterate observations made more than a decade earlier by representatives of the central government and by private observers like Wolf Ladejinsky and Daniel Thorner in the 1950s.

Reviewing the Progress in Agrarian Reform

In documents prepared for the conference (reflecting input from the Working Group on Land Reform set up in the Ministry of Food, Agriculture, Community Development and Cooperation for the formulation of proposals for agricultural development in the Fourth Five Year Plan and the Land Reforms Implementation Committee of the National Development Council) progress in agrarian reform and land reform was set forth in a way that reflected the central government's assessment of what the states individually and collectively had thus far accomplished.

Abolition of Intermediaries. In assessing progress in abolishing intermediaries, there was no exaggerated claim that the intermediaries (zamindars, jagirs and inams) had themselves been abolished. It was made plain that the intermediaries' erstwhile right to act for the state in the collection of land revenue was all that had been abolished, and that the intermediaries had also generally been permitted to retain "all of their home-farm lands".[12] At the same time, the somewhat misleading statement was made that "the principal tenants of intermediaries had acquired permanent and heritable rights ..." to the land in their

---

12. India, Ministry of Food, Agriculture, Community Development and Cooperation, "Chief Ministers' Conference on Land Reform -- Notes on Agenda," pp. 5-6.

possession, excepting only such land as could be claimed as home-farm land by the intermediaries.[13] This was misleading because, by this time, the Government of India itself, in its own reports, had repeatedly expressed concern that large numbers of tenants of intermediaries (already classified as permanent occupancy raiyats, virtual owners of the land in their possession) had either been ejected from their land by intermediaries or encouraged to surrender their land voluntarily. This not withstanding, the central government asserted, without any documentation, the widely repeated claim[14] that, when the intermediaries of India were abolished, "a large body of tenants, estimated at 20 millions ..." had "been brought in direct relationship with the State and enabled to become owners."[15]

Summarizing the progress of abolition of intermediary interests in the states, the conference organizers reported that Andhra had passed legislation to abolish zamindari tenures as early as 1948, and that additional steps had subsequently been taken to abolish the interests of other intermediaries (classified in Andhra as inams and jagirs). Similarly, permanently settled estates had been abolished (by means of legislation) in Assam. "In Bihar, Madhya Pradesh, Orissa, Rajasthan, Tamil Nadu, Uttar Pradesh and West Bengal all intermediary tenures have been abolished."[16] And, it was suggested that all but a few intermediary tenures had been liquidated in Gujarat, Maharashtra and Mysore, Haryana, and Punjab. In sum, the chief ministers were informed that the system of intermediary, "semi-feudal" tenures that had prevailed over at least 40 percent of the area of pre-independence India had virtually been eliminated. Whether intentionally or not, the presumption was implied in the conference papers that the legislation that had been enacted, by itself, had changed the behavior and customary practices of the ex-intermediaries so as to make obsolete their alleged "semi-feudal" practices

---

13. Ibid., p. 5.

14. I have sought documentation for this oft repeated claim for nearly thirty years and have found none that would explain how the number was computed.

15. India, Ministry of Food, Agriculture, Community Development and Cooperation, "Chief Ministers' Conference on Land Reform -- Notes on Agenda," p. 6. [As I have earlier emphasized, the use of the word "owners" is somewhat misleading. Within Indian law, it would have been more appropriate to suggest that the tenants had been accorded permanent occupancy rights in land, the rough equivalency of ownership rights.]

16. India, Ministry of Food, Agriculture, Community Development and Cooperation, "Chief Ministers' Conference on Land Reform -- Notes on Agenda," p. 6.

and had transformed them into modern entrepreneurial farmers in relation to the substantial home-farms they were permitted to retain within the frame of the legislation.

Reform of Tenancy. In the years preceding the Chief Ministers' Conference on Land Reform it had been widely assumed that land reform had given secure rights in land to tenant farmers throughout India. This assumption was rooted, partly, in the fact that, when discussing tenancy or tenancy reforms, people did not always make a distinction between cultivators who were de jure tenants and those who were de facto tenants. De jure tenants were recognized by the state; they were endowed with the virtual equivalency of ownership rights in land. De facto tenants, for example a cultivator who had taken-in land from a superior landholder on an oral lease as a sharecropper, had little prospect of ever acquiring a de jure right (even a tenurial right) to the land that they tilled. The former were few in number relative to the millions of de facto tenants who, like the bataidars of Bihar[17] and the bargadars of West Bengal, had no de jure rights in land. Policy makers and critics alike often made the mistake of using the word "tenants" or the phrase "tenant farmers" to describe a broad spectrum of people having any relationship to the land: a spectrum that included groups as disparate as, on the one hand, the so-called "tenants of the state" who had been accorded permanent occupancy rights in land and, on the other hand, cultivators who had "taken-in" land from a superior landholder and who had little or no de jure status as tenants.[18]

With unusual specificity, the organizers of the Chief Ministers' Conference on Land Reform outlined how reform measures in the states had affected the position of several types of tenants. They noted that many actual cultivators had been accorded permanent rights to land as tenants of the state. On the other hand, the organizers stated that sharecroppers, "sub-tenants and under-raiyats generally remained

---

17. Ironically, when some field officers of the Bihar Revenue Department sought to record such bataidars as de jure "tenants" in 1964, a controversial directive from the Bihar Revenue Secretary was issued to stop the practice. Upendra Baxi has cited this event, as reported by Wolf Ladejinsky, as an example of "governmental lawlessness" in the implementation of agrarian reform. For elaboration on this theme, see: Upendra Baxi, *The Crisis of the Indian Legal System,* (New Delhi: Vikas Publishing House Ltd., 1982), p. 24.

18. This obfuscational use of the word "tenants" is still prevalent today. See, for example, Inderjit Singh, "Tenancy in South Asia," World Bank Discussion Paper, (Washington, D.C.: The World Bank, 1988).

unaffected by reform measures."[19] In other words, vast numbers of actual cultivators remained outside of the scope of agrarian reform and land reform legislation.[20] The conference organizers, representing the central government, made a public admission that literally uncounted millions of sharecroppers, sub-tenants, and under-raiyats (cultivators with insecure, non-permanent rights in land) were not even within the purview of agrarian reform legislation as enacted in the states. The conference papers discussed the fact that some "informal" tenancy-like arrangements (sometimes called "veiled tenancies") resulted from sub-leasing agreements between landlords and cultivators. Such sub-leasing agreements were devoid of "any written document or record..."[21] and, therefore were difficult to identify and document. The conference papers classified such tenancy-like arrangements as a continuing problem.

The papers of the Chief Ministers' Conference also identified the problem for tenant farmers resulting from their landlords' right (as conferred on the landlords within the land reform legislation enacted in most of the Indian states) to resume land for personal cultivation. "The crux of the matter," it was suggested, "is that the ejectment of tenants takes devious forms and does not take place under the normal provisions governing eviction of cultivating tenants."[22] That is to say, it was recognized that reform laws permitting landlords to resume land for personal cultivation were being abused; tenants, whatever their potential claims to land, were being evicted by landlords using extra-legal means. In this context, it was noted that steps had been taken in a number of states to limit landlords' claims to tenants' lands and even, in certain instances, to restore tenants to lands taken from them by landlords. However, it was also made obvious that such steps had been taken only within the frame of legislation, as distinct from steps actually taken in the

---

19. India, Ministry of Food, Agriculture, Community Development and Cooperation, "Chief Ministers' Conference on Land Reform -- Notes on Agenda," p. 7.

20. This state of affairs continued for some years after the Chief Ministers' Conference on Land Reform. For example, it was not until the late 1970s and early 1980s that the Government of West Bengal sought to register the holdings of its sharecroppers (bargadars) and to give more than one million of them security of tenure on the land in their cultivating possession.

21. India, Ministry of Food, Agriculture, Community Development and Cooperation, "Chief Ministers' Conference on Land Reform -- Notes on Agenda," p. 7.

22. Ibid., p. 9.

field to monitor landlords' attempts to resume land from tenants or the states' attempts to restore to tenants lands taken illegally from them.

Ceilings on Landholdings. The conference papers exposed the complexity of the legislation enacted in the Indian states to effect ceilings on the size of landholdings. The papers showed that the ceilings that had been established in the states varied in size[23] and unit of measurement.[24] And, the papers illustrated how ceilings legislation had been drafted in the states to provide exemptions of certain categories of land from ceilings on the size of holdings. For example, plantations (tea, rubber coffee, cardamom and pepper) were exempted in a great number of states, including Assam, Bihar, Kerala, Uttar Pradesh, Madhya Pradesh, and West Bengal. Sugarcane farms operated by sugar factories were exempted from ceilings in many states, among them Andhra Pradesh, Assam, Bihar, Madhya Pradesh, Mysore, Orissa, Haryana, Punjab, Rajasthan and Uttar Pradesh.[25] Efficiently managed farms consisting of compact blocks and involving heavy investments or permanent structural improvements had been exempted from ceilings set in numerous states. These states included Assam, Haryana, Punjab, Gujarat and Rajasthan.[26] Lands held by religious and educational institutions, as well as charitable trusts, were exempted in many states, including Bihar, Gujarat, Andhra Pradesh, Tamil Nadu, Kerala, Uttar Pradesh, Haryana, Punjab, Maharashtra and West Bengal.[27] Cooperative farming societies were exempted in Andhra Pradesh, Jammu and Kashmir and Madhya Pradesh, as well as in other states on condition that each member of such a society

---

23. For example, Assam (fifty acres), Jammu and Kashmir (twenty-two and three quarters acres), West Bengal (twenty-five acres), Bihar (twenty to sixty acres depending on the class of land), Gujarat (nineteen to 132 acres depending on the class of land), and Maharashtra (eighteen to 126 acres depending on the class of land). [Ibid., p. 14.]

24. For example, in Assam, Gujarat, Kerala, Mysore, Rajasthan, and Tamil Nadu, the ceiling on the size of landholdings was defined to include the aggregate area held by all family members. In some states the ceiling applied to land held in the name of a single person. And, in Bihar and Madhya Pradesh, the ceiling unit was made applicable to the area of land held by a joint Hindu family.

25. India, Ministry of Food, Agriculture, Community Development and Cooperation, "Chief Ministers' Conference on Land Reform," p. 16.

26. Ibid., p. 17.

27. Ibid.

did not retain a right to land within the cooperative larger in size than the applicable ceiling.[28] In addition, it was confirmed that many other categories of land (including orchard land, specialized farms, lands awarded for gallantry in war, and lands held by industrial and commercial undertakings) had been exempted from the application of laws designed to put a ceiling on the size of agricultural holdings.

Notwithstanding the variable nature of the ceilings laws and the exemptions to those laws, the conference papers suggested that 10.7 million acres of land above applicable ceilings had been acquired and distributed by the states in the period beginning with the First Five Year Plan in 1952 and ending with the Third Five Year Plan in 1967. From the data presented, it is not clear whether the claimed surplus (10.7 million acres) included 4.3 million acres of land donated, allegedly, to the Bhoodan movement.[29] If the total does include the Bhoodan land, the aggregate claim can be sharply deflated (for reasons stated during our discussion of the Bhoodan movement in Chapter 3). In any event, the amount said to have been acquired and distributed is highly suspect, given what we have subsequently learned about the implementation of ceilings legislation. It can probably be said that, among the various measures enacted in India to effect agrarian reform and land reform, the ceilings legislation was the least effective in design and implementation. And, as the exemptions to the ceilings legislation listed above make plain, the laws were crafted in a way that limited not only the amount of land that might accrue to the states, irrespective of its quality, but also the amount of cultivable land that might become available for subsequent distribution to landless laborers.

Consolidation of Holdings and Prevention of Fragmentation. The papers prepared for the Chief Ministers' conference exposed the limited progress of efforts to effect the consolidation of holdings and to prevent the fragmentation of holdings. Not surprisingly, it was suggested that consolidation operations had been completed in the states of Haryana and the Punjab (part of the undivided Punjab prior to independence), the primary region of successful consolidation of holdings during the British colonial era. What was not said was that the success in Haryana and the Punjab no doubt reflected the fact that the quality of land in a given locality in those states was relatively homogeneous. In areas of the

---

28. Ibid.
29. Ibid., p. 19.

country that were experiencing difficulty in effecting consolidation, one of the inhibiting variables was the heterogeneous nature of the quality of the land. It was difficult to induce cultivators to agree to consolidation if their current holdings were heterogeneous in quality, especially when the cultivators feared that the consolidated blocks of land that they would acquire would each be of the same size as the sum of the parts of their fragmented holdings, but might well be of inferior quality when compared with their former holdings. Perhaps the most revealing statement in this context was one suggesting that, in contrast to the progress in consolidation demonstrated in the Punjab and Haryana, the Government of West Bengal had made provision only for legislation providing for voluntary consolidation, and that enforcement of such voluntary consolidation in West Bengal was, even at the end of the Third Plan, still only under consideration.[30]

Reviewing the Gaps in Agrarian Reform Legislation

Abolition of Intermediary Interests. The conference papers detailed various gaps in the legislation for agrarian reform and land reform in the states. They noted that, though the rights of intermediaries had, in the general case, been abolished, a number of "temporarily settled" estates in the hands of intermediaries in Assam had not been vested in the state, and special legislation needed to be enacted in Bihar that would apply to an important industrial region of the state, the Tatanagar Zamindari. The papers indicated that supplemental legislation seemed to be needed in other areas to ensure that forests and cultivable waste lands were vested in the state.[31] It was also suggested that some intermediaries had evaded provisions of legislation vesting their lands in the state, and had retained land that should have been settled with their tenants. In such circumstances, it was recommended only that the states should give additional scrutiny to such cases.[32]

Reform of Tenancy Regulations. The conference organizers expressed concern that tenants continued to be "altogether unprotected in

---

30. Ibid., p. 20.
31. Ibid., p. 22.
32. Ibid., p. 23.

Pondicherry," the former French colonial enclave in southern India, and that appropriate legislation to protect them needed to be enacted into law and implemented.[33] And, the organizers indicated that, notwithstanding action in a number of states to prevent the eviction of tenants and sharecroppers from lands tilled by them, steps needed to be taken to confer "substantial rights on such tenants and sharecroppers."[34]

Regarding the process by which landlords were resuming land for personal cultivation in many states, it was suggested that there was a need in some states for legislation that would require landlords to pay compensation to evicted tenants for improvements made by tenants prior to their eviction. Moreover, there was a recognized need (at least from the perspective of the central government) to pass legislation in the states that would enable tenants who had secured permanent occupancy rights in land to mortgage their land for the purposes of securing institutional credit for productive purposes.[35] There was also said to be a need for new legislation in the states that would discourage the process by which tenants had been pressured to give up their land voluntarily to their landlords.

The conference papers recorded progress in a number of states in enabling tenants to purchase permanent rights in land, but indicated that action was required in other states (including Bihar, Andhra Pradesh, Assam and the Punjab) that would permit the compulsory transfer of permanent rights in land to tenants.[36]

Ceilings on Landholdings. It was reported that ceilings on the size of landholdings, though enacted in most of the states, still needed to be enforced in a number of states, including Kerala, Mysore, Himachal Pradesh, and Manipur. Similarly, action was needed in other states to ensure that lands declared surplus were actually taken over by government and distributed to the landless. States in this latter category included Bihar, West Bengal, Madhya Pradesh and Assam.

Consolidation of Holdings. According to the conference papers, there was a need for action in respect to the consolidation of holdings in Andhra Pradesh, Bihar and Rajasthan -- especially with respect to lands

---

33. Ibid.
34. Ibid.
35. Ibid., p. 24.
36. Ibid., p. 25.

"falling within the command of major and medium irrigation projects."[37]
And, concern was expressed that steps be taken in other states, where
progress in the consolidation of holdings had been achieved, to prevent
the subsequent fragmentation of holdings.

Recognizing the Need for
Further State Action

The Need to Improve Intergovernmental Cooperation. The
conference papers, while acknowledging that agrarian reform and land
reform remained a state subject, emphasized the central government's
concern that steps continue to be taken, especially in the Fourth Five
Year Plan, to ensure that common land policies were instituted in the
states in consultation with other units of government, including the
Advisory Committee on Land Reforms in the Planning Commission and
the Working Group on Land Reforms set up in the Ministry of Food,
Agriculture and Community Development & Cooperation. It was
suggested in the papers that it would be appropriate for the states to set
up their own specialized advisory committees to assist them in the
planning and designing of land reform programs to meet national needs,
within the frame of local conditions and needs.

The Need to Reform Revenue Ministries. The conference forum was
used by the central government to make plain its frustration with the
work of revenue ministries in the states in implementing land reform.
In this context, the papers bluntly asserted, possibly for the first time in
a meeting involving all of the states' chief ministers, that "The normal
revenue agency, primarily responsible for the implementation of land
reforms, is neither adequate or suited for bringing about social change in
the rural areas through land reforms."[38] It was also suggested that special
attention needed to be given in the states to the training of revenue
department personnel to ensure that they were both functionally and
attitudinally prepared to carry out their duties. And, it was announced
that a Land Reform Centre would be established at the Gokhale Institute
of Politics and Economics at Pune (in Maharashtra) to offer orientation

---

37. Ibid., p. 26.
38. Ibid., p. 31.

courses for policy makers and administrators who were responsible for effecting land reform.[39]

The Need to Consult Actual Cultivators. Recognizing that the states had not taken steps either to solicit the views of actual cultivators before framing agrarian reform measures or to inform them, after legislation was enacted into law, concerning the scope of the legislation as it would affect their rights and interests in land, the central government now urged the states to develop orientation and education programs for persons whose rights in land would be affected by the implementation of reform measures. It was assumed by the central government that such efforts at orientation and education would facilitate implementation of reforms and minimize the evasion of reforms.[40] Whether this assumption was valid or not, it had been obvious for many years that the supposed beneficiaries of land reform were peculiarly separated from the entire process by which reform measures were conceived and implemented. The presumed beneficiaries of agrarian reform and land reform, in my experience, tended to feel that they were being acted upon by higher authority, and derived their sense of what was happening, or might happen, to affect their rights in land through rumors disseminated by informants, informants whose interpretations of reform laws often served to promote their own agendas in the countryside. Indeed, in the context of the agrarian unrest in India at the time of the Chief Ministers' Conference in 1969, it is understandable that the central government would urge the states to ensure that the presumed beneficiaries of agrarian reform or land reform better understood the official intent of reform measures.

The Need to Establish Up-To-Date Land Records. The conference papers recognized what had for many years been quite evident: that the lack of up-to-date land records in many states constrained the expeditious implementation of agrarian reform. The lack of up-to-date records of rights in land had been an impediment to the quick implementation of agrarian reform and land reform from the outset, especially in the permanent settlement region of East India where up-to-date records of cultivators' rights in land either did not exist or were incomplete. In 1969 there were a few states, notably Gujarat, Maharashtra and Uttar

---

39. Ibid., p. 32.
40. Ibid., p. 33.

Pradesh, that had "fairly reliable records of tenants and sharecroppers" that were being maintained on an up-to-date basis by means of annual revisions.[41] Nonetheless, the conference organizers reported what was already widely known in India and abroad: namely, that because the preparation of up-to-date land records involved elaborate Survey and Settlement Operations (requiring preparation of cadastral survey maps, preparation of records of rights in land, and preparation of estimates of revenue demand), and because there was fear that such operations might be disrupted in the countryside, Survey and Settlement Operations had "not been undertaken in some areas for as long as 30 years."[42] What is striking in this context is that there was no suggestion made that measures needed to be taken to expedite the development of up-to-date records by means other than the time-consuming Survey and Settlement Operations, operations still conducted in accordance with colonial era manuals of procedure. The general absence of attempts in India to develop alternative means by which land records could be quickly brought up-to-date provides support for the idea that the absence of up-to-date land records was not only an impediment to the quick implementation of such reforms as were enacted into law, but also a prime excuse for the non-implementation of agrarian reform and land reform in some states. In any event, it is an irony of the whole process by which reforms were conceived and implemented that post-independence India adhered slavishly to British colonial procedures: procedures recognized by the Government of India, itself, as constraining the implementation of reforms said to be essential to a development process linked to the twin goals of social justice and economic progress.

The lack of up-to-date land records, suggested the conference papers, also meant that land revenue had ceased to be a major source of income for the country. Revenue receipts, based on outdated records, were often too meager even to "finance the revenue collecting organization."[43] It had become politically fashionable after independence not to revise land revenue rates so that they conformed with existing land values. The failure to update land records and to correlate revenue demand with the increasing value of land meant that land revenue collections were so low by 1969 that "the revenue authority and the assessee alike ..." had

---

41. Ibid.
42. Ibid., p. 34.
43. Ibid.

learned "not to take the collections too seriously."[44] Ironically, the payment of land revenue had become important mainly because a cultivator who hoped to preserve or acquire a permanent occupancy right to land needed his "rent receipt as evidence of his interest in land."[45] Obviously, a cultivator (for example, someone classified as a "tenant-at-will") who had no rent receipts to confirm that he had met the state's revenue demand in respect to his holding could not successfully make a de jure claim to the land in his cultivating possession. And the rent receipt was as important to the ex-intermediary's claim to a permanent occupancy right to land as it was to the tenant farmer. Technically, following agrarian reform, both were legally rent-paying tenants of the state, the super-landlord in the hierarchy of interests in land.

The Need to Protect Tenant Cultivators. It was pointed out in the conference papers that the Government of India's effort to introduce new (Green Revolution) technology in agriculture toward the end of the 1960s had led to unprecedented increases in land values.[46] As a result, superior landholders (including traditional, non-tilling, absentee landlords) were taking whatever steps they could throughout India to resume land for personal cultivation. Superior landholders used liberal provisions in the agrarian reform laws that permitted them to resume land, even if this led to the eviction of cultivators who may have long presumed that they had a permanent right to the land that they tilled. While it had been well recognized for many years that personal cultivation clauses in agrarian reform laws had been used to evict tenant farmers from holdings claimed by their landlords, the conference papers indicated that the dramatic increase in land values accompanying the Government of India's endorsement of the new, technology-centered, strategy for rural development, seemed likely to produce another round of evictions of cultivators. And, it was likely that another round of evictions would exacerbate agrarian tensions. Reflecting the then current concern of the Home Ministry that agrarian tensions had been associated with the persistence of social and economic inequalities in the countryside, the central government used the occasion of the Chief Ministers' Conference to urge that measures be taken in the states to establish stringent safeguards for tenant cultivators so as to prevent such cultivators,

---

44. Ibid.
45. Ibid.
46. Ibid.

especially the smaller ones, from being overwhelmed "should another wave of resumptions occur."[47]

The Need to Provide Rural Credit Services. Sophisticated proponents of agrarian reform and land reform had earlier suggested that the redistribution of rights in land always needed to be associated with the development of supporting services (for example, institutionalized sources of credit) for the beneficiaries of reform. Now, in the context of the Chief Ministers' Conference, it was recognized, formally, that whatever reforms had been enacted into law in the states (including zamindari abolition) had left actual cultivators dependent mainly on superior landholders to meet their credit and other needs.[48] In other words, the reform measures had left the traditional hierarchy of socioeconomic power intact. For example, ordinary cultivators, whatever their de jure rights in land, were still reliant on superior landholders for agricultural credit, usually at usurious rates of interest. The Conference of Chief Ministers was used by the central government to send a message to the states that they needed not only to expedite the enactment and implementation of agrarian reform and land reform legislation, but also to recognize the need for complementary programs that would provide supporting services, including agricultural credit, to the beneficiaries of reform measures in order to free these beneficiaries from their traditional dependency on superior landholders for those services. The central government noted, in this context, that even cooperative credit institutions in the countryside had generally not provided credit to small landholders and that, therefore, such landholders' only source of agricultural credit would be local moneylenders, often superior landholders lending at usurious rates. The central government suggested that it was important to enact laws in the states that would permit small landholders (including tenant farmers and landholders belonging to scheduled tribes, scheduled castes and backward classes) the right to mortgage their land in order to obtain agricultural credit at non-usurious rates.

The Need to Monitor Agrarian Reform Progress. Within the context of the conference papers, the central government suggested the need for continuous review of the agrarian situation in the states with a view toward understanding the relationship between various agrarian reform

---

47. Ibid.
48. Ibid., p. 35.

measures and their long-term social and economic effects.[49] And, the central government said that, given the wide scope of the legislation that had thus far been enacted in the states and the differences in local conditions, it was desirable that the state governments, no less than the Research Programme Committee of the Planning Commission in New Delhi, monitor progress in agrarian reform and identify problems encountered in implementing the legislation in the countryside.

Encouraging a Link Between Agrarian Reform and Agricultural Development

In sharp criticism of the entire program of agrarian reform since independence, the conference organizers suggested that the reform measures that had been enacted into law in the states had been designed and undertaken in isolation from other programs of rural economic development. They had, therefore, been unrelated to the objectives of other programs aimed at agricultural development.[50] This criticism of the process in the states by which agrarian reform and land reform measures had been designed and enacted into law represented belated recognition within the central government of the policy bifurcation that had been maintained after independence between agrarian reform and agricultural development.[51] It had taken the Government of India twenty-two years and three five year plans (1952-67) to recognize that agrarian reform and land reform measures had never been designed specifically to complement efforts to transform traditional agriculture and to contribute to increases in agricultural productivity. This criticism showed belated recognition that agrarian reforms in the states had not been designed, necessarily, to meet national goals: that they had evolved as accretions to the land policy laws of the British colonial era, rather than as measures designed specifically to empower millions of cultivators, to give them a stake in economic progress, and to provide them with economic incentives to transform traditional agriculture. In effect, this government-generated criticism of agrarian reform, as implemented in India up to 1969, was as

---

49. Ibid., p. 36.

50. Ibid., p. 38.

51. This policy bifurcation, as noted earlier, had originated in the colonial era.

devastating as any criticism by concerned outsiders of India's land policy after independence.

The conference papers, amplifying on the criticism noted above, said that the reforms had not facilitated agricultural development,[52] while agricultural development measures had thus far served mainly to strengthen "the social and economic status of the rural elite."[53] The critique continued with the observation that, because agrarian reforms had not notably strengthened the social, economic and political status of sections of cultivators at the base of the agrarian hierarchy, they had "proved to be only eyewash."[54] In these circumstances, it had become imperative to design and implement a progressive program of agrarian reform that would be an integral part of a comprehensive approach to rural development. Toward this end, it was now necessary "to bring the cultivating tenant in direct contact with the State and confer on him permanent and transferable rights" in land.[55] This recommendation reflected recognition of the urgency of the moment, of the growing unrest in the countryside, and of the evident process by which landlords were resuming land for personal cultivation from landholders below them in the agrarian hierarchy. This recommendation was followed by the suggestion that action should be taken in the states to deny landlords who were not resident on their lands the right to retain such lands. Such lands, it was asserted, should be made available for distribution among bona fide cultivators in the same locality. It was noted that ex-intermediaries had "managed to retain extensive areas of land in many cases through questionable and fraudulent means."[56] Moreover, it was suggested that it was a common practice for such ex-intermediaries to continue to derive income from the land as they had in the past: giving the land out to unregistered tenants and sharecroppers for purposes of cultivation and expecting such tenants-at-will or sharecroppers to assume all of the risks of production and to perform all labor on the land, while, at the same time, giving the landlords unauthorized rents or shares of the produce. Accordingly, the central government made plain that there was a need

---

52. India, Ministry of Food, Agriculture, Community Development and Cooperation, "Chief Ministers' Conference on Land Reform -- Notes on Agenda," p. 39.
53. Ibid.
54. Ibid.
55. Ibid., p. 40.
56. Ibid., p. 41.

for the states to take action that would deny landlords the right to take possession of lands tilled by cultivators (including tenants-at-will and sharecroppers) who lacked security of tenure.[57] In effect, the central government, using the conference papers as its instrument, said that it should be an object of state policy to confer complete security of tenure on all cultivators, including those tenants-at-will and sharecroppers who had been most vulnerable to landlords' actions to resume land, under existing statutes, for personal cultivation.

Thus, in the conference papers, the central government communicated its judgement that the states should take adequate steps to design agrarian reform measures so as to integrate them with programs of agricultural development. The papers recognized that the country's rural development policies would benefit from efforts in the states designed to ensure that agrarian reform and agricultural development programs were integrated conceptually so as to be mutually reinforcing of overall development goals.

Recommending State Assistance for Landless Laborers

The Need to Provide Land for the Landless. The conference papers made reference to the fact that the ceilings laws as enacted in the states, even if implemented, would not make "available sufficient surplus lands for redistribution..." to landless agricultural laborers.[58] The papers suggested that there was no constitutional impediment to legislation that would further reduce ceilings on the size of landholdings.[59] And, the papers indicated that such new legislation seemed appropriate in the context of the national effort to introduce new technology in agriculture: new technology that was sufficiently scale neutral to ensure that, with assured irrigation, small landholdings (of one or two hectares) could become viable units of production.[60] Given the existing concentration of

---

57. Ibid.

58. Ibid., p. 42.

59. Ibid., p. 43.

60. Ibid. So far as I know, this is the first time after independence that the Government of India formally reversed the presumption contained in the Report of the Royal Commission on Agriculture in India, 1928, that efficient, modern

(continued...)

landholdings in the hands of a limited number of agriculturists and the existence of a large section of the rural population without secure rights in land, the conference papers made plain that the redistribution of rights in land by means of ceilings legislation had socioeconomic efficacy.[61] At the same time, the papers made clear that the central government was not prepared, even in the context of agrarian tensions in the countryside, to urge on the states a massive new program of redistributive land reform. Instead, the central government, having urged that land be provided for the landless, indicated that it could envision no solution to the problem of landlessness in India other than one based on increasing, over time, the proportion of non-farm jobs for landless agriculturists.[62]

The Need to Coordinate with the Bhoodan Movement. The Bhoodan movement was recognized within the frame of the conference papers as a non-official movement providing a favorable climate for land reform. Accordingly, the papers suggested that "To the extent feasible, land reform programmes of State Governments .... be coordinated with the Bhoodan" movement.[63] And, it was suggested that the recipients of Bhoodan land should be given high priority when states provided supporting services to new landholders, including those who received land made available through the implementation of ceilings on the size of agricultural holdings. Finally, the papers said that action should be taken to ensure that the recipients of surplus land were bona fide landless agricultural laborers, rather than influential persons (that is, persons who were already substantial landholders) who, it had been reported, were securing land that should have been allotted to others.[64]

The Need to Provide Programs for the Landless. Having suggested that there was insufficient land that could be made available to meet the needs of landless agriculturists, the papers of the Chief Ministers'

60.(...continued)
agriculture required, by definition, large units of production permitting economies of scale.

61. India, Ministry of Food, Agriculture, Community Development and Cooperation, "Chief Ministers' Conference on Land Reform -- Notes on Agenda," p. 43.

62. Ibid., p. 46.

63. Ibid., p. 44.

64. Ibid., p. 45.

Conference suggested a comprehensive strategy by which the needs of the landless could be addressed. The elements of such a strategy, as conceived by the central government, were outlined in the conference papers. The elements included fourteen points; among them were the following.[65]

1. Steps should be taken in the states to make scientific technology available to those small landholders who were prepared to engage in labor-intensive scientific farming.

2. Attempts should be made in the states to employ landless agricultural laborers in the development of social overhead capital (in the form of soil conservation, road building, and minor irrigation projects).

3. Steps should be taken to ensure that landless agricultural workers were covered progressively by the *Minimum Wages Act of 1948,* notwithstanding the fact that there were difficulties associated with enforcing the various provisions of the act in rural areas.

4. Steps should be taken in the states, where possible, to speed up the distribution of whatever land could be acquired through the enforcement of ceilings on the size of landholdings.

5. Attempts should be made in the states to prevent the eviction of cultivators from land tilled by them when superior landholders sought, inappropriately, to resume land under existing statutes for personal cultivation.

6. Measures should be taken in the states to enact and implement, where appropriate, tenurial reforms that would give security of tenure (as distinct from permanent occupancy rights in land) to cultivators of small holdings. It was explained in this context that the rationale for such tenurial reforms was enhanced by the prospect that small landholdings could yield a marketable surplus if the tillers of such holdings could be incorporated within the frame of the new agricultural strategy.

7. Action should be taken in the states to ensure that landless agricultural laborers receive permanent occupancy rights (the rough equivalency of ownership rights) to the land on which their huts ("homesteads") were placed.

---

65. Ibid., pp. 49-51.

8. Attempts should continue to ensure that the social status of landless laborers belonging to scheduled castes and tribes was enhanced within the frame of social legislation enacted in the states.

The Cycle Repeated

Escalated Rural Tensions

Notwithstanding the exhortations of the central government in the context of the Chief Ministers' Conference on Land Reform in November of 1969, agrarian tensions in rural India were not defused. By the Summer of 1970, a number of political parties had called for a land-grab movement to effect permanent changes in the agrarian structure. There was renewed fear of extensive violence. In Bihar, for example, state "government spokesmen pleaded for time to implement newly legislated reforms and indicated that measures would soon be taken (1) to effect ceilings on land holdings, (2) to distribute surplus lands among the landless, (3) to issue parchas (legal certificates) to the landless guaranteeing them a permanent right of occupancy to the scraps of land on which their huts stood, and (4) to inhibit the eviction of sharecroppers from lands tilled by them."[66] And, on July 1, 1970, the Government of Bihar ordered the urgent implementation of land reforms, suggesting as it did so that the failure to implement past legislation had contributed directly to agrarian unrest in the region.[67]

Tensions continued to escalate.

Newspapers carried reports that Communist-inspired mobs of peasants were taking possession of land in northern Bihar. In immediate reaction a kisan sabha (a farmers' organization, comprised of large landholders in this instance) was formed to resist the demands of the peasants for land. Meanwhile, the government published the names of 125 of the largest landholders in the state and announced that the ceilings act of 1961 would be brought into force against them and their cases disposed of summarily.

---

66. F. Tomasson Jannuzi, "India's Rural Poor: What Will Mobilize Them Politically?" in Henry C. Hart, editor, *Indira Gandhi's India,* (Boulder, Colorado: Westview Press, 1976), p. 192.

67. Bihar, Revenue Department, "D.O. No. 5LR-LA-224/70-5667-L.R." (Unpublished Document), (Patna, July 1, 1970).

Major landholders converged on Patna to hold lengthy strategy sessions and to lobby against the precipitate implementation of reforms that would impinge on their rights. Armed men, said to be Naxalites, attacked the holdings of a landlord in Bhagalpur district and forcibly harvested standing crops. Three days later, a Jan Sangh party worker was assassinated in Musahari development area in Muzaffarpur district in northern Bihar. This murder was widely considered to be part of the Naxalite strategy of mobilizing sections of the peasantry in violent revolt against landholders. Police were rushed to Musahari to forestall further violence.[68]

In the following years up to June of 1975, agrarian unrest became a persistent feature of life in rural India and, especially, in the state of Bihar. Musahari in Muzaffarpur District continued to be torn by violence. Still associated with the Bhoodan movement, "Jaya Prakash Narayan remained in Musahari until 1971 trying to resolve disputes peacefully and to lead a nonviolent struggle for social and economic justice. But, Narayan and his associates were no more successful in this effort than they and Vinobha Bhave had been in the Bhoodan campaigns. .... By June of 1975, there were ominous reports of continuing agrarian unrest and government repression of segments of the rural poor of Bihar in the name of anti-Naxalite activity."[69] And, on June 10, 1975, Arvind Narayan Das reported that a reign of terror had been let loose in rural Bihar by large landholders, their goondas (thugs) and elements of the local police.[70] Das indicated that the objects of repression were mainly landless agricultural laborers who had received land from the state government in 1970 only to have their lands repossessed subsequently by powerful landholders.[71]

Promised Government Action

On June 25, 1975 Prime Minister Indira Gandhi declared a state of emergency in India. Many factors above and beyond agrarian unrest

---

68. F. Tomasson Jannuzi, "India's Rural Poor: What Will Mobilize Them Politically?" in *Indira Gandhi's India,* p. 192.

69. Ibid., pp. 193-194.

70. Arvind N. Das, "Murder to Landlords' Order," *Economic and Political Weekly,* (June 10, 1975), pp. 915-917.

71. Ibid.

contributed to her decision to take this action.[72] Nevertheless, while her decision was not tied exclusively to issues linked directly to agrarian unrest, it is significant that, within five days of her declaration of a state of emergency, Mrs. Gandhi announced a Twenty Point Program of reform measures designed to meet the needs of people at the base of the agrarian hierarchy in the countryside. The program was a patchwork of measures that had been put forward many times previously. In effect, the central government, in the persona of Mrs. Gandhi, issued yet another pledge to urge the states to implement agrarian reform by updating land records, by ensuring that ceilings on the size of landholdings were enforced, by distributing surplus land to landless laborers, by providing household sites for landless agricultural laborers, by ending bonded labor in rural areas, by liquidating rural indebtedness, and by enforcing laws on minimum agricultural wages.[73] The thrust of these measures obviously could be interpreted as confirming that Mrs. Gandhi, as she sought to justify the state of emergency and to maintain her authority, considered it necessary to address directly the interests of sections of the cultivating peasantry who had demonstrated since the late 1960s that they were no longer prepared to accept their places at the base of the agrarian hierarchy and that they were now capable of working within and outside of the law to challenge not only the authority of the landholding elite, but also the authority of those in the Congress Party and in the Government of India who had acted to preserve and protect the interests of traditional landholders in the countryside.

72. For background on the factors that led to the declaration of the state of emergency, see Henry C. Hart, editor, *Indira Gandhi's India,* (Boulder, Colorado: Westview Press, 1976), pp. 1-36.

73. For elaboration on these and other measures see a collection of speeches by the then Minister of Finance, C. Subramaniam, and the Minister of Industry and Civil Supplies, T.A. Pai, in C. Subramaniam and T. A. Pai, *New Programme for Economic Progress: The Turning Point,* (New Delhi: Indraprastha Press, 1975).

5

The Ineffective Formulation
of Agrarian Reform Policy

The Recent Cycle of
Policy Drift and Rural Unrest

Government's Policy Drift
in the 1970s and 1980s

In the early 1970s, the central government seemed to demonstrate increased awareness of the need to address directly the interests of the cultivating peasantry. Prime Minister Indira Gandhi campaigned for election in the early 1970s on the platform of abolishing poverty and, following her declaration of a state of emergency in June, 1975, exhorted the states to implement her Twenty Point Program emphasizing agrarian reform. However, the power to initiate and implement agrarian reform continued to be the prerogative of state governments. The concern expressed by the central government was not translated sufficiently into action in the various states. Neither the government of Indira Gandhi nor the government that replaced it in 1977 was successful in expediting the implementation of agrarian reform in the Indian states and conveying benefits to people at the base of India's agrarian hierarchy, people roughly classified as the rural poor.[1] That is to say, notwithstanding the

---

1. I am referring generally here to those persons in the countryside who are low both in the social (caste) hierarchy and in the economic hierarchy: persons who are dependent on agriculture for income, but who lack either secure rights in land or any land at all. I am not concerned here with specifying whether
(continued...)

central government's urgent recommendations and exhortations concerning the need for immediate action for agrarian reform, there is little evidence to suggest that extraordinary steps were taken in the states to update land records, to enforce ceilings on the size of agricultural holdings, to give security of tenure to cultivators or to give land to the landless. Indeed, we now know that the recommended reform measures continued to be resisted, circumvented, diluted and denied by persisting coalitions of landholding interests. In some regions, associations of landlords, aided by local goondas in their employ, carried out acts of repression against those below them in the agrarian hierarchy, especially when such persons agitated for the enforcement of minimum wage laws or pressed, generally, for the implementation of agrarian reform. Landlords continued to employ the law, when possible, to evict peasant cultivators from holdings that the landlords wished to resume for personal cultivation, and, when not possible, to evict peasant cultivators using extra-legal means, including coercion and the threat of it. Local judges continued to grant stays of enforcement of agrarian reform legislation. And, state governments, influenced when not dominated by members of the landholding elite, continued to use colonial era procedures, when necessary, to impede the quick implementation of such reforms as had been enacted into law.

In the late 1970s the central government's public expressions of agrarian reform policy began to drift from aggressive initiatives stressing the urgent need for action by the states toward policies emphasizing rural development palliatives. The policy drift was reflected in the declining importance assigned to agrarian reform by the Planning Commission, the organ of the central government responsible for assessing progress in agrarian reform and for providing guidelines on policy issues pertinent to the implementation of land reform and agrarian reform in the states. This declining emphasis can be traced through several five year plans; each plan from the Fourth (1969-74) through the Seventh (1985-90) gave

---

1.(...continued)
such persons are technically below the poverty line or represent a given percentage of the rural population. For elaboration in this context, see the pioneering work of V. M. Dandekar, Nilakanta Rath and Amartya Sen. See, for example, V.M. Dandekar and Nilakanta Rath, "Poverty in India," *Economic and Political Weekly,* 8. Annual Number, February, 1973, pp. 245-54; and Amartya Sen, "Poverty, Inequality and Unemployment, Some Conceptual Issues in Measurement," *Economic and Political Weekly,* 9. Special Number, August 1973, pp. 1457-1466.

successively less attention to land reform and agrarian reform as important principles of state policy.

The Fourth Five Year Plan (1969-74) was the last of the plans to reiterate the urgent themes on land reform and agrarian reform as they had been set forth originally in the draft outline to the First Five Year Plan. The Fourth Plan's section on land reform recounted past successes, claiming that intermediary tenures had been "practically abolished,"[2] that "several million" acres of cultivable land had been distributed to landless agriculturists,[3] and that provisions for "security of tenure and regulation of rent" had been adopted.[4] At the same time, it reiterated old concerns. It admitted that there had been shortcomings in implementation and that progress had been slow in many states.[5] It also admitted that, notwithstanding claims made earlier that as many as 20 million tenant cultivators had gained secure rights in land, tenant cultivators who still lacked secure rights in land (i.e., those classified as tenants-at-will and as sharecroppers) constituted 82 percent of the tenants in India.[6] Finally, the Fourth Plan repeated the now familiar concerns of the central government: that the updating of records of rights in land should be completed in the plan period; that land reform laws should be implemented more effectively by revenue officials in the states; and that steps needed to be taken to ensure that progress in land reform and agrarian reform was constantly monitored in the states and, in due course, at a Land Reforms Centre to be established at the Gokhale Institute of Politics and Economics at Pune.[7]

The draft outline to the Fifth Five Year Plan, drawn up under the supervision of Professor D.T. Lakdawala, pointed out that the poorest 10 percent of rural households in India enjoyed secure rights in land on only 0.1 percent of the land in the country, while the richest 10 percent of rural households exercised control "over more than half of total assets in

---

2. India, Planning Commission, *Fourth Five Year Plan (1969-74)*, (New Delhi: India, Manager of Publications, 1969), p. 174.

3. Ibid.

4. Ibid.

5. Ibid.

6. Ibid., p. 177. The Fourth Five Year Plan indicated that these insecure and unprotected tenants were located mainly in Andhra Pradesh, Assam, Bihar, Haryana, Punjab, Tamil Nadu and West Bengal.

7. Ibid., pp. 182-183.

1971-72 as well as 1961-62."[8]   In a striking departure from past recommendations of the Planning Commission, the draft outline to the Fifth Five Year Plan recommended that steps be taken to establish village committees of the beneficiaries of land reforms to implement those reforms.   However, the Fifth Plan (1978-83) was not permitted to complete its course. It was replaced by the Sixth Five Year Plan (1980-85).

"The Sixth Plan .... was not even allowed to make a beginning, and much of the valuable work done was all but discarded."[9]   In any event, the Sixth Plan (1980-85) subordinated land reform and agrarian reform to an effort to provide benefits to the rural poor mainly by means of an Integrated Rural Development Program. Instead of addressing the needs of the rural poor by emphasizing land reform and agrarian reform, the Integrated Rural Development Program sought to address their needs mainly by means of Food for Work Programs and Special Area Development Programs.

By the time that the Seventh Plan (1985-90) was being formulated, land reform and agrarian reform had, virtually, been discarded as instruments of state policy.[10]   The Seventh Plan included only fifteen numbered paragraphs concerning land reform. And, while the plan gave lip service to the proposition that land reform would be looked upon as an intrinsic part of the plan's anti-poverty strategy, land reform was

---

8. India, Planning Commission, *Draft Five Year Plan, 1978-83,* (New Delhi: Manager of Publications, 1978), p. 11.

9. Tarlok Singh, "Planning and the Political Process," *Hindustan Times,* (Delhi), December 8, 1989.

10. D. Bandhyopadhyay, an officer of the Indian Administrative Services who had led the way to tenurial reform in West Bengal in the 1980s, told me (in private discussions while we were attending a "Workshop on Poverty in India" held at Oxford University in October of 1987) that he had had difficulty securing a place for agrarian reform and land reform in the Seventh Plan. He had fought successfully to include a brief statement in the Seventh Plan to the effect that land reform had efficacy both in the context of anti-poverty programs and rural development programs aimed at increasing productivity in agriculture. [D. Bandhyopadhyay, Interview, Oxford, England, October, 1987.]

Later, in February of 1989, K.B. Saxena, Joint Secretary for Rural Development (Land Reforms) in the Government of India, concurred with Bandhyopadhyay that an internal fight had had to be waged within the Government of India even to get land reform mentioned in the Seventh Plan. [K.B. Saxena, Interview, New Delhi, India, February 12, 1989.]

clearly made subordinate to a variety of anti-poverty programs emphasizing the generation of productive employment opportunities in rural areas.[11] Moreover, by the time the Seventh Plan was approved by the Government of India, there had been a progressive "weakening of the sense of partnership between the Centre and the States in working together to resolve the problems of the people within a broadly agreed long-range view of national and regional goals."[12]

Renewed Agrarian Unrest in the 1980s[13]

In the 1980s, agrarian unrest in the countryside increased, particularly in regions where agrarian reform measures had not been implemented but where rural expectations of change in existing conditions had grown.[14] As early as 1982, a central government team headed by Dr. Manmohan Singh was established to study extremist activities in the country and to suggest means by which such activities could be counteracted by the Government of India. That team reported that the renewed unrest in the countryside occurred in regions where land reform had not been effectively implemented and where landholders who enjoyed secure rights in land continued to exert authority over those who were below them in the rural hierarchy. And, to remedy the situation, the team suggested that there must be a vigorous drive to implement agrarian reform and

---

11. India, Planning Commission, *Seventh Five Year Plan, 1985-90*, (New Delhi: Manager of Publications, 1985), Vol. I, p. 23 and Vol. II, pp. 62-64.

12. Tarlok Singh, "Planning and the Political Process," *Hindustan Times*, December 8, 1989.

13. This section draws on data (including conversations with government officials) gathered by me in India in the 1980s, particularly in the Spring of 1989 when I was affiliated for several months as a visiting scholar with the Nehru Museum and Library in New Delhi.

14. As with the activities of the kisan sabhas in the 1930s, it is difficult to establish the degree to which agrarian unrest in the 1980s was rooted in local leadership or was promoted by activist outsiders, latter day "Naxalites" representing left-wing political factions. I believe that the unrest of the 1980s represented the work mainly of local persons, including people at the base of the agrarian hierarchy, who were at times aided and abetted by outsiders, including young, urban intellectuals seeking to establish their own nexus with poor and landless persons in the countryside.

land reform, to enforce minimum wage laws in the countryside, and to limit atrocities committed against agricultural laborers (especially Harijans) by the goondas of landholders, often in association with local police. Whether or not the central government acted on the team's recommendations is not clear. What is clear is that rural violence in some areas of India continued to increase.

By the late 1980s, one could not live in India without reading, almost daily, of agrarian tensions and rural violence, especially in the State of Bihar. While media reports often suggested that rural violence was a function of left-oriented terrorism, it was evident that disputes over rights in land were the source of the unrest and violence. Throughout Bihar, but especially in districts torn by violence in the 1980s, resident landholders (including Brahmin and Rajput ex-intermediaries) continued to cultivate their holdings using agricultural labor belonging generally to backward and dalit castes. Such landholders also typically gave out some land for cultivation by sharecroppers in disguised tenancies. In this arrangement, based usually on an oral agreement, the sharecropper performed all labor on the land, assumed all costs and risks of production, and gave the superior landholder at least 50 percent of any crop.[15] In addition to the resident landholders, there were also often absentee landlords. Such absentee landlords customarily continued to give out their land to sharecroppers for purposes of cultivation.

In the 1980s, claims by agricultural laborers for higher wages and claims by sharecroppers for secure rights in land continued to be denied by superior landholders. Sharecroppers who dared to demand that they be recorded as tenants were generally denied further temporary access to land and were relegated to the village pool of landless agricultural laborers. They were demoted to the base position in the agrarian hierarchy. Typically, the agricultural laborers were intimidated by those above them in the rural hierarchy; they were threatened with violence; they were physically punished; and, sometimes, they were killed.[16]

---

15. Describing the plight of such sharecroppers (bataidari in Bihar), the scholar/journalist B.G. Verghese has said, "In other words, the risks are his; the gains are disproportionately shared by others, parasites living on his sweat." [B.G. Verghese, *Beyond the Famine: An Approach to Regional Planning for Bihar,* (New Delhi: Super Bazar for the Bihar Relief Committee, 1967), p. 27.]

16. I am indebted to K.S. Subramanian, Senior Fellow, Centre for Contemporary Studies, Nehru Memorial Museum and Library, Teen Murti House, New Delhi, for his graphic descriptions of rural conditions in Bihar in

(continued...)

Agrarian tensions proliferated. Rural violence was endemic in rural Bihar, and there were increasing reports of atrocities, particularly in Patna, Nalanda, Bhojpur, Rohtas, Jehanabad and Aurangabad districts.[17] By October of 1988, elements of the Bihar Military Police, the Border Security Force, the Central Reserve Police Force and the Gujarat Armed Police had been deployed in many of these districts to defend the state not against the landlords but, rather, against sections of the peasantry who were now classified popularly as extremists.

Reviewing and commenting on the escalation of violence in rural India, a few courageous officers of the Government of India, like Shri K.B. Saxena,[18] reported that the agrarian unrest and rural violence were due mainly to the repressive actions of superior landholders bent on thwarting the implementation of agrarian reform;[19] bent on maintaining their own

---

16.(...continued)
the 1980s. Among current authorities on violence in rural India, I believe that none is more knowledgeable than Subramanian.

17. For a passionate account of contemporary rural violence in Bihar, see: Arun Sinha, *Against the Few: Struggles of India's Rural Poor,* (London: Zed Books Ltd., 1991). Though Sinha's book is methodologically marred by his use of class analysis to explain antagonisms in the countryside that are more complex than class analysis illuminates, his work does provide gripping descriptions of the rural violence that is a continuing phenomenon in Bihar.

18. In February of 1989, K.B. Saxena was Joint Secretary, Rural Development (Land Reforms), for the Government of India. I first interviewed him in New Delhi on February 12, 1989, after he was identified by mutual friends as an officer of the Indian Administrative Services, IAS, who was deeply interested in the implementation of agrarian reform. At that time, Saxena said that conditions in Bihar were rapidly deteriorating, and that little had changed in Bihar in more than thirty years. That is to say, he indicated that the ex-intermediaries, or zamindars, comprised mainly of Brahmins, Rajputs and Bhumiar Brahmins, continued to exercise significant power in rural areas, as they had in the past. At the same time, he said that, because land reform had provided some additional agriculturists (notably Yadavs and Kurmis among so-called Backward Castes) secure rights in land (as "tenants" of the state), such landholders were also now asserting their interests against the claims of those below them in the agrarian hierarchy -- unregistered tenants, or sharecroppers, and landless agricultural laborers.

19. About this time, Indu Bharti, writing in *Economic and Political Political Weekly,* argued that the violence resulted mainly from landless laborers "demanding implementation of the laws which the state government have enacted

(continued...)

power and authority over those who were below them in the agrarian hierarchy; and using violent means against sharecroppers and landless laborers, often in collusion with police and para-military forces. Others in New Delhi associated rural violence (not only in Bihar but also in Uttar Pradesh, Madhya Pradesh, Gujarat, Rajasthan and Tamil Nadu) with the failure to implement agrarian reform and with the increasing capacity of people near the base of the agrarian hierarchy to assert their rights, even if asserting their rights meant engaging in a one-sided struggle against superior forces. Some suggested that rural violence was precipitated mainly by the activities of leftist extremists acting to mobilize agricultural laborers against superior landholders and the state.[20] The Home Ministry was being told by its own investigators that the core issues precipitating rural unrest were those associated with the widespread perception in the countryside that agrarian reform and land reform had not been effectively or fairly implemented. In other words, no matter where the blame was placed, either on the superior landholders or on those lower in the agrarian hierarchy, the Government of India was told by many sources that agrarian reforms were at the root of the problem: that either the fear of further implementation of reforms or reaction to such reform as had been implemented had led landlords to use violence to protect their traditional rights in land; that dissatisfaction with unfair or inadequate implementation of reform had led those low in the agrarian hierarchy to use violence to assert their claims to land; or that both of these roots of violence were in effect in the countryside. Under these circumstances, it is not surprising that, as instruments of government

---

19.(...continued)
to dilute the inequitous pattern of landholdings. The powerful rural elements have tried to suppress every such demand by violent methods." [Indu Bharti, "Farce of Land Reforms in Jehanabad," *Economic and Political Weekly*, November 26, 1988, p. 2520.]

20. I believe that, unlike in the 1960s, those in authority in the late 1980s fully understood that the real threat of instability in the countryside was not caused mainly by leftist extremists. This is not to suggest that self-declared leftist organizations were not active in the countryside in the 1980s. Certainly, it was evident to me in India in 1989 that, in the case of Bihar, the Mazdoor Kisan Sangram Samity (MKSS), the Bihar Pradesh Kisan Sabha (BPKS), the Krantikari Kisan Committee (KKC), and the Bihar Kisan Samity (BKS) were among groups claiming varying degrees of credit for mobilizing agricultural laborers and others in direct action against superior landholders and representatives of the police and para-military forces.

policy, agrarian reform and land reform became increasingly less attractive.

Central Government's Response
in the 1980s

Abandonment of Radical Definitions of Agrarian Reform. By the beginning of the Seventh Plan (1985-90), it had become difficult for officers of the Government of India who were committed to agrarian reform to ensure that either agrarian reform or land reform would continue to be instruments of public policy. And, by the end of the Seventh Plan, it was uncertain whether land reform would be endorsed as a public policy in the Eighth Plan.[21]

In effect, even though some still associated agrarian unrest with the failure of government to implement meaningful programs of agrarian reform, the constituency within the Government of India that supported the need for agrarian reform and land reform had been narrowed considerably. Even officers advocating anti-poverty programs in rural areas tended to see such programs as palliatives that would not be enhanced by agrarian reform. It was clear by the end of the 1980s that rural economic development was not to be fostered in ways that would be linked to structural changes in the distribution of rights in land in rural areas. Instead, a decision had been made at the highest levels of the government of Rajiv Gandhi to address the needs of the rural poor by working within existing conditions (mainly by means of wage employment schemes), rather than by making agrarian reform a critical part of any anti-poverty strategy.[22] While some still dared to argue that poverty alleviation and equity-oriented policies and programs could not be pursued meaningfully in rural India except by attacking the existing system of rights in land,[23] the policies of the Government of India were moving in another direction.

---

21. K.B. Saxena, Interview, New Delhi, India, February 12, 1989.

22. See: D. Bandhyopadhyay, "Direct Intervention Programmes for Poverty Alleviation in India," Paper delivered at the Workshop on Poverty in India, International Development Centre, The University of Oxford, October 2-6, 1987, (Unpublished Manuscript).

23. M.L. Dantwala, "Growth and Equity in Agriculture," *Economic Times,* December 19, 1986.

The voices of K.T. Shah and of the Kumarappa Committee had long since been silenced. It was no longer fashionable to talk about the importance of "land to the tiller" as a construct of land policy, of rural economic development, or of poverty alleviation. There were no longer suggestions, as there had been in the 1950s (notably at the Nagpur convention of the Congress Party in 1959), that joint cooperative farming might be the sine qua non for transforming traditional agriculture in India (ensuring, according to its advocates, increases in productivity and, simultaneously, providing land for the landless, albeit in units to be farmed jointly by them).[24] Without a bang or a whimper, radical definitions of agrarian reform -- if the provision of permanent occupancy rights in land to actual tillers can be considered radical -- had quietly been abandoned by those who now governed India.

Separation of Agrarian Reform from Rural Economic Development.
A dichotomy was established in post-independence India between agrarian reform and rural economic development. That dichotomy was made plain in the colonial era within the frame of the recommendations of the Royal Commission on Agriculture in India, 1928, and it was reiterated in post-independence documents of state (especially the draft outline of the First Five Year Plan). It made agrarian reform and land reform policy instruments by which social justice might be conferred on people in the Indian countryside. At the same time, in the British tradition, it made rural economic development a function increasingly of technology-centered agricultural policies. The dichotomy between agrarian reform and rural economic development applied even to the processes by which public policies were implemented following independence. Revenue departments did the business of agrarian reform: drafting new laws affecting agrarian relations in the states within the frame of colonial era precedents in law and the dynamics of local politics. At the same time, agricultural departments focused on issues linked to the technological transformation of traditional agriculture.

There was no attempt at a synthetic strategy of rural economic development until 1969 when there was belated recognition within the

---

24. The fact that the Seventh Five Year Plan included one sentence ("Reform and revitalization of the cooperative movement would form an important plank in the programme of agricultural development.") endorsing cooperatives does not nullify the point made here. [Sentence quoted from India, Planning Commission, *Seventh Five Year Plan, 1985-90,* Volume I, p. 13.]

central government,[25] coincident with the decision of the Government of India to promote the introduction of new technology in agriculture,[26] that agrarian reform measures, if implemented, could complement and facilitate the introduction of the new technology.[27] It was only then that it became obvious to some that the new technology, when introduced in regions where gross inequalities in the distribution of assets (notably land) and income already existed, would tend to amplify existing inequalities[28] and thus could contribute to the growth of agrarian tensions. By the end of the Seventh Plan, however, there were few voices within the Government of India who were prepared to argue (as did M.L. Dantwala, from outside the government, and D. Bandhyopadhyay and K.B. Saxena from within it) that rural economic development and the alleviation of rural poverty would continue to require redistributive land reform and security of tenure. Given this background, it seems likely that agrarian

---

25. This was in the context of the Chief Ministers' Conference on Land Reform in 1969, as earlier noted in Chapter 4.

26. For a discussion of the role of foreign aid institutions, including the Rockefeller and Ford Foundations, in fostering the introduction of the new technology-driven strategy for rural development in India, see: F. Tomasson Jannuzi, *India in Transition: Issues of Political Economy in a Plural Society*, (Boulder, Colorado: Westview Press, 1989), pp. 83-90.

27. Central government policy makers for the first time recognized formally that even cultivators of small holdings, if they had secure rights in land, access to irrigation and non-usurious sources of credit, could become full participants in economic progress and produce marketable surpluses. Thus, it became less fashionable to argue, as had both the Royal Commission on Agriculture in India, 1928, and the independent Government of India, that efficient modern agriculture required the formation of large units of production (to be achieved by the consolidation of small holdings).

28. This has now been admitted even by ardent proponents of India's effort to introduce new (Green Revolution) technology in agriculture. Pinstrup-Anderson and Hazell (while attempting to repudiate, indirectly, the views of Vernon W. Ruttan, Francine Frankel, and others who had suggested in the 1970s that the Green Revolution had increased inequality of income and asset distribution in the Indian countryside) have themselves acknowledged that "Where existing institutions favor very unequal asset and income distributions, technological change has tended to amplify the inequality." [Per Pinstrup-Anderson and Peter B.R. Hazell, "The Impact of the Green Revolution and Prospects for the Future," as reprinted from *Food Reviews International*, Volume 1, No. 1, 1985, (Washington, D.C.: International Food Policy Research Institute) p. 20.]

reform, if it persists in any fashion as a goal of state policy in India in the 1990s, will again be separated conceptually and operationally from programs of rural economic development.

A Retrospective View of Agrarian Reform Policies

Inability to Establish a National Consensus

After independence, the Government of India sought to establish a national consensus in favor of legislating some variants of agrarian reform and land reform. However, even in the era of Congress Party dominance (1947-1967), the government had difficulty enunciating goals that were politically acceptable to a party and people whose leaders derived power, as in most agrarian societies, from the land. Moreover, the decision to make agriculture a state subject under the constitution meant that, at the outset, the central government relinquished its authority to dictate a national direction for agrarian reform and land reform in the states. During the first decade following independence the support for agrarian reform expressed within the central government and its Planning Commission derived inspiration from the constitution's Directive Principles of State Policy. However, no consensus emerged concerning the precise relationship that needed to be established between the content of agrarian reform and the goals of national development. Whatever commitment in favor of agrarian reform and land reform existed increasingly became rhetorical within the frame of successive five year plans. No consensus emerged concerning how agrarian reform should be defined or implemented. This lack of consensus would thereafter limit the scope and content of agrarian reform in the states.

Inability to Enact Revolutionary Legislation

Following independence, the Indian states enacted into law the largest body of complex legislation for agrarian reform and land reform ever enacted in the history of any country. This accomplishment can be put in perspective by reflecting on the fact that the legislation was effected by democratic, non-coercive means in state legislatures strongly influenced, if not dominated, by the landholding elites who were themselves the objects of the reform legislation. In such circumstances, the mountains of legislation enacted inevitably reflected both the interests of those who sought to change the traditional land systems of India and those who sought to thwart change in those systems. Consequently, the results of the legislation pleased neither the advocates nor the opponents of agrarian reform and land reform.

Agrarian reform, however conceived and implemented, is greater than the sum of its parts. Whether proposed as a means to social justice, as a spur to economic change, as a sine qua non for economic progress, or merely as one means by which rural economic development can be fostered, the concept of agrarian reform has revolutionary portent.

While not fully appreciating the potential implications of agrarian reform, those who sought to promote agrarian reform in India engaged themselves, for the most part unwittingly, in what could have been revolutionary activity. At its extreme, had the governing elites promoted a radical redistribution of rights in land in rural India, this revolutionary activity could have contributed to the transformation of India's traditional political economy: conferring new opportunities, political and economic, on long denigrated sections of the peasantry and transforming the structure of power in the countryside, and ultimately in the nation as a whole. Instead of engaging in such revolutionary activity, however, the governing elites decided warily to make marginal adjustments in the existing land systems -- striving to minimize political and economic turbulence in the process. They chose ultimately not to attempt to work a revolution, but to try to make, by means of legislation, incremental changes in colonial era laws governing the relationships of landlords and tenants. It was easier, after all, to amend and tinker with British legacy acts and ordinances than to strike out in new, threatening directions of public policy.

Agrarian reform in India has been characterized, ultimately, by a lack of willingness to establish new policy initiatives, especially if new initiatives threatened the inherited power and prerogatives of dominant landholders. Accordingly, much of the legislation not only was based on colonial era precedents in law, but also was deeply influenced by agrarian reform priorities (for example, those emphasizing the significance of consolidation of landholdings), economic principles (a belief that modern agriculture required, by definition, large units of production) and ideological precepts (a belief in the workability in rural India of all kinds of cooperatives) imbedded in colonial era reports and in external definitions of how traditional agriculture might best be transformed. Indeed, the sharpest criticism that can be made of India's post-independence measures for agrarian reform is that they were rooted mainly in the conventional wisdom of the colonial era.

Inability to Incorporate Alternative Approaches

Having established limited goals for agrarian reform, the promoters of agrarian reform and land reform were further constrained by the means adopted to implement such changes in the traditional land systems as were eventually enacted into law. As earlier emphasized, they used colonial legacy institutions to draft and implement reform legislation and they used colonial administrative procedures, rules, and regulations to gather data concerning rights in land. In the process, the advocates of agrarian reform in India pursued strategies that were peculiarly detached from other models of reform already evident. One searches in vain in the historical record for evidence that the Planning Commission, or other institutions of government in New Delhi and in the states, debated the advisability or feasibility within Indian conditions of concepts of agrarian reform that had been made operative elsewhere, especially in Japan.[29]

Failure to Learn from Procedures Used in Japan.
Because the post-World War II Japanese agrarian reform was carried out under a directive issued by a foreign power backed by an army of occupation, the Japanese experience of reform could have been dismissed by Indian policy makers as irrelevant to conditions in the Indian democracy following Indian independence. Whatever their reasons, the historical record suggests that, with the exception of recommendations made in the aborted Fifth Five Year Plan, Indian government officials did not give favorable consideration to the agrarian reform implementation techniques used successfully in Japan.

Nevertheless, agrarian conditions in India were comparable to conditions in pre-reform Japan. "In pre-reform Japan, for example,

---

29. This is not to ignore some attempts to derive inspiration from the agricultural policies of other countries -- for example, the laudatory description of collective farming in the People's Republic of China that was put forward in Nagpur in 1959 at the annual national meeting of the Congress Party.

tenant farmers generally assumed all risks of production. The tenants themselves, without any assistance from their landlords, provided the seed, the implements, and the labor. The tenants provided their own homesteads and sheds; they paid all taxes and assessments, except for the land tax, and were not compensated by landlords for improvements made on the land. Japanese tenants held land for short periods under contractual conditions that permitted landlords to evict them at will, and had to turn over to their landlords between fifty and sixty percent of the crop."[30] Clearly, these conditions in pre-reform Japan were similar to conditions in many regions of India when India gained freedom from Britain.

The implementation of agrarian reform measures in India could have benefitted from careful examination of the means by which agrarian reform was carried out in post-World War II Japan. Wolf Ladejinsky, the architect of that reform, realized that an effective reform must be quick and decisive. Accordingly, in the Japanese case, local land commissions were established at the village level and were designed, consciously, to favor persons near the base of the agrarian hierarchy. The local land commissions were comprised of five tenants, three landlords, and two owner-cultivators. These relative proportions were set by the state and elections were carried out at the village level. "The governing assumption was that the villagers themselves knew better than outsiders who owned and tilled the land in their own communities. This eliminated the time-consuming need to establish a complex and easily circumvented administrative apparatus."[31] Thus, the speedy nature of agrarian reform in Japan was derived from a bold and innovative plan to entrust village committees with the primary responsibility for making the decisions concerning the redistribution of 30 million plots of land.[32] The guiding principle was to confer on villagers the power and responsibility previously appropriated by landlords. And, the villagers of Japan demonstrated an ability not matched in courts of law to take the necessary steps to transform the land system. By contrast, whatever its intent, the

---

30. F. Tomasson Jannuzi and James T. Peach, *The Agrarian Structure of Bangladesh: An Impediment to Development,* (Boulder, Colorado: Westview Press, 1980), pp. 68-69.

31. Ibid., p. 69.

32. Louis J. Walinsky, editor, *Agrarian Reform as Unfinished Business: The Selected Works of Wolf Ladejinsky,* (London: Oxford University Press, 1977), p. 363.

Government of India, sought to carry out agrarian reform by giving authority to people and institutions who were unable to break free of rules, procedures, and precedents in law that could only delay and, therefore, deny the quick implementation of whatever reforms were enacted into law.

Failure to Respond to Definitions Offered by Wolf Ladejinsky. From the time of his first visit to India in 1952 until his death in India in 1975, Wolf Ladejinsky strove to convince all who would listen to him that agrarian reform and land reform were key instruments of public policy, instruments critical to the transformation of rural India and the economic development of the country as a whole. However, unlike Albert Mayer (a principal architect of India's Community Development program), Ladejinsky was unable to establish a close relationship with India's first Prime Minister, Jawaharlal Nehru -- a classic means during the first decade following independence of influencing public policy in India.[33] Moreover, notwithstanding his persistent efforts over the years, including his periodic reports to the Planning Commission and his published articles in the *Economic and Political Weekly* of Bombay, Ladejinsky never was able to shape bureaucratic perceptions of agrarian reform and land reform either within the central government of India or in the states. If Ladejinsky's record in fostering land reform in Japan was steeped in glory, his corresponding record in India was dismal, as he, himself, recognized. Indeed, he was known to have been moved to tears on at least one occasion[34] by his inability to convince officials in the Indian bureaucracy to pursue a program of agrarian reform rooted in his concept of "land to the tiller."

Failure to Respond to Definitions Offered by Erven J. Long. Erven J. Long, who worked in India in the 1950s, was a sensitive observer of

---

33. Contrasting Wolf Ladejinsky and Albert Mayer, Tarlok Singh (an influential Member of the Planning Commission from 1950 to 1967), who worked with both men, has said that "Ladejinsky focused narrowly on the peasant farmer and tenant and how they might be given secure rights in land, whereas Mayer had an extended vision concerning how an entire village community might be developed." [Tarlok Singh, Interview, New Delhi, January 23, 1989.]

34. As reported to the author in a New Delhi interview on March 11, 1989, by Tarzie Vitachi, a Sri Lankan journalist and former official of UNICEF, who had come to know Ladejinsky in the 1960s.

the Indian attempt to promote agrarian reform and land reform.[35] He argued at the time that agrarian reform and land reform should be designed not only to meet political requirements (including social justice), but also to ensure increases in productivity. Long suggested that social scientists, including agricultural economists, had been remiss in not establishing guidelines concerning precisely how various measures of agrarian reform might contribute to productivity goals in agriculture. Furthermore, he argued that, because the potential productivity effects of land reform had not been delineated, land reform legislation was being enacted in the Indian states "largely in an informational vacuum regarding its economic bases."[36]

For Long, the critical underlying issue with respect to agrarian reform had to do with the size of the unit of production in agriculture one ought to establish to meet productivity needs in a developing economy. And, he dared to question the then operative assumption in India that there was a tremendous efficiency advantage in large-scale operations. This assumption, which had been part of the conventional wisdom permeating the recommendations of the Royal Commission on Agriculture in India, 1928, reigned supreme in India in the 1950s. It was used by proponents of agrarian reform who favored consolidation of landholdings and the development of a range of cooperative institutions, including joint cooperative farming. The same assumption was also employed by opponents of land reform who argued against ceilings on the size of agricultural holdings on the grounds that ceilings would reduce the size of operational units and, thereby, reduce agricultural productivity. Meanwhile, Long saw that even proponents of "land to the tiller" were reluctant to predicate land reform on that construct alone for fear that the result would be the proliferation of small units of production, units already categorized as uneconomic holdings, the bane of traditional agriculture in India.

Long was not prepared, automatically, to accept reasoning based on the assumption of a highly positive relationship between size of farm operations and agricultural productivity. He argued that that assumption

---

35. In the 1950s, Long was the Group Leader of a University of Tennessee team working in India under contract to the International Cooperation Administration, a predecessor agency of the United States Agency for International Development.

36. Erven J. Long, "The Economic Basis of Land Reform in Under-developed Economies," *Land Economics* 37, no. 2, May 1961, pp. 113-125.

was based on a misinterpretation of the economics of so-called Western agriculture.[37] Long went on to suggest that his own research had shown that, though the size of a farm was, conventionally, "highly related to operator income, productivity per acre of land was inversely related to size of farm."[38] And, he said that, based on his own observations in India, even large state-owned farms produced little if any more per acre than small farms in the same locality.

Moreover, argued Long, data had now been gathered in India for samples of one hundred to two hundred farms per state in selected areas of West Bengal, Uttar Pradesh, the Punjab, Orissa, Andhra Pradesh, Bombay and Madras. And, this data "showed a very decided inverse relationship between the size of farm and value of output per acre."[39] This notwithstanding, Long was loathe to suggest that his data proved an inverse relationship between size of farm and productivity per acre. He said that he had cited the data "merely to prove that the general presumption of a highly positive relationship which underlies most land reform discussions is extremely suspect. This presumption is equally evident in the arguments for cooperative farming and in the argument that little can be done to increase the agricultural productivity of a nation of very small farms."[40] In short, Erven Long's sojourn in India left him with a belief, based on the weight of evidence that he had gathered, that the best outcome of land reform in India would be one that fostered the development of small farms (complemented by an agricultural research-extension program and a set of supporting services to be provided either by government or cooperative institutions). And, Long said that, on the basis of his observations and study in India, he suspected that "a system of owner-operated farms of such size as to require family labor only would contribute the maximum toward political and social stability."[41] What is striking about Long's observations, published in 1961, is their divergence from the conventional wisdom of the time, a time when it was presumed in the Planning Commission and elsewhere that large units of cultivation were inherently superior in their productivity potential than small units. There is no evidence to suggest that officials within the Government of India took cognizance of Long's dissenting judgement

---

37. Ibid., p. 115.
38. Ibid.
39. Ibid.
40. Ibid.
41. Ibid., p. 115.

concerning the then dominant paradigm or of his warning that land reform needed to be perceived as a public policy designed to contribute to productivity increases as well as to social justice.

Failure to Respond to Definitions Offered by Daniel Thorner. Daniel Thorner and his wife, Alice Thorner, were among the foreign scholars who demonstrated repeatedly their understanding of agrarian reform issues in the subcontinent. Together, they worked assiduously to gather first hand impressions and data from the countryside concerning the post-independence struggle in India to reach consensus about how the traditional land systems of the country could be restructured to serve the interests of actual cultivators in rural areas and to meet the national need for a more productive agricultural sector.

In the 1950s, Thorner's lectures at the Delhi School of Economics[42] confirmed his knowledge of the evolution of India's historical land systems, his understanding of the difficulties associated with any attempt made to transform those systems, and, above all, his empathy for people in the countryside, especially for those at the base of the agrarian hierarchy in land. Many of his observations then have stood the test of time and are relevant to any contemporary assessment of India's effort to restructure its agrarian society by means of agrarian reform.

In his later writings, Thorner not only assessed what had been achieved in agrarian reform, but also vigorously asserted his own sense of what had not been achieved and of what ought to be achieved if the Republic of India were to fulfill its promise to itself to empower the people in the country and, thereby, to enable them to be full participants in economic progress. By 1960, Thorner knew that, notwithstanding the immense and unprecedented wave of agrarian reform legislation in the first decade following independence, the hierarchy of interests in land in rural India remained essentially intact. Whereas he had hoped that large landholders who had been permitted to retain substantial holdings would be engaged in "the reorganization and intensification of production on their land," he saw that, instead, such landholders still found it "simpler and more lucrative to give out much of their land on rent ..." to petty tenants and sharecroppers.[43] Thorner also saw that there was a persistent

---

42. Daniel Thorner, *The Agrarian Prospect in India*, (Delhi: Delhi University Press, 1956).

43. Daniel Thorner and Alice Thorner, *Land and Labour in India*, (Bombay: Asia Publishing House, 1962), p. 3.

paradox operative in the countryside by which small landholders with insecure rights in land, still in the grip of large landholders, were denied the opportunity to develop lands tilled by them, while the large landholders did "far less than they might to modernize production on that part of their land" that they farmed directly, albeit with hired laborers.[44]

Describing conditions that he had observed in the countryside after the spate of legislation for agrarian reform, Thorner said that superior landholders continued the practice of giving out substantial portions of their holdings to sharecroppers for purposes of cultivation, and that "the work and costs of cultivation right through the eventual harvesting and threshing are borne by the cropsharers."[45] When it came time to harvest the crop, said Thorner, it was still the custom, legislation to regulate and reduce rents notwithstanding, for the landlord to demand a 50 percent share -- which, in practice, generally meant that he claimed at least two-thirds of the produce while the sharecropper retained about one-third.

Commenting on what had, thus far, been accomplished, Thorner expressed his dismay that the most basic aim of agrarian reform, to register actual tillers (as tenants having permanent occupancy rights to land) and to bring them into direct relationship with the state, had not happened. This was his way of saying also that landholding intermediaries had not been abolished, notwithstanding propaganda to the contrary. Instead, he noted, "intermediaries of one sort or another continue to remain very much present in India."[46] Even in Uttar Pradesh, where the *State's Zamindari Abolition Act of 1950* had been heralded as a landmark event, Thorner indicated that rights in land were still concentrated in the hands of traditional landholders. In summary judgement, Thorner said that, in essence, throughout India "the bigger people have held on to a lot of land, and they are getting others to cultivate it for them. In many states, in fact, tenancy continues to be open, blatant and flagrant (Punjab, Andhra, Madras, Mysore, etc.). In terms of their announced aims, the land reforms in India since 1947 have, by and large, failed."[47]

---

44. Ibid.

45. Ibid., p. 4.

46. Ibid., p. 5.

47. Ibid. Though Thorner's judgement concerning the failure of land reforms was made more than thirty years ago, only a few years before his premature death, it remains credible even in the 1990s -- the more so, perhaps,

(continued...)

In pronouncing the failure of land reform, Thorner made plain that the reform measures had not succeeded in providing secure rights in land for the actual tiller. It was central to Thorner's vision of agrarian reform and land reform that rights in land should not be conferred on ex-intermediaries, or other landholders, who did not themselves till the land in their possession (while also being resident in the vicinity of their holdings). He therefore deplored the fact that, even after reform measures had been enacted and implemented, non-tilling absentee landlords persisted throughout India.

Thorner understood that there was a widespread feeling in India that manual labor was degrading. "In the villages," he said, "there is one sure sign by which successful cultivators tend to show that their economic condition is improving and that they now wish to raise their social standing: they, and the members of their families, stop doing the field work; instead, they engage others to do it for them, or they give the land out to tenants or cropsharers."[48] But, stressed Thorner, "Once you absolve the so-called cultivator from tilling, you leave the door open for all manner of subterfuge and for easy violation of land reform acts."[49]

It was no surprise to Thorner that the legislation for agrarian reform and land reform that was enacted in the states was designed to preserve and protect the interests of large landholders. As he put it, "At all levels of government in India from the village to the state capital to the national capital, the larger holders have been very powerful."[50] However, he deplored the fact that the legislation in the states had permitted landholders to be registered as personal cultivators on lands actually tilled by sajhidars (that is, "helpers" functioning as sharecroppers, but lacking even that formal designation and recognition of their role). Concluded Thorner, India had not had a land reform "that could conceivably pave the way for a period of rapid agricultural development."[51] And, he regretted the fact that attempts had been made by the Government of India to make conditions in the countryside look better after reform legislation had been enacted by creating what he called an agricultural

---

47. (...continued)
because his principal criticisms have subsequently been echoed and endorsed, ironically, by the Government of India itself in the 1970s and 1980s.

48. Ibid., p. 6.
49. Ibid., pp. 6-7.
50. Ibid., p. 6.
51. Ibid., p. 8.

revolution by census redefinition. He said that if India's land problem was to be resolved it would "require more than census redefinition."[52]

Like Erven Long and Wolf Ladejinsky, Thorner derived his knowledge of conditions in rural areas of India by means of field investigations, including thousands of interactions with ordinary cultivators. Like his friend, Dr. Harold Mann, who had given testimony before the Royal Commission on Agriculture in India, 1928, Thorner believed that Indian agriculture would not reach its full potential until authority in the countryside was passed from vested interests to bona fide tillers.[53] And, like Mann, he recognized that there was no precedent for such a change in the modern history of India -- nor would there be in his lifetime.

Thorner's forthright assessment of the failure of agrarian reform and land reform in India and his vision of reform measures that would empower the actual tiller of the soil have been widely accepted by intellectuals within and outside of India. However, his judgments, advice, and counsel were not embraced by many key players in the shaping of post-independence land policy in India: key players including officials of the Government of India (for example, Tarlok Singh) and American exponents of technology-driven rural development (for example, Douglas Ensminger of The Ford Foundation) who considered Thorner to be too radical in his vision of what ought to be done to transform rural India.

Failure to Respond to Guidance Offered by Indigenous Critics. Whatever has been said by non-citizen critics of India's attempt to legislate and implement agrarian reform and land reform, indigenous criticism has known no bounds. It is a credit to India's system of democratic governance that, over time, the most pointed questions concerning the definition, the direction, and the scope of agrarian reform in India have persistently been generated endogenously by civil servants working within the structure of the government. Men like P.S. Appu,[54]

52. Ibid., p. 150.

53. In this context, see: Daniel Thorner, *The Shaping of Modern India,* (New Delhi: Allied Publishers Private Limited, 1980). This volume was put together by Alice Thorner after her husband's death.

54. P.S. Appu, a former Land Reforms Commissioner of the Government of India, was among the dedicated civil servants who believed that agrarian reform should be promoted in India not only to ensure social justice, but also to promote agricultural growth. He argued persistently that unless agrarian
(continued...)

B.S. Raghavan,[55] D. Bandhyopadhyay,[56] and K.B. Saxena[57] have raised questions concerning the possible causal relationship between failed reforms and outbursts of agrarian unrest, have provided evidence exposing the extra-legal means employed by the landholding elite to thwart the intent of land reform, and have offered guidance to the central government and to the states concerning the best means of implementing reforms, means that would simultaneously confer new rights in land to peasant cultivators and provide the basis for a more productive agricultural economy.

Moreover, many other persons both within and outside the Government of India have contributed over the years to the process by which agrarian reform and land reform efforts have been systematically evaluated. It truly can be said, then, that the perceived shortcomings in the design and implementation of agrarian reform and land reform in India occurred in spite of the fact that both adequate analysis of the problems and internal

---

54.(...continued)
structural change was effected in India, establishing a new man-land relationship in the countryside and "assuring to millions of small cultivators the fruits of their labour, investments and initiative ...", agriculture in many regions of the country would continue to stagnate. [The quotation included here is from an article written originally for *The Statesman,* July 30, 1973. The article was later incorporated in a volume containing other writings by Appu. See: P.S. Appu, *Agrarian Structure and Rural Development,* (New Delhi: India, Cabinet Secretariat, Department of Personnel and Administrative Reforms, May 1975).]

55. B.S. Raghavan (IAS), during his distinguished career as a civil servant, was a primary author of the 1969 report in the Ministry of Home Affairs, Research and Policy Division: "The Causes and Nature of Current Agrarian Tensions." That report first alerted the Government of India to the relationships between failed agrarian reform, raised expectations of change in existing conditions in rural areas, and agrarian unrest. The report's circulation within the Government of India led to the Chief Ministers' Conferences on Land Reform in 1969 and 1970.

56. D. Bandhyopadhyay was the IAS officer most responsible for helping to conceptualize and implement (in the late 1970s and 1980s) the tenurial reform known as Operation Barga in West Bengal.

57. K.B. Saxena (IAS) was for many years "a voice crying in the wilderness" of Bihar; later in the 1980s, he was the Joint Secretary, Rural Development (Land Reforms) in the central government of India. In his various roles within government, Saxena was a constant advocate for reform measures designed to benefit the rural poor (tenants-at-will, sharecroppers and landless agricultural laborers).

criticism of proposed solutions were available to policy makers. In taking stock now of what has and has not been accomplished in this sphere of public policy, one cannot ignore the fact that even the best internal advice and criticism could not, and did not, produce the necessary initiatives in the states either to implement such reforms as were in fact enacted into law or to establish the basis for new, more meaningful reforms. Even the most wise and dedicated of India's civil servants could not work a revolution from within the bureaucracy -- not in circumstances where the forces opposed to change in the existing structure of power continued to occupy the commanding heights of India's political economy at the village, state and national levels.

Inability to Digest
Operation Barga's Message

Even in the midst of failure to transform India's land systems, there were what might be called qualified success stories. One such was Operation Barga, a tenurial reform carried out in West Bengal in the late 1970s and early 1980s under the leadership of the Minister for Land Reforms, Shri Benoy Chowdhury, assisted by D. Bandhyopadhyay of the Indian Administrative Service.

Operation Barga was designed by the Left Front government in West Bengal along lines that would have been favored by the late Daniel Thorner who had argued for reforms, where appropriate, that would redistribute rights in land, as distinct from land. That is to say, Operation Barga did not employ the taking of land from one person (with or without compensation to the landholder) and the giving of it to another, either a sharecropper or landless agricultural laborer. Instead, Operation Barga involved only a tenurial reform by which sharecroppers were registered as the tillers of the land in their cultivating possession at a given time. Having been so registered, the sharecroppers (bargadars) were given security of tenure on the land. That is to say, the bargadars of West Bengal were given de jure status on the lands that they had taken in for purposes of cultivation from superior landholders (raiyats, including landlords, who had a permanent right to land, the rough equivalency of ownership). Bargadars could no longer be evicted from their sharecropped lands at the whim of a superior landholder, even though bargadars were still obligated to share their produce with the superior landholder.

Insufficient time has elapsed to confirm whether Operation Barga can be classified as an unqualified success story. Operation Barga has surely been a political success. It enabled the Left Front government in West Bengal to establish its bona fides with an important constituency of the rural poor, thereby paving the way for the Left Front's electoral success in recent general elections. Meanwhile, the economic returns on this tenurial reform remain, at best, inconclusive. Nevertheless, steps have been taken to ensure that the newly registered sharecroppers receive supporting services. For example, the Left Front government claims to have invested in the development of irrigation facilities. There were said to be only 78,000 shallow tube wells in West Bengal when the Left Front first came to power in 1977. Ten years later there were said to be 225,000 shallow tube wells. "And, while 65 percent of West Bengal's arable land remains unirrigated, the continuing investment in minor irrigation has already brought some positive results. In 1987, West Bengal became the second largest rice producer in India after the southern state of Andhra Pradesh."[58]

Measures complementary to Operation Barga were initiated by the Left Front government to regulate and reduce rental shares (paid by bargadars to their landlords), to secure improved wages for landless agricultural laborers, and to strengthen local government (village panchayat) institutions. While it cannot be claimed that rural West Bengal has been transformed by means of these measures, the Left Front has established its own nexus with more than a million sharecroppers and large numbers of landless laborers as well. This has enabled the government to solidify its hold on power -- not by retaining its traditional base in Calcutta but by following a rural-oriented strategy rooted in tenurial reform.

In the context of India's long-term effort to carry out agrarian reform and land reform, it is striking that it took thirty years for any Indian state to take concrete steps to give de jure recognition to the rights of sharecroppers. Without the persistent efforts of D. Bandhyopadhyay in the 1980s, it is doubtful whether this experiment in tenurial reform would have been put into effect. What is more, no other state in India has sought to emulate the West Bengal initiative, notwithstanding the obvious political returns to the Left Front government in West Bengal.

---

58. F. Tomasson Jannuzi, *India in Transition*, p. 58. [The quote cites data from Indranil Banerjie, "The Red Stranglehold," *India Today*, April 15, 1987, p. 46.]

A Lost Opportunity

The historical record of India's post-independence attempt to promote agrarian reform confirms that those policy makers who were prepared to legislate and implement reform measures never fully understood that they were engaged in revolutionary activity. At every level of government, especially in the first decade after independence when political leaders were filled with hubris at the prospect of transforming the agrarian structure of India within the period of a few five year plans, agrarian reform was contemplated as if it were "something that a government proclaims on any fine morning -- that it gives land to the tenants as it might give pensions to old soldiers or as it might reform the administration of justice."[59] In fact, to engage in agrarian reform (however defined) is to take a revolutionary step, one that "passes power, property, and status from one group in the community to another."[60] If the government of a country is dominated or strongly influenced by landholders, the very persons whose powers and prerogatives are to be curtailed by agrarian reform, no one should expect effective measures of reform to be enacted or, even if they could be successfully enacted, to be implemented.

If the proponents of agrarian reform never fully contemplated or understood the revolutionary implications of reform measures, we now know that the objects of those measures, those at the apex of the hierarchy of interests in land, fully appreciated that agrarian reform (however defined and implemented) had revolutionary portent. With this in mind, the opponents of reform have struggled for more than forty years to delay and deny by every conceivable means reforms that would threaten their traditional dominance in the countryside and their political power in the country as a whole. Moreover, because the proponents of agrarian reforms tried to effect them by permissive, non-coercive, democratic methods, the opponents of reform were accorded additional de jure means of resisting whatever change that could be contemplated in existing conditions. In such circumstances -- with the central government's coercive powers constrained by the constitution, and in the absence of rural organizations of tenants-at-will, sharecroppers and landless agricultural laborers pressing for change from below -- it was

---

59. J.K. Galbraith, "Conditions for Economic Change in Under-developed Countries," *Journal of Farm Economics,* Volume 33, 1951, pp. 689-96.
60. Ibid.

inevitable that the reforms would have negligible effect on the traditional hierarchy of interests in land.

In retrospect, the goals of agrarian reform and land reform, as designed and enacted in India, are amorphous. The achievements are obscure. The omissions are obvious.

First, agrarian reform and land reform legislation, as enacted in the states, did not alter significantly the traditional hierarchy of interests in land in rural India. Neither landholding intermediaries in East India nor landlords in other regions of India were abolished by means of agrarian reform or land reform.[61] This is not to ignore changes that have indeed occurred in the agrarian hierarchy of interests in land throughout India. Most of these changes have occurred for reasons that can be attributed to the indirect effects of agrarian reform: effects associated, for example, with the progressive process by which people at the base of the agrarian hierarchy have mobilized to express their interests and to promote change in existing conditions.[62] Moreover, while it can be said that many of the largest absentee landlords either no longer exist or have had their traditional powers curtailed, the legislation for agrarian reform and land reform enacted in the Indian states was designed, mainly, to preserve and protect to the extent possible the powers and prerogatives of the landholding elite. And, this it did accomplish.

Second, agrarian reform and land reform, however specified and enacted into law in the states, were not designed effectively to address the agricultural production goals imbedded in national policy documents. The belated recognition by the central government in 1969 that agrarian reform and land reform needed to be designed to complement technology-driven rural development programs was insufficient to reverse policies dating to the colonial era, policies that had maintained an administrative and conceptual dichotomy between agrarian reform and agricultural development.

Third, agrarian reform and land reform, as outlined in the various five year plans, were separated conceptually and literally from competing paradigms of economic development and poverty alleviation. Thus, neither the national program for Community Development during the First

---

61. The one possible exception to this generalization may be what happened to landlords in the State of Kerala, as earlier noted.

62. Change in the agrarian hierarchy of interests in land has been influenced by other phenomena as well, not least the worsening man-to-land ratio since independence as the country's population has more than doubled.

and Second Five Year Plans nor the Integrated Rural Development Program (IRDP) in the Sixth and Seventh Plans was linked conceptually or programmatically to agrarian reform and land reform as drafted and enacted into law in the states.[63]

Finally, agrarian reform and land reform, as conceived and as partially implemented, ignored generally the interests and needs of people at the base of the agrarian hierarchy of interests in land -- including tens of millions of tillers of the soil lacking secure rights in land both before and after reforms were legislated and partially implemented in the states. That is to say, agrarian reform and land reform did not generally confer new benefits on tenants-at-will, sharecroppers and landless agricultural laborers. These categories of actual tillers were placed outside of the scope of reform legislation as it was designed and implemented in the states, notwithstanding the periodic efforts to provide some land to the landless.

---

63. While men like D. Bandhyopadhyay warned that "IRDP and land reform should not be treated as two programmes operating in mutual exclusion ...," poverty alleviation programs, including the Integrated Rural Development Program (IRDP), in the Sixth and Seventh Plans were designed as if redistributive land reform and security of tenure had nothing to do with poverty alleviation. [See: D. Bandhyopadhyay, "Direct Intervention Programmes for Poverty Alleviation in India," (Unpublished Manuscript).]

6

The Persistent Dilemma

Establishing Consensus Definitions
of Economic Development,
Agrarian Reform and Land Reform

In its essence, the rhetorical commitment of those who led India to political freedom in 1947 was to take the steps necessary to ensure that India's post-colonial political economy was transformed. The stated goal was to establish a modern political economy within which new thresholds of opportunity would be crossed by millions of people within a socioeconomic environment conditioned by principles of social justice made operative under law. Regrettably, articulating that broad, rhetorical goal was easier than reaching consensus concerning the steps that would have to be taken by the independent Government of India to produce the favorable transformation.

The failure of the governing elites of India to reach consensus concerning how precisely they would work after independence to transform India's political economy should not surprise anyone. After all, modern economists still struggle to define economic development and have themselves reached no consensus concerning how best to achieve economic progress within an environment of social justice. Nevertheless, the absence of a persistent, consensus definition of economic development in modern India has meant that the governing elites have used a variety of terms -- modernization, economic growth, and growth with equity -- as if these terms implied similar processes and were synonymous in meaning. This has compounded confusion and has made it difficult for any Government of India to establish clearly understood development goals that were capable of implementation.

With the wisdom of hindsight, we now know that if a government hopes to implement economic development, it must establish a working consensus within its own counsels concerning the functional meaning of the term. After all, for any government, the definition employed will delineate goals and establish the means by which the state and the people can measure progress toward achieving them. The same principle holds, I believe, for the definitions employed for agrarian reform and land reform. From the time of the independence struggle, many Indian leaders included the transformation of India's traditional, hierarchical, inegalitarian agrarian economy as a part of their expressed goal of changing the post-colonial political economy. They often used the terms agrarian reform and land reform, but they established no consensus definition for these terms. Confusion was compounded. A lack of consensus definitions contributed to failures. It seems apparent that the prospects for economic development, agrarian reform and land reform in India would be considerably enhanced, even at this late date, if policy makers sought to establish consensus definitions of these and other terms that have been used casually and without precision of meaning for so many years.

Ideally, economic development needs to be perceived by those who govern as a holistic concept. It embraces the idea of aggregate increases in income within a region or country, even though its meaning extends beyond economic growth to imply changes in the social system of a society: changes that affect distribution of income, opportunity and power. Used this way, economic development suggests the need for changes in traditional institutions, including institutions within agrarian societies that govern the way people relate to the land. Used this way, economic development also suggests the need for fundamental changes in the way people perceive themselves in relation to others with whom they live and work. Above all, the term economic development connotes a dynamic process of change -- a process whose effects can be, at the same time, both benign (increasing peoples' economic well-being, for example) and disruptive (contributing to ferment, tension, and political and economic uncertainties).

Regrettably, following independence, India's policy makers in the central government did not recognize that economic development, defined as a process embracing the need for change in existing conditions, would have both benign and disruptive consequences. They did not appreciate that their invocations concerning the need for change in existing conditions would be perceived to have benign consequences only by those welcoming change and disruptive consequences by those fearing change. In particular, India's policy makers did not appreciate adequately that the leadership within the politically dominant Congress Party, derived substantially from the landholding elite, would itself fear any changes in existing conditions that seemed likely to diminish its own power and the prerogatives of power. We are better able today, as we reflect on the agrarian reform guidelines that were delineated by the central government and implemented variably in the states, to appreciate how the very idea of agrarian reform would be perceived by dominant landholders as having negative implications, disruptive of socioeconomic conditions favoring them, and by the prospective beneficiaries of agrarian reform as having positive implications, providing the promise of a new, more equitable socioeconomic order.

Reflecting on the decisions of those who articulated agrarian policy goals after independence and on the difficulty of realizing those goals within the then prevailing hierarchy of interests in land, I have had no illusions that agrarian reform and land reform could easily be implemented. At the same time, it has seemed evident to me that the promotion of rural economic development in India requires not only the application of modern science to agriculture, but also the transformation of the agrarian hierarchy so as to produce a new system of political economy within which the benefits of economic progress would accrue broadly to the actual tillers of the soil: a system which would ensure that those who labored on the land and invested in it received the full benefits of their labor and investment. Moreover, I have believed that there is no better means of establishing the preconditions for rural economic development in modern India than to foster programs of agrarian reform and land reform -- being careful in the process to design regionally differentiated reforms that take into account variations in India's historical land systems and variations in the socioeconomic conditions associated with those land systems.

In my writings, I have used agrarian reform within a broad definitional frame to refer to a constellation of national programs designed to effect structural changes in the hierarchy of interests in land: changes that transform historical land systems and the socioeconomic environments associated with those systems. Used this way, agrarian reform can be a comprehensive term applying to all of those programs promoted since independence by the Government of India to abolish certain kinds of landlordism; to effect tenancy reforms by which the interests of those lacking security of tenure on land can be enhanced; to consolidate agricultural holdings so as to produce larger units of production; to promote the development of cooperatives of various kinds; and to effect ceilings on the size of agricultural holdings with a view toward distributing lands made surplus by this process to landless laborers.

Land reform, within this definitional frame, can be subsumed within agrarian reform. It can be a component of agrarian reform by means of which structural change would be effected by taking land (with or without compensation payments) from a landholder who enjoys secure, de jure rights in land[1] and giving it to another person, or persons, under terms prescribed by law. And, even when it is associated with the breaking up of large holdings and their redistribution in smaller units, land reform does not necessarily lead to a reduction in market output or savings.

Agrarian reform, defined to encompass land reform, can be both equity oriented and consistent with those economic development goals that emphasize raising productivity and increasing employment. Indeed, when defined to encompass tenancy reforms as well, agrarian reform can encourage increased investment by those cultivators who become the beneficiaries of increased security. As The World Bank suggested,

The conversion of tenants into owner-operators generally leads to a more efficient and more equitable form of production organization than tenancy. .... Such reforms improve income distribution by shifting income away from the landlords to small-scale producers, often those among the lowest income groups. The more secure producers tend to invest part of their higher earnings in their holdings -- thus raising the level of investment in agricultural production -- whereas absentee landlords frequently invest in off-farm activities. Finally, greater security enables tenants to benefit from appropriate technological changes, instead of being displaced when landlords find it to their advantage to adopt a different technology. The financial returns to the landlords from using machines and hired labor may be high, but the returns to the economy are usually higher from labor-intensive operations undertaken by smallholders.[2]

---

1. In India, as earlier emphasized, to have de jure, occupancy rights in land is to enjoy the rough equivalent of ownership rights in the West.

2. The quotation is from an internal document of The World Bank issued in 1974. The views cited clearly conform to those of the late Wolf

(continued...)

Establishing a Conceptual Frame
for Agrarian Reform

There is still time for India to establish its own conceptual frame for agrarian reform -- a frame that derives broadly from an understanding of the content and record of agrarian reform in the twentieth century as it was conceived and implemented not only in India, but also in other countries, including Japan, Taiwan, South Korea, and even the Peoples's Republic of China, under varying conditions and different historical land systems.

If Indian leaders dared to establish anew their own conceptual frame for agrarian reform by assessing the successes and failures of agrarian reform within and outside of the country, it would become apparent that agrarian reform, however defined and made applicable within a specific context, can have many connotations. Agrarian reform can produce conditions in the countryside of a developing country that enhance the prospects of social justice. That is to say, it is obvious from the historical record that agrarian reform can be a means by which abstract notions of social and distributive justice can be made tangible -- conferring to its beneficiaries a new sense of human dignity and self-worth. Yet, however conceived and implemented, agrarian reform can be more than a means of fostering a more just and equitable agrarian society.

Agrarian reform need not be seen only as being equity oriented. Agrarian reform can have clearly defined economic implications. It

---

2.(...continued)

Ladejinsky, then a consultant to the Bank. In the same year, the Bank also laid down specific guidelines concerning the importance that it might attach to the promotion of land reform in some countries. Specifically, the Bank indicated that it might exclude from aid those countries that were not willing to promote land reform policies that the Bank considered to be necessary. [In this context, see: World Bank (IBRD), *Land Reform. A Policy Statement of the International Bank for Reconstruction and Development,* (Washington, D.C.: IBRD, 1974), and World Bank (IBRD), *The Assault on World Poverty,* (Washington,D.C.: IBRD, 1975).] The Bank's guidelines concerning land reform notwithstanding, Robert Cassen and Associates indicated in 1986 that there was little evidence "that the guidelines have significantly affected lending by the Bank or many other donors: few recipients have requested aid for land reform." [Robert Cassen and Associates, *Does Aid Work?* (Oxford: Clarendon Press, 1986), p. 59.]

can be a spur to economic efficiency and increased production by providing secure rights in land (the result either of land reform or tenurial reform) to cultivators who previously lacked incentives to invest in fixed improvements on the land in their cultivating possession. It can take land out of the hands of large landholders who hold land as property, but who are not engaged in agricultural operations, except in the sense that they retain a permanent occupancy right to their land while leasing it in small units to tenant cultivators, either on the basis of money rent or on the basis of sharecropping. In India, such large landholders, however they may appear in agricultural censuses, have little in common with farmers in the industrial economies of the West who engage in large-scale, capital intensive farming. As Doreen Warriner long ago emphasized, the most obvious characteristic of this kind of large landholder (in South Asia) is his monopoly power.[3] By subdividing the holdings of such large landholders and, thereby, eliminating their monopoly power, it is possible to achieve a more equitable distribution of income from the land, a more intensive use of the land, an increased demand for labor, and higher wages for the landless agricultural laborers in a given locality.

Agrarian reform, however conceived and implemented, can also be more than a spur to economic efficiency and increased production. In the Indian context, in which agricultural production and distribution are inextricably linked processes, agrarian reform can be, in some regions, the sine qua non for subsequent economic progress; in other regions, it may be unnecessary. That is to say, in regions where both the need for increasing agricultural output and the need for ensuring more equitable distribution of what is produced are obvious, agrarian reform, especially tenurial reform and/or land reform, can be an essential prerequisite for the transformation of the rural economy so as to foster economic development (as earlier defined). In other regions, like the Punjab, where land is already being tilled mainly by cultivators who enjoy secure rights in land, the land reform and tenurial reform components of agrarian reform may not be needed.

---

3. Doreen Warriner, *Land Reform and Economic Development,* National Bank of Egypt Fiftieth Anniversary Commemoration Lectures, Cairo, 1955, Lecture 2, as reprinted in Carl Eicher and Lawrence Witt, editors, *Agriculture in Economic Development,* (New York: McGraw-Hill, 1964), pp. 280-290.

Whether seen as a sine qua non for economic progress in some regions of India or not, and however defined or put into effect, agrarian reform should not be perceived as a panacea for economic development. As I see it, agrarian reform may be necessary in some regions of India, but it cannot, by itself, be sufficient for rural economic development. That is to say, agrarian reform can be a prerequisite for the introduction of fundamental, socioeconomic change in rural areas. However, it is only a means of promoting change conducive to economic development. Thus, agrarian reform cannot be made synonymous, conceptually, with the entire process of economic development, even when agrarian reform can be demonstrably conducive to rural economic development, as we have defined it.

I believe that agrarian reform should be perceived as being conceptually greater than the sum of its parts. Whether proposed as a means of promoting equity and social justice, as a means of fostering increases in productivity and improved distribution of income, as a prerequisite in some regions for subsequent economic progress, or as only one means by which economic development can be fostered in a society, the concept of agrarian reform has revolutionary portent. Inherently, it both promises and threatens profound change in the existing political economy: change in the existing distribution of rights in land and, as a result, change in the structure of power and status in an agrarian society.

Whatever specific elements of agrarian reform are proposed in a particular locality, the revolutionary portent of agrarian reform will contribute, at least temporarily, to increased unrest in an agrarian society. On the one hand, agrarian reform promises change and, therefore, raises expectations for those at the base of the agrarian hierarchy. These expectations will exceed what can be accomplished, producing frustration among the presumed beneficiaries of reform. Such is the case in some areas of contemporary India where agrarian reform has been promised, but not delivered sufficiently to satisfy the expectations of the rural poor. On the other hand, agrarian reform threatens change for those at the apex of the hierarchy and, therefore, raises fears that are bound to be exaggerated. The proponents of agrarian reform, however they define and qualify their intent, may well appear to those who are the targets of the reform to be promoting a revolutionary redistribution of economic assets and power. In such circumstances, resistance to agrarian reform will be obstinate and persistent over time by those who seek to preserve and protect their own traditional rights in land and related power prerogatives. Such was the case in India when some, after independence, sought to promote agrarian reform -- failing to appreciate at the time that such reforms would be perceived by some to be tantamount to instigating from New Delhi, without centrally administered coercive power under law, a non-violent revolution threatening the existing fabric of political and economic power in rural areas.

Implementing Agrarian Reform
in the 1990s

The Environment for
Central Government Action

Agrarian Reform Delayed Is Agrarian Reform Denied. Agrarian reform delayed is, obviously, agrarian reform denied.[4] There can be no question that the gradual enactment and implementation of India's legislation for agrarian reform and land reform over more than four decades have been, in themselves, an impediment to the process by which change in India's traditional land systems was sought. The quick and decisive implementation of agrarian reform is important if the reform is to have any prospect of effecting change in existing conditions. This means that a government seeking to implement agrarian reform within a democratic system of governance must be prepared, if necessary, to use all of its coercive powers under law to expedite the implementation of reform measures.[5] Gradualism is an enemy of agrarian reform, whatever its defining elements.

In the Indian case, the fact that agrarian reform and land reform were heralded prior to independence by Indian nationalists as means by which the rural economy and polity of India would be transformed was sufficient to cause the landholding elite in rural India to begin to take steps to protect their interests in land and the political power they

---

4. As Erik Eckholm has suggested, "Speed of implementation and the willingness and capacity to act forcefully, appear to be important to the success of reform policies." [Erik Eckholm, "The Dispossessed of the Earth: Land Reform and Sustainable Development," Worldwatch Paper 30, (Washington, D.C.: Worldwatch Institute, 1979), p.33.]

5. This was one of Wolf Ladejinsky's maxims.

derived from control of the land. Indeed, we know that major landholders began disguising the size of their holdings by various means long before independence and, obviously, long before anyone suggested that there should be legislation designed to place a ceiling on personal or family landholdings. In short, we know that Indian landholders, threatened by the prospect of future reforms, began devising means by which such reforms could be thwarted well before India gained freedom from Britain in 1947. Thus, it can also be said that agrarian reform that is anticipated is reform that can easily, thereafter, be nullified.

The Political Will No Longer Exists. There is little evidence to suggest that the Government of India will take meaningful steps in the 1990s, even within the limited ambit of its constitutional authority, to promote the implementation of agrarian reform measures that have already been enacted in law. So far as I know, there are few contemporary proponents of agrarian reform in the Government of India.

While agrarian reform may exist in the 1990s as a residual of state policy to which rhetorical adherence is sometimes given, it will be difficult to take seriously any further exhortations from the central government that ceilings on the size of holdings should be effected in order to give land to the landless or that the rights of tenants should be secured and their rents regulated. Similarly, it will be difficult to understand why in the 1990s the Government of India would continue to reiterate the conventional wisdom of the 1920s that consolidating landholdings remains everywhere important to the modernization of Indian agriculture.[6] What is more, it will be difficult to understand why in the 1990s the Government of India would once again suggest to the states that they take steps to expedite the updating of land records

---

6. As I have earlier emphasized, consolidation of holdings became a primary goal of agrarian reform in British India mainly because the "Terms of Reference" of the Royal Commission on Agriculture in India, 1928, eliminated for political reasons all references to other forms of agrarian reform. Moreover, consolidation of holdings, then and now, has efficacy only in circumstances where the quality of land in a given locality is relatively homogeneous, as in the Punjab and Haryana, where consolidation operations have always been more successful than elsewhere in India. In eastern India, by contrast, where the land quality is heterogeneous, consolidation operations have been difficult to effect for obvious reasons.

to facilitate the implementation of agrarian reform. The mere repetition of such central government exhortations will not at all confirm that anyone in government continues to have interest in promoting agrarian reform and land reform as policy instruments. Instead, one suspects that such exhortations, if repeated in the 1990s, will be in the form of a mantra disconnected from any residual political will to see reform measures implemented in the states.

The Coercive Power of Government Is Diminished. From the outset, the Government of India had limited coercive power under law to effect agrarian reform. The Indian constitution had made agriculture a state subject. Therefore, the primary responsibility for implementing agrarian reform rested with the states. The central government's powers were limited, as in the draft outline to the First Five Year Plan and subsequent five year plans, to providing general guidance to the states concerning the parameters of agrarian reform. It was understood that even this general guidance had to be qualified regionally, state by state, in accordance with the variability of the historical land systems of the subcontinent. The central government, however, was not equipped to offer detailed, variable instructions to the states concerning the appropriate purposes and content of agrarian reform in order to address conditions within their boundaries.

Still constrained in its role by the constitution, the central government is today even less able than earlier either to give explicit guidance to the states concerning the scope and direction of agrarian reform or to compel them to effect specific reforms. Moreover, while the Indian system of governance was originally designed to ensure the dominance of the union government, the federal nature of The Republic of India has been reinforced over many years following the decision in 1956 to redraw the internal boundaries of India in order to establish "linguistic states." The formation of linguistic states had the effect, gradually, of enlarging the powers of states relative to those of the central government. In the 1990s it is evident that the powers of the central government are increasingly being devolved on the states. Indeed, there seems to be a growing approval within India of a system of governance that is based on decentralization of authority and power -- with efforts being made to shift major responsibilities not only from the central government to the states, but also from the states to village-based units of governance. If this process continues, as I suspect it will, the central government will be even weaker than it has been in the past forty years to give direction to programs, including agrarian reform, that are to be effected in the states. In the days ahead, therefore, if agrarian reform and land reform are to be promoted, it appears that the initiative for such reforms -- prompted possibly by village-based proponents of reform measures -- will have to originate with the states.

The Prospect of Providing Land to the Landless is Diminished. Even if ceilings legislation on the size of landholdings were implemented more effectively than in the last several decades, it is unlikely in the days ahead that sufficient land could be made available to the landless and near-landless to provide them with economically viable holdings. There are too many millions of people in these categories to meet their needs for land. While I do not believe that adequate data exist concerning the incidence of landlessness in India in the 1990s, it appears that the landless and near-landless may well constitute the rural majority. If they are the rural majority, it is difficult even to contemplate implementing programs for the landless and near-landless that would be of sufficient magnitude to do more than ameliorate conditions for a few of them. Certainly, there is no past precedent within the frame of existing legislation for agrarian reform of providing more than token amounts of land to some of the landless (and even then mainly without supporting services that could enable the recipients of land to become economically viable landholders). Clearly, for these reasons, there is a diminished prospect of providing land for the landless -- even if there were evidence that providing land to the landless had high priority in contemporary India.

The Prospect of
Central Government Action

Assuming Congress Party-led Governments. The Congress Party has an illustrious history. It is the party of the Independence Movement. It is the party whose leaders and members, even prior to independence, dared to suggest repeatedly that political freedom was a necessary, but not sufficient condition, for economic freedom in the country. It is the party that suggested that agrarian reform could be the critical means by which economic freedom might be conferred on people in rural areas -- particularly those of low social (caste) and economic status at the base of the socioeconomic hierarchy of interests in land. It is also the party whose leaders and policy makers, faced with the problems of governance after independence and with the need to preserve a ruling coalition of diverse interests, progressively diminished the content and meaning of agrarian reform, especially of land reform -- responding in this process to those among its members who were agents of the status quo, rather than agents of change. The proponents of the status quo in the Congress Party had powerful voices in the deliberative bodies of government at the center and in the states, while the proponents of change in India's historical land systems were few in number and, until the late 1960s, were unsupported by voices from the countryside. Moreover, as noted earlier, it was not until 1969 that the Congress Party was formally confronted (by means of a report compiled by the Home Ministry of the Government of India) with the idea that there were rural constituencies of poor peasants who were increasingly prepared to assert their interests and to press (sometimes violently) for secure rights in land and for the enforcement of minimum wages laws.

The response of the Congress Party to pressures from constituencies at the base of the agrarian hierarchy was swift and sure. The party promised to banish poverty in the 1970s and, as the ruling party of government, urged the states to complete expeditiously the programs of agrarian reform and land reform that had earlier been enacted into law. At the same time, the party (using the instruments of governance that it controlled at the center) took steps increasingly to bolster the forces of "law and order" in the countryside, differentiating aribitrarily between the legitimate and illegitimate demands of constituencies of peasants. In the process, there was obvious confusion in the states, and in the body politic, as to whether the central government sought to respond to demands from below by ensuring that changes in existing conditions were effected by means of agrarian reform or by repressing dissent and denigrating dissenters as terrorists seeking to overthrow democratic systems of governance.

In short, the response of the Congress Party to pressure from below in the 1970s and 1980s has been ambivalent; alternately, it has responded to this pressure by employing the policies of the carrot (the development of palliative programs like "Food for Work") and the stick (the use of Border Security Forces to augment the powers of local police to repress "terrorists" in rural areas). As a result, the party, if it clings to power in the 1990s, is ill-equipped institutionally to give new direction to agrarian reform as an instrument of state policy. Its credibility with the people in the countryside is greatly diminished.[7] It is doubtful, given the historical record, that the party can use exhortation for agrarian reform as means of refurbishing its public image in the near future.

Assuming Bharatiya Janata Party led Governments. The Bharatiya Janata Party (BJP) has emerged in recent years as a possible alternative to the Congress Party. Though the party had only two seats in Parliament in 1989, it acquired 119 seats in the general elections of 1991. This notwithstanding, the party's greatest strength has been in northern, Hindi-speaking states, and it seems doubtful that it can form a government at the center in the near future, except in coalition with other parties.

At the present time, The BJP's core members are drawn mainly from urban, rather than rural areas. The party has yet to establish its bona fides in the countryside, except possibly as the party of Hindu revivalism.[8] Its followers are self-described Hindu nationalists who indicate that they would like to alter drastically the system of governance in the country -- amending the constitution so that India ceases to be a secular, democratic republic and is transformed into a Hindu state.[9] The BJP's agenda for action in India is profoundly disturbing of the status quo. Currently, the party is attempting to mobilize votes by encouraging Hindus to assert their identity and to take back their country from the "residual Muslims" of the Mogul era and the "residual secularists" of the British era.

---

7. Gone forever are those days in the 1950s when tenants-at-will, sharecroppers and landless laborers could be summoned by their landlord (a still potent, if legally abolished, zamindar and Congress politician) and instructed, with decisive effect, to vote for the "Party of Gandhi and Nehru."

8. I have consciously referred here to the BJP as a party of Hindu revivalism, rather than as a party of "Hindu fundamentalism." It is an oxymoron to refer to the BJP as a Party of Hindu fundamentalism, as is commonly done. [See, for example, Edward A. Gargan's article entitled "In India, Nationhood Rips Along Old Seams," in *The New York Times,* February 28, 1993, p. E 3.] This is because Hinduism is essentially an inchoate system of belief -- one that does not have core, or fundamentalist, principles.

9. For many members of the Bharatiya Janata Party (BJP), the Indian constitution is mainly a colonial-legacy document, a derivative of the British *Government of India Act of 1935.* The constitution's substantial revision or abrogation could, therefore, be expected if the BJP came to power.

It is possible that in the future the BJP may see strategic advantage in broadening the base of its support in rural areas.[10] This could be attempted by addressing the needs of constituencies of the rural poor (including tenants-at-will, sharecroppers and landless laborers), instead of addressing the interests of the traditional, landholding elites whose allegiance has been to the Congress Party. The fact that the Bharatiya Janata Party has never drawn support from the landholding elite in the countryside could make it easier for the BJP to focus its attention on the rural poor and to promote variants of agrarian reform. However, it is difficult to conceive of the Bharatiya Janata Party, as presently constituted, committing itself to the implementation of existing or new programs of agrarian reform; the party has yet to delineate its agenda in a fashion that would confirm any interest whatsoever in agrarian reform.

Following Operation Barga. The prospects for most programs of agrarian reform, especially land reform modeled after existing legislation in India, are not high in the years ahead, but some scope remains for programs of tenurial reform along lines already partially implemented in West Bengal. This is not to suggest, of course, that land policy in the whole of India can be derived out of the peculiar conditions that have applied in that state. The whole of India cannot be fitted to the Procrustean bed of tenurial policy in any single state.

Having said this, there is a governing principle that can be derived from the record of Operation Barga in West Bengal: namely, that it is easier to effect changes in rights in land than to engage in a full-fledged exercise in land reform -- even in the face of stubborn resistance from superior landholders. That is to say, if a reform is to be implemented in contemporary India within the rule of law, it must be the sort of reform that redistributes rights in land, not land.[11] In this way, resistance from superior landholders can be minimized. After all, tenurial reform need not threaten landholders' permanent

---

10. I am indebted to my fellow economist and colleague in the field of South Asian Studies, Brian Trinque, for raising seriously the notion that the BJP could establish its own nexus with rural constituencies in ways that would amplify its power. [Brian Trinque, Interview, Austin, Texas, February 27, 1993.]

11. Of course, this formulation owes much to the work of the late Daniel Thorner.

occupancy rights in land. It need not even deny landholders the right to give out land for purposes of cultivation to sharecroppers. What it does do, when effected, is to confer new, de jure rights in land to sections of the cultivating peasantry who have thus far been denied such rights in land. This is, of course, a minimum kind of agrarian reform. It is not a radical reform,[12] as envisioned by men like K.T. Shah prior to India's independence. It is not a reform that confers permanent occupancy rights in land to actual tillers who are subordinate to superior landholders. However, it is a "land to the tiller" program, a program that confers additional security of tenure on the tiller. What is more, it is probably the only kind of agrarian reform that could be implemented in contemporary India, assuming that policy makers and opinion leaders in the states had the will to promote it.

Establishing New Means. In any event, if a decision were made in a state to implement tenurial reform (a reform designed, as was Operation Barga, to give security of tenure to actual tillers in the Indian countryside who are not now registered as tenants, and who are outside the scope of existing laws that would protect their interests), the implementation should be effected by new means. That is to say, the implementation should be swift and decisive. There should be no reliance on colonial era rules and procedures: rules and procedures used effectively in the past by opponents of reform to delay and deny reform measures.

One way of expediting tenurial reform would be the issuance of an executive order by the chief minister of a state outlining the scope of the proposed reform. This order would be followed immediately by a declaration of at least the equivalency of a martial law administration in the countryside and the stationing of police and para-military forces in every district of the state.[13]

---

12. Though Operation Barga was instituted by a Left Front government in West Bengal, the reform was enacted into law and implemented within the frame of democratic governance. Moreover, Operation Barga has been criticized by some Marxists as a "bourgeois" democratic reform unworthy of a left-oriented government.

13. This approach need not be inconsistent with the rule of law in a democratic society. As noted earlier, the historical record of agrarian reform, especially land reform, confirms that reforms that are implemented

(continued...)

The next step would be to transfer primary responsibility for implementing the tenurial reform from the state's revenue ministry to village committees comprised of representatives of the local hierarchy of interests in land. Each committee would be elected locally. The policy directive would specify that the committee be comprised of five members, only two of whom could be representatives of landholders who already enjoyed permanent occupancy rights to land. In this way, the majority of committee members would be persons whose rights in land were tenuous or nonexistent.

Entrusting village committees with the responsibility for awarding security of tenure to cultivators would obviate the need for elaborate pre-reform exercises, including cadastral surveys. The governing assumption here is that the villagers themselves in any given locality know better than outsiders who actually tills what holdings in their own communities.[14]

The final step in the process would be the registering of cultivators on the land by representatives of the government and the commitment of the state to the provision of supporting services (including credit at non-usurious rates) for the beneficiaries of the reform.

Electing Minimum Goals. Tenurial reform, if effected along lines indicated above, would not transform the historical land systems of India. It would not transform radically the existing hierarchy of interests in land. It would not be a redistributive land reform that would transfer power and status from traditional landholders (having permanent occupancy rights in land) to new landholders. The window of opportunity for radical reform, if it ever really existed, is long gone. What tenurial reform would do, however, is to confer enhanced rights in land to millions of actual tillers of land in their temporary (unregistered) possession -- land taken in for purposes of cultivation by

---

13.(...continued)
gradually over time are reforms that are easily nullified. The suggested means here is one that recognizes that reform measures that accord power or status in an agrarian society cannot, generally, be effected unless the coercive power of a state is fully mobilized.

14. The speedy execution of land reform in Japan after World War II benefitted from the same approach by which village committees (local land commissions in the case of Japan) were given the primary responsibility for decisions concerning the redistribution of more than 30 million plots of land.

cultivators from superior landholders, usually on contractual understandings that are oral and informal.

The emphasis of such tenurial reform, as noted above, would be on redistributing rights in land, rather than on redistributing land. In the process, tenurial reform would also recognize the importance of small units of production. Indeed, it would validate small farms as appropriate units of production in a country where such units clearly predominate. And, when complemented by supporting services, tenurial reform would demonstrate modern policy makers' awareness that "Land-saving technologies -- improved seed varieties, fertilizers, insecticides and improved weeding -- can usually be applied equally well and efficiently on small farms."[15] Such tenurial reform would make plain that policy makers realize that, under conditions of rapid population growth and abundant supplies of labor, there is economic efficacy in promoting agricultural development emphasizing small farms tilled by labor intensive means -- farms where productivity could be measured per unit of land instead of per unit of labor. Such tenurial reform would recognize that under existing conditions -- where sharecroppers rights in land are insecure,[16] where superior landholders take more than 50 percent of whatever is produced, and where superior landholders do not share the risks and costs of production -- it is difficult to expect that such non-registered tenants, lacking de jure rights in land, will be engaged in agricultural innovation leading to increasing yields. Finally, tenurial reform might put a halt to efforts in many regions of India to eliminate small units of production by promoting consolidation of holdings. Such efforts have not been very successful. They have been resisted by tillers of small farms. They have been favored "mainly by large landholders as a means of getting rid of small farmers ..."[17] and by those in government who still cling to the colonial era notion that only large farms can be farmed

---

15. Peter Dorner, *Land Reform and Economic Development,* (Middlesex, England: Penguin Books, 1972), p. 119.

16. Sharecroppers' rights in land are not merely insecure, of course; they are virtually non-existent. For many years now, it has been said that the incidence of sharecropping has been declining. However, I suspect that data suggesting a decline in sharecropping documents mainly the process by which superior landholders have sought to disguise sharecroppers as hired laborers. If there is a decline in sharecropping in rural India, it may be a decline linked to "definitional obfuscation."

17. K.B. Saxena, Interview, New Delhi, India, February 12, 1989.

efficiently, and that small holdings remain the bane of Indian agriculture.

Looking Ahead to
the Twenty-first Century

The Environment for
Central Government Action

Whatever coalition of interests rules India in the years ahead, it is likely to be distracted for some time from issues pertaining to agrarian reform by other pressing problems. For example, there will be problems posed by the continuing unrest in Kashmir. There will be problems posed by the persistence of communal tensions between Hindus and Muslims in the aftermath of the destruction of the mosque at Ayodhya in 1992 and the subsequent pogrom by Hindu extremists against the Muslims of Bombay. And, there will be problems posed by the persistence of internal debate concerning economic restructuring in the aftermath of pressures in the late 1980s from institutions like the World Bank: pressures designed to encourage the Government of India to liberalize its economy, to reduce the role of state planning, and to minimize bureaucratic controls in the ordering of development priorities. Nevertheless, early in the twenty-first century, if not sooner, there will be increased pressure on any Government of India to come to grips with its land problem. This pressure will be difficult to ignore.

The pressure on the Government of India will be generated anew by people in the countryside: people at the base of the agrarian hierarchy who, already in the early 1990s, constitute the rural majority. Like their counterparts in the late 1960s, 1970s, and 1980s, they will place new demands on those who are above them in the hierarchy of power. With the continuing pressure of population on the land, the stiffening of the terms of tenancy, the continuing evictions of bona fide tenants from the land, the widespread denial of sharecroppers of de jure rights in land, and the growth of landlessness, there will be renewed tension between those who hold land and power and those who struggle below them for subsistence. Within the agrarian hierarchy, there will be a new cycle of violence from below and counter-violence from above. This can be anticipated because the people at the base of the agrarian hierarchy have embraced the idea of the possibility of change in existing conditions. Indeed, it is one of the paradoxes of failed measures of agrarian reform and land reform that they have served, above all, to generate such a potent idea in the Indian countryside -- the idea of the possibility of change in existing conditions. This idea, already evident in the 1960s, is continuing to gain currency in rural India. And, the actions spurred by such an idea will not be as easily contained, as in the past, by government policies based only on the carrot (poverty alleviating palliatives) or the stick (the mobilization of police and para-military forces to repress new demands).

Meanwhile, the power of the traditional elites in the agrarian hierarchy is fading. We have emphasized that agrarian reform, as designed and partially implemented in the post-independence period, has not altered substantially the traditional hierarchy of interests in land. The agrarian reform legislation was designed, to the extent possible, to preserve and protect the interests of superior landholders. Nonetheless, the powers and prerogatives of superior landholders, including absentee landlords, have been eroded progressively over time. They, themselves, threatened by the prospect of change, have taken steps to diversify their portfolios: to rely less on income from land and to invest in manufacturing enterprise and in urban properties. At the same time, persons at or near the base of the agrarian hierarchy have increasingly had the courage to challenge the authority of superior landholders and, occasionally, to acquire secure rights in land for themselves. In the process, lower caste landholders have become a potent force in rural areas -- especially in electoral contests where they have demonstrated their numerical strength relative to higher caste landholders. Thus, the traditional landlord is no longer as dominant a figure in the countryside as he was forty years ago.

This is not to suggest that superior landholders in India have gone quietly into the night of history. They have resisted change in existing conditions by every conceivable means. Indeed, superior landholders, using their own goondas (armed thugs, augmented from time-to-time by local police) and para-military forces, have continued to engage in ruthless repression of all who are below them in the agrarian hierarchy, especially low caste landless laborers (persons conveniently classified as terrorists by those who would deny them even minimum wages as specified in law).

The Prospect of
Central Government Action

Early in the twenty-first century, the Government of India, whatever its ideological roots, will take stock of what has happened in rural areas and what is continuing to happen there. Such a government will understand that votes in general elections[18] cannot be won only by relying on vote banks mobilized within the ambit of the declining coercive power of superior landholders. In such circumstances, recognizing the fading power of traditional landholders, any government at the center[19] will be compelled to establish a nexus with representatives of the rural majority -- those toward the base of the agrarian hierarchy. And, by then, it should be obvious to those who rule that establishing such a nexus can best be done by effecting variants of agrarian reform (as has been demonstrated by the successful land reform in Kerala in the 1970s and by the the successful tenurial reform in the 1980s in West Bengal): variants of reform that address the needs and interests of people whose support the government will need to maintain or to acquire power.

Finally, any future Government of India will have to cope with the pressures posed by a kind of neo-Malthusian crisis. India's population is continuing to grow at an alarming rate -- one that could make India the world's most populous country by the middle of the next century. Even if India does not continue to pursue a policy of self-sufficiency with regard to food grains in the years ahead, it is assumed here that there cannot be exclusive reliance on imported food grains to fill gaps in local production. This will hold true, especially, if scarce foreign exchange must be allocated for such imports. In such circumstances, there will be a need not only to rely on increases in agricultural productivity that may continue to be generated in states like the Punjab

---

18. I am assuming here the continuance of the post-independence system of governance -- a system, however flawed, that has served to give expression to the interests of people at virtually every level of the body politic. Such an assumption may not be warranted in the days ahead, especially if the Bharatiya Janata Party is able to form a government and to alter the existing system of governance.

19. Even a BJP government would read the same tea leaves and, I believe, reach the same general conclusion.

and Haryana,[20] but also to rely on other states, and especially those in eastern India (the region least affected by attempts in the 1970s and 1980s to introduce and disseminate new technology in agriculture).[21] In short, to meet the food needs of a rapidly growing population, any future Government of India must ensure that increases in productivity are generated in a full spectrum of states (in the east, south and west, as well as the northwest) and among all categories of rural cultivators. When this realization sinks in, there is the prospect that such a future government will want to take vigorous steps in concert with state governments to design variegated programs of agrarian reform that will be complementary to productivity needs.

For all these reasons -- the need to respond to new pressures from the base of the agrarian hierarchy, the need to recognize the fading power of traditional landholders, the need to establish a working nexus with the rural majority, and the need to facilitate the spread of new technology in agriculture, both regionally in India and among new sections of the cultivating peasantry -- a future Government of India will be challenged to take meaningful action concerning agrarian reform. Early in the twenty-first century, if not sooner, any remaining proponents of agrarian reform and land reform may finally have their day, and meaningful steps may be taken to resolve India's persistent dilemma in its agrarian sector.

---

20. There has been evidence in the 1980s that the momentum of the Green Revolution is declining in the Punjab and Haryana for reasons quite apart from the political strife and turbulence in the Punjab. Moreover, for India as a whole, the "Growth of agricultural yields is at risk of stalling even in the 25% of districts where it has been rapid. Yield potentials for main food crops .... have grown at less than 1% per year -- for rice, not at all -- since the mid-1960s, and there is no major breakthrough on the horizon." [Robert Cassen, Vijay Joshi and Michael Lipton, "Stabilization and Structural Reform in India," *Contemporary South Asia,* 2(2)., (1993), pp. 165-198.]

21. This was a major concern of the Government of India in the 1980s. [See, for example: India, Reserve Bank, Committee on Agricultural Productivity in Eastern India, *Agricultural Productivity in Eastern India,* Volumes 1 and 2, (Bombay: Reserve Bank of India, 1984).] It has been a continuing puzzlement to the Government of India that the growth in agricultural productivity in the eastern region -- comprised of eastern Uttar Pradesh, Bihar, West Bengal and Orissa -- has been quite modest and well below levels considered attainable in view of the region's agronomic potential, a potential exceeding that of the Punjab and Haryana.

Selected Bibliography

Anstey, Vera. *The Economic Development of India.* Fourth Edition. London: Longmans, Green and Company Ltd., 1957.

Appu, P.S. Article in *The Statesman.* (July 30, 1973) as reprinted in P.S. Appu, *Agrarian Structure and Rural Development.* New Delhi: India, Cabinet Secretariat, Department of Personnel and Administrative Reform, May 1975.

Baden-Powell, B.H. *Indian Village Community.* London: Longmans, Green and Company, 1896.

_____. *The Land Systems of British India.* Volumes I and II. Oxford: Clarendon Press, 1892.

_____. *Land Revenue and Tenure in British India.* Second Edition. Oxford: Clarendon Press, 1913.

Bandyopadhyay, D. "Direct Intervention Programmes for Poverty Alleviation in India." Paper delivered at the Workshop on Poverty in India, International Development Centre, The University of Oxford, October 2-6, 1987. Unpublished manuscript, 1987.

_____. Interviews. Oxford, England. October, 1987.

Bardhan, Pranab. *The Political Economy of Development in India.* Oxford: Basil Blackwell Publisher Ltd., 1984.

_____. "The So-Called Green Revolution and Agricultural Labourers." Unpublished Manuscript, 1970.

Baxi, Upendra. *The Crisis of the Indian Legal System.* New Delhi: Vikas Publishing House Ltd., 1982.

_____. Interviews. New Delhi, India. January, 1990.

_____. Interviews. Oxford, United Kingdom. June, 1991.

Bharti, Indu. "Farce of Land Reforms in Jehanabad." *Economic and Political Weekly.* (November 26, 1988), pp. 2519-2520.

Bhave, Vinobha. *Bhoodan Yajna (Land-Gifts Mission).* Ahmedabad: Navajivan Publishing House, 1953.

_____. Interview. Sarvodaya Sammelan, Kerla, India. June 13, 1957.

_____. *Principles and Philosophy of the Bhoodan Yagna.* Tanjore, India: Sarvodaya Prachuralaya, March 1956.

Bihar. Revenue Department. "D.O. No. 5LR-LA-224/70-5667-L.R." Unpublished document. Patna: July 1, 1970.

Bose, P.K. and M. Mukherjee. eds. *P.C. Mahalanobis Papers on PLanning.* Calcutta: Statistical Publishing Society, 1985.

Boserup, Ester. *The Conditions of Agricultural Growth: The Economics of Agrarian Change under Population Pressure.* London: George Allen and Unwin, 1965.

Brayne, F.L. *The Remaking of Village India.* London: Oxford University Press, 1929.

Brecher, Michael. *Nehru, A Political Biography.* London: Oxford University Press, 1959.

Byres, T.J. "The Dialectic of India's Green Revolution." *South Asian Review,* 5:2. (January 1972), pp. 99-116.

Cassen, Robert, and Associates. *Does Aid Work?* Oxford: Clarendon Press, 1986.

Cassen, Robert, Vijay Joshi and Michael Lipton. "Stabilization and Structural Reform in India." *Contemporary South Asia.* 2(2). (1993), pp. 165-198.

Chakravarty, Sukhamoy. *Development Planning: The Indian Experience.* Oxford: Clarendon Press, 1987.

Congress Party. All India Congress Committee (AICC). *AICC Economic Review.* Selected Volumes. (New Delhi, 1954).

_____. Economic Programme Committee. *Report of the Economic Programme Committee.* Submitted to The Congress President, AICC, New Delhi, January 25, 1948.

Cummings, Ralph W. Jr. and Susanta K. Ray. *Policy Planning for Agricultural Development.* Delhi: Tata McGraw-Hill Publishing Company, 1971.

Dandekar, V.M. and N. Rath. "Poverty in India." *Economic and Political Weekly* 8 Annual Number (February 1973), pp. 245-54.

Dantwala, M.L. "Agricultural Credit in India -- The Necessary Link." *Pacific Affairs,* 25. (December 1952), pp. 349-359.

_____. "Growth and Equity in Agriculture." *Economic Times.* (December 19, 1986).

_____. "Prospects and Problems of Land Reform in India." *Economic Development and Cultural Change,* 6, No. 1. (October 1957/58), pp. 3-15.

Dantwala, M.L. and C.H. Shah. *Evaluation of Land Reforms with Special Reference to the Western Region of India.* Chicago: Aldine Press, 1969.

Darling, Malcolm Lyall. *Punjab Peasant in Prosperity and Debt.* London: Oxford University Press, 1925.

Darling, Sir Malcolm. "Report on Certain Aspects of the Cooperative Movement in India." Under the auspices of the Government of India Planning Commission. New Delhi: Government of India Publishers, 1957.

_____. Interviews. London, United Kingdom, January, 1958.

Das, Arvind N. "Murder to Landlords Order." *Economic and Political Weekly.* (June 10, 1975), pp. 915-917.

Dasgupta, Sugata. *A Great Society of Small Communities: The Story of India's Land Gift Movement.* Varanasi: Sarva Seva Sangh Prakashan, 1968.

219

Dobbs, Peter. "Ideas in Agrarian History: Some Observations on the British and Nineteenth-Century Bihar." *Journal of the Royal Asiatic Society,* No. 1. (1990), pp. 17-43.

Dore, Ronald Philip. *Land Reform in Japan.* London: Oxford University Press, 1959.

Dorner, Peter. *Land Reform and Economic Development.* Middlesex, England: Penguin Books, 1972.

Dutt, R. Palme. *India Today.* Bombay: People's Publishing House Ltd., 1949.

Eckholm, Erik. "The Dispossessed of the Earth: Land Reform and Sustainable Development." Worldwatch Paper 30. Washington, D.C.: Worldwatch Institute, 1979.

Epstein, T. Scarlett. *Economic Development and Social Change in South India.* Manchester: Manchester University Press, 1962.

_____. *South India: Yesterday, Today and Tomorrow.* London and Basingstoke: Macmillan, 1973.

Frankel, Francine. "Agricultural Modernisation and Social Change." *Mainstream.* (November 29, 1969).

_____. *India's Green Revolution.* Princeton: Princeton University Press, 1971.

Frykenberg, Robert E. ed. *Land Control and Social Structure in Indian History.* Madison: University of Wisconsin Press, 1969.

_____. ed. *Land Tenure and Peasant in South Asia.* Delhi: Orient Longman, 1977.

Galbraith, J.K. "Conditions for Economic Change in Under-developed Countries." *Journal of Farm Economics.* Volume 33. (1951), pp. 689-696.

Gandhi, Mohandas K. *Collected Works of Mahatma Gandhi.* Volume 19. Ahmedabad: Government of Gujarat, 1966.

Gargan, Edward A. "In India, Nationhood Rips Along Old Seams." *The New York Times.* (February 28, 1993), p. E 3.

George, P.T. *Ceiling on Landholdings: A Study on Utilisation of Surplus Land.* Hyderabad: National Institute of Rural Development, 1981.

Ghate, Prabhu. *Direct Attacks on Rural Poverty: Policy, Programmes and Implementation.* New Delhi: Naurang Rai Concept Publishing Company, 1984.

Gopal, S. *Jawaharlal Nehru: A Biography.* A Project of the Jawaharlal Nehru Memorial Fund. Volume 1. New Delhi: Orient Longman, Ltd., 1972.

_____. *Jawaharlal Nehru: A Biography, 1889-1947.* Volume 1. Delhi: Oxford University Press, 1981.

_____. *Jawaharlal Nehru: A Biography, 1947-1956.* Volume 2. Delhi: Oxford University Press, 1979.

Griffin, K. and A.R. Khan. eds. *Poverty and Landlessness in Rural Asia.* Geneva: ILO, 1977.

Gupta, Amit Kumar. "The Leftists and the Rural Poor in India, 1934-39." Draft Manuscript. New Delhi, 1989.

Hart, Henry. ed. *Indira Gandhi's India.* Boulder, Colorado: Westview Press, 1976.

Herring, Ronald J. *Land To The Tiller: The Political Economy of Agrarian Reform in South Asia.* New Haven: Yale University Press, 1983.

————. "Explaining Anomalies in Agrarian Reform: Lessons from South India." in Roy L. Prosterman, Mary N. Temple and Timothy M. Hanstad, eds., *Agrarian Reform and Grassroots Development: Ten Case Studies.* Boulder, Colorado: Lynne Rienner Publishers, 1990.

Hirschman, A.O. and M. Rothschild. "The Changing Tolerance for Income Inequality in the Course of Economic Development." *Quarterly Journal of Economics,* 87. (1973).

India. Administrative Reforms Commission. *Report of the Study Team on Agricultural Administration.* Annexures, Volumes I and II. Delhi: Manager of Publications, 1967.

India. Ministry of Community Development and Cooperation. *Report on India's Food Crisis and Steps to Meet It.* Delhi: Manager of Publications, 1959.

India. Ministry of Food and Agriculture. *Report of the Committee on Large-sized Mechanical Farms: First Report, 1961.* Delhi: Manager of Publications, 1961.

————. *Report of the Committee on Large-sized Mechanical Farms: Second Report, 1964.* Delhi: Manager of Publications, 1964.

————. *Report of the Indian Delegation to China on Agricultural Planning and Techniques.* Delhi: Manager of Publications, 1956.

————. *Report of the Working Group of the Government of India and Food and Agriculture Organization of the United Nations on Methods for Evaluation of Effects of Agrarian Reorm.* Delhi: Manager of Publications, 1958.

————. *Report on Intensive Agricultural District Programme, 1961-63.* New Delhi: Manager of Publications, 1964.

————. Economic and Statistical Adviser. *Agricultural Legislation in India.* Volume I: "Regulation of Money-lending," 1951. Volume II: "Consolidation of Holdings," 1950. Volume III: "Agricultural Production and Development," 1952. Volume IV: "Land Reforms -- Abolition of Intermediaries," 1953. Volume V: "Village Panchayats," 1954. Volume VI: "Land Reforms -- Reforms in Tenancy," 1955. Delhi: Manager of Publications, 1950+.

————. *A Bibliography of Indian Agricultural Economics.* Delhi: Manager of Publications, 1952.

India. Ministry of Food, Agriculture, Community Development and Cooperation. "Chief Ministers' Conference on Land Reform -- Notes on Agenda." Mimeographed report. New Delhi: Department of Agriculture, 1969.

India. Ministry of Home Affairs. *Report, 1986-87.* New Delhi: Ministry of Home Affairs, 1987.

————. Research and Policy Division. "The Causes and Nature of Current Agrarian Tensions." Unpublished Report, 1969.

India. Ministry of Information and Broadcasting. *Jawaharlal Nehru's Speeches.* Volume 1 (September 1946-May, 1949). Fourth Edition. Delhi: Director, Publications Division, May, 1983.

India. Ministry of Law. *The Constitution of India.* As modified up to the 1st May 1965. Delhi: Manager of Publications, 1965.

————. *The Constitution of India.* As on the 1st November 1988. New Delhi: Manager of Publications, 1988.

India. Planning Commission. *Appraisal and Prospects of the Second Five Year Plan.* New Delhi: Manager of Publications, 1958.

————. *Consolidation of Holdings (Methods and Problems).* New Delhi: Manager of Publications, 1957.

India. Planning Commission. *Draft Five Year Plan (1978-83).* New Delhi: Manager of Publications, 1978.

————. *Fifth Five Year Plan (1974-79).* New Delhi: Manager of Publications, 1974.

————. *First Five Year Plan.* New Delhi: Manager of Publications, 1952.

————. *First Five Year Plan (Draft Outline).* New Delhi: Manager of Publications, 1951.

————. *Five Year Plan Progress Report for 1954-55.* New Delhi: Manager of Publications, 1955.

————. *Fourth Five Year Plan (1969-74).* New Delhi: Manager of Publications, 1969.

————. *Fourth Five Year Plan (A Draft Outline).* New Delhi: Manager of Publications, 1966.

————. *Implementation of Land Reforms: A Review by the Land Reforms Implementation Committee of the National Development Council.* New Delhi: Government of India Press, 1966.

————. *Review of the First Five Year Plan.* New Delhi: Manager of Publications, 1957.

————. *Second Five Year Plan.* New Delhi: Manager of Publications, 1956.

————. *Seventh Five Year Plan (1985-90).* Volumes I and II. New Delhi: Manager of Publications, 1985.

————. *Sixth Five Year Plan (1980-85).* New Delhi: Manager of Publications, 1983.

————. *Third Five Year Plan.* Delhi: Manager of Publications, 1962.

————. *Third Five Year Plan (A Draft Outline).* New Delhi: Manager of Publications, 1960.

————. Panel on Land Reforms. *Reports of the Committees of the Panel on Land Reforms.* Delhi: Manager of Publications, 1959.

222

India. Planning Commission. Programme Evaluation Organization. *Evaluation Report on Working of Community Projects and N.E.S. Blocks.* P.E.O. Publication No. 10. New Delhi: Government of India Press, April 1956.

_____. *Progress of Land Reform.* New Delhi: Ministry of Information and Broadcasting, January 1956.

_____. *Progress of Land Reform.* New Delhi: Manager of Publications, 1963.

_____. *Report of the Indian Delegation to China on Agrarian Cooperatives.* New Delhi: Government of India Press, May 1957.

_____. *Studies in Co-operative Farming.* P.E.O. Publication No. 18. New Delhi: Government of India Press, December, 1956.

_____. *The Fifth Evaluation Report on Working of Community Development and National Extension Service Blocks.* New Delhi: Manager of Publications, 1958.

India. Reserve Bank. Agricultural Credit Department. *Review of the Co-operative Movement in India 1952-54.* Bombay: Reserve Bank of India, 1956.

India. Reserve Bank. Committee on Agricultural Productivity in Eastern India. *Agricultural Productivity in Eastern India.* Volumes 1 and 2. (Bombay: Reserve Bank of India, 1984.

Jannuzi, F. Tomasson. *Agrarian Crisis in India: The Case of Bihar.* Austin, Texas and London: The University of Texas Press, 1974.

_____. *India in Transition: Issues of Political Economy in a Plural Society.* Boulder, Colorado: Westview Press, 1989.

_____. "India's Rural Poor: What Will Mobilize Them Politically?" in Henry C. Hart, ed., *Indira Gandhi's India.* Boulder, Colorado: Westview Press, 1976.

_____. "Land Reform in Bihar, India: The Agrarian Structure in Bihar." in United States Agency for International Development, *Spring Review of Land Reform, June 1970.* Volume 1. Second Edition. Washington,D.C.: USAID, 1970.

_____. "Land Systems, Economic Growth and Social Justice: The Permanent Settlement Region." in Paul Wallace, ed., *Region and Nation in India.* New Delhi, Bombay and Calcutta: Oxford and IBH Publishing Company, 1985.

_____. "Toward Food Security in South Asia." in W. Ladd Hollist and F. Lamond Tullis, eds., *Pursuing Food Security: Strategies in Africa, Asia, Latin America, and the Middle East.* Boulder, Colorado: Lynne Reinner Publishers, 1987.

Jannuzi, F. Tomasson, and James T. Peach. *The Agrarian Structure of Bangladesh: An Impediment to Development.* Boulder, Colorado: Westview Press, 1980.

Jha, L.K. "The 11th Govind Ballabh Pant Memorial Lecture." Delivered in New Delhi, India on December 10, 1986, at the India International Centre.

Johnson, A.A. *The Intensive Agricultural District Program (IADP): An Evaluation.* New Delhi: The Ford Foundation, 1975.

King, Russell. *Land Reform: A World Survey.* Boulder, Colorado: Westview Press, 1977.

Krishna, Raj. "Agrarian Reform in India: The Debate on Ceilings." *Economic Development and Cultural Change,* 8, No.3. (April 1959), pp. 258-278.

_____. "Some Aspects of Land Reform and Economic Development in India." in Walter Forelich, ed., *Land Tenure, Industrialization and Social Stability.* Milwaukee: Marquette University Press, 1961.

_____. "The Economic Outlook for India." Unpublished manuscript. A version of the manuscript was published in James R. Roach, ed., *India 2000: The Next Fifteen Years.* Riverdale, Maryland: The Riverdale Company Inc., 1986.

Kumar, Dharma, and Meghnad Desai. eds. *The Cambridge Economic History of India.* Volume 2. Cambridge: Cambridge University Press, 1983.

Kumarappa, J.C. Chairman. *Report of the Congress Agrarian Reforms Committee.* New Delhi: The All India Congress Committee, 1949.

Kurien, C.T. *Poverty, Planning and Social Transformation.* Bombay, Calcutta, Madras, New Delhi, Bangalore: Allied Publishers Private Limited, 1978.

Ladejinsky, Wolf. "Agrarian Reform in Asia." *Foreign Affairs,* 42. (April 1964), pp. 475-487.

_____. Letter to F. Tomasson Jannuzi. May 30, 1974.

Leaf, Murray J. "The Green Revolution in a Punjab Village." *Pacific Affairs,* LIII4. (Winter 1980-81).

Lipton, Michael. *Why Poor People Stay Poor: Urban Bias in World Development.* London: Temple Smith, 1977.

_____. "New Strategies and Successful Examples for Sustainable Development in the Third World." Testimony presented at a hearing on Sustainable Development and Economic Growth in the Third World held by the Joint Economic Committee of the U.S. Congress, Subcommittee on Technology and National Security, June 20, 1989. Reprint No. 170 of the International Food Policy Research Institute, Washington, D.C.

Long, Erven J. "The Economic Basis of Land Reform in Underdeveloped Countries." *Land Economics,* 37, no. 2. (May 1961), pp. 113-125.

Lewis, W.A. "Economic Development with Unlimited Supplies of Labour." *Manchester School,* 22. (1954), pp. 139-91.

_____. *The Theory of Economic Growth.* Homewood, Illinois: Irwin, 1955.

Lucas, Robert E.B. and Gustav F. Papanek. *The Indian Economy: Recent Development and Future Prospects.* Boulder, Colorado: Westview Press, 1988.

Mahalanobis, P.C. Interview. Indian Statistical Institute, Calcutta, India. February 17, 1957.

_____. "Science and National Planning." *Sankhya,* Volume 20, Parts 1 and 2. (September 1958).

Malaviya, H.D. *Land Reforms in India.* Second Edition. New Delhi: All India Congress Committee, 1955.

Mann, Harold H. *The Social Framework of Agriculture.* Daniel Thorner, ed. Bombay: Tri Printers, 1967.

Mayer, Albert. with Mckim Marriott and Richard Park. Foreword by Pandit Govind Ballabh Pant. *Pilot Project India: The Story of Rural Development at Etawah, Uttar Pradesh.* Berkeley: University of California Press, 1958.

Mehta, Jagat. Interview. New Delhi, India. February 2, 1989.

Meier, Gerald M., and Dudley Seers. eds. *Pioneers in Development.* New York: Oxford University Press, 1984.

Mellor, John W. *The New Economics of Growth: A Strategy for India and the Developing World.* Ithaca and London: Cornell University Press, 1976.

Mellor, John W., Uma J. Lele, and R. Sheldon Simon. *Developing Rural India: Plan and Practice.* Ithaca: Cornell University Press, 1968.

Menon, V.K.N. "The New Anchal Adhikari System in Bihar." *Indian Journal of Public Administration,* 2, No. 2. (April-June 1956).

Minhas, B.S. *Planning and the Poor.* New Delhi: S. Chand & Co. (Pvt.) Ltd., 1974.

Moreland, W. H. *The Agrarian System of Moslem India.* Cambridge: W. Heffer, 1929.

Mukherjee, Radhakamal. *Land Problems of India.* Calcutta University Readership Lectures. London: Longmans, Green and Company, 1933.

Myrdal, Gunnar. *Asian Drama: An Inquiry into the Poverty of Nations.* New York: Random House, 1968.

Narayan, Jaya Prakash. "The Bhoodan Movement in India." *Asian Review.* (October 1958), pp. 271-274.

_____. Interviews. Patna, Bihar, India. December 1956.

_____. Interviews. Sarvodaya Ashram, Sukhodeora, Bihar, India. January 1957.

_____. Interviews. Patna, Bihar, India. March 1968.

_____. Interviews. Muzaffarpur, Bihar, India. August 1970.

_____. Interviews. New Delhi, India. June 1975.

_____. "Planning for Sarvodaya (Draft Plan)." Issued under the auspices of the Bhoodan movement. New Delhi: Ananda Press, 1957.

National Front Manifesto -- Lok Sabha Elections, 1989. New Delhi: Shri V.P. Singh, Convenor, National Front, 1989.

Neale, Walter C. *Economic Change in Rural India: Land Tenure and Reform in Uttar Pradesh, 1800-1955.* New Haven: Yale University Press, 1962.

_____. "Land Is To Rule." in R. E. Frykenberg, ed., *Land Control and Social Structure in Indian History.* pp. 3-15. Madison: University of Wisconsin Press, 1969.

_____. "Land Reform in Uttar Pradesh, India." in United States Agency for International Development, *Spring Review of Land Reform, June 1970.* Volume 1. Second Edition. Washington,D.C.: USAID, 1970.

Nehru, Jawaharlal. "Disciplined and Effective Work at a Grave and Urgent Moment." Nehru's letter dated May 26, 1954, to the All Pradesh (State) Congress Presidents. *AICC Economic Review,* Volume VI., No. 4. (June 15, 1954), pp. 3-5.

_____. *Mahatma Gandhi.* Calcutta: Signet Press, 1949.

Nehru, Jawaharlal. *Selected Works of Jawaharlal Nehru.* Second Series, Volume 2. New Delhi: Jawaharlal Nehru Memorial Fund, 1984.

Nurkse, Ragnar. *Problems of Capital Formation in Underdeveloped Countries.* Oxford: Basil Blackwell Publisher Ltd., 1953.

Overstreet, Gene D., and Marshall Windmiller. *Communism in India.* Berkeley: University of California Press, 1959.

Pai, T.A. *New Programme for Economic Progress: The Turning Point.* New Delhi: Indraprastha Press, 1975.

Parthasarathi, G. ed. *Jawaharlal Nehru: Letters to Chief Ministers 1947-1964.* Volume 4. London: Oxford University Press, 1988.

Pinstrup-Anderson, Per, and Peter B.R. Hazell. "The Impact of the Green Revolution and Prospects for the Future." as reprinted in *Food Reviews International,* Volume 1, No. 1. Washington, D.C.: International Food Policy Research Institute, 1985.

Raj, K.N. *Indian Economic Growth, Performance and Prospects.* New Delhi: Allied Publishers, 1965.

Ranga, N.G., and P.R. Paruchuri. *The Peasant and Co-operative Farming.* New Delhi: Indian Peasants' Institute, July 1968.

Raychaudhuri, Tapan, and Irfan Habib. eds. *The Cambridge Economic History of India.* Volume 1. Cambridge: Cambridge University Press, 1982.

Ridker, Ronald G. *Land Reform and Rural Poverty in India.* Washington, D.C.: USAID, 1970.

Robb, Peter. "Ideas in Agrarian History: Some Observations on the British and Nineteenth-Century Bihar." *Journal of the Royal Asiatic Society,* No. 1. (1990).

Rosenstein-Rodan, Paul. "Problems of Industrializatioin in Eastern and Southeastern Europe." *Economic Journal,* 53. (1943), pp. 202-11.

Royal Commission on Agriculture in India, Abridged Report. London: His Majesty's Stationery Office, 1928.

Royal Commission on Agriculture in India, 1928. Volumes 1-14. London: His Majesty's Stationery Office, 1928.

Rosen, George. *Democracy and Social Change in India.* Berkeley: University of California Press, 1966.

_____. *Western Economists and Eastern Societies: Agents of Change in South Asia, 1950-1970.* Baltimore and London: The Johns Hopkins Press, 1985.

Ruttan, Vernon W. "The Green Revolution: Seven Generalizations." *International Development Review.* (December, 1977), pp. 16-22.

Sahay, K.B. Interviews. Patna, Bihar, India. November, 1956; April, May, and November 1957; December 1967; and March 1968.

226

Saxena, K.B. Interview. New Delhi, India. February 12, 1989.

Sen, Amartya. "Poverty, Inequality and Unemployment, Some Conceptual Issues in Measurement." *Economic and Political Weekly* 9. Special Number. (August 1973), pp. 1457-1466.

_____. *Resources, Values and Development.* Oxford: Basil Blackwell Publisher Ltd., 1984.

Sethi, J.D. *India's Static Power Structure.* Delhi: Vikas Publications, 1969.

_____. Interview. New Delhi, India. February 2, 1989.

_____. "Poverty, Inequality and Unemployment, Some Conceptual Issues in Measurement." *Economic and Political Weekly,* 9 Special Number. (August 1973), pp. 1457-1466.

Sen Gupta, Bhabani. *Communism in Indian Politics.* New York and London: Columbia University Press, 1972.

Schultz, Theodore W. ed. *Distortions of Agricultural Incentives.* Bloomington and London: Indiana University Press, 1978.

Shah, K.T. ed. *Land Policy, Agricultural Labour and Insurance.* Report of the Sub-Committee of the National Planning Committee Series. Bombay: Vora and Co., Publishers Ltd., July, 1948.

_____. ed. *Labour.* Report of Sub-Committee of the National Planning Committee. Bombay: Vora and Co., Publishers Ltd., 1947.

_____. ed. *Report, National Planning Committee.* Bombay: Vora and Co., Publishers Ltd., 1949.

Shankar, Kripa. *Status of Land Reforms.* Allahabad: Govind Ballabh Pant Social Science Institute, 1988.

Shourie, Arun. "Growth, Poverty and Inequalities." Reprinted from *Foreign Affairs.* (January 1973), pp. 340-352.

Shukla, Tara. ed. *Economics of Underdeveloped Agriculture.* Bombay: Vora and Co., 1969.

Singer, Hans W. "The Mechanics of Economic Development." *Indian Economic Review.* (1952); reprinted in A.N. Agarwala and A.P. Singh. eds. *The Economics of Underdevelopment.* London: Oxford University Press, 1958.

Singh, Inderjit. "Tenancy in South Asia." World Bank Discussion Paper. Washington, D.C.: The World Bank, 1988.

Singh, Tarlok. *India's Development Experience.* Delhi: The Macmillan Company of India Limited, 1974.

_____. Interviews. New Delhi, India. December, 1967; June, 1975; January and February, 1989; and January, 1990.

_____. "Planning and the Political Process." *Hindustan Times.* (December 8, 1989).

_____. *Poverty and Social Change.* Second Edition. Delhi: Orient Longmans, 1969.

_____. "Reassessing Nehru's Perspective on Planning." Public Address. New Delhi: November 16, 1974.

Singh, Tarlok. *Towards an Integrated Society: Reflections on Planning, Social Policy and Rural Institutions*. Calcutta: Orient Longman Ltd., 1969.

Sinha, Arun. *Against the Few: Struggles of India's Rural Poor*. London: Zed Books Ltd., 1991.

Subramaniam, C. *The New Strategy in Indian Agriculture*. New Delhi: Vikas Publishiung House Private Ltd., 1979.

Subramaniam, C., and T.A. Pai. *New Programme for Economic Progress: The Turning Point*. New Delhi: Indraprastha Press, 1975.

Srinivas, M.N. *Social Change in Modern India*. Berkeley: University of California Press, 1956.

_____. "On Living in a Revolution." James R. Roach, ed., *India 2000: The Next Fifteen Years*. Riverdale, Maryland: The Riverdale Company, Inc., 1986.

Taylor, Carl C. *A Critical Analysis of India's Community Development Programme*. New Delhi: The Community Development Administration, 1956.

Taylor, Carl C., Douglas Ensminger, Helen W. Johnson, and Jean Joyce. *India's Roots of Democracy*. Bombay, Calcutta, Madras and New Delhi: Orient Longmans, 1965.

The Second Congress of the Communist International: Proceedings. Moscow, 1920.

Thorner, Alice. Interview. New Delhi, India. January 26, 1989.

Thorner, Daniel. *The Agrarian Prospect in India*. Delhi: Delhi University Press, 1956.

_____. *The Shaping of Modern India*. New Delhi: Allied Publishers Private Limited, 1980.

Thorner, Daniel, and Alice Thorner. *Land and Labour in India*. Bombay: Asia Publishing House, 1962.

Trinque, Brian. Interview. Austin, Texas. February 27, 1993.

United Nations. *Progress in Land Reform, Fourth Report*. New York: United Nations, 1966.

United Nations. Department of Economic Affairs. *Progress in Land Reform (Analysis of replies by governments to a United Nations questionnaire)*. New York: United Nations Publication, January 12, 1954.

_____. Economic and Social Commission for Asia and the Pacific. *Role of Participatatory Organizations in Agrarian Reform*. New York: United Nations, 1985.

United States. Department of State. Agency for International Development. *Spring Review of Land Reform, June 1970*. Volumes 1-12. Second Edition. Washington, D.C.: USAID, 1970.

Verghese, B.G. *Beyond The Famine: An Approach To Regional Planning for Bihar*. New Delhi: Super Bazar for the Bihar Relief Committee, 1967.

Vitachi, Tarzie. Interview. New Delhi, India. March 11, 1989.

228

Walinsky, Louis J. ed. *Agrarian Reform as Unfinished Business: The Selected Works of Wolf Ladejinsky*. London: Oxford University Press, 1977.

Warriner, Doreen. *Land Reform and Economic Development*. National Bank of Egypt Fiftieth Anniversary Commemoration Lectures. Lecture 2. Cairo, 1955. Reprinted in Carl Eicher and Lawrence Witt, eds., *Agriculture in Economic Development*. pp. 280-290. New York: McGraw-Hill, 1964.

West Bengal. Department of Information and Cultural Affairs. *Left Front Government of West Bengal and Land Reforms*. Calcutta: Government of West Bengal, 1984).

World Bank (IBRD). *Land Reform. A Policy Statement of the International Bank for Reconstruction and Development*. Washington, D.C.: IBRD, 1974.
_____. *The Assault on World Poverty*. Washington, D.C.: IBRD, 1975.

Zinkin, Maurice. *Development for Free Asia*. Fair Lawn, New Jersey: Essential Books, Inc., 1956.

About the Book
and Author

This study shows that the failure of successive Indian governments to effect meaningful agrarian reforms has led to a political economy in rural India that is shaped, as it was prior to independence, largely by the interests of an elite minority of landholders. This group, Jannuzi argues, has worked both to deny the socioeconomic changes promised by modern India's own founders and to thwart the needs and interests of the rural majority who continue to lack secure rights in land. Examining the government's inability to establish a coherent national program for agrarian reform, the author focuses on the failure of a process that, on the one hand, has guaranteed India's landholding elites strong and continuous representation in the shaping of such agrarian reforms as were legislated and partially implemented and, on the other, has given no meaningful voice to the people at the base of what he calls "the hierarchy of interests in land" in rural India.

The author skillfully interweaves three major themes: (1) the remarkable continuity in the thinking of policy makers in both colonial and independent India as they struggled to articulate and promote agrarian policies; (2) the persistence of economic arguments for agrarian reform that emphasize the idea that large units of cultivation offer inherent productive efficiency advantages over small holdings; and (3) the role of both British and Indian decision makers in maintaining a conceptual dichotomy between the issue of increasing productivity and the issue of distributive justice. Noting the expanding political participation of India's rural poor as well as the continuing need for increased agricultural productivity, Jannuzi asserts that future Indian leaders must emphasize the complementarity of the goals of productivity growth and distributive justice. As they seek to form a political nexus with the rural majority, future leaders will be challenged to implement agrarian policies that actually transform the political economy of rural India.

F. Tomasson Jannuzi is professor of economics and Asian studies at the University of Texas at Austin.

Index

Agarwal, S.N., 87-88

Agrarian Crisis in India: The Case of Bihar (Jannuzi), 108(n16)

Agrarian Prospect in India, The (Thorner), 112

Agra Tenancy Act of 1926, 49

Agriculture

  assumptions concerning, 69, 78, 95, 183-184

  development. *See* Rural economic development

  displaced labor from, 75

  investments in, 80-81, 82, 83, 86, 149, 191, 198

  landless laborers, 22, 31, 43, 50, 64-65, 75, 77, 78-79, 79(n53), 106, 107, 108, 111, 130, 135, 136, 139, 142, 143, 144, 160-163, 164, 165, 168, 172, 173, 174, 191, 194, 200, 205, 213. *See also* Bonded laborers; Sharecroppers; Tenancy

  large scale farming, 10. *See also* Agriculture, production units; Consolidated holdings

  new strategy in, 94

  production/productivity, 39, 42, 59, 75, 76, 83, 94, 95, 96, 96(nn 94, 95, 96), 138, 158, 183-184, 198, 211, 214, 215, 215(nn 20, 21)

  production units, 2(n3), 62-63, 69, 76-77, 79, 127, 128-129, 130, 161(n60), 179, 183-184, 211-212. *See also* Agriculture, small farmers; Consolidated holdings; Landholdings, sizes/

  types of

    scientific, 3, 4, 38, 39, 87, 94, 95, 127, 162. See also Green Revolution; Technology

    small farmers, 87-88, 111, 143, 177(n27), 184, 198, 211. *See also* Agriculture, production units; Kisans

    tillers of the soil, 2, 4, 20, 22, 28, 45, 46, 48, 49, 51, 60-61, 62, 63, 66, 72, 73, 103, 106, 107, 112, 113, 115, 119, 119(n43), 135, 137, 142, 154, 176, 182, 183, 185, 188, 190, 194, 197, 209, 210. *See also* Agriculture, landless laborers

  See also Collective/cooperative farming

AICC Economic Review, 87, 132

AIKS. *See* All India Kisan Sabha

All India Kisan Sabha (AIKS), 31-32, 31(n51), 32, 33

Ambedkar, B.R., 35(n)

Andhra/Andhra Pradesh, 118, 123, 141, 146, 149, 152, 169(n6), 184, 191

Andhra Provincial Ryots Association, 31

Anstey, Vera, 1(n), 44(n75)

Appu, P.S., 188

Assam, 118, 120, 141, 146, 149, 149(nn 23, 24), 151, 152, 169(n6)

Assassinations, 164

Atrocities, 172, 173

Awadh, 36

Ayodhya mosque, 212